D1515590

StdWnds

The StdWnds unit defines two standard types of windows: TDlgWindow and T-FileWindow. A TDlgWindow merges the features of windows and dialog boxes, producing a new type of object called a dialog window. This object allows the user to provide both structured input (via buttons and checkboxes) and nonstructured (text) input for the program. A TFileWindow provides a simple text-editing window that can read from and write to files.

WinCRT

The WinCRT unit has one primary function: to make it possible for standard Turbo Pascal programs to run as Windows applications. You can use the WinCRT unit any time you need to port a DOS-based Turbo Pascal program to Windows and have to do it with a minimum of recoding. The only difference is that DOS programs name the CRT unit in the USES clause, while the Windows version names the WinCRT unit.

WinDOS

The WinDOS unit provides a variety of routines for working with MS-DOS and handling files; it corresponds to the DOS unit in standard Turbo Pascal. Many of these operations are (or should be) handled by calls to Windows functions instead of directly through the DOS unit.

Strings

The Strings unit provides a variety of routines for the use of null-terminated strings, a string type that is required by the Windows API but foreign to standard Turbo Pascal.

In standard Turbo Pascal, a string is treated as an array of characters with the first position (array[0]) containing the current length of the string. It has a maximum size of 255 characters and can occupy from 1 to 256 bytes of PC memory. A null-terminated string, on the other hand, has no length byte to indicate where the string ends. Instead, it indicates the end of the string with a NULL (#0) character. This means that it can contain up to 65,535 characters, much more than a standard string.

Computer users are not all alike.
Neither are SYBEX books.

We know our customers have a variety of needs. They've told us so. And because we've listened, we've developed several distinct types of books to meet the needs of each of our customers. What are you looking for in computer help?

If you're looking for the basics, try the **ABC's** series. You'll find short, uninitmidating turorials and helpful illustrations. For a more visual approach, select **Teach Yourself,** featuring screen-by-screen illustrations of how to use your latest software purchase.

Learn Fast! books are really two books in one—a tutorial to get you off to a fast start and a reference to answer your questions when you're ready to tackle advanced tasks.

Mastering and **Understanding** titles offer you a step-by-step introduction, plus an in-depth examination of intermeditate-level features, to use as you progress.

Our **Up & Running** series is designed for computer-literate consumers who want a no-nonsense overview of new programs. Just 20 basic lessons, and you're on your way.

We also publish two types of reference books. Our **Instant References** provide quick access to each of a program's commands and functions. SYBEX **Encyclopedias** and **Desktop References** provide a *comprehensive reference* and explanation of all of the commands, features, and functions of the subject software.

Our **programming** books are specifically written for a technically sophisticated audience and provide a no-nonsense value-added approach to each topic covered, with plenty of tips, tricks, and time-saving hints.

Sometimes a subject requires a special treatment that our standard series doesn't provide. So you'll find we have titles like **Advanced Techiques, Handbooks, Tips & Tricks,** and others that are specifically tailored to satisfy a unique need.

We carefully select our authors for their in-depth understanding of the software they're writing about, as well as their ability to write clearly and communicate effectively. Each manuscript is thoroughly reviewed by our technical staff to ensure its complete accuracy. Our production department makes sure it's easy to use. All of this adds up to the highest quality books available, consistently appearing on best-seller charts worldwide.

You'll find SYBEX publishes a variety of books on every popular software package. Looking for computer help? Help Yourself to SYBEX.

For a brochure of our best-selling publications:

SYBEX, Inc. 2021 Challenger Drive, Alameda, CA 94501
Tel: (510) 523-8823/(800) 227-2346 Telex: 336311
SYBEX   Fax: (510) 523-2373

SYBEX is committed to using natural resources wisely to preserve and improve our environment. As a leader in the computer book publishing industry, we are aware that over 40% of America's solid waste is paper. This is why we have been printing the text of books like this one on recycled paper since 1982.

This year our use of recycled paper will result in the saving of more than 15,300 trees. We will lower air pollution effluents by 54,000 pounds, save 6,300,000 gallons of water, and reduce landfill by 2,700 cubic yards.

In choosing a SYBEX book you are not only making a choice for the best in skills and information, you are also choosing to enhance the quality of life for all of us.

PROGRAMMER'S INTRODUCTION TO

TURBO PASCAL
FOR
WINDOWS

PROGRAMMER'S INTRODUCTION TO
TURBO PASCAL®
FOR WINDOWS™

Scott D. Palmer

SYBEX®

SAN FRANCISCO ■ PARIS ■ DÜSSELDORF ■ SOEST

Acquisitions Editor: David Clark
Editor: Doug Robert
Technical Editor: Lillian Chen
Word Processors: Susan Trybull, Ann Dunn
Book Series Designer: Suzanne Albertson
Screen Graphics: Delia Brown, Cuong Le, Richard Green
Desktop Publishing Production: Len Gilbert
Proofreader: Rhonda M. Holmes
Indexer: Ted Laux
Cover Designer: Ingalls + Associates
Cover Photographer: David Bishop
Screen reproductions produced with Collage Plus

Collage Plus is a trademark of Inner Media Inc.

SYBEX is a registered trademark of SYBEX, Inc.

TRADEMARKS: SYBEX has attempted throughout this book to distinguish proprietary trademarks from descriptive terms by following the capitalization style used by the manufacturer.

SYBEX is not affiliated with any manufacturer.

Every effort has been made to supply complete and accurate information. However, SYBEX assumes no responsibility for its use, nor for any infringement of the intellectual property rights of third parties which would result from such use.

Copyright ©1992 SYBEX Inc., 2021 Challenger Drive, Alameda, CA 94501. World rights reserved. No part of this publication may be stored in a retrieval system, transmitted, or reproduced in any way, including but not limited to photocopy, photograph, magnetic or other record, without the prior agreement and written permission of the publisher.

Library of Congress Card Number: 91-67558
ISBN: 0-7821-1022-3

Manufactured in the United States of America
10 9 8 7 6 5 4 3 2 1

This book is dedicated to—

Victor Meladze, Reuven Goren, and Michael Stabler—each of whom, in his own way, is a man of destiny;

And to Jim and Lynne Rock, who are the best friends I could ever wish for.

ACKNOWLEDGMENTS

Many people contribute to a good book, and this book is no exception. First among those who contributed was Doug Robert, my editor at Sybex, who is both an excellent collaborator and, I'd like to think, a good friend. Also essential were the efforts of Lillian Chen, Sybex technical reviewer, whose astute comments brought about much improvement from the original manuscript. I also owe thanks to David Clark, acquisitions editor at Sybex, for helping to launch this project, and of course to Rudolph Langer.

Nan Borreson and Karen Giles at Borland International were also very helpful. Zack Urlocker, Borland's product manager of Turbo Pascal for Windows, provided a bit of technical advice.

As always, my family and friends were patient and supportive during the writing of this book, and my debt to some of them is reflected in the dedication.

CONTENTS AT A GLANCE

TABLE OF CONTENTS

INTRODUCTION

This book is your introduction to the best tool you'll find anywhere for learning Windows programming—Borland International's *Turbo Pascal for Windows*. Unlike better-known Windows platforms, such as Microsoft C and even Borland C++, Turbo Pascal for Windows shields you from much of the complexity of Windows programming, letting you learn a little bit at a time as you become more comfortable with the Windows Application Programming Interface. At the same time, Turbo Pascal for Windows is a full programming language and development environment that enables you to write complete, full-featured programs, unlike end-user-oriented tools such as Borland's ObjectVision or Microsoft's Visual BASIC. TPW thus provides an ideal middle ground between too much complexity and too little power. As a result, not only is it ideal for *learning* Windows programming, but it may be the only Windows programming platform you'll ever need.

About the Book

In writing this book, I assumed only that my readers would have a basic familiarity with programming concepts and that they've done at least a little programming in some high-level language—ideally, Turbo Pascal. Beyond that, everything is explained.

A Self-Contained Tutorial

This book is also self-contained—that is, it contains *all* the information you need to get started programming in Turbo Pascal for Windows. Are you a little rusty on the basic language features of Pascal and Turbo Pascal? Turn to Chapter 2 for a quick review of Turbo Pascal. Are you a little hazy about the concepts and techniques of object-oriented programming? Turn to Chapter 3 for a tutorial on OOP basics and how they evolve from standard structured programming. Want more general information about the Windows programming environment? Turn to Chapter 4, where all the basic concepts are presented in a clear, step-by-step fashion.

This book also covers TPW-specific topics that the Borland TPW manuals either covered inadequately or completely ignored, such as how to get data out of a dialog box and pass it back to a TPW program. At each stage, the emphasis is on learning the governing concepts and techniques with an absolute minimum of unnecessary complication. Simple examples are used to spotlight specific TPW programming features, and each example is accompanied by a step-by-step explanation of what is going on in the program source code.

Program Listings on Disk

The companion disk included with the book contains all the program listings presented in the examples. Use the disk to get started with your own applications or simply to save typing as you follow along with the examples.

How the Book Is Structured

I have structured the book in such a way that you can read as much or as little as you need. If you wish, you can work straight through the book from front to back to get a thorough introduction to all aspects of Windows programming with Turbo Pascal for Windows. Or, if you prefer, you can read only those chapters that interest you, dipping into the others as needed for reference information and examples of techniques.

Part I, "Overview of Turbo Pascal Programming," is designed as a review and reference section for the basics of Turbo Pascal, Windows, and object-oriented programming. If you're in need of help with any of these areas, you should go directly to this section. On the other hand, if you're comfortable with Turbo Pascal, Windows, and object-oriented programming, you might want to skip all the chapters in this section except for Chapter 1, which covers the Turbo Pascal for Windows Integrated Development Environment (IDE).

Part II, "Essential Turbo Pascal for Windows," explains and demonstrates the basic features of TPW and Windows programming. It shows how to create windows, display data, and use menus and simple dialog boxes. It also introduces the Whitewater Resource Toolkit, a package included with Turbo Pascal for Windows version 1.0 that lets you create and edit Windows resources.

Part III, "Intermediate-Level Windows Programming Skills," teaches skills for more sophisticated use of Windows resources, including resources for dialog boxes, accelerator keys, bitmaps, icons, cursors, and string tables. It also explains the basics of using Turbo Debugger for Windows to find any hidden bugs in your TPW programs.

Part IV, "Advanced Windows Programming Skills," shows how to use some of the most sophisticated Windows features, such as memory management, graphics, dynamic link libraries, and the Windows Multiple Document Interface.

Finally, the *appendices* discuss TPW-related topics that can help extend your skills in Windows programming. Appendix A shows the basic features of the Borland Resource Workshop, a resource editor similar to the Whitewater Resource Toolkit. Appendix B surveys some other important Windows programming tools and how they compare to Turbo Pascal for Windows, such as Microsoft C, Borland C++, and Actor. Appendix C provides basic reference information on TPW's ObjectWindows object hierarchy drawn from the Turbo Pascal for Windows WOBJECTS unit.

Throughout, the emphasis is on learning all the most useful Windows programming skills with the least amount of pain and complication.

PART I

Overview of Turbo Pascal Programming

1 The Turbo Pascal IDE

2 A Quick Review of Turbo Pascal

3 Structured and Object-Oriented Programming

4 The Windows Programming Environment

The Turbo Pascal IDE

- **Advantages of Windows Programming**

- **The IDE Main Window**

- **A Quick Demonstration**

- **Using the IDE Menus**

There's good news and better news about programming with Turbo Pascal for Windows. The good news is that if you know how to write Pascal programs, you can—with very little adjustment—learn to write Turbo Pascal programs for Microsoft Windows. The even better news is that if you have a little experience in Turbo Pascal 6 and "Turbo Vision," then the ideas, techniques, and even the terminology of Turbo Pascal for Windows programming will be almost completely familiar.

Until recently, if you wanted to do Windows programming, you had two main choices. You could use the C programming language with the Microsoft Windows Software Developers' Kit (SDK), which is flexible but difficult, or you could use end-user packages such as Toolbook, which is easy but inflexible. There was no middle ground.

Turbo Pascal for Windows solves that dilemma. It provides full high-level support for all the Windows functions—both in the user interface and behind the scenes—but it does so through familiar Pascal constructs that mask much of the complexity of the Windows *application programming interface* (*API*). At the same time, it provides much more programming flexibility than end-user packages such as Toolbook or Microsoft Visual BASIC.

This book assumes that you have a basic familiarity with Pascal programming and can get by with a brief review, which is presented in the next two chapters. If you don't yet know Pascal programming, you should first work through one of the excellent books on the subject, such as *Mastering Turbo Pascal 6* (SYBEX, 1991).

Advantages of Windows Programming

Although the user interface of Microsoft Windows has received the most attention, it is only a small part—and arguably the least important part—of what Windows has to offer. For the programmer, Windows offers multitasking, memory management, device independence, inter-process communication ("Dynamic Data Exchange"), and a standard "look and feel" for all application programs. This not only provides more features for less programming work, but it lets you focus on the unique aspects of your own program instead of the details of how it should look.

Just as much as MS-DOS, Windows qualifies as a PC operating system. It manages the PC's memory, controls access to the processor and schedules tasks, and serves as an intermediary between application programs and the physical devices (screen, printers, etc.) that they use. At present, of course, Windows sits on top of MS-DOS and works together with it; in the future, we can expect a more and more intimate relationship between the two.

One cautionary note. Turbo Pascal for Windows, just like Windows itself, is designed for use with a mouse or some other pointing device (trackball, joystick, etc.). If you don't like using a mouse, I sympathize; I'm a keyboard man myself, and I've held out against using a mouse for quite a few years. But a mouse is almost essential for working with Windows and Windows programs. You can get by (barely) without one, but it's a waste of effort. Therefore, in this book, I'll assume that you're using a mouse or some other pointing device so that when you need to "click on" a button or "drag" a window, you'll know what to do.

The IDE Main Window

Once you've installed Turbo Pascal for Windows, you start it up from within Windows by opening the *TPW program group* and double-clicking on the *TPW icon*. The TPW program group also includes icons for the **Whitewater Resource Toolkit** and **Turbo Debugger for Windows**, but we'll cover those later on in the book. For now, just start Turbo Pascal for Windows. The opening screen is shown in Figure 1.1.

The first screen you see is the "main window" of the Turbo Pascal for Windows *integrated development environment*, or *IDE*. This allows you to interactively develop, test, and debug your Windows programs, and it works almost exactly like the IDE in the standard DOS version of Turbo Pascal.

Within this main IDE window, you can open or create multiple "child" windows that contain source code files. These windows can be moved and resized as you wish, using standard Windows user-interface guidelines. Whenever a window is less than full size, it has a button at the top right to *zoom* the window to fill the screen (by using the mouse to click on the up arrow). When a window is already full size, the up-arrow zoom button changes to a double-headed arrow: clicking on this button will restore the window to its most recent size and position. You can also reduce the window to an icon by clicking on the down-arrow button next to the corner button.

FIGURE 1.1:

The TPW main window

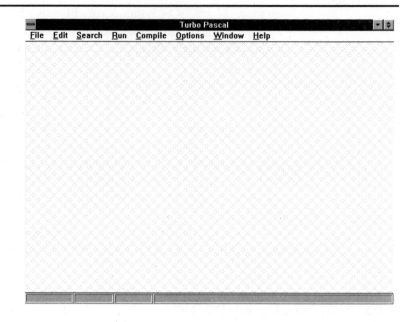

Likewise, each window has a device at the top left to open a menu offering options permitting the user to switch to other windows or to reduce the current window to an icon. Clicking on this "control bar" displays the menu shown in Figure 1.2.

The window-control menu has seven menu options:

Restore: If a window has been *minimized* (reduced to an icon), this restores it to its most recent size and position on the screen.

Move: This allows you to move a window by using the cursor (arrow) keys on the keyboard. First you select "Move," then you use the cursor keys to move the window to its new location, and then you press *Enter.* The move operation can be performed more easily with a mouse, however, and without resorting to the window-control menu, by simply dragging the window by its top border.

Size: This allows you to resize a window by using the cursor keys; the method is the same as for moving a window. This operation is also easier to perform with the mouse: to resize a window vertically, you simply drag its bottom border up or down; to resize a window horizontally, you grab its right border and drag it left or right.

FIGURE 1.2:

The window-control menu

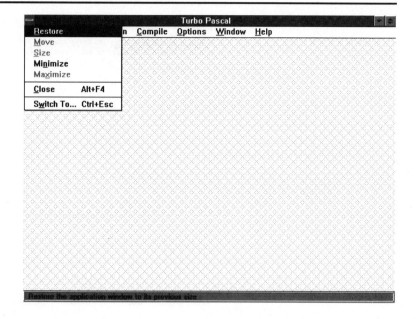

Minimize: This shrinks a window to an icon on the screen.

Maximize: This zooms a window to take up the entire screen.

Close: This closes the current window. If the current window is Turbo Pascal's main window, it closes down Turbo Pascal, releasing the PC resources used by the program; as shown on the menu, you can also use *Alt+F4* as a speed key to perform the close operation. Note that this is different from minimizing the Turbo Pascal main window, which leaves the program still open and running—albeit in the background, and shown on the screen as an icon.

Switch To: This opens a Microsoft Windows *task list*, showing all the programs that are currently running. This option allows you to switch temporarily to another program without shutting down Turbo Pascal.

Because the main window is simply a "desktop" on which other windows can be displayed (opened), it lacks some of the features to be found in the *editing windows*, as shown in Figure 1.3. (You can open an editing window by selecting "New" from the File menu.)

FIGURE 1.3:

An editing window

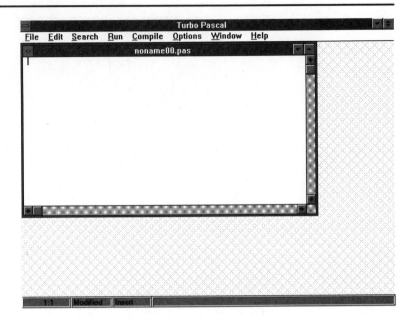

Actually, I cheated just a bit with Figure 1.3. The vertical scroll bar doesn't appear when you first open a new window, because there's no content in the window that would allow you to scroll up or down. It appears immediately, however, as soon as you add a line to the window. The scroll bars, which appear on the bottom and right borders of the window, help you to move around inside the window. To see more contents from the left or right, you use the mouse to grab the square device between the two arrows in the bottom border and drag it in the appropriate direction. Likewise, to see more contents from above or below, you grab the square on the right border and drag it up or down.

Apart from its scroll bars, and from the fact that you enter text into it, the editing window has the same features as the main window. There's a window-control button at the top left, the name of the window (currently *noname00.pas*) in the center of the top border, and the zoom and minimize buttons at the top right. There is one difference in the editing window's window-control menu: instead of "Switch To," which allows you to switch from Turbo Pascal to another program, the menu has "Next," which allows you to switch from the current editing window to another one within Turbo Pascal.

A Quick Demonstration

Now that we have an editing window open, it's a good time for a demonstration of how simple it is to write Windows programs with Turbo Pascal for Windows. Enter Listing 1.1 into the "noname00.pas" editing window and, from the File menu, save it as

`LST01_1.PAS`

You don't need to add the .PAS extension; Turbo Pascal uses it automatically unless you specify otherwise.

Listing 1.1

```
{Listing 1.1: The "Hello" program
in Turbo Pascal for Windows}
PROGRAM Listing1_1;
USES WINCRT;
BEGIN
   WRITELN('Hello, new Windows programmer!');
END.
```

Once you've entered and saved this program, compile it by opening the Compile menu from the menu bar and selecting "Compile." A dialog box will appear that gives you information about the progress of the compilation process, as shown in Figure 1.4. In this case, of course, the process is almost instantaneous because the program is so short.

To run the program, just open the Run menu and select "Run." The program creates a Windows-style window and displays the text Hello, new Windows programmer! inside, as shown in Figure 1.5.

Note the most interesting thing about Listing 1.1 and what it produced: We did very little Windows-specific work. Except for the WinCRT unit that is named in the USES statement, this is a perfectly ordinary Turbo Pascal program. There's a BEGIN and an END, and a WRITELN statement in between. And yet, we've made a program that creates a Windows-style window, complete with zoom/minimize buttons, scroll bars, and a window-control menu. All we needed to know was a little Pascal; Turbo Pascal took care of all the Windows-specific details for us through the WinCRT unit.

FIGURE 1.4:

The Compile Status dialog box

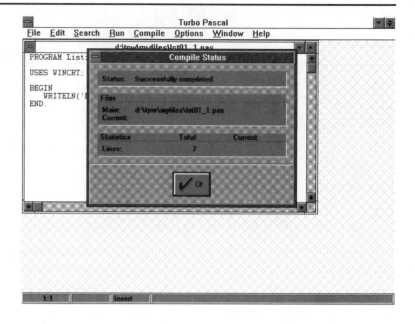

FIGURE 1.5:

Result of running Listing 1.1

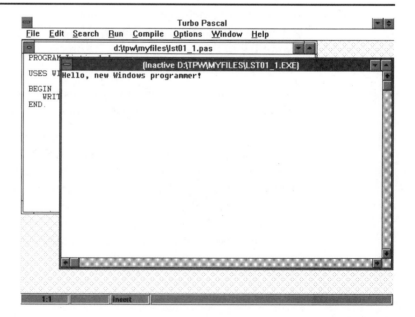

This pattern—writing a program that leaves all the Windows details to Turbo Pascal for Windows—will be repeated in most of the program listings in this book. Turbo Pascal for Windows shields the programmer from unneeded details of the Windows API, doing most of the behind-the-scenes work. It gives you access to low-level Windows function calls when you need them, but you can do most Windows programming in straight object-oriented Turbo Pascal with the TPW Object-Windows library.

Using the IDE Menus

The Turbo Pascal IDE provides drop-down menus that take care of virtually every normal programming task. You open a menu by using the mouse to click on its name in the menu bar or by pressing the *Alt* key and the underlined letter in the menu name, e.g., *Alt+F* to open the File menu.

The IDE also provides "speed keys" for many operations (such as *Alt+F9* to compile a program file) that are more efficient than going through the menus to achieve the same result. A summary of the IDE menu speed keys appears in Table 1.1.

TABLE 1.1:   Standard Turbo Pascal IDE Speed Keys

	Menu Item	Speed Key	Operation
Window Control Menu	Switch To	Ctrl+Esc	Switch to different Windows task
File Menu	Exit	Alt+F4	Quit Turbo Pascal for Windows
	Close	Ctrl+F4	Close current file window
Edit Menu	Undo	Alt+Backspace	Undo last editing change to file in current window
	Cut	Shift+Delete	Delete selected text from file in current window, but copy it to the clipboard
	Copy	Ctrl+Insert	Copy selected text from file in current window to clipboard, but don't delete original
	Paste	Shift+Insert	Paste contents of clipboard to current cursor position in current file window
Search Menu	Search/Search Again	F3	Search or repeat search

TABLE 1.1: Standard Turbo Pascal IDE Speed Keys (continued)

	Menu Item	Speed Key	Operation
Run Menu	Run	Ctrl+F9	Run program in current file window
Compile Menu	Compile	Alt+F9	Compile program in current file window
	Make	F9	Compile program in current file window, as well as related files that need recompilation
Window Menu	Window name	Ctrl+F6	Switch to next TPW file window
	Tile	Shift+F5	Display file windows in " tiled" format
	Cascade	Shift+F4	Display file windows in " cascading" format
Help Menu	Index	F1	Open Help window
	Index	Shift+F1	Open Help Index
	Topic Search	Ctrl+F1	Open help window with information on item at current cursor location

The Turbo Pascal menus provide a full range of program development facilities beyond what is available through the speed keys. The specific features of each menu are discussed below.

File

The File menu, shown in Figure 1.6, allows you to perform the usual file operations.

New   opens a new, empty editing window in which a new file can be created.

Open   enables you to open a previously created file in an editing window. When you choose the "Open" menu choice, the **File Open** dialog box (Figure 1.7) is displayed. (The speed key to open a file in the non-Windows version of Turbo Pascal is *F3*, but this isn't a standard speed key here because Turbo Pascal for Windows follows IBM's *"Common User Access"* (*CUA*) standard for its user interface. If you wish, you can still use *F3* as a speed key for opening files by first choosing the *Alternate* IDE interface—in the **Preferences** dialog box from the Options menu — instead of the CUA-compliant interface.)

FIGURE 1.6:

The File menu

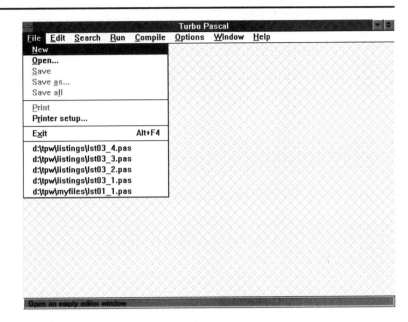

FIGURE 1.7:

The File Open dialog box

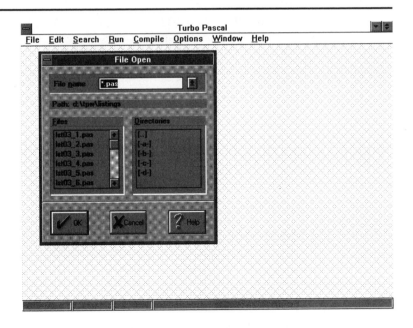

The dialog box has several parts: boxes that list file names and directories, and buttons to perform various operations. With a mouse, you simply click on the part of the dialog box that you want. With the keyboard, you move from one part of a dialog box to another by pressing *Tab* or *Shift+Tab* and then move within that part by tapping the appropriate cursor keys. You select a file or directory either by double-clicking on it with the mouse or, from the keyboard, by highlighting it and pressing *Enter.*

Near the top of the dialog box is a box where you can enter the name of the file you want to open. You can also enter a file name with wildcard characters, such as `*.pas` or `t*.*`, so that only files whose names match the pattern you entered will be displayed in the *Files* list at the lower left.

If you are reopening a file you used previously, you can simply click on the down arrow at the right end of this box to choose from a list of recently used files; from the keyboard, you can press *Alt* and the down-arrow key. Underneath the *File name* box is displayed the path of the current disk directory, and under that is a list of the files in the current directory that match the wildcard specification in the *File name* box.

If the file you want to open is not in the current disk directory, then highlight and open the appropriate directory in the *Directories* box at the right. With the mouse, simply double-click on a directory to open it; with the keyboard, use the *Tab* and cursor keys to highlight the directory, then press *Enter.* As soon as a directory is opened, its files will be displayed in the list on the left.

The three buttons across the bottom of the dialog box are standard equipment for every dialog box in Turbo Pascal for Windows. Selecting the *OK* button tells Turbo Pascal that it should perform the action according to the criteria indicated in the dialog box—in this case, opening the file whose name is displayed in the *File name* box. The *Cancel* button means that you've changed your mind about performing the operation, and tells Turbo Pascal to close the dialog box without doing anything. The *Help* button opens a help window with information about the various parts of the dialog box and what you can do with them.

Save   saves the file in the currently active editing window. (In non-Windows Turbo Pascal, *F2* is the speed key for this operation, but it's not supported in the standard CUA interface. To use *F2* as a speed key for saving files, you must use the *Alternate* user interface definition from the Options/**Preferences** dialog box.) If you're saving a new file that hasn't been named yet, Turbo Pascal will bring up the **File Save As** dialog box with a default name, "noname#.pas."

Save As allows you to save an existing file under a new file name or in a different directory. It opens up a dialog box that allows you to rename or relocate the file; this dialog box works the same as the **File Open** dialog box discussed earlier.

Save All saves all open files that have been changed since they were last saved to disk, regardless of whether or not they are in the current editing window.

Print prints out a hard copy of whatever file is in the current editing window.

Printer Setup opens a dialog box that lets you select which printer you want to use to print your program files. One of the advantages of Microsoft Windows is that it has its own printer drivers, so Turbo Pascal for Windows does not itself need to include printer drivers for different printers. Instead, you simply select which of the Microsoft Windows printer drivers you want to use. Turbo Pascal then sends the print job to Microsoft Windows, which uses the appropriate printer driver and routes it to the selected printer. Through this menu option, you can also set up special paper sizes and use other features (which must be supported by your printer) for printing program listings.

Exit shuts down Turbo Pascal and releases the memory that it occupied, making it available for use by other programs. The speed key for this is *Alt+F4*; the old speed key, *Alt+X*, is available only through the *Alternate* user interface definition from the Options/**Preferences** dialog box.

(List of Previous Files) At the bottom of the File menu is a "pick list" of up to five recently used editor files. If you wish to reopen one of these files, you can simply select it like any other menu option, thereby bypassing the extra steps involved in using the File Open dialog box.

Edit

The Edit menu provides options that let you cut, copy, and paste selected blocks of text in editing windows. There are two main ways to select a block of text for these operations. Most of the choices in the Edit menu operate on blocks of text that have first been selected in one way or another. With a mouse, you can position the mouse cursor at the beginning of the text you want to select, hold down the left mouse button, and then simply drag the mouse cursor to the end of the text. This highlights the block of text that has been selected, as shown in Figure 1.8. An equivalent method with the keyboard is to position the keyboard cursor at the beginning of the text to be selected, then hold down the *Shift* key while pressing the cursor keys.

Undo   reverses the most recent editing change or cursor movement. For example, if you deleted a block of text, choosing "Undo" would restore the deleted text. Selecting "Undo" again will not "undo the undo," as in some packages, but will undo the editing change preceding the one that was just undone. Thus, you can undo a whole series of changes by choosing "Undo" repeatedly. All editing changes in the current editing session can be undone, but not any changes from previous sessions. Speed key: *Alt+Backspace.*

Redo   reverses the most recent "Undo" command. For example, if a block of text was deleted and then restored with "Undo," selecting "Redo" would re-delete the block of text. There is no speed key for this operation.

Cut   deletes a selected block of text and copies it to the clipboard—an area of memory set aside by Windows. Text can then be pasted from the clipboard into another editing window or even into another active Microsoft Windows program. Speed key: *Shift+Delete.*

FIGURE 1.8:

Selected text in an editing window

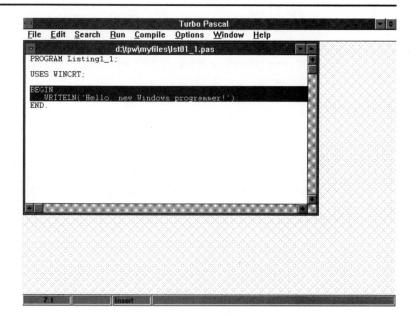

Copy   copies a selected block of text to the clipboard, but does not delete it from the current editing window. It can then be pasted to another location, just as with the Cut command. Speed key: *Ctrl+Insert.*

Paste   takes whatever is in the clipboard and copies it to the current location of the keyboard cursor (not the mouse cursor). This operation does not, however, delete the contents of the clipboard, so the same material can be pasted into multiple locations. Speed key: *Shift+Insert.*

Clear   deletes a selected block of text from the current editing window, but does not copy it to the clipboard—thereby leaving the clipboard's current contents undisturbed. This operation is equivalent to deleting a selected block of text by pressing the Delete key. Speed key: *Ctrl+Delete.*

Search

The Search menu provides a variety of features that allow you to search for text strings, specific locations in your file, and simple programming errors:

Find   lets you search for a particular text string in the current editing window. Choosing "Find" opens up the **Find Text** dialog box, as shown in Figure 1.9.

You enter the text string you want to find in the *Text to find* box. In the *Options* part of the dialog box, you can tell Turbo Pascal if you want the search to be case sensitive—e.g., to treat writeln and Writeln as different strings—and if it should look for whole words only—e.g., if the search target is Write, it should not consider Writeln a match. By checking the *Regular expression* box, you can also tell it to use wildcard characters, such as * and ?, in its search process.

The *Scope* radio buttons determine if Turbo Pascal will search the entire file or just a selected block of text. The *Direction* buttons are self-explanatory. If the cursor is in the middle of the file, the *Origin* buttons tell Turbo Pascal either to search the entire file or text block ("Entire scope") or just up or down beginning from the cursor.

Replace   This menu choice not only finds a text string for you, but lets you replace it with a different text string. It works through the **Replace Text** dialog box, shown in Figure 1.10.

FIGURE 1.9:

The Find Text dialog box

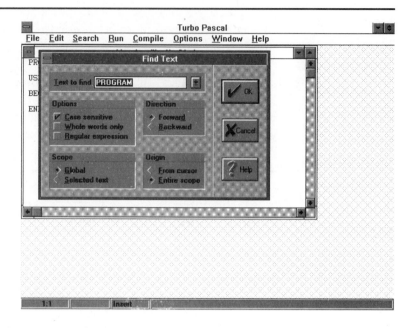

The dialog box is fairly self-explanatory, particularly if you already know how to use the **Find Text** dialog box. You enter the text to find in the *Text to find* box at the top, and enter the replacement text in the *New text* box underneath it. All the other buttons are identical, except for *Prompt on replace*, which, if checked, will cause Turbo Pascal to stop each time it finds the search text and ask if you want to replace it.

Search Again   simply repeats whatever search (or search/replace) command you entered last—thereby avoiding the extra steps involved in using the **Find Text** dialog box.

Go to Line Number   lets you jump directly to a line in a long program file—assuming, of course, that you know the line number to jump to.

Show Last Compile Error   moves the cursor to the location of the last compilation error (i.e., syntax error) that occurred with the current program, even if the error occurred in a different file, such as a unit.

FIGURE 1.10:

The Replace Text dialog box

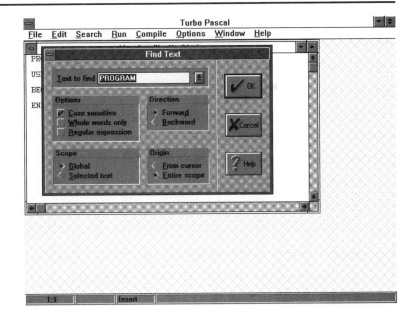

Find Error   moves the cursor to the location of the last run-time error (e.g., file not found) with your current program.

Run

The Run menu, as you might expect, lets you run your program from within the IDE, and provides features to assist you in testing and debugging it. The menu choices are:

Run   compiles your program and runs it from within the IDE.

Debugger   helps you debug your program by using **Turbo Debugger for Windows**. To use the Debugger, you should make sure that "Debug Info in EXE" (in the Options/Linker submenu) is set *ON* so that the compiled program will have the debugging information that Turbo Debugger needs.

Parameters   lets you pass command-line parameters to your program, just as if you were starting it from the Windows Program Manager.

Compile

The Compile menu provides various ways of compiling your program—ranging from compiling only the current editor file to recompiling all files linked to the program, whether they need it or not. The menu choices are:

Compile   compiles the program in the current editing window. As we saw earlier when we compiled Listing 1.1, a compilation status dialog box (Figure 1.4) reports on the progress of the compilation and any problems that are encountered.

Make   compiles the file in the current editing window (or the "primary file," if one has been named with the "Primary File" option). It also checks any files on which the compiled file depends, such as units, and recompiles them if needed.

Build   compiles the current editor file or primary file, as well as all files on which it depends—whether or not the other files are up to date.

Primary File   opens a dialog box that lets you specify a "primary file" to be compiled by the Make and Build commands. It is particularly useful when working on large programming projects that involve many linked files.

Clear Primary File   clears a primary-file specification so that a primary file is no longer specified.

Information   displays statistics on the last compilation that occurred. It is similar to, but provides more extensive information than, the compilation status dialog box that is displayed while compilation takes place.

Options

The Options menu lets you specify a wide range of preferences for how you want Turbo Pascal to work. The menu choices are as follows:

Compiler   opens a dialog box that lets you set various options for how programs, units, etc. should be compiled. The **Compiler Options** dialog box is shown in Figure 1.11.

The most important compiler options for program development and debugging are *Range checking, Stack checking, I/O checking, Debug information,* and *Local symbols.* All

FIGURE 1.11:

The Compiler Options dialog box

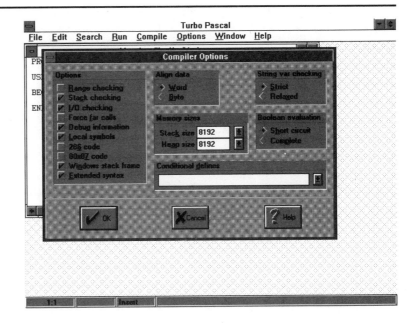

of these should be turned *ON* during the program development process to catch errors on compilation and to aid **Turbo Debugger**. They can be turned off when the final version of the program is compiled; this will produce a smaller .EXE file than if they are turned on. Other features of the Compiler Options dialog box, such as the ability to generate 80x87 code for numeric coprocessors or the ability to change the default sizes of the stack and the heap, will already be familiar to Turbo Pascal programmers.

Linker opens the **Linker Options** dialog box, shown in Figure 1.12, with which you can control how your program files are linked.

During program development, the *Map File* option should be *ON* to produce a detailed map file for use with **Turbo Debugger for Windows**. Likewise, the *Debug info in EXE* box should be checked, but turned off again for compilation of the final version of the program. The *Link buffer file* feature lets you speed up compilation by using memory (the default) for a link buffer, but you can specify a disk buffer if your program is large and you might run out of memory during compilation.

FIGURE 1.12:

The Linker Options dialog box

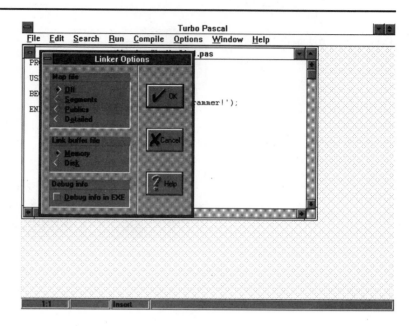

Directories lets you specify the directories where Turbo Pascal will put or look for .EXE files and units, including files, object files, and resource files.

Preferences opens a dialog box (shown in Figure 1.13) that lets you set options for making backups, using the TPW program editor, and determining which Turbo Pascal command set to use.

It is highly advisable to use the *CUA* (Common User Access) command set instead of the *Alternate* command set, even though the latter may be more familiar to users of the non-Windows version of Turbo Pascal. CUA is the standard for user interfaces in Windows programs; if you use a different interface in Turbo Pascal itself, you're defeating the whole purpose of having a standard.

Open allows you to load a different set of options than are found in the default configuration file. If you change the options, you can use "Save As" (see below) to save them under a different configuration file name. You can then reload them by loading that file with "Open."

Save saves the current IDE options to the default configuration file.

FIGURE 1.13:

The Preferences dialog box

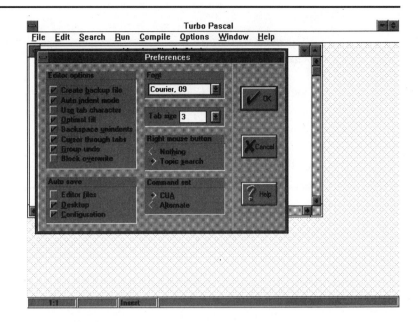

Save As lets you save the current options in a file different from the default configuration file.

Window

The Window menu provides options for arranging windows and icons on the Turbo Pascal desktop. The menu choices are as follows:

Tile arranges open windows so that they do not overlap, with some of the screen reserved for each window. Speed key: *Shift-F5.*

Cascade arranges open windows so that they are "diagonally stacked," with windows overlapping, but a portion of each window visible. Speed key: *Shift-F4.*

Arrange Icons arranges any icons on the Turbo Pascal desktop, just as in Microsoft Windows itself. No speed key.

Close All closes all open windows on the Turbo Pascal desktop. You will, however, be prompted to save any unsaved files. No speed key.

Help

The Help menu provides different ways to open Turbo Pascal's on-screen help system. The menu choices are:

Index opens an index to all the help topics available. To see information about any topic, you simply click on it with the mouse or highlight it and press *Enter.* Speed key: *Shift+F1.*

Topic Search shows information about any Pascal word at the current cursor position. Speed key: *Ctrl+F1.*

Using Help provides general information about the structure of the help system and how to use it.

SUMMARY

Turbo Pascal for Windows is a remarkably easy to use programming environment that lets you create Microsoft Windows programs in the familiar idiom of Turbo Pascal. Most of the details of the Windows API are handled "behind the scenes" by Turbo Pascal, although the programmer can make direct calls to Windows functions on those infrequent occasions when they are needed.

A Quick Review of Turbo Pascal

- Turbo Pascal Identifiers

- Reserved Words

- Rules for Identifiers

- Overall Program Structure

- Specific Features of Turbo Pascal Programs

Before you can start using Turbo Pascal for Windows, you must be familiar with the Turbo Pascal language, as well as with the concepts and techniques of structured and object-oriented programming. This chapter gives a brief overview of the Turbo Pascal language for people who can already write programs in Pascal or Turbo Pascal, but need a review or a handy reference.

Because Turbo Pascal for Windows really is just an extended version of Turbo Pascal, most of the discussion in this chapter applies equally to both Windows and non-Windows Turbo Pascal.

Turbo Pascal Identifiers

The fundamental building blocks of a Turbo Pascal program are "identifiers," which are names for different parts of the program. Each part of the program must have its own identifier, and, with a few exceptions related to the scope of identifiers, no two parts of a program can have the same identifier.

Reserved Words

Turbo Pascal's vocabulary includes its own built-in set of identifiers called *reserved words*. These are words such as BEGIN, PROCEDURE, TYPE, UNIT, and VAR.

In addition to reserved words, there are also *standard identifiers* such as WRITELN and WINCRT. These are the names of predefined procedures, functions, and Turbo Pascal *units* (precompiled libraries of subroutines, definitions, and data types; see below for more about units). Depending on which units you use in your program, standard identifiers can also be the names of predefined record or object types. In any event, you need to be aware of which standard identifiers are "active" for a particular program you are writing.

You should not use reserved words or standard identifiers to name parts of a program you create. If you do it with reserved words, the program won't compile. If you do it with standard identifiers, the program probably will compile, but won't run correctly, because you've redefined one or more of Turbo Pascal's standard identifiers.

A list of Turbo Pascal for Windows' reserved words is shown in Figure 2.1

FIGURE 2.1:

TPW reserved words

AND	GOTO	RECORD
ASM	IF	REPEAT
ARRAY	IMPLEMENTATION	SET
BEGIN	IN	SHL
CASE	INLINE	SHR
CONST	INTERFACE	STRING
CONSTRUCTOR	LABEL	THEN
DESTRUCTOR	LIBRARY	TO
DIV	MOD	TYPE
DO	NIL	UNIT
DOWNTO	NOT	UNTIL
ELSE	OBJECT	USES
END	OF	VAR
EXPORTS	OR	WHILE
FILE	PACKED	WITH
FOR	PROCEDURE	XOR
FUNCTION	PROGRAM	

Rules for Identifiers

Just like identifiers in any programming language, Turbo Pascal identifiers must follow certain rules. A Turbo Pascal identifier

1. must begin with a letter or _ (underline)

2. cannot contain any spaces or other special characters, including . ! ? # or -

3. can have any combination of letters, digits, and underlines after the first character

4. can be as long as you like, but Turbo Pascal only pays attention to the first 63 characters.

Thus, the following are examples of legal user-defined identifiers:

Legal Identifier

`ClientRecord`

`_AnyOldThing`

`Number_Of_Loops`

`mrspeel`

`COUNTER`

`file2read`

The following, on the other hand, are examples of illegal identifiers:

Illegal Identifier	Mistake
`Client Record`	contains a space
`2motleycrue`	doesn't start with a letter or underline
`Number-Of-Loops`	contains hypens—illegal characters
`Begin`	same as a Pascal reserved word
`data.txt`	contains period—an illegal character

Overall Program Structure

Unlike programs in BASIC and other unstructured languages, Turbo Pascal programs must follow a very definite structure. Each program is broken up into sections:

The PROGRAM Statement This gives the name of the program and marks the beginning of the program for Turbo Pascal or any other Pascal compiler.

The USES Clause   This tells Turbo Pascal what units the program uses. Units are separately compiled libraries of routines and/or object types. By naming a unit in your USES clause, you can use material from the unit without having to include it in your program. If Turbo Pascal can't find a given subroutine (or object type) in the current program, it looks in the units named by the USES clause to find them. Turbo Pascal for Windows comes with units, such as WINCRT, that provide Windows objects and perform many Windows programming tasks automatically.

The LABEL Section   In this section, you can declare line labels for use with GOTO statements. Then, you can begin a line with the label, followed by a colon. When Turbo Pascal encounters the statement GOTO <linelabel>, it will make the program jump to the line named in the GOTO statement. In standard Pascal, labels must be integers in the range 0–9999, and leading zeros don't count (e.g., 000125 and 125 are considered the same label). Turbo Pascal also lets you use ordinary identifiers for labels, such as DestinationLine, though of course they must be unique within your program (or at least within a subroutine).

This feature should be used sparingly, and Turbo Pascal limits GOTO's jumping capabilities so that a program can only jump within a *code block* (e.g., within a subroutine). Thus, a GOTO statement in a subroutine can only jump to somewhere else in the same subroutine, not to another subroutine or to the main body of the program.

The CONST (Constant) Section   In this section, you declare any constants used by your program. Constants can be either simple or complex expressions, such as

```
10
'stockfile'
CHR(13)
1000 div 5
```

Each constant gets its own identifier. The number 10, for example, could be NumberOfClients. In this section, you can also declare *typed constants,* which are not really constants, but are variables whose initial value is preset in the constant section.

The TYPE Section   In this section, you can create and declare your own data types beyond those supported by Pascal. While Turbo Pascal supports data types of numbers, text, etc., the TYPE section can be used to create customized data types that are tailored to a specific program, such as:

```
TYPE
String10 = STRING[10];        { needed for passing }
String15 = STRING[15];        { string variables to }
String20 = STRING[20];        { subroutines        }

DaysOfWeek = (Sunday, Monday, Tuesday, Wednesday,
                  Thursday, Friday, Saturday);

Digits = 0..9;
FirstSixLetters = 'A'..'F';
Weekdays = Monday..Friday; { uses "DaysOfWeek" type }

WorkDays = ARRAY[Monday..Friday] of String20;

Client = RECORD
        Firstname,
        Lastname : string[15];
        Address  : string[30];
        City     : string[15];
        State    : string[2];
        Zipcode  : string[5];
        Balance  : real;
        PaidUp   : Boolean      { True/False }
        END;
```

It's important to remember that merely defining a data type in the TYPE section doesn't automatically put that type to use in your program. The above section does not, for example, create a variable named "Client" for use in a program; for that, you must declare a variable of the Client data type—a job you can do in the VAR section, which comes next.

Remember that you don't have to declare any simple Pascal types in this section—only types that you create.

The VAR (Variable) Section   In this section, you declare the names and data types of variables you use in the program. A variable name can be any legal identifier, and the data type can be a standard Turbo Pascal data type or a data type you defined in the TYPE section. The only variables not declared in this section are a special type of variables called "dynamic" variables, which get created while the program is actually running.

The Procedures and Functions Section   This is the section for the program's subroutines, and it's the only section of the program that does not begin with an explicit section label. Technically, you can spread procedures and functions throughout your program ad libitum, as long as each is declared before it is used. In practice, however, it's better to keep them together.

The Main Body of the Program   In a well-designed program, this part is usually only a few lines long. The main body of the program should show only the overall structure of what happens in the program, leaving all the details to the subroutines. In many of the object-oriented programs we'll write in Turbo Pascal for Windows, this part is exactly three lines long:

```
BEGIN
     myprog.init;
     myprog.run;
     myprog.done;
END.
```

Specific Features of Turbo Pascal

The overall structure of a Turbo Pascal program is filled out through a powerful set of specific language features. Here is an overview of those features.

BEGIN and END

To understand the functions of BEGIN and END in a Pascal program, you have to grasp an odd idea: A Pascal program is just a single big statement.

A Pascal program is a large compound statement composed of simpler statements. By using BEGIN and END, you signal to Pascal where a compound program statement is supposed to begin and end. Semicolons are used in the same way that the word "and" works in English: to combine two simpler statements into a compound statement. Thus, you only need to use BEGIN and END to show the start and finish of a compound statement. Here are some legal Pascal statements:

```
WRITELN(' This is a simple statement.');      { simple }
```

```
IF a = 1 THEN DoOneThing ELSE DoAnotherThing; { simple }

IF a = 1                                    { simple IF..}
    THEN BEGIN                              { THEN which }
        WRITELN(' a = 1');                  { contains a }
        pause                               { compound }
        END                                 {THEN clause }
    ELSE WRITELN(' a doesn''t equal 1');

BEGIN                                       { compound }
    WRITELN(' This block is a compound statement.');
    WRITELN(' Sub-statements are linked by semicolons.');
    WRITELN(' There''s no semicolon right before the END');
    WRITELN(' because there''s no next statement from');
    WRITELN(' which the last line must be separated.')
END;
```

Any time you're constructing a compound statement out of simpler statements, you should start with BEGIN, separate the simpler statements with semicolons, and finish with END. Moreover, because each `BEGIN..END` sequence is itself a statement, it needs to be separated from other statements by a semicolon after the word END. The only exception is at the very end of the whole program, when you put a period after END.

Simple Data Types

Pascal supports both simple and complex data types. You can use the simple data types as building blocks to define your own complex data types. In essence, Pascal's simple data types come down to *numbers, text, truth-values,* and *"pointers."*

Numeric Data Types

Numeric data types are divided into integers (whole numbers) and real numbers (numbers with a decimal point). Turbo Pascal's integer type ranges from –32,768 to 32,767; so examples of Pascal integers are 123, 5, 30000, and – 555. Real numbers in Turbo Pascal go from 2.9 times 10^{-39} to 1.7 times 10^{38}, an astronomical range. Each type has several subtypes. Real numbers can be formatted for clearer display by specifying the number of digits and decimal points you want. For example, where n=12.5, then you would write in Pascal

```
n:0:1
```

that is, one digit to the right of the decimal point and a variable number of total digits. If you don't specify a format, the number will be displayed in scientific notation as

```
1.2500000000E+01
```

Text Data Types

There are two text data types in Turbo Pascal: characters (called "CHAR") and strings. A *character* is any single letter, digit, or special symbol, such as 'g', 'P', '5', '&', or '+'. Each character must be enclosed in single quote marks. A *string* is an ordered sequence of characters, such as 'U.S.S. Enterprise' or 'Pascal'. A string must also be enclosed in single quote marks. In fact, strings are practically indistinguishable from arrays of characters (see below for a discussion of arrays).

You'll use characters often to get the user's answer to on-screen prompts, such as Proceed (Y/N)? You'll use strings most often to display text and get text input from the user, such as

```
WRITE(' Enter your name: '); { displays a string }
READLN(Name);                 { gets input string }
```

There's also a data type actually called "text" that is used to represent unstructured disk files. This is discussed with file types, below.

Truth-Value Data Types

In Pascal, truth values are denoted by the words "true" and "false." You can use Boolean variables and expressions to control the flow of your program. For example, if PaidUp is a Boolean variable, then you could write

```
IF PaidUp = TRUE
   THEN SendThankYou
   ELSE BugForMoney;
```

Pointer Data Type

The pointer data type is different from the others we've discussed so far. Instead of holding something ordinary, like a number or a text string, a pointer holds the memory address of a variable—usually, a record or an object variable. Thus, one declares a pointer type in the TYPE section as follows:

```
TYPE
    studentptr = ^student;
```

```
student = RECORD
            name : string10;
            GPA  : REAL;
            next : studentptr;
            END;
VAR
     firststudent : studentptr;
```

Firststudent, of course, is a pointer variable, not a student record variable. This means that it is capable of holding the memory address of a student record variable, but it is not itself a student record and cannot hold the actual student information. To create a student record variable and point the firststudent pointer at its memory address, you use the Pascal NEW procedure, as follows:

```
NEW(firststudent);
```

The firststudent pointer can then be "de-referenced" in order to refer to the variable it points to. To do this, simply add a caret to the end of the pointer name. To illustrate, firststudent is a pointer, but firststudent^ is the student record variable that the pointer points to. The fields of this record (see the section on records, later in this chapter) can be referred to by the dot notation or via a WITH statement, as in:

```
firststudent^.name := 'Philippe';
```

```
WITH firststudent^ DO
     BEGIN
     name := 'Bill';
     GPA  := 4.00
     END;
```

The variables created with the NEW procedure and pointers are called *dynamic variables* because they are created while the program is actually running. When a dynamic variable is no longer needed, the memory it occupies can be freed up by using DISPOSE, as in

```
DISPOSE(firststudent);
```

After using DISPOSE, the firststudent pointer no longer refers to a dynamic variable. Pointers not associated with a particular dynamic variable are called "dangling" pointers and are very dangerous. Any time a pointer variable is not in use, it should be set to NIL with a statement of the following form:

```
studentptr := NIL;
```

The pointer can be reactivated by another call to the NEW procedure.

Structured Data Types

There are four main structured types: *arrays, records, objects,* and *file types.* Arrays are used to hold static lists of data, while records and objects can be used to create your own customized data types. Files represent disk files or hardware devices, such as printer ports.

Arrays

An array is like a row of slots into which you can fit data items of a single type. Thus, an array can hold numbers, text items, truth values, pointers, and even user-defined types such as records and objects.

To declare an array, you must specify three things: the *name* of the array, the *number* of slots, and the *type* of data item that the slots will need to hold. Note, however, that since ARRAY is a built-in data type, you do not strictly have to declare it in the type section. Either of the following will do fine:

```
TYPE
Enrollment = ARRAY[1..100] of Student;
{ where Student is a previously  defined data type }
VAR
StudentList : Enrollment; { declares variable }
```

or, more economically,

```
VAR
StudentList : ARRAY[1..100] of Student;
```

You refer to the individual items in an array by using the name of the array variable combined with its array index. To refer to the fifth element in an array named Text-List that holds text strings, for example, we would write `TextList[5]`. With the StudentList array, which holds records, it's a bit more complicated: to refer to the name part of the student record in position 5, we would write `Student-List[5].Name`.

Records

Records are used in Pascal to hold together different pieces of information that can be of different types. For example, a student record would hold name and address (strings), grade point average (a real number), and an indication of whether the student was on academic probation (a Boolean value). A record is defined in the

TYPE section by naming the record type, defining its data slots (called "fields"), and ending the definition with END—for example,

```
TYPE
    Student = RECORD
            Name      : STRING[20];
            Address   : STRING[30];
            City      : STRING[10];
            State     : STRING[2];
            Zipcode   : STRING[5];
            GPA       : real;
            Probation : Boolean
            END;
```

You can then create variables of this type and use them as follows:

```
VAR
    Pupil : Student; { declares individual variable }
                     { of Student record type }
    StudentList : ARRAY[1.100] of Student;
                     { declares an array of student }
                     { records                      }
BEGIN
    Pupil.Name := 'Gerald Ford';
    Pupil.Address := '30 Rockefeller Center'
    StudentList[1].Name := 'Jimmy Carter';
    StudentList[1].Address := '10 Maple Street';
    StudentList[1].City := 'Plains'
    StudentList[1].State := 'California'
    StudentList[1].Zipcode := '90069'
    StudentList[1].GPA := 4.00;
    StudentList[1].Probation := false
END;
```

Objects

Objects are the central data type used by Turbo Pascal for Windows to create Windows-specific program features. They look similar to records, but they have very special properties:

- Object types include their own subroutines (procedures and functions).

- Object types can be derived from previously defined object types and inherit the features of those types (their "ancestor" types).

- Object types can override the features of their ancestor types and add their own new features, including new data fields and subroutines.

Object types are discussed in detail in Chapter 3.

File Types

There are two main file types in Turbo Pascal: *text files* and *typed files*. Text files contain text data and are structured only into lines and characters; typed files contain data items of a specific type, and these data items are arranged sequentially in the file. Any file used in a program must be associated with a file variable declared in the VAR section. Thus, the following creates one text file and one typed file (a file of integers):

```
VAR
    thisfile: TEXT;
    thatfile: FILE OF INTEGER;
```

Several Turbo Pascal procedures apply to files. The most important of these are as follows:

Assign: Associates a file or device with a file variable used in the program—for example

```
Assign(filvar, 'student.dat');
```

Reset: Opens a text file for reading; opens a typed file for reading or writing

Rewrite: Creates a new text file and opens it for writing; if the file already exists, this destroys any data already in the file

Append: Opens an existing text file and positions the file pointer at the end of the file to add new data

Close: Writes to disk any file data still in memory and closes the file (text or typed)

Constants and Variables

A constant is a data item that never changes its value during a run of the program; a variable can have new values assigned to it at any time. Both can be any legal Pascal data type and can be denoted by any legal Pascal identifier.

Declaring Constants

You declare constants in your program as we've already seen, by assigning values to them in the CONST section of your program. Some typical constant declarations might be found as:

```
CONST
     MaxCount = 100;
     Interest = 0.18;
     Space = ' ';
```

Declaring Variables

Before a normal variable can be used in a program, it has to be named and its type has to be declared. A variable can be any data type—for example a built-in type or a user-defined type that's been declared in the TYPE section. To declare a variable, you simply give its name, a colon, and then its type:

```
VAR
     Counter        : INTEGER;
     StudentList    : ARRAY[1..100] of Student;
     String20       : STRING[20];
     YesNo          : CHAR;
```

Typed Constants

The term "typed constant" is actually misleading, but it is the standard way that pre-initialized variables are referred to in the Pascal literature. A typed constant is a variable that is declared in the CONST section along with its initial value; for example,

```
CONST
     CustomerBalance : REAL = 0.00;
```

Statements

There are several different statement types in Turbo Pascal. The most important are *assignment statements, input/output (I/O) statements,* and *control statements.*

Assignment Statements

Assignment statements assign a value to a variable. Pascal uses a combination of the colon and the equals sign to make its assignment operator. Some examples of assignment statements are listed below:

```
counter := 15;

Name := 'Zardoz';

PaidUp := TRUE;

StudentList[5].Name := 'Parker Lewis';
```

Input/Output Statements

Input/output (I/O) statements are used to transfer data from one place to another; for example, to get it from the keyboard, display it on the screen, write it to a disk file, or print it on a printer. Examples are:

```
WRITELN(' This displays text on the screen.');

READLN(Name); { Gets a string from the keyboard }

WRITELN(myfile, 'This writes text to a disk file.');
```

There are two things to notice in these examples. First, you can use I/O statements to assign values to variables. In line 2 of the example, the READLN statement not only gets a string from the keyboard, but puts that string into the variable Name. Second, the WRITELN statement at the bottom writes a line of text to a disk file that's denoted by the file variable myfile. WRITELN and READLN can take the name of a file as the destination (with WRITELN) or the source (with READLN) of the information they use; if you don't specify a file name, Pascal assumes that you want to READ from the keyboard and WRITE to the screen. For example,

```
WRITELN (myfile, 'Doug')
```

writes the string 'Doug' to the disk file or device represented by the file variable 'Doug'. On the other hand,

```
WRITELN ('Doug')
```

simply displays the string 'Doug' on the screen.

Control Statements

Control statements are used to direct the flow of your program in one direction or another based on the value of some variable. The most important are summarized here.

IF..THEN..ELSE   You use IF..THEN..ELSE (or just IF..THEN when you don't need an ELSE) when you want the program to go in one of two directions based on an either/or situation. For example:

```
IF PaidUp = true
 THEN SendThankYou
 ELSE BugForMoney;
```

In this case, PaidUp is either true or it isn't; there is no third alternative. For situations in which a statement must deal with several alternatives, it is usually better to use a CASE statement.

CASE Statements   A CASE statement is used when the program must branch in one of several directions based on a variable which can have several different values. For example,

```
CASE varval OF
     1 : FirstRoutine;
     2 : SecondRoutine;
     3 : ThirdRoutine;
     4 : FourthRoutine;
     ELSE DoError;
     END;
```

This is a typical CASE statement and causes the program to execute the First-Routine procedure if the value of varval is 1, SecondRoutine if the value is 2, and so on. If the value does not match any of the values specified in the CASE statement, then the ELSE clause (DoError) is executed. Unlike IF statements, however, CASE statements can only be used with ordinal data types; they cannot, for example, be used with a string variable as the CASE selector.

FOR Loops   FOR loops repeat a simple or compound statement a certain number of times. A good example of using a FOR loop is to assign initial values to the slots in an array:

```
VAR
     Letters = ARRAY[1..50] of char;
```

```
    Counter : integer;
BEGIN
 FOR counter := 1 to 50 DO
     Letters[counter] := ' '
END;
```

This assigns initial values to the Letters array so that each slot has a space in it. Notice that we needed an integer-type counter variable. In the FOR statement itself, we used the assignment operator and not the equals sign. The DO part of the statement can be any legal Pascal statement, whether simple (as in the example) or compound (a BEGIN..END statement).

WHILE and REPEAT Loops   WHILE and REPEAT statements are quite similar. In both cases, you want to repeat a certain statement or series of statements based on the value of a single control variable. The difference is that with a WHILE statement, the variable is evaluated before the loop ever executes, so a WHILE loop might never execute at all. In a REPEAT statement, however, the variable is evaluated at the end of each loop, so a REPEAT loop will always execute at least once. Examples of WHILE and REPEAT loops are as follows:

```
WHILE paidup DO statement;

WHILE paidup DO
     BEGIN
     statement1;
     statement2
     END;

REPEAT
     statement1;
     statement2;
     statement3;
UNTIL GPA > 3.00;
```

The other significant difference between WHILE and REPEAT loops is that a WHILE loop only repeats the first statement after the WHILE statement; this is why the second example used BEGIN..END to make two statements into a single compound statement. A REPEAT loop, on the other hand, will execute all the statements up to the UNTIL statement, which indicates the end of the loop.

Procedures and Functions

Procedures and functions are both named subroutines that process values and return them to the calling part of the program. Each can have its own local types, variables, constants, procedures, and functions. For example,

```
PROCEDURE CheckBalance(VAR balance: REAL);
 CONST Tax = 1.05;
 BEGIN
 IF balance <> 0.00
     THEN balance := balance * Tax
 END;

FUNCTION PaidUp (balance: real) : Boolean;
 BEGIN
     IF balance <= 0.00
      THEN PaidUp := TRUE
      ELSE PaidUp := FALSE
 END;

{ main body of program }
BEGIN
     CheckBalance(215.00);
     IF PaidUp(215.00) THEN DoSomething;
END.
```

In this example, when you pass a value 215.00 to the procedure CheckBalance, it multiplies the value by 1.05 to add 5-percent sales tax. When you pass the same value to the function PaidUp, it returns a value of false, which you can then use in an IF..THEN statement.

Parameters and Scope

If a procedure or function is to handle any values from outside, they should be declared as parameters, just as in the two examples above. Notice that you declare each type of value that goes into and comes out of the procedure when you first define the procedure. You then pass the values as parameters to the procedure by calling the procedure and listing the appropriate variables in parentheses after the procedure name. Outside variables that must be changed by a procedure must be declared as VAR parameters, as in the example.

Note that parameters and local variables inside procedures and functions are not visible to any part of the program outside those procedures and functions. Thus, in the example above, the constant `Tax` can only be used inside the `CheckBalance` procedure, not in the `PaidUp` function or in the main part of the program.

Turbo Pascal Units

Turbo Pascal allows the creation of separately compiled libraries of subroutines called *units.* Each unit can have its own variables, constants, data types, procedures, and functions in both a public part (the INTERFACE part of the unit) and a private part (the IMPLEMENTATION part). The private part is only accessible by routines in the unit itself.

Turbo Pascal for Windows comes with several predefined units of object types and routines. These units form the heart of its Windows-handling capabilities. These include the `WObjects Strings, System, WinCrt, WinDos, WinProcs,` and `WinTypes` units. We will discuss all of these units in detail later on.

Program Comments

Program comments in Turbo Pascal are delimited by two types of brackets, illustrated below:

```
{ This is a comment. }
(* This is another comment. *)
```

The only thing to be careful about is that a comment begun with one type of bracket cannot be terminated with the other type of bracket. As with other programming languages, comments are for human eyes, and are ignored by Turbo Pascal.

Structured and Object-Oriented Programming

- **Basic Concepts of Structured Programming**

- **From Structured to Object-Oriented Programming**

- **Methods and Encapsulation**

- **Inheritance**

- **Static and Virtual Methods**

- **Dynamic Object Variables and Pointers**

Programming with Turbo Pascal for Windows requires a firm understanding of the concepts and techniques of object-oriented programming (OOP). OOP is a new approach, one that builds on the ideas of traditional structured programming that Pascal was designed to teach. Because most people—even most programmers—are still unfamiliar with OOP, this chapter provides a complete discussion of the object-oriented techniques needed in using Turbo Pascal for Windows, showing how these techniques grow out of structured programming concepts.

Although our examples will be Windows programs, we will deliberately avoid getting involved in any Windows-specific details at this stage so that Windows features won't be confused with more generally applicable OOP techniques.

Basic Concepts of Structured Programming

The basic idea of structured programming is that the overall job of the program should be divided into subtasks, and that each of these subtasks should be handled by its own subroutine. The precise details of how each task is performed are hidden inside its subroutine, so that no knowledge of those details is needed to design and code the rest of the program.

Of course, knowing that you should "split the program into subroutines" isn't enough: the question is, *what* subroutines? How should different program tasks be divided up so that the overall goal of the program is achieved efficiently and with clear, easy-to-understand code?

State What the Program Should Do

The first step is to summarize in one sentence what the program is supposed to do. Let's use Turbo Pascal for Windows as an example. (Although it's a tool for creating other programs, it is itself a PC program.)

> Turbo Pascal for Windows should allow the user to write Turbo Pascal programs that will run under Microsoft Windows.

That is, of course, a very general statement. It doesn't tell us anything about how the programs will be written, debugged, and compiled, or if Turbo Pascal for Windows will itself be a Windows program.

Divide the Main Task into Subtasks

As a second step, we'll make our problem definition a little more specific.

> Turbo Pascal for Windows should display a Windows-compliant graphic user interface, have an integrated development environment (consisting of menu-driven program editor, compiler/linker, and debugger), and take advantage of Windows' program and memory management capabilities.

Notice that we haven't said anything about how these features should be implemented in program code; we've simply identified the major tasks that the program has to perform. At this stage, there are three main ideas to follow:

1. Subdivide the program's tasks until each subroutine performs a clear logical step, such as opening a file.

2. Avoid getting involved in language details. Focus on what the program is supposed to accomplish.

3. Don't forget about housekeeping details, such as setting up the program to run and explaining the program to the user. Each of those may need its own subroutine.

Decide on Broad Implementation Details

Once you have a good outline of the jobs that the program should perform and how they're divided into subroutines, you must consider the specifics of how the program is to be implemented:

What Needs to Be Global, and What Can Be Local?

Remember that the code inside each subroutine is "hidden" from the main program and the other subroutines. Parts of the program that are hidden inside a subroutine are local to that subroutine because they aren't accessible to other parts of the program. Things that aren't in a subroutine, on the other hand, are considered global.

The operative principle is so important that it deserves special emphasis as a rule of thumb:

Within reason, hide everything you can.

This means that the main structure of the program shouldn't be mucked up with a lot of details about how various parts of the program work. Those details should be hidden inside subroutines, which can contain their own variables, data structures, and local subroutines.

Some things do need to be global. If a variable is shared by several subroutines, it must be global so that it's accessible to all those subroutines. Hiding it inside one of the subroutines just wouldn't make sense. Likewise, a subroutine to pause the program, which will be called by many other subroutines, must be global. Anything that doesn't really need to be global, however, should be hidden inside a subroutine.

Decide on Data Structures

At this stage, you simply need to decide what the data structures must do—never mind how they get coded in a particular language.

Which Language Is Best for the Program?

There are currently several tools available for Windows programming: Borland C++, Microsoft C with the Windows SDK, Smalltalk/Windows, and Toolbook. Not all of these, however, are powerful enough to write a compiler, let alone a compiler with integrated development and debugging facilities. Either Borland C++ or Microsoft C/Windows SDK are plausible choices; we could even, with some extra effort, do it in assembly language or Turbo Pascal!

From Structured to Object-Oriented Programming

In object-oriented programming, any minimally sophisticated data structure includes two things:

- A particular arrangement of data items, such as an array or a linked list, and

- A set of operations that manipulate those data items.

For example, without Push and Pop routines, an array is just an array. When you add those routines, you create a stack data structure. If, instead, you add the routines appropriate for a queue or for a hash table, then you turn the array into a queue or a hash table.

In standard Pascal there is no way to weld the routines right into the data structure—there's no way to create a stack, queue, hash table, or other data structure that is smart enough to take care of itself and does not need outside routines to help it. Instead, you have a passive array on which external routines operate to create a stack or other data structure. Object-oriented programming, on the other hand, lets us create a data structure that contains within itself everything it needs to behave as it should. For example, instead of adding an item to a stack by passing the stack to a Push routine, you send a message to a stack object to add an item to itself. What makes this tricky is that it involves a totally new way of structuring and thinking about our programs.

Object-oriented programming originally came out of ideas in the Simula programming language of the 1960s. Most of the research work that developed the object-oriented approach, however, was done at Xerox Corporation's Palo Alto Research Center (PARC) in a 10-year project that developed Smalltalk, the first truly and completely object-oriented programming language. Xerox PARC is perhaps most famous for developing the "Xerox Star" microcomputer and its icon-based screen interface, which provided the inspiration for Microsoft Windows and the Apple Macintosh. The difficulty of creating such a screen interface was a key motivation in the development of object-oriented programming techniques, even though object-oriented programming has no necessary connection with icon-based screen displays.

Turbo Pascal for Windows traces its object-oriented heritage from Xerox PARC's original work on Smalltalk, through Apple's Object Pascal and AT&T's C++ programming languages, as well as from the non-Windows version of Turbo Pascal itself. The great advantage of object orientation, particularly in programming for Microsoft Windows, is that it lets you use predefined *object types* for windows, buttons, icons, and other Windows features—modifying these object types as needed.

In creating a Windows application, for example, you can use a single *parent window* object type (TWindow) that already knows how to do all the basic window tasks, such as moving, responding to mouse clicks, displaying a menu, and closing itself.

You can then create as many specialized window types as you need, based on this parent type, without repeating any code from the parent type. Each specialized data type, called a *child* of the parent type, inherits all of the features of the parent type and can add its own new features. It can even cancel out parent features that don't apply to it. Extending the parent/child metaphor, a type that is derived from an earlier object type is called its *descendant*, while the earlier object type, likewise, is called the descendant type's *ancestor*.

Because these object data types inherit the characteristics of their ancestor types, you can extend the capabilities of already compiled units of library routines even if you do not have the source code. You simply create new object types as descendants of already existing object types, and then add new features or cancel inherited features as needed. Procedures designed to work with ancestor object types will work with their descendant object types as well.

Basic Concepts of Object-Oriented Programming

Those are the general ideas behind object-oriented programming. Now, let's look at the specifics. Object-oriented programming introduces several new concepts:

- **Objects** Objects look similar to records, but they contain their own procedures and functions, both of which (in an object type) are called *methods*.

- **Object types** define particular object data types and their capabilities.

- **Encapsulation** binds procedures and functions into a data structure along with the data they process.

- **Messages** are instructions sent to objects to tell them to carry out their built-in methods.

- **Inheritance** means that the characteristics of an object type are passed along to its descendant object types.

- **Polymorphism** is the ability of different objects to respond in their own unique ways to the same program command.

- **Extensibility of code** This property enables already compiled units to be used as a basis for creating and using new objects that were unknown at compile time.

Appropriately enough, the fundamental concept in object-oriented programming is that of the object. An object looks very much like a Pascal record, except that it has its own procedures and functions. Consider Listing 3.1, which shows a conventional structured programming approach to loading values into a student record.

Listing 3.1

```
PROGRAM Listing3_1;
{ Shows standard structured programming techniques for
entering data into a student record and displaying the
data. }

USES winCRT;

CONST space = #32;

TYPE
string15 = STRING[15];
studentrec = RECORD
    fname,
    lname : string15;
    GPA   : REAL;
    END;
VAR
    student : studentrec;

PROCEDURE Pause; { Pauses program until user presses a key. }
VAR
    Proceed : char;
    BEGIN
    Writeln;
    Write(' Press any key to continue ... ');
    Proceed := readkey;
    Writeln; Writeln
    END;

PROCEDURE init(var student : studentrec);
BEGIN
    WITH student DO
    BEGIN
fname := space;
lname := space;
    GPA    := 0.00
    END
```

```
    END;

PROCEDURE FillRecord(var student : studentrec);
BEGIN
    WITH student DO
    BEGIN
write(' Enter the student''s first name: ');
readln(fname);
write(' Enter the student''s last name: ');
readln(lname);
write(' Enter the student''s current GPA: ');
readln(GPA);
    END
    END;

PROCEDURE DisplayInfo(student : studentrec);
BEGIN
    CLRSCR;
    WITH student DO
    BEGIN
WRITELN(' Student name is: ', fname, space, lname, '.');
WRITELN(' Student GPA is: ', GPA:0:2, '.');
    pause
    END;
    END;

BEGIN
    CLRSCR;
    init(student);
    fillrecord(student);
    pause;
    displayinfo(student)
END.
```

The student record itself uses the RECORD data type to bind together two string fields (for first name and last name) with a real-number field for grade point average (GPA). Routines are defined to initialize the record, load it with data, and then display the data on the computer screen, as shown in Figure 3.1. If the student's GPA is over 3.5, then a letter of congratulations is printed.

It's in the main body of the program that we will see the most dramatic change when we go from structured to object-oriented programming. In Listing 3.1, the program clears the screen and then passes the student record variable to the Init routine, which initializes its data fields with "blank" values. The variable is then

FIGURE 3.1:

Output screen from Listing 3.1

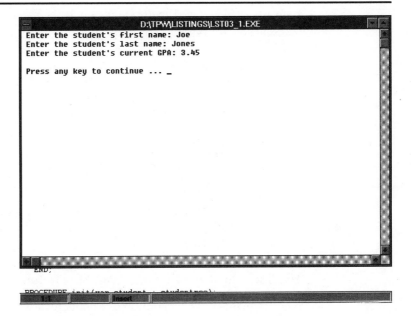

```
                              D:\TPW\LISTINGS\LST03_1.EXE
Enter the student's first name: Joe
Enter the student's last name: Jones
Enter the student's current GPA: 3.45

Press any key to continue ... _
```

```
   END;

PROCEDURE init(var student : studentrec);
```

passed to the FillRecord routine, which loads name and GPA information into its data fields. Finally, it is passed to the DisplayInfo routine, which takes the information in its data fields and displays it on the computer screen.

Throughout all this, the student record variable is a passive spectator that has things "done to it," like a hospital patient lying on a cart who gets wheeled from one examining room to the next. Poked, prodded, and (we imagine) slightly humiliated by all this, the student record variable nonetheless provides what we need.

Methods and Encapsulation

A neater way to accomplish the goals of the preceding program is to declare the student record type as an *object type* instead of as an *object* (a record type). This allows us to include all the procedures and functions needed to manipulate the data in the object itself—an approach called *encapsulation* because it creates a hermetically sealed object "capsule" that includes all the data fields and methods it needs. To declare an object type, you simply use the Turbo Pascal reserved-word object and then list its fields and methods in much the same way as you would do with a standard record-type declaration:

```
TYPE
studentrec = OBJECT
         fname,
         lname : string15;
         GPA   : REAL;
         PROCEDURE init;
         PROCEDURE fillrecord;
         PROCEDURE SendHonorsLetter;
         PROCEDURE DisplayNameAndGPA;
         END;
```

All the data fields must be listed in the type definition before any methods are listed, as in the example above. A quirk of object-type declarations is that the last method or field declaration before the END must be followed by a semicolon; this is the only place in Pascal where a semicolon must be used right before an END. You'll see a lot of these "extra" semicolons in Turbo Pascal for Windows programs.

Of course, this type declaration does not create an object, any more than declaring a record type creates any records. To create an object, you must declare *a variable of the object type*—for example,

```
VAR
     student : studentrec
```

At some point, either before or after you declare the object variable, you must spell out the details of the object's methods, just as you would with any other subroutines. There are, however, two key differences from the way in which you would declare ordinary subroutines:

- First, the name of each method must be preceded by the name of the object type. When we declare the details of our Init method for the studentrec object type above, for example, we would write the subroutine header as

  ```
  studentrec.init
  ```

  to make it clear that the subroutine is a method in the studentrec object type.

- Second, the header for a method does not need to take an object variable itself as a parameter. For example, in the Init declaration from Listing 3.1, which uses standard structured programming, the record variable must be declared as a parameter because it is passed to the Init subroutine. With an object type, however, the Init routine is part of the object variable, so it automatically "knows" which variable it should initialize—i.e., itself. Therefore, instead of

```
Init(student: studentrec)
```

as in Listing 3.1, the declaration can be simply

```
studentrec.init
```

The best way to understand these concepts is to look at a simple example, as shown in Listing 3.2. This is exactly the same program as in Listing 3.1, but with a crucial difference: it is coded using object-oriented techniques.

Listing 3.2

```
PROGRAM Listing3_2;
{ Shows object-oriented approach to entering data into a
student record (an object) and displaying the data.
Principal feature demonstrated: ENCAPSULATION. }

USES winCRT;

CONST
    formfeed = #12;
    space    = #32;

TYPE
    string15 = STRING[15];
    studentrec = OBJECT
    fname,
    lname : string15;
    GPA : REAL;
    PROCEDURE init;
PROCEDURE fillrecord;
PROCEDURE SendHonorsLetter;
PROCEDURE DisplayNameAndGPA;
END;

VAR
    student : studentrec;

PROCEDURE Pause; { Pauses the program until user presses a key. }
VAR
```

```
    Proceed : char;
    BEGIN
    Writeln;
    Write(' Press any key to continue ... ');
    Proceed := readkey;
    Writeln; Writeln
    END;

PROCEDURE studentrec.init;
    BEGIN
    fname := space;
    lname := space;
    GPA    := 0.00
    END;

PROCEDURE studentrec.FillRecord;
    BEGIN
    CLRSCR;
    WRITE(' Enter the student''s first name: ');
    READLN(fname);
    WRITE(' Enter the student''s last name: ');
    READLN(lname);
    WRITE(' Enter the student''s current GPA: ');
    READLN(GPA);
    END;

PROCEDURE studentrec.SendHonorsLetter;
VAR
    letterfile: TEXT;
    counter : INTEGER;
    BEGIN
    ASSIGN(letterfile, 'prn');
    REWRITE(letterfile);
FOR counter := 1 TO 10 DO WRITELN(letterfile);
WRITELN(letterfile, 'Dear Mr./Ms. ', lname, ':');
WRITELN(letterfile);
WRITELN(letterfile, 'Your grade point average is over 3.5. This');
WRITELN(letterfile, 'means that you will graduate cum laude from');
WRITELN(letterfile, 'this institution. Congratulations.');
WRITELN(letterfile);
WRITELN(letterfile, 'Sincerely,');
WRITELN(letterfile);
WRITELN(letterfile, 'V. Wormer');
WRITELN(letterfile, 'Dean of Students');
WRITELN(letterfile, formfeed);
```

```
CLOSE(letterfile)
   END;

PROCEDURE studentrec.DisplayNameAndGPA;
BEGIN
   CLRSCR;
WRITELN(' The student''s name is: ', fname, space, lname, '.');
WRITELN(' The student''s GPA is:  ', GPA:0:2, '.');
IF GPA > 3.5 THEN SendHonorsLetter;
   END;

BEGIN
   student.init;
   student.fillrecord;
   student.displaynameandGPA
END.
```

In most of the program code, the differences seem fairly minor. Instead of declaring studentrec as a record type, we declare it as an object type. We include as methods in the object type all of the procedures that were formerly separate from the student record; this is an example of encapsulation. When we get to declaring the details of the methods, again, everything looks pretty much the same. The Init method initializes the object's data fields with a "blank" value, the FillRecord method loads data into the data fields, the DisplayNameAndGPA method shows the name and GPA on the screen, and if the GPA is over 3.5, then the SendHonorsLetter prints a congratulatory letter.

It is when we get to the main body of the program that the dramatic difference becomes clear. Instead of passing the student record variable to the init routine, which would then initialize it (as in Listing 3.1), we send a message to the variable and tell it to initialize itself. It knows how to do this because it has a built-in init method. We then tell the variable to get some data from the user and load the data into its fields. Finally, we tell it to display its data on the screen and, if appropriate, send a congratulatory letter to the student.

Note how we called the methods in the object: by using the name of the object variable (not the object type), a dot, and then the name of the method. The variable name tells the program which object variable is to get a message, and the method name tells the variable which of its methods it should use.

Which Methods to Include

In the preceding simple example, we can see that object-oriented programming gets rid of the traditional passive data structures that we saw in structured programming. In their place, it puts active, intelligent data structures that know how to do every task that they will be called on to perform.

This leads to a key principle of object design: make sure that your object type has all the methods it needs to manipulate the data in its fields. It is possible in Turbo Pascal (but not in most other languages that support object-oriented programming) to access an object's fields directly. For example, instead of sending a message to the student variable to use its Init method, you could initialize its fields as follows:

```
student.fname := space;
student.lname := space;
student.GPA := 0.00;
```

As you might suspect, you can also use the WITH notation, just as you can with a record variable:

```
WITH student DO
    BEGIN
    fname      := space;
    lname      := space;
    GPA        := 0.00;
    END;
```

Now, if student were a record variable, there would be nothing wrong with this; indeed, it would be the only way to initialize the record's data fields. But student is not a record variable. It is an object that has built-in methods to handle any task involving its data fields. A major benefit of encapsulation is that it allows us to hide even more information inside various compartments of the program. Just like using global variables in a subroutine without declaring them as parameters, any attempt to manipulate an object's fields without using its methods violates the principle of information hiding and must be avoided whenever possible.

The key to avoiding it, and thereby preserving the integrity of your object variables, is to make sure that your object type definition includes all the methods that the object will need in order to manipulate the data in its fields. If one or more methods are left out of your object type definition, then you will have no choice but to manipulate object fields directly, which you don't want to do.

Obviously, which methods an object will require depends on the purpose of the object. Our student object variable needs methods to initialize its fields, to load them with data, to report that data to the screen, and to print out a letter when appropriate. A stack object variable would also need an Init method, but it would also need methods to do Pushes and Pops.

Because you can create descendant object types and add methods that are not in their ancestor types, you can even do this with precompiled libraries of objects, as we will see in the next section.

Inheritance

Just as human children inherit characteristics from their parents—hair color, height, etc.—Pascal objects inherit fields and methods from their parent objects, as well as from all their other ancestor objects up the line. In this section, we will discuss how to create and use descendant object types that are derived from already existing object types.

The first thing we want to do is put the object and method declarations from Listing 3.2 into a unit. Listing 3.3 shows how to do this.

Listing 3.3

```
UNIT my_objs;

INTERFACE

USES winCRT;

CONST
    formfeed = #12;
    space    = #32;

TYPE
    string15 = STRING[15];
    studentrec = OBJECT
    fname,
    lname : string15;
    GPA    : REAL;
    PROCEDURE init;
PROCEDURE fillrecord;
```

```
PROCEDURE SendHonorsLetter;
PROCEDURE DisplayNameAndGPA;
END;

IMPLEMENTATION

PROCEDURE studentrec.init;
    BEGIN
    fname := space;
    lname := space;
    GPA   := 0.00
    END;

PROCEDURE studentrec.FillRecord;
    BEGIN
    CLRSCR;
    WRITE(' Enter the student''s first name: ');
    READLN(fname);
    WRITE(' Enter the student''s last name: ');
    READLN(lname);
    WRITE(' Enter the student''s current GPA: ');
    READLN(GPA);
    END;

PROCEDURE studentrec.SendHonorsLetter;
VAR
    letterfile: TEXT;
    counter : INTEGER;
    BEGIN
    ASSIGN(letterfile, 'prn');
    REWRITE(letterfile);
FOR counter := 1 TO 10 DO WRITELN(letterfile);
WRITELN(letterfile, 'Dear Mr./Ms. ', lname, ':');
WRITELN(letterfile);
WRITELN(letterfile, 'Your grade point average is over 3.5. This');
WRITELN(letterfile, 'means that you will graduate cum laude from');
WRITELN(letterfile, 'this institution. Congratulations.');
WRITELN(letterfile);
WRITELN(letterfile, 'Sincerely,');
WRITELN(letterfile);
WRITELN(letterfile, 'V. Wormer');
WRITELN(letterfile, 'Dean of Students');
WRITELN(letterfile, formfeed);
close(letterfile)
    END;
```

```
PROCEDURE studentrec.DisplayNameAndGPA;
BEGIN
   CLRSCR;
WRITELN(' The student''s name is: ', fname, space, lname, '.');
WRITELN(' The student''s GPA is:  ', GPA:0:2, '.');
IF GPA > 3.5 THEN SendHonorsLetter;
   END;

END.
```

Once you have typed in Listing 3.3, save it as MY_OBJS.PAS. Go into Turbo Pascal's Compile menu and compile the unit to generate MY_OBJS.TPU, copying the compiled .TPU file to your Turbo Pascal for Windows program directory (probably C:\TPW).

You can see in Listing 3.3 that, from the standpoint of creating a unit, there is nothing unusual about setting up a unit with object types. The object type definition itself goes in the INTERFACE section of the unit, while the details of the methods go in the IMPLEMENTATION section, just as you would expect.

The trick comes in Listing 3.4, a program which uses the object type and method definitions in the unit. In this program, we create a GradStudentRec object type which is a descendant of the StudentRec object type. To do this, we simply include the identifier StudentRec in parentheses after the word OBJECT in the object type definition.

Listing 3.4

```
PROGRAM Listing3_4;
{ Shows how the creation of descendant object types saves
considerable programming work. Principal features shown:

    INHERITANCE, whereby an object type automatically includes
    fields and methods from its ancestor types; and

    OVERRIDING, whereby an object type can (but does not have to)
replace methods from ancestor types with more appropriate
methods for itself. }

USES winCRT, my_objs;

TYPE
   gradstudentrec = OBJECT (studentrec)
```

```
    PhDcandidate : BOOLEAN;
    PROCEDURE init;
    PROCEDURE FillRecord;
    PROCEDURE SendHonorsLetter;
    END;

VAR
    gradstudent : gradstudentrec;

PROCEDURE Pause; { Pauses the program until user presses a key. }
VAR
    Proceed : char;
    BEGIN
    Writeln;
    Write(' Press any key to continue ... ');
    Proceed := readkey;
    Writeln; Writeln
    END;

PROCEDURE gradstudentrec.init;
    BEGIN
    CLRSCR;
    studentrec.init;
    PhDcandidate := FALSE;
    WRITELN(' PhDcandidate field has been initialized to false.');
    pause
    END;

PROCEDURE gradstudentrec.fillrecord;
    VAR candidate : CHAR;
    BEGIN
    studentrec.fillrecord;
    WRITE(' Is the student a Ph.D. candidate (Y/N)? ');
    READLN(candidate);
    IF UPCASE(candidate) = 'Y'
    THEN PhDcandidate := TRUE
    ELSE PhDcandidate := FALSE
    END;

PROCEDURE gradstudentrec.SendHonorsLetter;
    VAR
    letterfile: TEXT;
    counter : INTEGER;
    BEGIN
    ASSIGN(letterfile, 'prn');
```

```
   REWRITE(letterfile);
FOR counter := 1 TO 10 DO WRITELN(letterfile);
WRITELN(letterfile, 'Dear Mr./Ms. ', lname, ':');
WRITELN(letterfile);
WRITELN(letterfile, 'Your grade point average is over 3.5. This');
WRITELN(letterfile,
'means that you will receive your Ph.D. "with');
WRITELN(letterfile, 'distinction" from this institution.');
WRITELN(letterfile, 'Congratulations.');
WRITELN(letterfile);
   WRITELN(letterfile, 'Sincerely,');
   WRITELN(letterfile);
   WRITELN(letterfile, 'V. Wormer');
   WRITELN(letterfile, 'Dean of Students');
   WRITELN(letterfile, formfeed);
   CLOSE(letterfile)
   END;

BEGIN
   gradstudent.init;
   gradstudent.fillrecord;
   gradstudent.displaynameandGPA;
   pause
END.
```

Notice that we declared three methods in the GradStudentRec object type: Init, Fill-Record, and SendHonorsLetter. Because these methods have the same names as methods in their ancestor type, they override the methods from the ancestor type. If we create a variable of type GradStudentRec and send it a message to initialize itself, it will use its own Init routine; likewise for the other methods.

The DisplayNameAndGPA method did not need to be changed, so we did not have to declare it in GradStudentRec at all. Because it is part of the StudentRec object type, it is inherited by the GradStudentRec object type.

Another trick demonstrated by Listing 3.4 is that, in an object type's methods, you can make explicit calls to the methods of ancestor types by using the dot notation with the name of the ancestor type. In the GradStudentRec.init method, for example, there is no need to repeat the code that gets the student name and GPA, because this code is part of the ancestor type StudentRec. Instead, we simply include an explicit call to StudentRec's Init routine inside the GradStudentRec's Init routine. When this line of code is reached, StudentRec.init executes just like any other subroutine. The rest of the

GradStudentRec.init routine then gets the information that is unique to the GradStudentRec type. The same trick is used in the GradStudentRec.fillrecord method.

In summary, to override a method from an ancestor object type, you simply declare a new method in the descendant object type with the same name as the method in the ancestor type. To add a new method or field, as we did with the PhDCandidate field in the GradStudentRec type, simply add it to the descendant type declaration.

Note one very important point: only *methods* can be overridden, not data fields. The data fields of an ancestor type are an ineradicable part of all its descendant types, and this cannot be changed. If some of your descendant types will need a certain field and others will not, you should simply leave that field out of the ancestor type.

Once you have typed in Listing 3.4, compile and run it. You will see that, as advertised, the GradStudentRec methods collect the information and process it as needed—that is, with one exception. It fails to execute the GradStudentRec.SendHonorsLetter method; instead it executes the method from the ancestor StudentRec object type. Something has clearly gone wrong.

Static and Virtual Methods

The problem with the preceding example is that the DisplayNameAndGPA method, which calls the SendHonorsLetter method, is inherited from the ancestor object type. When the program is compiled, the DisplayNameAndGPA method is given the memory address of the SendHonorsLetter method that it should use. Because the copy of DisplayNameAndGPA we are using is part of the StudentRec object type, it naturally uses the SendHonorsLetter method that is also part of the StudentRec object type. Because everything is determined at compile time, this is called an example of *early binding*: the method call is "bound" to a certain copy of the SendHonorsLetter method when the program is compiled, and this cannot be changed later when the program is run. Methods that are bound at compile time are called *static methods* because they cannot be changed after compilation.

The obvious solution to the problem is to put a new method declaration for DisplayNameAndGPA into the GradStudentRec object type. Then, when the program is compiled, this method is part of the GradStudentRec type, so it is bound to the appropriate copy of the SendHonorsLetter method. This solution is demonstrated in Listing 3.5.

Listing 3.5

```
PROGRAM Listing3_5;
{ Shows a static-method solution to the problem of the inherited
"DisplayNameAndGPA" method calling the ancestor object type's
"SendHonorsLetter" routine instead of the current object type's
"SendHonorsLetter" routine. This approach requires more code
than the virtual method solution. }

USES winCRT, my_objs;

TYPE
    gradstudentrec = OBJECT (studentrec)
    PhDcandidate : BOOLEAN;
    PROCEDURE init;
    PROCEDURE FillRecord;
PROCEDURE SendHonorsLetter;
PROCEDURE DisplayNameAndGPA;
END;

VAR
    gradstudent : gradstudentrec;

PROCEDURE Pause; { Pauses program until user presses a key. }
VAR
    Proceed : char;
    BEGIN
    Writeln;
    Write(' Press any key to continue ... ');
    Proceed := readkey;
    Writeln; Writeln
    END;

PROCEDURE gradstudentrec.init;
    BEGIN
    CLRSCR;
    studentrec.init;
    PhDcandidate := FALSE;
    WRITELN(' PhDcandidate field has been initialized to false.');
    pause
    END;

PROCEDURE gradstudentrec.fillrecord;
```

```
    VAR candidate : CHAR;
    BEGIN
    studentrec.fillrecord;
    WRITE(' Is the student a Ph.D. candidate (Y/N)? ');
    READLN(candidate);
    IF UPCASE(candidate) = 'Y'
    THEN PhDcandidate := TRUE
    ELSE PhDcandidate := FALSE
    END;


PROCEDURE gradstudentrec.SendHonorsLetter;
    VAR
    letterfile: TEXT;
    counter : INTEGER;
    BEGIN
    ASSIGN(letterfile, 'prn');
    REWRITE(letterfile);
FOR counter := 1 TO 10 DO WRITELN(letterfile);
WRITELN(letterfile, 'Dear Mr./Ms. ', lname, ':');
WRITELN(letterfile);
WRITELN(letterfile, 'Your grade point average is over 3.5. This');
WRITELN(letterfile,
'means that you will receive your Ph.D. "with');
WRITELN(letterfile, 'distinction" from this institution.');
WRITELN(letterfile, 'Congratulations.');
    WRITELN(letterfile);
    WRITELN(letterfile, 'Sincerely,');
    WRITELN(letterfile);
    WRITELN(letterfile, 'V. Wormer');
    WRITELN(letterfile, 'Dean of Students');
    WRITELN(letterfile, formfeed);
    CLOSE(letterfile)
    END;


PROCEDURE gradstudentrec.DisplayNameAndGPA;
    BEGIN
    CLRSCR;
WRITELN(' The student''s name is: ', fname, space, lname, '.');
WRITELN(' The student''s GPA is:  ', GPA:0:2, '.');
IF GPA > 3.5 THEN SendHonorsLetter;
    END;
```

```
BEGIN
    gradstudent.init;
    gradstudent.fillrecord;
    gradstudent.displaynameandGPA;
    pause
END.
```

This approach will work: if you run the program in Listing 3.5, you will see that the correct copy of the SendHonorsLetter method is being used. However, notice that apart from the fact that it is in the GradStudentRec object declaration, there is no difference between the DisplayNameAndGPA routine in Listing 3.5 and the DisplayNameAndGPA routine in the ancestor StudentRec type. This means we are writing the same code all over again.

One of the advantages of object-oriented programming was supposed to be that it reduces the amount of code we have to write. If we have to keep rewriting the same methods in each descendant object type just to make sure that they are bound to the appropriate copies of other methods, then it would seem that we should sue somebody for false advertising: interesting as it is, object-oriented programming would not be making good on its promises. However, there is a better solution than repeating the same method code in each descendant type (or suing somebody): using *virtual methods,* which are not bound at compile time. Declaring a method as virtual tells Turbo Pascal that it is unknown at compile time which copy of the method will need to be used, and that this decision should be put off until the program is actually run—an approach called *late binding.*

To declare a method as a virtual method, we add the Turbo Pascal reserved word `virtual` at the end of the method header in the object type definition. Listing 3.6 shows how we can change the MY_OBJS unit so that it makes SendHonorsLetter a virtual method.

Listing 3.6

```
UNIT my_objs2;
{ Changes the unit in Listing 3.3 to make SendHonorsLetter
a virtual method instead of a static method. Principal
features illustrated:

VIRTUAL METHODS, whereby a program can choose at
run-time which method should be executed, and

    A CONSTRUCTOR routine, which is absolutely required
in any object type that uses virtual methods. An object
```

variable's constructor MUST be called to set up the VMT
before any calls are made to the object's other methods. }

```
INTERFACE

USES WINCRT;

CONST
    formfeed = #12;
    space    = #32;

TYPE
    string15 = STRING[15];
    studentrec = OBJECT
    fname,
    lname : string15;
    GPA   : REAL;
    CONSTRUCTOR init;
    PROCEDURE fillrecord;
PROCEDURE SendHonorsLetter; VIRTUAL;
PROCEDURE DisplayNameAndGPA;
END;

PROCEDURE Pause; { Pauses program until user presses a key. }

IMPLEMENTATION

PROCEDURE Pause;
    VAR
    Proceed : char;
    BEGIN
    Writeln;
    Write(' Press any key to continue ... ');
    Proceed := readkey;
    Writeln; Writeln
    END;

CONSTRUCTOR studentrec.init;
    BEGIN
    fname := space;
    lname := space;
    GPA   := 0.00
    END;
```

```
PROCEDURE studentrec.FillRecord;
   BEGIN
   CLRSCR;
   WRITE(' Enter the student''s first name: ');
   READLN(fname);
   WRITE(' Enter the student''s last name: ');
   READLN(lname);
   WRITE(' Enter the student''s current GPA: ');
   READLN(GPA);
   END;

PROCEDURE studentrec.SendHonorsLetter;
   var
   letterfile: text;
   counter : integer;
   BEGIN
   assign(letterfile, 'prn');
   rewrite(letterfile);
for counter := 1 to 10 do WRITELN(letterfile);
WRITELN(letterfile, 'Dear Mr./Ms. ', lname, ':');
WRITELN(letterfile);
WRITELN(letterfile, 'Your grade point average is over 3.5. This');
WRITELN(letterfile, 'means that you will graduate cum laude from');
WRITELN(letterfile, 'this institution. Congratulations.');
WRITELN(letterfile);
   WRITELN(letterfile, 'Sincerely,');
   WRITELN(letterfile);
   WRITELN(letterfile, 'V. Wormer');
   WRITELN(letterfile, 'Dean of Students');
   WRITELN(letterfile, formfeed);
   close(letterfile)
   END;

PROCEDURE studentrec.DisplayNameAndGPA;
   BEGIN
   clrscr;
WRITELN(' The student''s name is: ', fname, space, lname, '.');
WRITELN(' The student''s GPA is:  ', GPA:0:2, '.');
IF GPA > 3.5 THEN SendHonorsLetter;
   END;

END.
```

Notice that there are two key differences between Listing 3.6 and Listing 3.3. First, of course, we have added the word virtual after the SendHonorsLetter method in the object type definition. Second—and this is vitally important—we have a new name for the Init routine: instead of being called a procedure, it is now called a *constructor.*

Let's review the situation to see why this is so important. When the program is compiled, any calls to static (non-virtual) methods are given the memory addresses where those methods can be found—an instance of early binding. However, with virtual methods, it is not known at compile time which virtual method will be needed by a particular method call: the method call is not given the memory address of a virtual method because it isn't known which address (i.e., the address of which method) is going to be needed. This means that when the program is compiled, these method calls do not know where to find the virtual methods that they are supposed to call. When the program is finally run, we need a way to tell those method calls where to find the methods they need.

This task is performed by the constructor routine. When the program is run, an object variable's constructor routine must be called before any calls are made to the object's virtual methods. The constructor routine sets up a *virtual method table* (*VMT*) that tells the program where to find the object variable's virtual methods. If you fail to put in a call to the constructor routine before calling a virtual method, your program will crash.

The good news is that all this work is done simply by the word constructor. As long as you call a routine designated as an object's constructor, the VMT will automatically be set up. You don't have to worry about it. This means that, even though the studentrec.init routine in Listing 3.6 does some other work as well, you could have a constructor routine that did nothing except set up the VMT, as in

```
CONSTRUCTOR AnotherInitMethod;
   BEGIN
      END;
```

A call to this routine will set up the VMT and make it possible for the object variable to use virtual methods, even though it doesn't do anything else. It's simply the word *constructor* that is important in setting up the VMT.

This is so important it must be repeated:

> Every object variable that uses virtual methods must have a constructor method, and the program must call that method before attempting to use any of the object variable's virtual methods. Failure to abide by this rule can result in disaster.

Now, let's recode the program from Listing 3.5 and make the SendHonorsLetter method a virtual method. First, save Listing 3.6 as MY_OBJS2.PAS and compile it to disk. Second, compile MY_OBJS2.PAS to generate the MY-OBJS2.TPU. Then, type in the program in Listing 3.7. Be sure that you name MY-OBJS2, not MY_OBJS, in the USES clause of Listing 3.7.

Listing 3.7

```
PROGRAM Listing3_7;
{ Shows how the creation of descendant object types saves
considerable programming work. Principal features shown:

    INHERITANCE, whereby an object type automatically includes
    fields and methods from its ancestor types; and

    OVERRIDING, whereby an object type can (but does not have to)
replace methods from ancestor types with more appropriate
methods for itself. }

USES winCRT, my_objs2;

TYPE
    gradstudentrec = OBJECT (studentrec)
    PhDcandidate : BOOLEAN;
    CONSTRUCTOR init;
    PROCEDURE FillRecord;
    PROCEDURE SendHonorsLetter; VIRTUAL;
    END;

VAR
    gradstudent : gradstudentrec;

CONSTRUCTOR gradstudentrec.init;
    BEGIN
    CLRSCR;
    studentrec.init;
    PhDcandidate := FALSE;
    WRITELN(' PhDcandidate field has been initialized to false.');
    pause
    END;
```

```
PROCEDURE gradstudentrec.fillrecord;
   VAR candidate : CHAR;
   BEGIN
   studentrec.fillrecord;
   WRITE(' Is the student a Ph.D. candidate (Y/N)? ');
   READLN(candidate);
   IF UPCASE(candidate) = 'Y'
   THEN PhDcandidate := TRUE
   ELSE PhDcandidate := FALSE
   END;

PROCEDURE gradstudentrec.SendHonorsLetter;
   VAR
   letterfile: TEXT;
   counter : INTEGER;
   BEGIN
   ASSIGN(letterfile, 'prn');
   REWRITE(letterfile);
FOR counter := 1 TO 10 DO WRITELN(letterfile);
WRITELN(letterfile, 'Dear Mr./Ms. ', lname, ':');
WRITELN(letterfile);
WRITELN(letterfile, 'Your grade point average is over 3.5. This');
WRITELN(letterfile,
'means that you will receive your Ph.D. "with');
WRITELN(letterfile, 'distinction" from this institution.');
WRITELN(letterfile, 'Congratulations.');
WRITELN(letterfile);
   WRITELN(letterfile, 'Sincerely,');
   WRITELN(letterfile);
   WRITELN(letterfile, 'V. Wormer');
   WRITELN(letterfile, 'Dean of Students');
   WRITELN(letterfile, formfeed);
   CLOSE(letterfile)
   END;

BEGIN
   gradstudent.init;
   gradstudent.fillrecord;
   gradstudent.displaynameandGPA;
   pause
END.
```

In Listing 3.7, we declare the Init method as a constructor method and make Send-HonorsLetter into a virtual method. Now, because SendHonorsLetter is virtual (in both the studentrec and gradstudentrec object types), its memory address is not bound to the method call in DisplayNameAndGPA when the program is compiled. The decision on which version of SendHonorsLetter to use is put off until the program is run. When a call is actually made to SendHonorsLetter during a program run, the program first checks to see what type of object is making the method call. It then calls the correct SendHonorsLetter method for that object type. In the case of Listing 3.7, SendHonorsLetter is being called by a gradstudentrec-type object, so it gets the version of SendHonorsLetter from the gradstudentrec object declaration.

By using virtual methods, we can avoid repeating code in descendant object types. Object-oriented programming has made good on its promise to reduce the amount of code we must write.

Example: An Object-Oriented Stack

As one more illustration, let's look at an object-oriented version of a stack. As you probably know, a stack is a list in which all additions and deletions are made at one end of the list. Here, we will create an array-based stack by using object-oriented techniques.

Listing 3.8

```
PROGRAM Listing3_8;
{ Demonstrates an object-oriented version of a stack. The program
prompts the user to enter enough characters to fill up the stack,
then pops them off the stack in reverse order.}

uses wincrt, my_objs2;

const max = 5;

type
    { GENERIC LIST OBJECT TYPE }
{ The list type is an abstract object type. This means that
we never intend to create any variables of the list type
itself. The list type is created only as an ancestor type
```

for other list object types, such as stacks and queues. We will actually create variables of these descendant types. Here, we demonstrate a stack object which is a descendant of the abstract list type. }

```
    list = OBJECT
listitem : array[1..max] of char;
count : 0..max;
    procedure init;
    function full : Boolean;
    function empty: Boolean;
    end;

    { STACK OBJECT TYPE }
stack = object (list) { stack type is descendant of list}
{ Because the top of the stack will always be the same
as the "count" field inherited from the list object
type, there is no need for a separate stacktop field.}
    procedure push(item : char);
    procedure pop(var item : char);
    end;

{ METHODS FOR THE LIST OBJECT TYPE }

procedure list.init;
    var counter : integer;
    begin
    clrscr;
    for counter := 1 to max do listitem[counter] := space;
    { recall that "space" is defined in the MyUtils unit. }
count := 0
    end;

function list.full : Boolean;
    begin
    if count = max then full := true else full := false
    end;

function list.empty : Boolean;
    begin
    empty := (count = 0)
```

```
   end;

{ METHODS FOR THE STACK OBJECT TYPE }

procedure stack.push(item : char);
   begin
   if full
   then begin
   writeln(' Sorry, full stack.');
   exit
   end
   else begin
   count := count + 1;
   listitem[count] := item
   end
   end; { of push procedure }

procedure stack.pop(var item : char);
   begin
   if empty
   then begin
   writeln(' Sorry, empty stack.');
   exit
   end
   else begin
   item := listitem[count];
   listitem[count] := space;
   count := count - 1
   end
   end; { of pop procedure }

{ VARIABLE DECLARATION SECTION }
VAR charlist : stack;

{ NON-OBJECT-ORIENTED PROCEDURES TO DISPLAY RESULTS ON PC'S SCREEN
}

procedure pushitemsonstack(var charlist : stack);
var
   newitem : char;
   counter : integer;
```

```
begin
for counter := 1 to max do
begin
write(' Enter a character to push onto the stack: ');
readln(newitem);
charlist.push(newitem);
writeln
end
end; { of pushitemsonstack routine }

procedure popitemsoffstack(var charlist : stack);
var
    counter : integer;
    item : char;
    begin
    clrscr;
writeln(' The stack items are popped off in reverse order');
writeln(' because a stack is a last-in-first-out list.');
writeln;
write(' Items popped from the stack: ');
for counter := 1 to max do
    begin
    charlist.pop(item);
    write(item, space)
    end
    end; { of popitemsoffstack routine }

{ MAIN BODY OF THE PROGRAM }
begin
    charlist.init;
    pushitemsonstack(charlist);
    popitemsoffstack(charlist);
    pause
end.
```

We first create a generic ("abstract") object type that can serve as an ancestor type for both stacks and queues; we call this abstract type list. This type contains the data fields and methods that will be common to all the list object types that we plan to create. Having created this ancestor type, all we need to add when we declare the stack object type are methods for pushing items onto the stack and popping items off of the stack.

Note that the methods for pushing and popping only have to take a single parameter: the character that is being pushed or popped. It is not necessary to include the stack object as a parameter, because, as we discussed earlier, the Push and Pop routines are part of the stack object, not external to it. When a call is made to an object's Push or Pop methods, it automatically knows that it is supposed to do a push or pop on its own listitem data field.

We also include routines to prompt the user for input and display the results in a window on the computer screen. These routines are external to the stack object and, therefore, the object is passed to them as a parameter.

The rest of the stack operations go pretty much as expected. We first tell the stack object charlist to initialize itself. Then, we call the PushItemsOnStack and PopItemsOffStack routines to get input and display it. These routines, in turn, instruct the stack object to push items onto its listitem data field and pop them off. The result is shown in Figure 3.2.

FIGURE 3.2:

Output from an object-oriented stack

Dynamic Object Variables and Pointers

Although it's a little more complicated, objects can be used with pointers just like any other variables:

```
TYPE
   studentrecptr = ^studentrec;
   studentrec = OBJECT
                  { object fields and methods }
                  END;
VAR
   student : studentrecptr;
BEGIN
   New(student);
   { ... other program statements }
END.
```

With objects, Turbo Pascal for Windows extends the New procedure so that you can create a dynamic object variable and initialize it in a single step. You can still do things the traditional way, as in

```
New(student);
student.init;
```

but you can also include the initialization method in the call to the New procedure, as in

```
New(student, init);
```

You'll see this kind of thing often in Turbo Pascal for Windows. Often, the dynamic object variable is a window or a dialog box, and the Init procedure takes parameters, as in

```
AButt := New(PButton, Init(@Self, id_Push1, 'State of Check Box',
   88, 48, 296, 24, False));
```

This is also an example of using the New procedure as a function—a capability that is unique to Turbo Pascal and Turbo Pascal for Windows.

In addition, Turbo Pascal for Windows also extends the Dispose procedure to do extra work in handling object variables. Because objects are more complicated than other data types, you can include a shutdown routine called a *Destructor* in your object type definition to handle any special cleanup chores that are needed. Dispose can now call this destructor method at the same time as it de-allocates a dynamic object variable. If your destructor method is called Done, then it would be written as:

```
Dispose(student, done)
```

No amount of explanation can substitute for practical experience in object-oriented programming. Next, after a brief look at the Windows environment itself, we'll see how to apply these techniques in actual Turbo Pascal for Windows programs.

SUMMARY

Object-oriented programming provides an immensely powerful tool to reduce the amount of work required in complex programming projects. An object is a "smart" data structure that encapsulates in itself all the subroutines (called *methods*) that it needs to operate. Any object type can also have descendants which inherit all of its data fields and methods. The methods of an ancestor type can be overridden when different methods are needed for the descendant type, and virtual methods allow the postponement until the program is run of a decision on which methods are used.

Turbo Pascal extends the capabilities of the New and Dispose procedures for use with dynamic object variables, allowing initialization and shutdown to be handled in the same program commands as allocation and de-allocation of a dynamic object.

The Windows Programming Environment

4

- A Queued, Event-Driven Architecture

- Multitasking

- Memory Management

- Interprocess Communication

- Device-Independent Graphics

- Graphic User Interface

- Programming in Windows

Before we get into the specifics of programming with Turbo Pascal for Windows, we need to take a brief look at the Windows programming environment, as well as how Windows applications differ from standard DOS application programs.

Microsoft Windows is commonly referred to as a *graphic user interface* (*GUI*), and the implication is that its most important feature is what you see on the PC's screen. The GUI aspect of Windows is indeed important, but it is arguably the least important feature that Windows has to offer.

The fact is that Windows provides a complete operating environment in which application programs can run, offering features that are not available in the MS-DOS operating system. These features include:

A queued, event-driven architecture: an environment in which hardware and software events, such as key presses and mouse clicks, are intercepted by Microsoft Windows, which then sends the appropriate instructions ("messages") to the desired application program in its window.

Multitasking: the ability to run multiple programs at the same time, all sharing the PC's memory, processor, and other system resources.

Interprocess communication: the ability to exchange data between different programs while they are running, either under the user's control or under Windows' control.

Device-independent graphics: a single graphics device interface, under the control of Windows, which insulates application programs from the details of the device used for graphics output—whether it is a printer, plotter, Hercules monochrome screen, VGA color screen, or some other device unknown at the time the application program was written.

A graphic user interface: a screen display in which the user issues commands by pointing at on-screen pictures and clicking or dragging the mouse.

Each of these features has significant implications for the way in which Windows programs must be structured and written. Let's take a closer look at each.

A Queued,
Event-Driven Architecture

When a standard application program runs under MS-DOS, it gains exclusive control of and access to the PC's system resources—memory, keyboard, screen, ports, and so on. Any input, such as a key being pressed by the user, is passed by MS-DOS directly to the application. If the application is not prepared to receive input at that time, the input might or might not get lost.

Consider a traditional Turbo Pascal program running under MS-DOS. It accepts input from the keyboard primarily through READLN and related procedures. If you have set up a menu, for example, you might have a series of statements like the following in your code:

```
WRITELN(' Main Menu');
WRITELN(' -----------------');
WRITELN(' 1. Create');
WRITELN(' 2. Edit');
WRITELN(' 3. Quit');
WRITELN;
WRITE(' Enter your choice (1/2/3): ');
READLN(menuchoice);
```

If your program has reached this READLN or another input statement when the user decides to press a key, everything works fine. However, if your program is busy doing something else, then the keypress goes into DOS's keyboard buffer and might or might not be used by your program.

A Windows program, however, is different. Because more than one program may be running at the same time, Windows must intercept input events and route them to the correct application program in a usable format. Hence, Windows monitors *all* the sources of input events to programs. When such an event occurs, Windows generates a message, such as *wm_KeyDown* for a key press, and this message goes into a message queue for the appropriate application program. When the program is ready for input, it reads its messages from the input queue provided by Windows.

Likewise, when the program needs to create output—whether displaying something on the screen or printing a document—it sends a message to Windows, which then carries out the request by using the appropriate hardware device. A Windows application, therefore, must be able to both (1) understand input messages that it receives from Windows and (2) generate the appropriate output messages to send to Windows when it wants to do something.

Significantly, because all input events are intercepted and managed by Windows, and Windows provides an insulating layer between the program and the hardware it's running on—a traditional operating system function—different versions of Windows could theoretically be created to run on radically different hardware platforms, from PCs to mainframes. And because the application programs are insulated from hardware and operating system details by the Windows environment itself, a PC program could in principle run without alteration on an IBM mainframe or a DEC minicomputer.

Multitasking

Windows can run multiple application programs at the same time, meaning that system resources must be shared by all the active programs and by Windows. The screen is only the most obvious of these resources: Windows limits each application's use of the screen to the application's own window and "client area," which is the area inside the window. Likewise, Windows schedules different programs' access to the PC's processor, allocates and de-allocates memory for applications and their data, and controls interactions between the different programs. An example of this type of situation is shown in Figure 4.1.

This means that a Windows application must not attempt to access any of these devices (the processor, memory, the screen, etc.) directly. For example, in order to display text on the screen, an application must go through Windows to make sure that the text is displayed in the application's client area—not in another window or on the Windows desktop. Likewise, an application should not try to directly manipulate data in processor registers, because it would almost certainly interfere with Windows' concurrent use of the processor with other applications.

This differs considerably from standard DOS programs, which typically have exclusive access to the processor, the screen, all memory not used by DOS or TSR programs, and all other system resources. "Ill-behaved" DOS programs such as WordPerfect, which also have Windows versions, achieve considerable performance gains in slower machines by bypassing DOS/BIOS calls and writing directly to the hardware (such as the screen). However, such ill-behaved programs normally

FIGURE 4.1:

Windows manages multiple concurrent programs in different windows

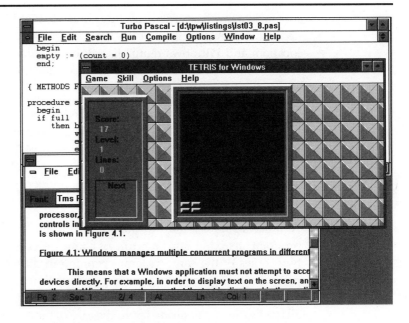

cannot be multitasked under Windows; in addition, their faster performance is less of an issue with the high-end PCs needed to run Windows in the first place.

Memory Management

Another aspect of the multi-tasking situation is how Windows handles PC memory. In effect, multi-tasked programs under Windows are all "resident" programs that can be popped up on the screen at any time. Under DOS, the order of resident programs in memory is static; that is, they cannot be shuffled and moved around in the PC's memory. Once a program and its data areas occupy a certain part of memory, they must remain there until the program is unloaded. Moreover, resident DOS programs must be unloaded in an order opposite to that in which they were loaded: if you load a print spooler, a macro program, SideKick, and a word processor, you must unload the word processor first, then SideKick, then the macro program, and then the print spooler.

Windows applications suffer from no such limitations. They can be loaded and unloaded in any order, and Windows itself takes care of allocating and managing memory for each one. This means, however, that Windows applications must not access memory directly. If you write a program that sets up a pointer to a memory location, and Windows reorganizes the allocation of memory, then your pointer will no longer point to the correct memory address of the data you need.

To manage dynamic memory, Windows uses "handles." Every object in a Windows program and in Windows itself has a handle, which is a special kind of pointer (represented as a number) that is managed by Windows. Programs, windows, icons, devices, and the client areas inside windows are all referred to by their handles. But never fear: Turbo Pascal "handles the handles" behind the scenes, so that in your own code, you can use traditional Pascal pointers and operations such as the NEW and DISPOSE procedures.

Another aspect of Windows' memory management is its ability to let more than one program share the same module of compiled code. For example, you might have two copies of the same program running in different windows, or two different programs that can use the same import/export routines. In both of these cases, Windows would keep one copy of the shared code in memory, making it available to all applications that needed it. In the case of the import/export routines, the shared code would be called a *dynamic link library* (*DLL*)—a special kind of .EXE file that can be created in Turbo Pascal. DLLs can be loaded and unloaded as they are needed.

Interprocess Communication

"Interprocess communication" means that Windows applications can exchange data with each other—either under the user's control or behind the scenes under Windows' control.

The most obvious form of interprocess communication is the Windows clipboard, a feature already familiar to users of memory-resident utility programs under DOS. The clipboard allows the user to select a block of text (or graphics) from one window, copy it to a buffer area in memory, and then paste it from the buffer into another window. Under DOS, this type of feature is supported by programs such as SideKick, which can pop up over an application's screen and copy material from the screen. The Windows clipboard is not limited to copying the currently displayed screen of information; however, information copied to the clipboard must be in one of several special formats (which we will examine later in this book).

The more sophisticated type of interprocess communication is called *dynamic data exchange* (*DDE*). This is a feature through which two applications in different windows are able to send information back and forth to each other without the user's direct intervention. For example, a Windows spreadsheet in one window might update a copy of a worksheet in a Windows word processing document that is in another window.

DDE is not the easiest thing in the world to implement, but, as usual, Turbo Pascal does its best to hide the messy details. As with the clipboard, the information to be exchanged must be in a standard format, and the cooperating applications must know how to start, conduct, and terminate the exchange by sending the appropriate messages.

Device-Independent Graphics

Another way that Windows insulates application programs is by providing a common *graphics device interface* (*GDI*) that programs can use regardless of the output device to which they are sending information.

That's very abstract, but in practice it's quite simple. Under DOS, programs must be equipped with a different software driver for every hardware device to which they might need to send output. That much is familiar even to users of word processing packages, who must specify the type of monitor and printer they have when they first install the software. Likewise, Turbo Pascal and Turbo C++ programmers are familiar with the need to include all the appropriate .BGI (Borland Graphics Interface) drivers for different types of video adapters and screen displays; in addition to your program itself, you'll typically include (on the diskette) drivers for IBM monochrome, Hercules graphics, CGA, EGA, and VGA video equipment.

Windows makes all this unnecessary. Because Windows insulates application programs from the underlying hardware, the programs can simply write to the Windows GDI. Windows then formats the output appropriately and routes it to the desired output device, such as a video display, printer, plotter, or modem. When each user installs Windows, the Windows program itself sets up all the drivers needed for a particular hardware configuration; application programs no longer need to worry about them.

Graphic User Interface

Finally, Windows provides a graphic user interface by which the user can interact with application programs. This means that application programs

- must be able to respond to mouse clicks and movements as well as keyboard input;

- must use Windows-standard GUI screen objects, such as dialog boxes, buttons, menus, and scroll bars; and

- must respond to input events in Windows-standard ways, e.g., by opening a menu in response to a mouse click on the menu name.

Turbo Pascal for Windows makes it easy to do all of these things with the predefined objects in its ObjectWindows class library. Object types that are defined in ObjectWindows already contain most of the required Windows behaviors, so you can simply "inherit" them in your own application programs and modify them as needed.

Programming in Windows

The key to Windows programming with Turbo Pascal is to understand the relation between the Windows API and ObjectWindows. Windows provides about 600 different functions that can be used by application programs. These functions, originally designed to work with the C programming language and Microsoft's Windows **Software Developers Kit (SDK)**, are often complex and difficult to deal with in writing a program.

ObjectWindows provides an easier way of approaching the multitude of functions in the Windows API. Because object types inherit data fields and methods from their ancestor types, the object types in ObjectWindows provide all of the Windows features needed, so that you can concentrate on developing new features that are unique to your application program. To use a particular object type defined in ObjectWindows, you simply

- declare the relevant ObjectWindows unit in a USES clause, and

- define a new object type as a descendant of the ObjectWindows object type.

The new type inherits all the fields and methods of the ObjectWindows type. You can add new fields and methods, or override methods, from the predefined type so that the new object type fits your program's needs. You don't need to worry about defining methods for basic Windows behaviors or screen objects; those are already taken care of for you by the predefined object type.

The result is twofold. First, you have a much easier time dealing with the Windows API, because Turbo Pascal and ObjectWindows do most of the work for you. Second, you can develop your programs in object-oriented Turbo Pascal without needing to be concerned about many of the program details that would take up a great deal of time if you were working in C or assembly language and making calls directly to the API.

We saw the clearest example of this in Chapter 1, where we created a standard Pascal "Hello, world" program as a Windows program simply by declaring the WINCRT unit in a USES clause. Except for naming WINCRT, this program is a perfectly ordinary Turbo Pascal program, using a WRITELN statement to display text on the screen. However, the text from the WRITELN statement is routed into the program's window—specifically, into its client area. The window in which it resides can perform all of the expected Windows functions, such as displaying a window-control menu, using scroll bars, and responding to mouse clicks. Although most Turbo Pascal for Windows programs are more complex than this one, the principle is the same: Let the predefined types in ObjectWindows handle the details and fill in the blanks while you concentrate on the features you want to add or modify.

PART II

Essential Turbo Pascal for Windows

ObjectWindows and Other Turbo Pascal Units

5

- **ObjectWindows Units**

- **Other TPW Units**

- **ObjectWindows Object Types**

- **Using Windows Functions with ObjectWindows**

ObjectWindows is the library of predefined object types that comes with Turbo Pascal for Windows. The great advantage of ObjectWindows is that its object types already include all the basic Windows devices and behaviors. This makes Object-Windows the single most important feature of Turbo Pascal for Windows. All you need to do, as a programmer, is know how to use the inherited features and then add the unique features that your own program requires.

To use these predefined types, you simply declare new object types in your program as descendants of the ObjectWindows types, modifying them as needed. If you have already written programs in the DOS version of Turbo Pascal using the "Turbo Vision" object library, then the ObjectWindows types will seem quite familiar.

All the object types included with ObjectWindows begin with the letter *T*.

ObjectWindows Units

The ObjectWindows object types are organized into several special Turbo Pascal *units*. Each unit provides object types for a specific purpose, for example, different units provide Windows-related procedures and functions, specialized data types, and dialog boxes. The units are precompiled, but because they contain object types, it is not necessary to see their source code to create new object types based on them. You simply declare any new object type as a descendant of the predefined object type, then modify it as needed.

WObjects

It's with the WObjects unit that serious Turbo Pascal for Windows applications begin. This unit, which is the heart of ObjectWindows, defines all the standard object types needed for Windows applications, as well as object types for *collections* and *streams*, which are the object-oriented counterpart of files. Because of its central role, this unit must be named by all programs that use any of the special TPW object types—that is, by all programs except DOS applications that have simply been ported to Windows by naming the WinCRT unit (discussed later in this chapter).

WinProcs

The WinProcs unit allows you to call Windows *functions* directly, providing procedure and function headers for every routine in the Windows API. Windows has over six hundred functions ("function" is the generic term used in Windows to refer to any of its API routines), and the WinProcs unit provides a way for your application to use them directly. When taken along with the WinTypes unit (see below), this gives the complete Turbo Pascal implementation of the Windows Application Programming Interface.

In general, ObjectWindows will take care of all the underlying details for you. The ObjectWindows object types include *methods* that call Windows API functions; in addition, the object types usually have *data fields* that contain any information that must be passed as parameters to the Windows functions that they call. When a TPW object method calls a Windows function, the required parameters are passed automatically. The most obvious example is a function that must act on a particular window: in order to know what window it should act on, the function must receive that window's *handle* as a parameter when it is called by the application.

WinTypes

The WinTypes unit contains declarations of the Turbo Pascal counterparts for the data types used by routines in the Windows API. These include both simple data types and more complex data types (such as records), as well as standard Windows constants for such things as styles, messages, and flags. Data types from this unit that you will see fairly often in TPW programs include:

HWnd, which defines a handle data type for particular window handles.

PHandle, which defines a pointer to a generic Windows handle.

THandle, which defines a generic Windows handle type.

THandleTable, which defines an array of handles.

TMDICreateStruct, which is a record type containing data for the creation of an MDI (Multiple Document Interface) child window.

StdDlgs

Unlike windows, which provide mostly unstructured interaction with the user, dialog boxes are designed for structured input through buttons and checkboxes. The StdDlgs unit defines two standard types of dialog boxes: **TFileDialog** and **TInputDialog**.

The TFileDialog object type allows you to create dialog boxes in which the user can select a file name for saving or loading. The TInputDialog object type provides a less structured dialog box that lets the user type in a text response to a query from the program.

StdWnds

The StdWnds unit defines two standard types of windows: **TEditWindow** and **TFileWindow**. A TEditWindow provides a simple text-editing window. A TFile-Window also provides a simple text-editing window, but one that can read from and write to files.

Other TPW Units

Although the ObjectWindows units constitute Turbo Pascal's most powerful tool for creating Windows programs, several other units play key roles that are not specifically related to creating Windows objects. These correspond to the units in the DOS version of Turbo Pascal: **WinCRT, System, WinDOS**, and **Strings**.

WinCRT

The WinCRT unit is the least complicated of all the units to use. That's because it has only one function: to make it possible for standard Turbo Pascal programs to run as Windows applications. Of course, although these programs are Windows applications in the sense that (a) they run under Windows, and (b) they obey Windows rules for staying in an on-screen window and not hogging the processor, it's really more accurate to call these programs "Windows-compatible" applications, since they don't really take advantage of any of Windows' special features.

You can use the WinCRT unit any time you need to port a DOS-based Turbo Pascal program to Windows and have to do it with a minimum of recoding. The listings in Chapter 3 are a good example: they will compile and run under either DOS Turbo Pascal or Turbo Pascal for Windows. The only difference is that DOS programs use the CRT unit in the USES clause, while the Windows programs use the WinCRT unit.

WinCRT does provide most—but not all—of the standard CRT unit routines, including such standards as CLRSCR, GotoXY, and READKEY. It does lack a few of the less-often-used routines, such as DELAY, so you'll need to do a little modification of non-Windows programs that use these routines.

System

The System unit provides basic Turbo Pascal procedures, functions, and definitions that are used by virtually all programs. It is automatically linked to every TPW program when it is compiled, so you never need to explicitly name the System unit in a USES clause.

WinDOS

The WinDOS unit provides a variety of routines for working with MS-DOS and handling files; it corresponds to the DOS unit in standard Turbo Pascal. When using TPW you should provide for as many of these operations as possible to be handled by calls to Windows functions instead of directly through the DOS unit. For example, although the WinDOS unit (like the DOS unit) has routines and data types for manipulating processor registers and software interrupts, these activities can interfere with the operation of other Windows applications that may be running concurrently with your program.

Strings

The Strings unit provides support for the use of *null-terminated strings*, a new string type that is required by the Windows API.

In standard Turbo Pascal, a string is treated as an array of characters with the first position (array[0]) containing the current length of the string. It has a maximum size of 255 characters and can occupy from 1 to 256 bytes of PC memory. A null-terminated string, on the other hand, has no length byte to indicate where the string ends. Instead, it indicates the end of the string with a NULL (#0) character. This means that it can contain up to 65,535 characters, much more than a standard string.

Like most Windows objects, you access a null-terminated string through a handle to that string. This is more similar to standard Turbo Pascal than it might seem, because when you use a string variable in standard Turbo Pascal, you are actually performing a pointer operation—with the details taken care of by Turbo Pascal itself.

ObjectWindows Object Types

There are several different object types included in ObjectWindows. Each type serves a different kind of function in Windows programming—from top-level "abstract" types such as TApplication, which are never implemented without modification, to types for windows and dialog boxes. The hierarchy of the types is shown in Figure 5.1.

Top-Level Abstract Object Types

The base object type in ObjectWindows is the **TObject** type. This is an abstract type that serves as the ancestor for all other ObjectWindows types, and, as such, it is never actually implemented in any of your TPW programs. It defines basic *constructor* and *destructor* methods.

TApplication is another abstract object type that serves as the basis for defining your own Windows applications. When you create a Windows program, you'll usually declare the main object type as a descendant of TApplication, adding (at least) your own version of the inherited InitMainWindow method.

FIGURE 5.1:

The ObjectWindows object type
hierarchy

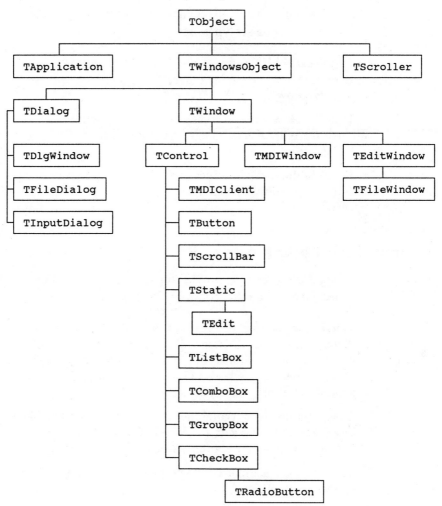

Window Object Types

The window object types in ObjectWindows take care of setting up various types of windows and the controls that operate them. You can also, when needed, create many of the controls yourself if you need to add some special functionality to them. The main window object types are:

TWindow, which serves as the basis for general-purpose windows that can be used to hold or display other things, such as graphics or an application's child windows.

TEditWindow, which serves as the basis for windows that provide basic text entry and editing capabilities, but without the ability to read from or write to files.

TFileWindow, which serves as the basis for windows that provide basic text entry and editing capabilities, and also have the ability to read from and write to files.

Dialog-Box Object Types

The dialog-box object types provide for structured interaction with the user via buttons, checkboxes, and other controls. The object types are:

TDialog, an abstract object type which serves as the basis for all Windows dialog boxes. Each TDialog object type has an associated resource file that describes the appearance and location of the dialog box's control objects. TDialog includes methods to initialize, run, and shut down the dialog box, as well as for other tasks such as interacting with files.

TDlgWindow, which combines characteristics of both dialog boxes and windows, and can include traditional dialog box elements as well as icons and cursors, which are most often associated with windows.

TFileDialog, a standard dialog box type that prompts the user to select a file to open, edit, or save.

TInputDialog, which defines a dialog box for the input of a single item of text.

Control Object Types

Unlike windows, which have mostly standard control devices, dialog boxes merely provide a backdrop for control devices that you specify. You don't need to define these control devices, of course, because their basic appearance and behaviors are already defined in the ObjectWindows object types; however, you must choose which devices will appear and what text they will display—for example, displaying Yes, No, and Cancel buttons. The basic control object types are:

TControl, an abstract type that serves as the basis for all other Windows control types. This contains the necessary functions for creating controls and processing messages for all its descendant control-device object types.

TButton, which serves as the basis for creating push buttons.

TListBox, which serves as the basis for creating general-purpose Windows list boxes.

TComboBox, which adds editing control to the TListBox type.

TCheckBox, which serves as the basis for creating checkboxes.

TRadioButton, which serves as the basis for creating radio buttons.

TGroupBox, which serves as the basis for creating *group boxes.* (A group box, usually found within a dialog box, serves to group together several related buttons or controls.)

TEdit, which serves as the basis for text-processing capabilities in an editing control.

TScrollBar, which serves as the basis for creating stand-alone scrollbar controls. Scrollbar controls are normally included in window object types (descendants of TWindow), so you usually won't need a separate operation to create them.

TStatic, which provides methods to set, query, and clear the text in an output-only ("static") control.

MDI Object Types

Windows defines a standard set of behaviors for setting up multiple documents within a single window. This standard is called the *Multiple Document Interface* (*MDI*). The ObjectWindows MDI types provide a way to set up and manipulate MDI windows. An MDI application has a main window and one or more child windows, each of which can be opened, closed, moved, resized, or reduced to an icon. The object types are:

TMDIWindow, which serves as the basis for creating the main MDI window.

TMDIClient, which serves as the basis for creating child windows and their client (internal) areas.

Using Windows Functions With ObjectWindows

The **WinProcs** and **WinTypes** units provide all you need to call Windows API functions from Turbo Pascal programs. To use a Windows function in a program, you simply call the corresponding Turbo Pascal procedure or function from the WinProcs unit. Windows functions typically require that one or more parameters be passed to them when they are called: a typical example is the creation of a Windows *MessageBox* in which you specify the types of buttons (such as Yes, No, and Cancel) and an icon that shows the kind of message box that it is. ObjectWindows takes care of many of these parameters, but you must specify others yourself.

SIX

Creating a Window

- **Creating a Bare-Bones Windows Application**

- **Responding to Mouse Clicks**

- **Handling Null-Terminated Strings**

6

We've already created several Windows programs in the course of the first five chapters. However, these programs have been meant to illustrate specific non-Windows points, such as object-oriented programming. As a result, the programs we have written so far are "Windows programs" only by virtue of using the WinCRT unit and running in a window. They haven't really taken advantage of the tremendous power that Turbo Pascal for Windows puts at your fingertips.

Now that the groundwork has been taken care of, we are ready to get down to some serious Windows programming. In this chapter, we'll look at how to create a more flexible and powerful Windows application than you can create by merely using the WinCRT unit. We'll see how to set up a main window, how to respond to mouse clicks and other input events, how to display text in a window, and how to use some of the predefined object types and methods that are provided in ObjectWindows. In later chapters, we'll return to each of these techniques to explore them in more detail.

Creating a Bare-Bones Windows Application

The first thing you must do to create a Windows application is to create a main window for that application. In itself, creating a main window is remarkably simple: you simply declare the WOBJECTS unit in a USES clause and inherit what you need. Later, you can define more powerful main-window types, but let's take things one step at a time. The code to set up an application's main window is shown in Listing 6.1, which is a complete—if rather spartan—Windows program in itself.

Listing 6.1

```
PROGRAM Listing6_1;
    { Creates a Windows application and the main window
        of the application. Features demonstrated:
        1. Using the TApplication object type.
        2. Using the inherited InitMainWindow procedure.
        3. Initializing the main window with NEW used
            as a function.
        4. The significance of the main window title. }

USES WOBJECTS;
```

```
TYPE
    TMyFirstApp = OBJECT (TApplication)
        PROCEDURE InitMainWindow; VIRTUAL;
        END;

PROCEDURE TMyFirstApp.InitMainWindow;
    BEGIN
    MainWindow := NEW(PWindow, Init(NIL, 'First TPW Program'));
    END;

VAR
    MyFirstApp : TMyFirstApp;
{ Main body of the program }
BEGIN
    MyFirstApp.Init('MyFirst');
    MyFirstApp.Run;
    MyFirstApp.Done;
END.
```

When you enter, compile, and run the program, it should display a screen like that shown in Figure 6.1. A main window should appear, titled "First TPW Program." The basic window-control devices should be present, including maximize/minimize buttons at the top right and a control-menu button at the top left. The actual size and position of the program window may be different from the figure, depending on the type of system you have.

Let's take this program a line at a time, because even though it's a simple program, there's a great deal to notice about it. The first line is a standard Pascal program statement, declaring "Listing6_1" as the program name. The second line (ignoring the comment, of course) is a USES clause that names the WOBJECTS unit. This unit provides three predefined object types that we need to use in this program:

TApplication, which is the object type that controls the behavior of the overall program.

TWindow, which is the object type for the main program window. This object type is used by the inherited method *TApplication.InitMainWindow* unless you override it and specify a different type of window.

PWindow, which is a predefined handle (i.e., "pointer") type that can point to an object of type *TWindow*.

FIGURE 6.1:

Running the program in Listing 6.1

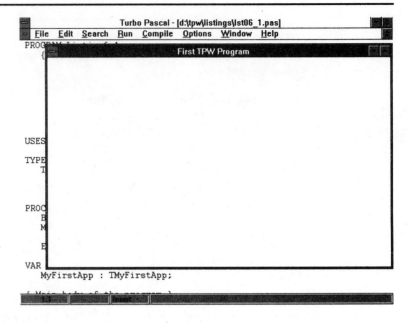

In the TYPE section of the program, we declare *TMyFirstApp* as an object that is a descendant of *TApplication*. This means that it inherits all of *TApplication*'s fields and methods, including *InitMainWindow*, which we override (as you normally will) with a new *InitMainWindow* method. If it is not overridden, the inherited *InitMain-Window* method will produce a generic *TWindow* main window with no title. Note that our new version of the *InitMainWindow* routine is declared as a *virtual* method. This is an example of the point made in Chapter 3 that once a method is declared as virtual (as *InitMainWindow* is in the *TApplication* object type), then it must remain a virtual method in all object types that are descended from the base type.

In the *TMyFirstApp.InitMainWindow* method, we assign the title "First TPW Program" to the main window, and thereby to the application task itself. The procedure header is a standard object method header: first it gives the name of the object type that the method goes with, then the name of the method. The body of the method consists of a single line to set up the *MainWindow* variable, which is a predefined pointer type (a handle) that points to the main window object.

Notice that the statement uses Turbo Pascal's extended syntax for the NEW procedure, both using NEW as a function and including a call to the dynamic object's Init method. In this case, the *PWindow* parameter is a predefined object type that points to a *TWindow* object. The *TWindow.Init* method takes two parameters itself: first, a handle to the window's parent window, if any, and second, the window title. The first parameter is NIL here because this is the main application window and, therefore, there is no parent window. The second parameter provides the window title that appears in the top border of the application window, as shown in Figure 6.1.

It's worth noting that the main window title doesn't appear only in the top border of the application window. When you call up the Windows task-switching menu, the task for your application is listed under the main window title, as shown in Figure 6.2.

Next in the program comes the VAR section, where we declare a variable of the *TMyFirstApp* object type. And though everyone knows it, it's worth reminding ourselves once more that type declarations, no matter how intricate, do not create any variables of the types declared. The application that we run in this program is not *TMyFirstApp*, which is a data type, but *MyFirstApp*, which is an object variable of that type.

FIGURE 6.2:

The main window title appears in the task-switching menu.

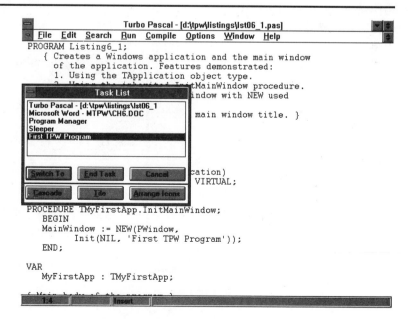

107

Finally, the main body of the program calls *MyFirstApp*'s Init, Run, and Done methods. We've defined the Init method, of course, and the Run and Done methods are inherited from *TApplication*. The Run method sets up the application's message loop as a task under Windows. The Done method disposes of the application's (dynamic) main window object and then shuts down the application.

That may all seem complicated for a program that just opens a window on the screen, but look at what we got for our 17 lines of code. We got a program that runs as a task under Windows, has its own window-control buttons, and has its own window title in the Windows task list. It even has a predefined window-control menu, as shown in Figure 6.3. All in all, that's remarkably little work for a remarkably sophisticated result.

One other point is worth mentioning. If you've tried out the program in Listing 6.1, you know that it can also respond to mouse clicks and drags. When you click the left mouse button on a device, it responds; when you hold down the mouse button and drag the window or one of its borders, the window or border moves just as you would expect. We have not, however, *defined* any methods to respond to mouse

FIGURE 6.3:

MyFirstApp's window-control menu

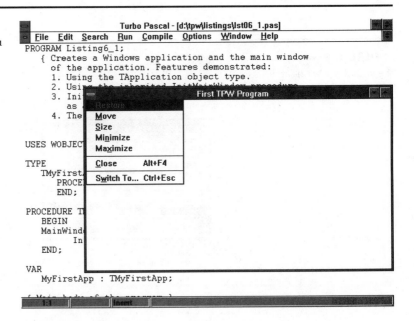

input; these are all inherited from the ancestor *TWindow* object that is created by *InitMainWindow*. In the next section, we'll add a method to respond to a left mouse click.

Responding to Mouse Clicks

The program in Listing 6.1 is impressive enough, considering the sophistication of what it does. However, if you click a mouse button when the mouse cursor is in the *middle* of the window—that is, not on one of the window-control buttons or on the border—then nothing happens.

This is because the *TWindow* object type used by *TApplication* includes a method to respond to mouse clicks, but only for left-button clicks and only when the cursor is on a control button or in the window's border. To respond to clicks in the interior of the window—the area called the window's "client area"—we must define our own mouse-click response methods. In this section, we'll look at two ways of doing that. Both ways use the same basic approach—an approach that is, in fact, used to respond to all Windows messages of all types—but they differ in their results.

Displaying a Message Box in Response to a Mouse Click

The first way of defining mouse-click responses is shown in Listing 6.2. In this program, we set up a method that displays a message box in the window when the click occurs. The code is short, but fairly intricate. Therefore, as we did earlier, we'll look at it line by line. First, however, you should enter and run the program to see what it does. Your result should look like Figure 6.4.

Listing 6.2

```
PROGRAM Listing6_2;
  { Demonstrates how to set up a mouse-click response
    method that displays a message box in the interior
    of a window. }

USES WINTYPES, WINPROCS, WOBJECTS;
```

FIGURE 6.4:

Displaying a message box in
response to a mouse click

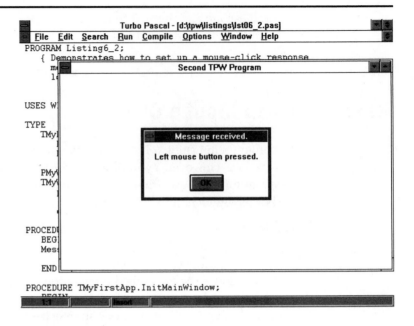

```pascal
TYPE
    TMyFirstApp = OBJECT (TApplication)
        PROCEDURE InitMainWindow; VIRTUAL;
        END;

    PMyWindow = ^TMyWindow;
    TMyWindow = OBJECT (TWindow)
        PROCEDURE WMLButtonDown(VAR Msg : TMessage);
                VIRTUAL wm_First + wm_LButtonDown;
        end;

PROCEDURE TMyWindow.WMLButtonDown(VAR Msg : TMessage);
    BEGIN
    MessageBox(HWindow, 'Left mouse button pressed.',
            'Message received.', mb_OK);
    END;

PROCEDURE TMyFirstApp.InitMainWindow;
    BEGIN
        MainWindow := NEW(PMyWindow,
                        Init(NIL, 'Second TPW Program'));
```

```
    END;

VAR

    MyFirstApp : TMyFirstApp;

BEGIN
    MyFirstApp.Init('MyFirst');
    MyFirstApp.Run;
    MyFirstApp.Done;
END.
```

Apart from the program name, the first difference between Listing 6.2 and Listing 6.1 is that Listing 6.2 adds the WINTYPES and WINPROCS units to the program's USES clause. We need these because our mouse-click response method, defined later on in the listing, uses Windows API functions and associated Object-Windows data types: the former are handled by the WINPROCS unit and the latter by the WINTYPES unit.

Next, the declaration of the *TMyFirstApp* object type is the same as in Listing 6.1. This doesn't need to change at all. We begin to see a difference right below it, however, where we declare a pointer (*PMyWindow*) to a new window type (*TMyWindow*). In Listing 6.1, we simply accepted the inherited, generic *TWindow* object type that is used by the *TApplication* object type. Here, though, we want to add features to the main application window, so we define a new window type based on *TWindow* and add our own method to respond to clicks of the left mouse button.

The mouse-click response method itself deserves considerable study. First, the name *WMLButtonDown* indicates that this is intended to override the *TWindow* inherited method of the same name. Because the *TWindow* method that it overrides is virtual, this method must also be virtual. The new *WMLButtonDown* method takes one parameter, *Msg*, that is of the *TMessage* record type. This is a variant record type that has a field for a handle to the window where the mouse-click occurs, as well as for the X and Y coordinates of the mouse-click inside the window.

After VIRTUAL, the final part of the method header is

```
wm_First + wm_LButtonDown
```

This is called the *extension* of the method header and it tells Turbo Pascal which Windows messages this method is intended to respond to. The first part of the extension, *wm_First*, really doesn't do much of anything: it has a value of zero and is included merely because you'll see it in the TPW sample programs. Don't worry about it; it isn't documented in the TPW manuals, anyway, and you'll search for it in vain if you try to find it in the *Windows Reference Manual* from Microsoft.

The second part of the extension is the important part, because it tells which Windows message this method responds to. All Windows messages are referred to in TPW by identifiers in the same format:

`wm_`*identifier*

Here, *wm_LButtonDown* is a predefined identifier that says "This method responds to left-button mouse clicks." If we had used *wm_RButtonDown* instead, the method would respond to right-button mouse clicks.

Now we get to the actual definition of the *TMyWindow.WMLButtonDown* method. The body of the method consists of a single line, which calls the TPW *MessageBox* function. This function creates a *message box*—kind of a read-only version of a dialog box. A message box takes four parameters:

1. A **handle** (pointer) to the window (the "parent window") in which the message box is supposed to appear.

2. The **message** to be displayed in the message box. This is a special kind of string used by Windows, called a *null-terminated string*. We'll discuss null-terminated strings in more detail in the next section.

3. The **title** of the message box, also in the form of a null-terminated string.

4. One or more **identifiers** that display icons or buttons in the message box.

In this case, *HWindow* is the handle to the parent window. The identifier *HWindow* itself is a predefined window-handle identifier from the WOBJECTS unit that points to whatever window is associated with the mouse click. `'Left mouse button pressed.'` is the message to be displayed in the window, while `'Message received.'` is the window title. Finally, *mb_OK* is a predefined button identifier that displays the OK button in the message box, as shown in Figure 6.4. There is a variety of predefined pushbutton identifiers that you can use in message boxes and dialog boxes, including such identifiers as *mb_YesNo* (displays Yes and No buttons) and *mb_IconQuestion* (displays a non-interactive questionmark icon).

In most respects, the *TMyFirstApp.InitMainWindow* method is just as it was in Listing 6.1, with the exception that the *MainWindow* function calls NEW with a *PMyWindow*-type window handle instead of the generic *PWindow* window handle. As before, NEW is called as a function and uses extended Turbo Pascal syntax to initialize the main window. The rest of the program is the same as Listing 6.1.

Displaying Text in Response to a Mouse Click

Now that we've seen how to create and customize a main application window, let's make our example a little more sophisticated. Instead of displaying a message box when the user clicks the left mouse button, the new application will display a plain-text message at the location of the mouse click inside the window. To see how this works, enter, compile, and run Listing 6.3. After you've clicked the mouse in the window a few times, the result should look like Figure 6.5.

Listing 6.3

```
PROGRAM Listing6_3;
    { Demonstrates how to display text at the location
       of a mouse click. Specific features demonstrated:
            1. The TextOut procedure.
            2. Null-terminated strings vs. regular strings.
            3. The StrPCopy procedure.
            4. Getting and releasing a display context. }

USES WINTYPES, WINPROCS, WOBJECTS, STRINGS;

TYPE
    TMyFirstApp = OBJECT (TApplication)
        PROCEDURE InitMainWindow; VIRTUAL;
        END;

    PMyWindow = ^TMyWindow;
    TMyWindow = OBJECT (TWindow)
        PROCEDURE WMLButtonDown(VAR Msg : TMessage);
            VIRTUAL wm_First + wm_LButtonDown;
        END;

PROCEDURE TMyWindow.WMLButtonDown(VAR Msg : TMessage);
```

```
VAR
    dc : HDC;
    s  : ARRAY[0..20] OF CHAR;
BEGIN
    StrPCopy(s, 'Left Button Clicked.');
    dc := GetDC(HWindow);
    TextOut(dc, Msg.LParamLo, Msg.LParamHi, s, strlen(s));
    ReleaseDC(HWindow, dc);
END;

PROCEDURE TMyFirstApp.InitMainWindow;
    BEGIN
        MainWindow := NEW(PMyWindow,
                          Init(NIL, 'Third TPW Program'));
    END;

VAR
    MyFirstApp : TMyFirstApp;

{ main body of program }
BEGIN
```

FIGURE 6.5:

Displaying text in a window at the location of a mouse click

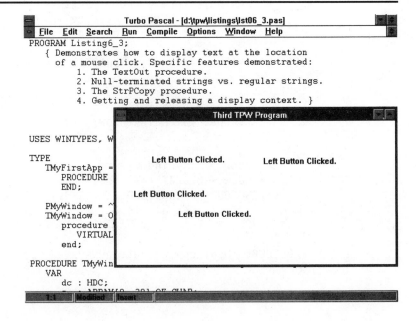

114

```
   MyFirstApp.Init('MyThird');
   MyFirstApp.Run;
   MyFirstApp.Done;
END.
```

As before, this adds several new wrinkles to the previous program listing. The first is the addition of the STRINGS unit to the USES clause: this is needed to handle the null-terminated string that we will use to display the text in the window. To understand the idea of null-terminated strings, it's useful to contrast them with standard Turbo Pascal strings.

In standard Turbo Pascal, a string is treated as a special case of an array of characters. Thus, for example, a string of type

```
STRING[20]
```

is really an

```
ARRAY[0..20] OF CHAR
```

The array slots numbered 1..20 are used to store the characters in the string, and the zero array slot holds the current length of the array. Thus, if a string of type STRING[20] only held five characters, such as "Susan", then the zero slot would hold the length 5. This is how standard Turbo Pascal normally determines where the string ends.

Windows, however, uses a different approach. It uses an ASCII NULL character (#0) to mark the end of the string. Thus, for example, a string with "Susan" in it would actually be a character array containing 'S', 'u', 's', 'a', 'n', #0. This is a more important difference than you might think, and it can get you into trouble if you forget it, as we'll see in Listing 6.4 where we deliberately forget it.

The declaration of the *PMyWindow* window handle and the *TMyWindow* object type are the same as in Listing 6.2. This is only to be expected, of course, because if we're encapsulating our method details properly, making a minor change in the method should not require any change in the object type declaration.

The details of the *WMLButtonDown* method, however, are very different. As before, it takes a parameter of type *TMessage*, but that's about the only similarity. First, it declares two local variables, *dc* and *s*:

- **dc** is a variable to hold the handle for a *display context* for the text we are going to display in the window. Any text or graphics drawn in a window must have a display context, which serves as the "drawing surface" on which the text or graphic is created. The data type of the variable, HDC, is the Windows equivalent of a Turbo Pascal WORD data type, and is the appropriate type for a handle to a display context.

- **s** is a 21-slot array to hold the 20-character string

  ```
  'Left Button Clicked.'
  ```

  The final slot of the array holds the NULL character that marks the end of the string.

In the main body of the method, the first action is to call the *StrPCopy* procedure from the STRINGS unit. This copies the standard string 'Left Button Clicked.' into the array *s* and turns it into a null-terminated string.

Next, we create a display context and load its handle into the *dc* variable by calling the *GetDC* function with the current (parent) window's handle. This gets a display context and associates it with the appropriate window so that when the text is displayed, it goes into the correct window.

Next, we call the *TextOut* procedure. This writes the string contained in array *s* (the fourth parameter) to the current cursor location in the window. It takes five parameters:

1. The **display context** on which the text is to be drawn in the window.

2. (and **3.**) The **window coordinates** of the mouse cursor when the click occurs. *Msg*, you may recall, is a *TMessage*-type variant record. Two of its fields, *LParamLo* and *LParamHi*, can be used to get the current mouse position at a mouse click.

4. The **array** containing the null-terminated string to be drawn on the display context.

5. The **length** of the string. Here, we have used the *StrLen* function to return this value; it would have worked just as well simply to use the integer 20 for a 20-character string.

Finally—and this is very important—we release the display context that we called earlier in the method: the two parameters are the handle to the current window and the handle to the display context.

> **NOTE** Display contexts are analogous to dynamic variables in standard Turbo Pascal. When a dynamic variable is no longer needed in a program, you always dispose of it to free up the memory it required. If you fail to do so, your program can run out of memory because most of the memory is allocated to dynamic variables that aren't being used. Likewise, you must dispose of any display context immediately after using it: otherwise, you will run out of display contexts. The problem is a little more acute with display contexts than with dynamic variables: you might have plenty of memory to waste on unused dynamic variables, but Windows 3.0 limits you to only five display contexts—that's the total number that can be active in a Windows session. Thus, you have to be a real stickler for releasing display contexts the moment they are no longer being used.

The rest of the code in Listing 6.3 is unproblematic and is the same as in Listing 6.2.

Handling Null-Terminated Strings

Let's close this chapter with a demonstration of what can happen if you forget the difference between standard Turbo Pascal strings and null-terminated strings. Listing 6.4 is identical to Listing 6.3 in every respect but one, and yet it produces buggy output. If you enter and run the program, your output should look like Figure 6.6.

Listing 6.4

```
PROGRAM Listing6_4;
{ Demonstrates how failure to remember the
  difference between null-terminated strings
  and standard strings can lead to puzzling
  program bugs. }

USES WINTYPES, WINPROCS, WOBJECTS, STRINGS;

TYPE
    TMyFirstApp = OBJECT (TApplication)
        PROCEDURE InitMainWindow; VIRTUAL;
        END;

    PMyWindow = ^TMyWindow;
```

```
TMyWindow = OBJECT (TWindow)
   PROCEDURE WMLButtonDown(VAR Msg : TMessage);
        VIRTUAL wm_First + wm_LButtonDown;
   end;

PROCEDURE TMyWindow.WMLButtonDown(VAR Msg : TMessage);
   VAR
      dc : HDC;
      s  : ARRAY[0..19] OF CHAR;
   BEGIN
      StrPCopy(s, 'Left Button Clicked.');
      dc := GetDC(HWindow);
      TextOut(dc, Msg.LParamLo, Msg.LParamHi, s, strlen(s));
      ReleaseDC(HWindow, dc);
   END;

PROCEDURE TMyFirstApp.InitMainWindow;
   BEGIN
   MainWindow := NEW(PMyWindow,
                       Init(NIL, 'Buggy TPW Program'));
   END;

VAR
   MyBuggyApp : TMyFirstApp;

{ main body of program }
BEGIN
   MyBuggyApp.Init('MyThird');
   MyBuggyApp.Run;
   MyBuggyApp.Done;
END.
```

Now, because I've pointed out the bug, it should be obvious. The array *s* is now only a 20-character array: big enough to hold the string 'Left Button Clicked.' but *not* big enough to hold that string plus a NULL character to terminate the string. In this case, the extra characters displayed to the right of the 'Left Button Clicked' message are just whatever characters happen to be in the next memory locations after the string is supposed to end. (Note, however, that if the string had been only 19 characters—e.g., 'Left Button Clicked', omitting the period—then everything would be fine, because the 20-slot array would have an empty slot at the end to hold the string-terminating NULL. But failing to remember the extra slot for the NULL can lead to incorrect output.)

FIGURE 6.6:

Buggy output from Listing 6.4

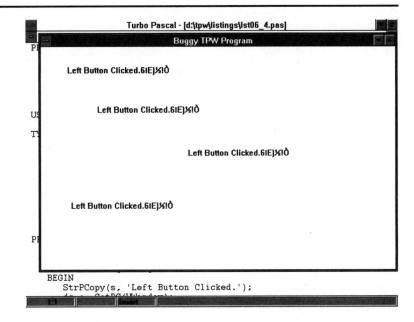

CHAPTER
SEVEN

Displaying Data
in a Window

- **Different Pushbutton Identifiers**

- **Adding File-Save Protection**

- **Formatting Data for Display**

- **Drawing in a Window**

We've already created a simple Windows application in Chapter 6, complete with predefined menu and a message box. In this chapter, we'll extend the features shown in Chapter 6, showing how to display informative icons in a message box, add file-save protection to your applications, and display graphic data in a window.

Different Pushbutton Identifiers

Let's start by trying some different features in the dialog box (actually a "message box") we created in Chapter 6. Although that dialog box simply informs the user that the left mouse button has been pressed and displays an *OK* pushbutton, we can make some interesting changes quite easily.

One of the simplest things to do is to enhance the dialog box by adding an icon to show the user what kind of dialog box it is. For example, a dialog box that asks the user for information might display a question mark, a warning box might display a stop sign, or a box that provides information might show an "I" for "Information."

Let's take things one step at a time and just make a simple change. Enter and run Listing 7.1, which enhances the dialog box from Listing 6.2. Notice that the only difference is the addition of a new identifier in the *TMyWindow.WMLButtonDown* method. When it calls the predefined *MessageBox* method to create the dialog box, it adds the identifier *mb_IconExclamation* to the identifier for the *OK* pushbutton. The result is shown in Figure 7.1.

Listing 7.1

```
PROGRAM Listing7_1;
     { Demonstrates how to set up informative icons
       in a dialog box. }

USES WINTYPES, WINPROCS, WOBJECTS;

TYPE
     TMyFirstApp = OBJECT (TApplication)
         PROCEDURE InitMainWindow; VIRTUAL;
         END;

  PMyWindow = ^TMyWindow;
  TMyWindow = OBJECT (TWindow)
```

```
       PROCEDURE WMLButtonDown(VAR Msg : TMessage);
             VIRTUAL wm_First + wm_LButtonDown;
             END;

PROCEDURE TMyWindow.WMLButtonDown(VAR Msg : TMessage);
   BEGIN
   MessageBox(HWindow, 'Left mouse button pressed.',
     'Message received.', mb_OK or mb_IconExclamation);
   END;

PROCEDURE TMyFirstApp.InitMainWindow;
   BEGIN
   MainWindow := NEW(PMyWindow,
     Init(NIL, 'Listing 7.1'));
   END;

VAR
   MyFirstApp : TMyFirstApp;

{main body of program}
BEGIN
```

FIGURE 7.1:

Adding an icon to the "Left mouse button pressed" dialog box

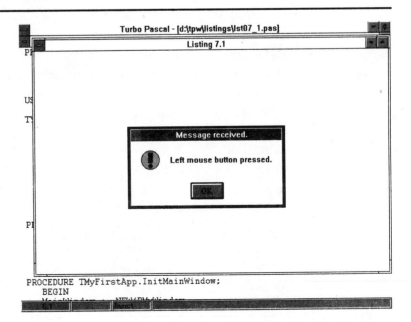

```
    MyFirstApp.Init('Listing7_1');
    MyFirstApp.Run;
    MyFirstApp.Done;
END.
```

Of course, there's no substitute for trying things on your own, but this shows how easy it is to change a dialog box. ObjectWindows provides predefined identifiers for the most common things you want to do in a dialog box; these are shown in Table 7.1. As usual, we've used upper and lowercase letters to make things easier for you to read. It doesn't matter if you use upper or lowercase in your programs.

TABLE 7.1: Predefined identifiers for use with the *MessageBox* function

Identifier	Result
mb_AbortRetryIgnore	Displays pushbuttons for *Abort, Retry,* or *Ignore* in the current operation.
mb_ApplModal	Creates a modal message box.
mb_DefButton1	Makes the first (leftmost) button the default button.
mb_DefButton2	Makes the second button the default button.
mb_DefButton3	Makes the third button the default button.
mb_IconAsterisk	Displays an " I" icon for an information box.
mb_IconExclamation	Displays an exclamation-mark icon.
mb_IconHand	Displays a stop-sign icon.
mb_IconInformation	Displays an " I" icon for an information box.
mb_IconQuestion	Displays a question-mark icon to prompt the user for information.
mb_IconStop	Displays a stop-sign icon.
mb_OK	Displays an *OK* pushbutton.
mb_OKCancel	Displays *OK* and *Cancel* pushbuttons.
mb_RetryCancel	Displays *Retry* and *Cancel* pushbuttons.
mb_SystemModal	Creates a modal message box that suspends Windows; for use in emergency situations.
mb_TaskModal	Creates a modal message box when no parent window is available. You should specify 0 as the parent window parameter. All top-level windows (tasks) in the application will be suspended.
mb_YesNo	Displays *Yes* and *No* pushbuttons.
mb_YesNoCancel	Displays *Yes, No,* and *Cancel* pushbuttons.

Adding File-Save Protection

Let's look at another example that shows both how to modify pushbuttons and to remind the user to save work before closing an application. Enter and run the program in Listing 7.2; the result is shown in Figure 7.2.

Listing 7.2

```
PROGRAM Listing7_2;
       {      Demonstrates how to set up a dialog box
              that prompts the user to save files when
              closing the window. Also demonstrates how
              to modify the pushbuttons in a dialog box. }

USES WINTYPES, WINPROCS, WOBJECTS, STRINGS;

TYPE
     TMyFirstApp = OBJECT (TApplication)
           PROCEDURE InitMainWindow; VIRTUAL;
           END;

     PMyWindow = ^TMyWindow;
     TMyWindow = OBJECT (TWindow)
           FUNCTION CanClose: BOOLEAN; VIRTUAL;
           PROCEDURE WMLButtonDown(VAR Msg : TMessage);
                     VIRTUAL wm_First + wm_LButtonDown;
           END;

FUNCTION TMyWindow.CanClose: BOOLEAN;
VAR
     Reply: Integer;
BEGIN
     CanClose := TRUE;
     Reply := MessageBox(HWindow,
                         'Do you want to save your work?',
                         'Window content has changed',
                         mb_YesNoCancel or mb_IconQuestion);
     IF (Reply = id_Yes) OR (Reply = id_Cancel)
              THEN CanClose := FALSE;
END;

PROCEDURE TMyWindow.WMLButtonDown(VAR Msg : TMessage);
     VAR
           dc : HDC;
```

```
        s  : ARRAY[0..20] OF CHAR;
    BEGIN
        StrPCopy(s, 'Left Button Clicked.');
        dc := GetDC(HWindow);
        TextOut(dc, Msg.LParamLo, Msg.LParamHi,
                         s, strlen(s));
        ReleaseDC(HWindow, dc);
    END;

PROCEDURE TMyFirstApp.InitMainWindow;
    BEGIN
    MainWindow := NEW(PMyWindow,
        Init(NIL, 'Listing 7.2'));
    END;

VAR
    MyFirstApp : TMyFirstApp;

{main body of program }
BEGIN
    MyFirstApp.Init('Listing7_2');
    MyFirstApp.Run;
    MyFirstApp.Done;
END.
```

Listing 7.2 has several new features that need explaining. The first difference appears in the definition of the *TMyWindow* object type. A new method (a function) has been added called *CanClose*. This is a predefined Boolean function in Object-Windows, but with a twist: *how* it acts is predefined, but the details of *why* it acts are left up to you. If *CanClose* is false, then any attempt to close the current window (of type *TMyWindow*) is canceled; if it's true, then the window can be closed. However, the details of when it is set to false or true are left to be defined by you.

The details of the *CanClose* function are also illuminating. First, we define a local variable called *Reply* of type integer. Then, using the *MessageBox* method as a function, we assign its result to the *Reply* variable.

When *MessageBox* is used in this way, the value it returns depends on which buttons have been put into it. In this case, for example, we have included *Yes, No,* and *Cancel* buttons by using the predefined identifier *mb_YesNoCancel*. Clicking on each of these buttons will cause a different value to be assigned to *MessageBox* and, thereby, to the *Reply* variable.

FIGURE 7.2:

Adding a file-save dialog box

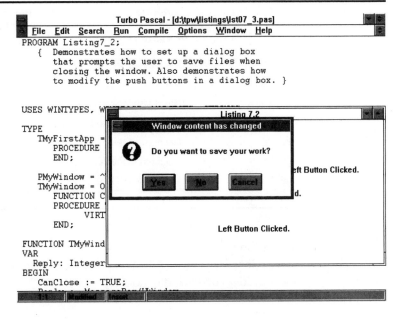

The final line of the *CanClose* method's main body tests the value of the *Reply* variable that was returned by the *MessageBox* function. If the user clicked on either the *Yes* or the *Cancel* button, then *CanClose* is set to *false;* otherwise, it remains true and the window is closed.

The identifiers *id_Yes* and *id_Cancel,* as you probably guessed, are predefined ObjectWindows identifiers for the values returned by various pushbuttons. Each type of button (see Table 7.1) causes its own particular value to be assigned to *MessageBox.* The buttons' return values are shown in Table 7.2.

Formatting Data for Display

Another way to display data in a window is to format information and read it into a buffer by using the *WVSPrintF* procedure. You may recall that Windows was originally designed to work with the C programming language: as a result, even Turbo Pascal for Windows has a few "C-like" features, and *WVSPrintF* is one place they show up. Along the way, we'll see some new aspects of the *Msg* parameter that we've been using to handle mouse clicks.

TABLE 7.2: Values returned to *MessageBox* by different types of buttons

Identifier	Meaning
id_Abort	User pressed the Abort button.
id_Cancel	User pressed the Cancel button.
id_Ignore	User pressed the Ignore button.
id_No	User pressed the No button.
id_OK	User pressed the OK button.
id_Retry	User pressed the Retry button.
id_Yes	User pressed the Yes button.

To see how *WVSPrintF* works, enter and run Listing 7.3. The output window should look like Figure 7.3. (The actual coordinates, of course, depend on where in the window you click the mouse.)

Listing 7.3

```
PROGRAM Listing7_3;
        {     Demonstrates how to format data for display
              by using the WVSPrintF procedure. Specific
              features demonstrated:
                   1. How to use the WVSPrintF procedure.
                   2. How to format data with WVSPrintF (not
                         documented in the Borland TPW manuals).
                   3. The contents of the MSG parameter
                         passed with a Windows message. }

USES WINTYPES, WINPROCS, WOBJECTS, STRINGS;

TYPE
     TMyApp = OBJECT (TApplication)
          PROCEDURE InitMainWindow; VIRTUAL;
          END;

     PMyWindow = ^TMyWindow;
     TMyWindow = OBJECT (TWindow)
          FUNCTION CanClose: BOOLEAN; VIRTUAL;
          PROCEDURE WMLButtonDown(VAR Msg : TMessage);
                    VIRTUAL wm_First + wm_LButtonDown;
```

```
            END;

FUNCTION TMyWindow.CanClose: BOOLEAN;
VAR
  Reply: Integer;
BEGIN
    CanClose := TRUE;
    Reply := MessageBox(HWindow,
                           'Do you want to save your work?',
                           'Window content has changed',
                           mb_YesNoCancel or mb_IconQuestion);
    IF (Reply = id_Yes) OR (Reply = id_Cancel)
                 THEN CanClose := FALSE;
END;

PROCEDURE TMyWindow.WMLButtonDown(VAR Msg : TMessage);
    VAR
          dc : HDC;
          s  : ARRAY[0..20] OF CHAR;
    BEGIN
          WVSPrintF(s, 'Click at: %d,%d', Msg.LParam);
          dc := GetDC(HWindow);
          TextOut(dc, Msg.LParamLo, Msg.LParamHi, s, StrLen(s));
          ReleaseDC(HWindow, DC);
    END;

PROCEDURE TMyApp.InitMainWindow;
    BEGIN
    MainWindow := NEW(PMyWindow,
          Init(NIL, 'Listing 7.3'));
    END;

VAR
    MyApp : TMyApp;

{main body of program }
BEGIN
    MyApp.Init('Listing7_3');
    MyApp.Run;
    MyApp.Done;
END.
```

True to the spirit of modular programming, the only differences are in the *WMLButtonDown* method. As before, the method is defined in such a way that it

FIGURE 7.3:

Mouse-click coordinates displayed as formatted with WVSPrintF

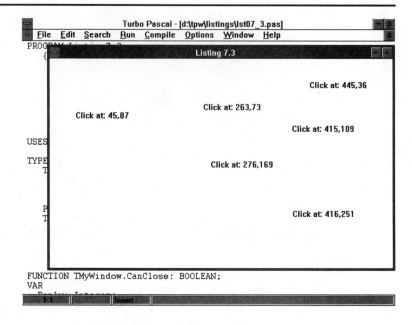

responds to left-button mouse clicks. It has a local variable, *dc*, for a display context, and another local variable, *s*, which is an array to hold a null-terminated string.

The first line in the main body of the method invokes the *WVSPrintF* procedure, which is similar to the *printf( )* function in C. It takes three parameters:

- A buffer, normally an array, to hold some data.
- A format string that shows how the data should be stored in the buffer.
- A variable that provides the data for the buffer.

The buffer here is *s*, our local character array. The format specification may look familiar if you've programmed in C: *%d* says that the data should be stored in decimal format. In the format string, you can also include other (non-reserved) characters and strings that you want to go with the data: here, we've put in "Click at:" to indicate that the numbers stored (and later displayed) are the coordinates of a mouse click.

Unfortunately, the format specifiers for the data are not documented in the TPW manuals, though they're an easy guess for C programmers. The format specifiers in TPW are a subset of those in C, and are shown in Table 7.3.

TABLE 7.3: Predefined data format specifiers for use with *WVSPrintF*

Specifier	Format
%d	Decimal
%s	String
%c	Char
%i	Integer
%ld	Long signed decimal
%u	Unsigned integer
%lu	Long unsigned integer
%x	Unsigned hex integer
%lx	Long unsigned hex integer

The final parameter in *WVSPrintF* is a variable that holds the data to be put into the buffer. Here, that variable is *Msg.LParam*—one of the fields of the *Msg* parameter that is passed to mouse-click response methods. Previously, we haven't needed to look at this parameter very closely, but now its features become important.

The *Msg* parameter is a record of type *TMessage*, as defined in the WOBJECTS unit. *TMessage* is a variant record type which contains fields for the X and Y coordinates of a mouse click or other user event. *LParam* is a long INTEGER type field (32 bits) that can be subdivided into a low-order part and a high-order part, each of which contains a 16-bit WORD value. Here, we simply load the whole *LParam* value into the buffer, depending on the format specifier to make it display properly.

If you're not familiar with dividing a sequence of bits into low-order and high-order parts, here's an example. Consider the sequence

0000000011111111

This is a 16-bit sequence; however, it can be divided into a low-order part, *00000000*, and a high-order part, *11111111*, each of which has a different value. This means that in a single memory location, you could store any of the following values, depending on how you retrieved the data:

0000000011111111
00000000
11111111

If you can do this, it's obviously more efficient in certain situations.

In the case at hand, *LParam* contains a single 32-bit value that can be split into a low-order part (the X coordinate of the mouse click) and a high-order part (the Y coordinate of the mouse click). We simply load the whole thing into the buffer, then read it out in the format we need.

The next lines simply get a display context, use the *TextOut* procedure to display the text string from the buffer at the coordinates of the mouse click, and release the display context. Everything else in the program is identical to Listing 6.3.

Drawing in a Window

As a final example in this chapter, we'll look at a program to draw lines in a window. While line-drawing itself is not of major importance for most applications, this program does illustrate some key features of Windows programming and provides a jumping-off point for features we'll discuss in later chapters. To get started, enter the program in Listing 7.4.

Listing 7.4

```
PROGRAM Listing7_4;
   {   Demonstrates using the mouse to draw in a window.
      Features shown:
         1. Overriding the parent object type's
            CONSTRUCTOR method.
         2. The InvalidateRect method.
         3. The SetCapture and ReleaseCapture methods.
         4. The MoveTo method.
         5. The LineTo method. }

USES STRINGS, WINTYPES, WINPROCS, WOBJECTS;

TYPE
   TMyApp = OBJECT (TApplication)
            PROCEDURE InitMainWindow; VIRTUAL;
            END;
   PMyWindow = ^TMyWindow;
   TMyWindow = OBJECT(TWindow)
            dc: HDC;
            LButtonDown: BOOLEAN;
```

```
                        CONSTRUCTOR Init(AParent: PWindowsObject;
                            ATitle: PChar);
                        FUNCTION CanClose: BOOLEAN; VIRTUAL;
                        PROCEDURE WMLButtonDown(VAR Msg: TMessage);
                            VIRTUAL wm_First + wm_LButtonDown;
                        PROCEDURE WMLButtonUp(VAR Msg: TMessage);
                            VIRTUAL wm_First + wm_LButtonUp;
                        PROCEDURE WMMouseMove(VAR Msg: TMessage);
                            VIRTUAL wm_First + wm_MouseMove;
                        END;

{TMyWindow methods}
CONSTRUCTOR TMyWindow.Init(AParent: PWindowsObject;
                            ATitle: PChar);
    BEGIN
        TWindow.Init(AParent, ATitle);
        LButtonDown := FALSE;
    END;

FUNCTION TMyWindow.CanClose: BOOLEAN;
    VAR
        Reply: INTEGER;
    BEGIN
        CanClose := TRUE;
        Reply := MessageBox(HWindow,
                'Do you want to save your work?',
                'Window content has changed',
                mb_YesNoCancel or mb_IconQuestion);
        IF (Reply = id_Yes) OR (Reply = id_Cancel)
            THEN CanClose := FALSE;
    END;

PROCEDURE TMyWindow.WMLButtonDown(VAR Msg: TMessage);
    BEGIN
        InvalidateRect(HWindow, NIL, TRUE);
        IF not LButtonDown
        THEN    BEGIN
                LButtonDown := TRUE;
                SetCapture(HWindow);
                dc := GetDC(HWindow);
                MoveTo(dc, Msg.LParamLo, Msg.LParamHi);
                END;
    END;

PROCEDURE TMyWindow.WMMouseMove(VAR Msg: TMessage);
```

```
      BEGIN
         IF LButtonDown
         THEN LineTo(dc, INTEGER(Msg.LParamLo),
                     INTEGER(Msg.LParamHi));
      END;

PROCEDURE TMyWindow.WMLButtonUp(VAR Msg: TMessage);
   BEGIN
   IF LButtonDown
   THEN   BEGIN
          LButtonDown := FALSE;
          ReleaseCapture;
          ReleaseDC(HWindow, dc);
          END;
   END;

{TMyApp methods}
PROCEDURE TMyApp.InitMainWindow;
   BEGIN
      MainWindow := New(PMyWindow,
      Init(NIL, 'Listing 7.4'));
   END;

{global object variable for application}
VAR
   MyApp: TMyApp;

{main body of program}
BEGIN
   MyApp.Init('Listing7_4');
   MyApp.Run;
   MyApp.Done;
END.
```

When you run this program, it will open a window on the PC's screen. If you hold down the left mouse button and move the mouse cursor around, it will draw a line in the window, as shown in Figure 7.4. Of course, the line you get will depend on how you move the mouse.

When you release the left mouse button, the line stops. If you click the button again, or move or resize the window, the original drawing disappears, leaving a blank window in which you can enter a new drawing.

FIGURE 7.4:

Drawing a line in a window

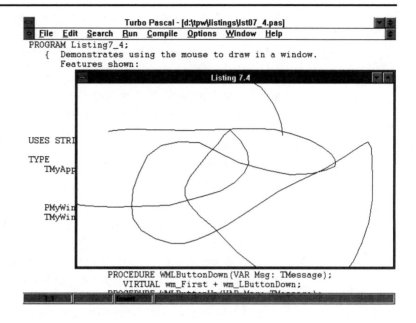

```
Turbo Pascal - [d:\tpw\listings\lst07_4.pas]
File  Edit  Search  Run  Compile  Options  Window  Help
PROGRAM Listing7_4;
    {  Demonstrates using the mouse to draw in a window.
       Features shown:
```

Listing 7.4

```
USES STRI
TYPE
    TMyAp
    PMyWi
    TMyWi
```

```
PROCEDURE WMLButtonDown(VAR Msg: TMessage);
       VIRTUAL wm_First + wm_LButtonDown;
```

There are several new features in Listing 7.4. First, notice that we have added a new Boolean variable, *LButtonDown*: this is needed so that Windows knows if the left mouse button is being held down or not. On the basis of this variable's value, your program knows whether or not to draw a line.

We've also overridden the *Init* method that *TMyWindow* inherits from its predefined ancestor object type, *TWindow*. As such things often are, this is to make a fairly small change. In the definition of the new *Init* method, we simply call the ancestor *Init* method and then set the *LButtonDown* Boolean variable to *false*.

The WMLButtonDown Method

The *WMLButtonDown* method is quite different. It begins by calling *InvalidateRect*, a predefined ObjectWindows routine that operates on an area inside a window. This takes three parameters: a handle to the window in which *InvalidateRect* should work, a *TRect* type variable indicating the region in the window on which it should work, and a Boolean variable indicating whether or not the region should be erased. In this case, the window handle is of course the current window. The second parameter is set to NIL, indicating that *InvalidateRect* should apply to the entire client area of the window instead of just a region within that client area. The third parameter is set to *true*, indicating that the region should be erased. This is why the previous drawing disappears when you click the left mouse button again.

The *WMLButtonDown* method then sets up an IF statement to see if the mouse button is already depressed. If it is, then you don't want to execute the statements in the THEN part, such as getting a new display context. Without this test, the program would crash almost instantly as it ran out of new display contexts. In the THEN part itself, we first set the *LButtonDown* variable to *true*. Then we call a predefined procedure you haven't seen before: *SetCapture*, which tells Windows that all user input should be restricted to the current window.

The importance of using *SetCapture* is shown in Figure 7.4. Earlier, you may not have noticed, but several of the lines go to the window border, stop, and then re-appear at the window border in a different place. This is the result of trying to continue drawing a line outside of the current window. What *SetCapture* does is make sure that all the lines you draw are restricted to the window specified in the program, so that other windows won't be affected even if you move the mouse cursor over their locations on the screen. Later in the program, of course, we'll call *ReleaseCapture*, which cancels the effect of *SetCapture*.

The next step is to get a display context, which is fairly familiar. Then, we call the (predefined) *MoveTo* method, which moves the mouse cursor to the location of the click. The first parameter is the current display context, while the second and third parameters are the X and Y coordinates of the mouse click—the low and high-order parts of one of the *Msg* fields, as we saw earlier in this chapter.

WMMouseMove Method

In this program, the mouse doesn't just get clicked and released. As long as the mouse button is held down, we want a line to be drawn from the point at which it was originally pressed to the current location of the mouse cursor. That's what this method does. Notice, in the object type definition near the top of the listing, that this method is set to respond to the Windows message *wm_MouseMove*.

This method first checks to see if the left mouse button is depressed. If it is, it calls the predefined *LineTo* method. This draws a line from the previous location of the mouse cursor to its current location. It takes three parameters. The first parameter is the current display context. The second and third parameters are the X and Y coordinates of the current mouse cursor location. However, *LineTo* requires that these be integers, so we use the *Integer()* function to convert *LParamLo* and *LParamHi* (which are both of type WORD) to integers.

WMLButtonUp Method

Because the mouse button is being held down while drawing in the window, we need a method to take care of things when the button is released. This method is defined so that it responds to the Windows message *wm_LButtonUp*. First, it checks to see if the button has, in fact, been held down—i.e., whether or not the *LButton-Down* Boolean variable is set to *true*. If it is, then (because a *wm_LButtonUp* message has just been received by the program), it sets the variable to *false*. It then calls *ReleaseCapture*, which we explained earlier, and releases the display context that was being used for drawing in the window.

Main Body of the Program

The rest of the program is fairly standard. We define an *InitMainWindow* method based on the predefined *InitMainWindow* method in ObjectWindows. Then, we set up an object variable to represent the entire program, and do the usual init-run-done sequence.

CHAPTER
EIGHT

Getting User
Input with Menus

- **Preparing a Program to Use a Menu**

- **Using the Whitewater Resource Toolkit**

- **Variations in Menu Formats**

8

So far, we've done some remarkable things with remarkably little effort. We've created application programs that run under Windows, respond to mouse clicks, display a predefined window-control menu, and draw text or lines in the window.

One thing we haven't done, however, is add customized menus to our application. The only menu we've seen so far is the window-control menu that comes predefined.

Setting up menus in Turbo Pascal for Windows is quite a bit different from setting them up in a standard Pascal program, though there are some similarities. In most programs, regardless of whether they are in standard Pascal, BASIC, or some other language, a menu structure requires the inclusion of a case statement in the program's source code—for example,

```
WRITELN(' Main Menu');
WRITELN(' ------------------');
WRITELN(' 1. Edit');
WRITELN(' 2. Save');
WRITELN(' 3. Quit');
WRITE(' Enter your choice (1/2/3): ');
READLN(menuchoice);

CASE menuchoice OF
    1 : EditFile;
    2 : SaveFile;
    3 : QuitProgram
    ELSE Error
    END;
```

In a Windows program, however, a menu is a *resource* that is defined apart from the main program. There is still the equivalent of a CASE statement in the source code itself, though you'd hardly recognize it. The menu structure itself is defined in a separate file called a *resource file*. Although you can define resources in Turbo Pascal itself, the easiest way to do it is to use the **Whitewater Resource Toolkit** that is included with the TPW package. Then, by naming the resource at the top of your program and going through a few other gyrations, you get a Windows-compatible drop-down menu in your program.

Getting User Input with Menus

Preparing a Program to Use a Menu

The basic moves for setting up a program to use a menu are shown in Listing 8.1. We won't be able to run this program until we actually create a menu resource in the Whitewater Resource Toolkit, but we can see how it *will* run when it finally does. This listing, by the way, extends the features of Listing 7.4 from the previous chapter.

Listing 8.1

```
PROGRAM Listing8_1;
   {  Shows how to set up a program to use a menu
      resource created in the Whitewater Resource
      Toolkit. Features demonstrated:
         1. Naming the resource.
         2. Defining command constants for the various
            menu commands.
         3. Activating the menu with the LoadMenu
            function.  }

USES STRINGS, WINTYPES, WINPROCS, WOBJECTS, STDDLGS;
{$R MyRes1.res }

CONST
   cm_New    = 101;
   cm_Color = 102;
   cm_Style = 103;
   cm_Thick = 104;
   cm_Help   = 901;

TYPE
   TMyApp = OBJECT(TApplication)
      PROCEDURE InitMainWindow; VIRTUAL;
      END;

   PMyWindow = ^TMyWindow;
   TMyWindow = OBJECT(TWindow)
      dc: HDC;
      LButtonDown: BOOLEAN;
      CONSTRUCTOR Init(AParent: PWindowsObject;
         ATitle: PChar);
      FUNCTION CanClose: BOOLEAN; VIRTUAL;
```

```
        PROCEDURE WMLButtonDown(VAR Msg: TMessage);
            VIRTUAL wm_First + wm_LButtonDown;
        PROCEDURE WMLButtonUp(VAR Msg: TMessage);
            VIRTUAL wm_First + wm_LButtonUp;
        PROCEDURE WMMouseMove(VAR Msg: TMessage);
            VIRTUAL wm_First + wm_MouseMove;
        PROCEDURE NewDraw(VAR Msg: TMessage);
            VIRTUAL cm_First + cm_New;
        PROCEDURE ChangeColor(VAR Msg: TMessage);
            VIRTUAL cm_First + cm_Color;
        PROCEDURE ChangeStyle(VAR Msg: TMessage);
            VIRTUAL cm_First + cm_Style;
        PROCEDURE ChangeThickness(VAR Msg: TMessage);
            VIRTUAL cm_First + cm_Thick;
        PROCEDURE Help(VAR Msg: TMessage);
            VIRTUAL cm_First + cm_Help;
        END;

{TMyWindow methods}
CONSTRUCTOR TMyWindow.Init(AParent: PWindowsObject;
                               ATitle: PChar);
    BEGIN
        TWindow.Init(AParent, ATitle);
        Attr.Menu := LoadMenu(HInstance, PChar(100));
        LButtonDown := False;
    END;

FUNCTION TMyWindow.CanClose: BOOLEAN;
    VAR
        Reply: INTEGER;
    BEGIN
        CanClose := TRUE;
        Reply := MessageBox(HWindow,
                    'Do you want to save your work?',
                    'Window content has changed',
                    mb_YesNoCancel or mb_IconQuestion);
        IF (Reply = id_Yes) OR (Reply = id_Cancel)
            THEN CanClose := FALSE;
    END;

PROCEDURE TMyWindow.WMLButtonDown(VAR Msg: TMessage);
    BEGIN
        InvalidateRect(HWindow, NIL, TRUE);
        IF not LButtonDown
        THEN  BEGIN
```

```
                        LButtonDown := TRUE;
                        SetCapture(HWindow);
                        dc := GetDC(HWindow);
                        MoveTo(dc, Msg.LParamLo, Msg.LParamHi);
                        END;
            END;

PROCEDURE TMyWindow.WMMouseMove(VAR Msg: TMessage);
    BEGIN
        IF LButtonDown
        THEN LineTo(dc, INTEGER(Msg.LParamLo),
                    INTEGER(Msg.LParamHi));
    END;

PROCEDURE TMyWindow.WMLButtonUp(VAR Msg: TMessage);
    BEGIN
        IF LButtonDown
        THEN  BEGIN
                LButtonDown := False;
                ReleaseCapture;
                ReleaseDC(HWindow, dc);
                END;
    END;

PROCEDURE TMyWindow.NewDraw(VAR Msg: TMessage);
    BEGIN
    END;

PROCEDURE TMyWindow.ChangeColor(VAR Msg: TMessage);
    BEGIN
    END;

PROCEDURE TMyWindow.ChangeStyle(VAR Msg: TMessage);
    BEGIN
    END;

PROCEDURE TMyWindow.ChangeThickness(VAR Msg: TMessage);
    BEGIN
    END;

PROCEDURE TMyWindow.Help(VAR Msg: TMessage);
    BEGIN
    END;

{TMyApp methods}
```

```
PROCEDURE TMyApp.InitMainWindow;
   BEGIN
   MainWindow := NEW(PMyWindow, Init(NIL, 'Listing 8.1'));
   END;

{global object variable for application}
VAR
  MyApp : TMyApp;

{main body of program}
BEGIN
   MyApp.Init('Listing8_1');
   MyApp.Run;
   MyApp.Done;
END.
```

Including a Resource File

The first new wrinkle in Listing 8.1 has nothing much to do menus: it's an additional unit, *STDDLGS*, that we declare in the USES clause. This will enable us to create an interactive dialog box with more features than the simple message boxes we've seen so far. We'll return to this when we create a dialog box later in the chapter.

After the USES clause comes a compiler directive that looks very much like one used to insert an "include file"—an older Turbo Pascal programming feature that was replaced by *units* in versions 4 and later—at that point in the code. In fact, it does insert an include file, but it's an include file of a very special kind. The compiler directive *$R*, when used together with a file name, is called a *resource file directive*, and it names a precompiled resource file that is used by the program. A resource file is a standard type of Windows file that defines characteristics of some windowing object, such as an icon or a menu.

If we were using the Windows SDK, we would create a resource file in source-code form and compile it with the **Windows Resource Compiler**. However, it's much easier to accomplish the same goal with the **Whitewater Resource Toolkit**, as we'll see later in the chapter. In either case, the file will have the same format, since it's a standard Windows resource file. The default filename extension is .RES.

Note that the resource file directive does not specify a disk directory where the resource file can be found. You can specify a directory path if the file isn't in the current directory. If you don't specify a directory path, then when it compiles the program, Turbo Pascal will first look for the resource file in the current directory, then in the directories (if any) you specified in the Resource Directories box that you open from the Options menu.

Defining Command Constants

The next thing in the program that may be unfamiliar (unless you've used Turbo Vision with the DOS version of Turbo Pascal) is the CONST section where we define command constants for the various menu choices:

```
CONST
    cm_New   = 101;
    cm_Color = 102;
    cm_Style = 103;
    cm_Thick = 104;
    cm_Help  = 901;
```

There are a couple of things to notice about this. First, each command constant begins with *cm_*. This marks the identifier as a command constant, just as the prefix *wm_* marks an identifier as corresponding to a Windows message. Object methods that name the cm_ identifiers in their extensions are *command-response methods*.

Second, each command constant is assigned an integer value. These are the values that we'll assign to the corresponding menu choices when we create the menu resource file. If we wanted to, we could simply use the integer values and forget about defining the command constants. However, defining the command constants makes our code much easier to read, particularly when we get to the extensions for the method headers. The point, however, is that we use the command constants to set up a link between the menu choices defined in the resource file and the method that each one executes.

For example, the value *101* will appear in the WRT next to the menu choice "New Drawing." The command constant *cm_New* is defined as having the same value, and this command constant is named in the extension of the method to create a new drawing in the window. Thus, the method is connected—albeit indirectly—to the menu choice that calls it.

Setting Up Command-Response Methods

The *TMyApp* object type definition is the same as in Listing 7.4, and except for the addition of some new methods, so is the definition of *TMyWindow*. The new methods are the command-response methods that will carry out our menu choices. Notice that each method header has an extension that begins with *cm_First*, identifying it as a command-response method, and then names the command constant for the particular menu choice. In other respects, however, these method headers are pretty typical of what we've seen so far.

If you look farther down in the listing, you'll see that we've simply put in empty BEGIN..END statements ("stubs") for the details of each method definition. We'll work out those details later on. This way, however, we can get the main framework of the program up and running without needing to define precisely how the methods will work.

Loading the Menu Resource

Just as a file must first be named in the program and then officially "opened," a menu resource must be named in the resource-file compiler directive and then "loaded" with the *LoadMenu* function. Here,

```
CONSTRUCTOR TMyWindow.Init(AParent: PWindowsObject;
                            ATitle: PChar);
   BEGIN
      TWindow.Init(AParent, ATitle);
      Attr.Menu := LoadMenu(HInstance, PChar(100));
      LButtonDown := False;
   END;
```

not only initializes the window and the *LButtonDown* variable, but loads the menu resource as well.

The crucial line, of course, is

```
Attr.Menu := LoadMenu(HInstance, PChar(100));
```

Let's look at each part of this line in turn.

> **Attr.Menu** The predefined *TWindow* object type, on which our *TMy-Window* type is based, has a field called *Attr* that contains the attributes of any particular instance of that type. The *TWindow.Attr* field is itself a record structure that has fields of its own to hold the different attributes,

such as (1) the window's associated text, style, extended style, position, and size; (2) the window's handle; and (3) the window's control ID. One of the fields of *Attr* holds a handle to the window's menus: that field is *Attr.Menu*.

LoadMenu() This is a Windows API function that returns a handle to a menu resource. It takes two parameters: first, a handle to the program or resource module that contains the menu resource; and second, a null-terminated string that gives the menu's resource ID, which you specify when you create the menu resource. What this line does is to load the menu handle into the *Attr.Menu* field of an object variable of type *TMyWindow*.

HInstance This is a handle to the menu resource.

PChar(100) Normally, *PChar* denotes a pointer to a null-terminated string. Here, however, it's used as a function that takes the integer resource ID of the menu (100) and recasts it into a null-terminated string. Thus, this expression returns a null-terminated string 100#0.

Nothing else about Listing 8.1 is particularly remarkable, apart from the fact that it won't run until we use the **Whitewater Resource Toolkit** to create a menu resource. The methods for the specific menu options, at this point, are empty BEGIN..END statements, just as they would be at this stage if we were doing a standard structured program under DOS instead of Windows. We create a *TMyApp*-type variable, just as in Listing 7.4, and then initialize it, run it, and shut it down in the main body of the program.

Starting the Whitewater Resource Toolkit

The next step is to use the **Whitewater Resource Toolkit (WRT)** to create the menu resource. This package, which is included with Turbo Pascal for Windows, can be used to create resources for use by any Windows application, regardless of whether it was created in Turbo Pascal for Windows. The WRT was created by The Whitewater Group (Evanston, Illinois), which makes several other valuable tools for Windows programming—including **ObjectGraphics**, which makes it easier to put art and graphics into your Turbo Pascal for Windows applications.

Before you start the WRT, it will save you some trouble if you write down the menu choices and their corresponding command constants in Listing 8.1. You'll need that information to create the menu resource, and this will save you from needing to switch back and forth between the WRT and Turbo Pascal for Windows. In this case, of course, the number of menu choices and command constants is trivial and easy to remember, but when you have got multiple menus and lots of choices, it can be a problem.

To start the WRT,

1. Switch to the Windows Program Manager and double-click on the WRT icon in the Turbo Pascal for Windows program group, as shown in Figure 8.1.

2. Click on the minimize button in the Program Manager so that you will be able to see the TPW document you are working with. The WRT main control screen will appear, as shown in Figure 8.2.

Using the WRT Menu Editor

There are several different things we can do with the WRT, but at the moment, we're only interested in using the menu editor. (We'll discuss the rest of the WRT and its other features later in the book.) To start up the menu resource editor, click on the

FIGURE 8.1:

Starting the WRT from the Windows Program Manager

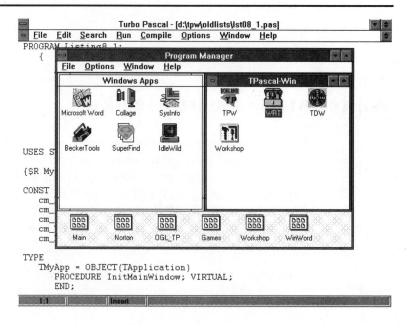

FIGURE 8.2:

The WRT main control screen

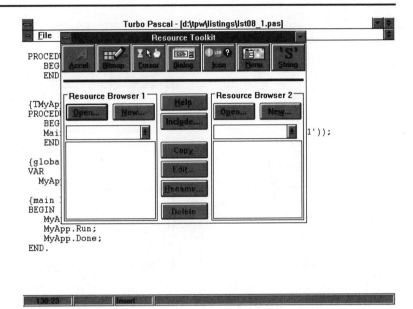

icon button marked "Menu" in the icon palette underneath the window's title bar. The menu editor will open, as shown in Figure 8.3.

Each part of the menu editor screen plays its own role in creating or editing a menu resource. The large boxes in the middle are where you fill in a menu's content—in the *Item Text* column, the menu title and its menu choices; in the *Value* column, the command values to be passed to the application that owns the menu.

When the menu editor starts up, the cursor is on the first line of the Item Text column. To create a menu, you simply type the name of the menu. If you wish to highlight one of the letters in the menu, so that the menu can be opened by pressing the *Alt* key and that letter, you precede the letter with an ampersand (&). (The highlighted letter can be any letter in the menu item text.)

The arrow buttons above the Item Text column enable you to change an item's level in the menu hierarchy. The leftmost position is reserved for menu *titles*; menu *choices* must be indented, by clicking once on the right-arrow button. (The left-arrow button reverses the effect of the right-arrow button, "promoting" the cursor position from menu choices to menu names.)

FIGURE 8.3:

The WRT menu resource editor

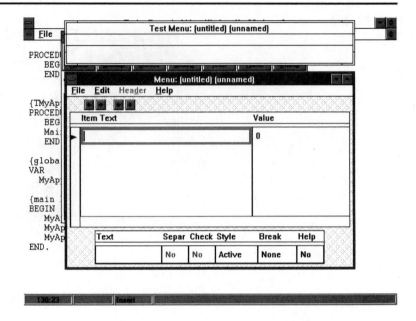

Remember that you must assign each menu item (except the menu title, which automatically gets a value of zero) its own command value in the Value column. These must be the same as the command constants assigned in the program's source code. (There is no need to indent items in the Values column.)

To create a second menu, simply click on the left-arrow button above the Item Text column to move the cursor back to its leftmost position. Figure 8.4 shows how the menu editor appears when we've created the two menus ("Line" and "Help") for the program in Listing 8.1.

Testing the Menu Resource

Creating the menu is one thing, but being sure that it will work is something else again. One way to test it would be to save the menu resource to disk and then run Listing 8.1. If the listing compiled and ran correctly, then we would know that the menu resource is okay. If it didn't, however, then we could get into a time-consuming cycle of switching back and forth between the menu editor and Turbo Pascal for Windows.

FIGURE 8.4:

Menu editor with menu data for Listing 8.1

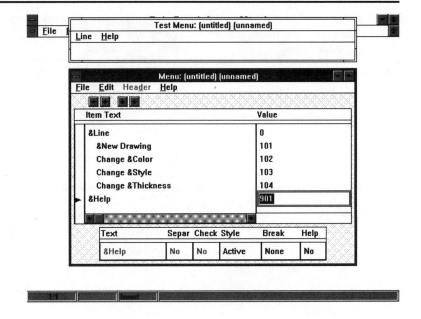

Fortunately, the menu editor provides a way to test a menu resource "live" without having to run it in an actual program. The window across the top of the menu editor is the **Test Menu** window. By clicking in this window and then clicking on the menu choices that it displays, you can see if the menu resource has been set up to work the way you want—particularly to see if it returns the correct value for its corresponding command constant in the TPW program. A test of the menu resource we've just created is shown in Figure 8.5.

There's one important point to remember about the testing window: it tests *only* the menu resource itself, not how well (or if) the menu choices will work in your program. The latter depends on the code you write in Turbo Pascal for Windows, defining the methods correctly and linking them with the appropriate command constants.

Saving the Menu Resource

The final step, once you've verified that the menu works correctly, is to save the menu as a resource file. To do this, you select "Save" from the File menu in the menu editor. This will open up the **File Save As** dialog box shown in Figure 8.6.

FIGURE 8.5:

Testing a menu resource in the
Test Menu window

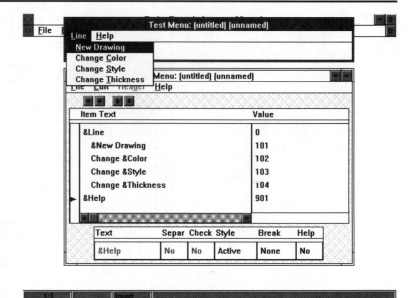

FIGURE 8.6:

The File Save As dialog box

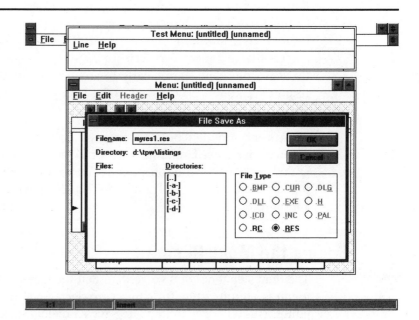

The File Save As dialog box is pretty self-explanatory. You type the name you want for the menu resource file in the *Filename:* text box at the top. In this case, name the resource file MyRes1. The current directory path is shown underneath that box, and you can change the directory by double-clicking on the one you want in the *Directories:* box. The *File Type* group box at the lower right shows the different kinds of resource file you can create. At this point, only two types, .RC and .RES, are available, and the .RES type (compiled resource file) is the default. Be sure to save the resource file either to the same directory as Listing 8.1 or to the default directory: that way, Turbo Pascal for Windows will be able to find the menu resource when it compiles the program.

Because we want to save the menu as a .RES resource file, simply click on *OK.* The next thing to appear on the screen will be the **Resource Attributes** dialog box, shown in Figure 8.7. In this dialog box, we assign the resource identifier (the default is *A_RESOURCE*) that the *LoadMenu* function will use to access the menu for the application's main window *Attr* record. Because we used the integer *100* in the program, type 100 into the *Name:* text box and click on OK.

FIGURE 8.7:
The Resource Attributes dialog box

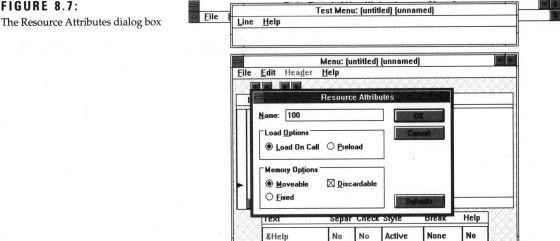

Running the Menu

Now that we've created and saved the menu resource, we can see the result in our program. The program still won't do much of anything—the methods corresponding to the menu choices are still empty—but we can verify that the main program works just fine. After switching back to Turbo Pascal for Windows, compile and run Listing 8.1. The result is shown in Figure 8.8.

Variations in Menu Formats

The menu we set up in Listing 8.1 was fairly simple, of course, and quite adequate for our purposes. However, there are several other things you can do with menu resources in TPW. Your menus can have submenus that pop open when certain choices are selected, menu choices can be checked or unchecked to indicate the current status of the operations they represent, and menus can have more than one column of choices in a single menu.

FIGURE 8.8:

Running Listing 8.1 with a menu resource

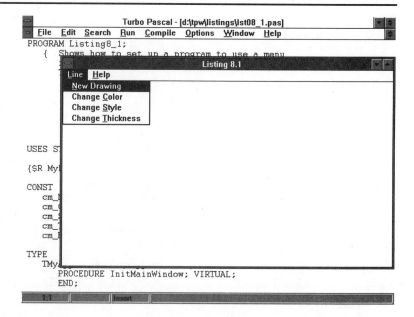

Let's look at how we might modify the menus in Listing 8.1 and the *MyRes1.Res* menu resource. We're not going to use these modifications in future chapters, so you might want to save both the listing and the resource file under different names—say, LST8_2.PAS and MyRes1A.Res. The modified listing follows the discussion of these modifications.

Creating Multilevel Menus

The easiest variation is multilevel menus. This allows individual menu choices to activate submenus that pop open just to the right of the original menu. To do this, we'll need to add the appropriate command constants and menu-response methods to Listing 8.1. Then, we'll simply add an indented level of menu choices under one of the existing menu choices in the WRT.

Let's start by changing the name of the menu resource included in the compiler directive statement to MyRes1A.Res, then adding the required code to Listing 8.1 for the added menu choices. We'll create three new menu choices, so we'll need three new command constants in the CONST section of the program. Add them (indented, for clarity) under the *cm_Thick* command constant, as follows:

```
cm_Thin    = 201;
cm_Medium  = 202;
cm_RealThick   = 203;
```

Then, add empty menu-response methods for each of the new menu choices. The code is trivial, but is included here for completeness. The method headers should be placed under the header for *TMyWindow.ChangeThickness* in the declaration of the *TMyWindow* object type. The empty method definitions should be placed in the code under the declaration of the details for *TMyWindow.ChangeThickness*.

```
{ New menu-response method headers}
ROCEDURE Thin(VAR Msg: TMessage);
    VIRTUAL cm_First + cm_Thin;
PROCEDURE Medium(VAR Msg: TMessage);
   VIRTUAL cm_First + cm_Medium;
 PROCEDURE RealThick(VAR Msg: TMessage);
    VIRTUAL cm_First + cm_RealThick;

{Empty-method definitions}
PROCEDURE TMyWindow.Thin(VAR Msg: TMessage);
   BEGIN
   END;
```

```
PROCEDURE TMyWindow.Medium(VAR Msg: TMessage);
   BEGIN
   END;

PROCEDURE TMyWindow.RealThick(VAR Msg: TMessage);
   BEGIN
   END;
```

The next step is to modify the menu resource. In the WRT, add three new menu choices, indented another level, under "Change Thickness." The menu choices should correspond to the three new command constants in the TPW program, and have the appropriate values (201, 202, and 203). The WRT screen with the new menu items is shown in Figure 8.9, while the result of running the program is shown in Figure 8.10.

Checking/Unchecking Menu Choices

Allowing certain menu choices to be checked (with a ✓ mark) or unchecked can be helpful, particularly when the choice is too simple to warrant using a dialog box. A typical example is the "Full Menus" choice that one sees in the Options menus of

FIGURE 8.9:

Submenu choices added to the menu resource editor

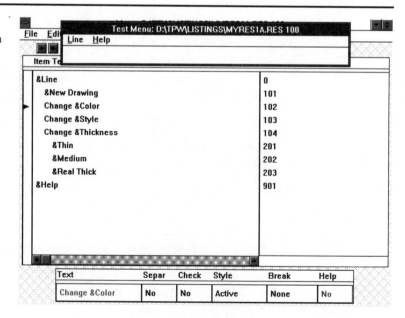

FIGURE 8.10:

A submenu added to the TPW
program first created in Listing 8.1

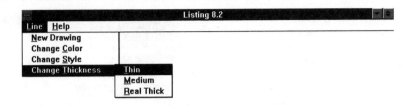

many programs. If "Full Menus" is not checked, then only short, abbreviated menus suitable for inexperienced users are displayed. If "Full Menus" is checked, then all the menu choices are displayed when a menu pops open.

To check and uncheck menu choices, you need to learn the following:

- How to set up the menu resource so that a desired menu choice is either checked or unchecked as the default.

- How to use the methods *GetMenuState* and *CheckMenuItem* defined in the TPW WINPROCS unit.

Let's take each of these points in turn.

Setting the Checked/Unchecked Status in the Menu Resource

The resource file itself can indicate whether a menu choice should initially be checked or unchecked. In the WRT, you can set this option by selecting the *Check* box at the bottom of the WRT menu resource editor, then toggling it to Yes or No by pressing the spacebar. The default value is No, meaning that the normal value for the menu choice is unchecked. Figure 8.11 shows a new menu choice, "Full Menus," with a

FIGURE 8.11:

A default checked menu choice, set using the "Check" feature of the menu resource editor

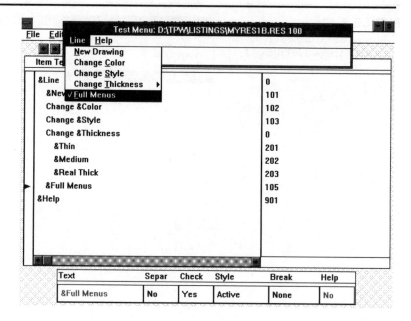

checkmark next to it. Note that the third column along the bottom of the screen, *Check*, has been toggled to Yes.

Using GetMenuState and CheckMenuItem

GetMenuState and *CheckMenuItem* are two routines defined in the WINPROCS unit. *GetMenuState* allows you to retrieve the current status of a particular menu choice—in this case, in regard to whether it's checked or unchecked. *CheckMenuItem* allows you to change the checked/unchecked status of a particular menu choice.

GetMenuState takes three parameters: a handle to the menu, the control ID of the menu choice you want to inspect, and how the program should find the menu choice. The menu handle will typically be the *Attr.Menu* field of the parent window's *Attr* record. The second item is either the menu choice's control ID or its position in the menu. For example, if the "Full Menus" choice is assigned a control ID of 105, then that is the value which would be passed to *GetMenuState*. If you'd rather the program find the "Full Menus" choice by its position in the menu, then, because it's the fifth item in the menu and the first item is in position #0, you would pass 4 to the *GetMenuState* routine. Under normal circumstances, however, it makes more sense to use the menu choice's control ID.

The third and final parameter passed to *GetMenuState* tells the routine whether the previous parameter is the menu choice's control ID or if it is its position in the menu. You can pass one of two values in this parameter: *mf_ByCommand*, which indicates that you're using the control ID, or *mf_ByPosition*, which indicates that you're using the position in the menu. Thus, for example, we might check the new "Full Menus" choice with

```
GetMenuState(attr.menu, 105, mf_ByCommand);
```

where *attr.menu* is the handle to the parent window's menus, 105 is the control ID for the "Full Menus" choice, and *mf_ByCommand* indicates that the control ID 105 is the flag, not the position in the menu. *GetMenuState* can be used to check for more than checkmarks. It can also be used to determine if a menu choice is enabled, disabled, and other status information.

The other important routine, *CheckMenuItem*, can be used to check or uncheck a menu choice. It takes three parameters: a handle to the menu, the control ID or the position of the menu item to be checked or unchecked, and what status it should be set to by the routine (i.e., checked or unchecked). To check a menu choice, you pass the predefined value *mf_Checked* as the third parameter; to uncheck a menu choice, you pass the predefined value *mf_UnChecked*. There's no reason in principle why you couldn't pass a value of *mf_Checked* to a menu choice that was already checked (or *mf_unChecked* to one that was unchecked), but I see no practical value in doing so.

To utilize these two routines (functions, actually) in a program, you simply need to add a little bit of code to the menu-response method that corresponds to the menu choice that should be checked or unchecked. Of course, checking or unchecking a menu choice doesn't always make a great deal of sense. There would be little point in putting a checkmark next to the "Change Color" menu choice, because that menu choice is meant to open a dialog box that lets the user choose from among many colors for the line drawn in the window. Checkmarks are also inappropriate unless the checked/unchecked status of a menu choice indicates an ongoing state of the program rather than a specific event that happens and then terminates.

Setting Up Multicolumn Menus

Sometimes, you may want an individual menu to have two columns. This will most often be the case when you have numerous menu choices or when you anticipate that the user will need to see the part of the screen that would otherwise be covered by a deep single-column menu.

Setting up two columns is easy with the WRT menu editor. You simply highlight, in the *Item Text* box, the menu choice that you want to be at the top of the new column, then you select the *Break* box at the bottom right of the menu resource editor (column 5 in the bottom-line menu). By pressing the spacebar, you can toggle it between three values:

None: No column break between the current menu choice and the one above it.

Column: The highlighted menu choice should appear at the top of a new column in the menu.

Bar: The highlighted menu choice should appear at the top of a new column in the menu, and the new column should be separated from the previous column by a vertical bar, as shown in Figure 8.12.

In Listing 8.2, we add the new "Full Menus" option to the Line menu, along with a method to check or uncheck the menu choice. A full implementation would need additional code to carry out specific menu-handling tasks, but this shows how the operations discussed in the preceding discussions are performed.

Listing 8.2

```
PROGRAM Listing8_2;
{  Shows how to set up menus with different
   formats. Specific features demonstrated:
        1. Multilevel menus.
        2. Checked/unchecked menu items.
        3. Two-column menus. }

USES STRINGS, WINTYPES, WINPROCS, WOBJECTS, STDDLGS;

{$R MyRes1b.res }

CONST
   cm_New   = 101;
   cm_Color = 102;
   cm_Style = 103;
   cm_Thick = 104;
      cm_Thin        = 201;
      cm_Medium      = 202;
```

FIGURE 8.12:

Inserting a column break in a menu
with the menu resource editor (top),
and the resulting menu when
Listing 8.2 is run (bottom)

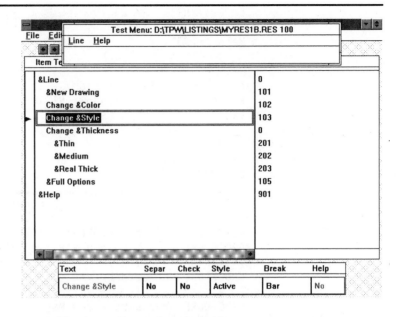

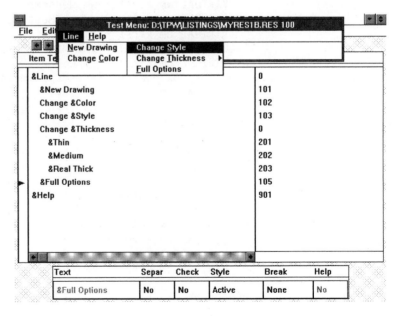

```
      cm_RealThick   = 203;
   cm_FullOptions = 105;
   cm_Help  = 901;

TYPE
   TMyApp = OBJECT(TApplication)
      PROCEDURE InitMainWindow; VIRTUAL;
      END;

   PMyWindow = ^TMyWindow;
   TMyWindow = OBJECT(TWindow)
      dc: HDC;
      LButtonDown: BOOLEAN;
      CONSTRUCTOR Init(AParent: PWindowsObject;
         ATitle: PChar);
      FUNCTION CanClose: BOOLEAN; VIRTUAL;
      PROCEDURE WMLButtonDown(VAR Msg: TMessage);
         VIRTUAL wm_First + wm_LButtonDown;
      PROCEDURE WMLButtonUp(VAR Msg: TMessage);
         VIRTUAL wm_First + wm_LButtonUp;
      PROCEDURE WMMouseMove(VAR Msg: TMessage);
         VIRTUAL wm_First + wm_MouseMove;
      PROCEDURE NewDraw(VAR Msg: TMessage);
         VIRTUAL cm_First + cm_New;
      PROCEDURE ChangeColor(VAR Msg: TMessage);
         VIRTUAL cm_First + cm_Color;
      PROCEDURE ChangeStyle(VAR Msg: TMessage);
         VIRTUAL cm_First + cm_Style;
      PROCEDURE ChangeThickness(VAR Msg: TMessage);
         VIRTUAL cm_First + cm_Thick;

      {New menu-response method headers}
      PROCEDURE Thin(VAR Msg: TMessage);
         VIRTUAL cm_First + cm_Thin;
      PROCEDURE Medium(VAR Msg: TMessage);
         VIRTUAL cm_First + cm_Medium;
      PROCEDURE RealThick(VAR Msg: TMessage);
         VIRTUAL cm_First + cm_RealThick;
      PROCEDURE FullOptions(VAR Msg: TMessage);
         VIRTUAL cm_First + cm_FullOptions;

      PROCEDURE Help(VAR Msg: TMessage);
         VIRTUAL cm_First + cm_Help;
      END;
```

```
{TMyWindow methods}
CONSTRUCTOR TMyWindow.Init(AParent: PWindowsObject;
                              ATitle: PChar);
    BEGIN
        TWindow.Init(AParent, ATitle);
        Attr.Menu := LoadMenu(HInstance, PChar(100));
        LButtonDown := False;
    END;


FUNCTION TMyWindow.CanClose: BOOLEAN;
    VAR
        Reply: INTEGER;
    BEGIN
        CanClose := TRUE;
        Reply := MessageBox(HWindow,
                    'Do you want to save your work?',
                    'Window content has changed',
                    mb_YesNoCancel or mb_IconQuestion);
        IF (Reply = id_Yes) OR (Reply = id_Cancel)
            THEN CanClose := FALSE;
    END;


PROCEDURE TMyWindow.WMLButtonDown(VAR Msg: TMessage);
    BEGIN
        InvalidateRect(HWindow, NIL, TRUE);
        IF not LButtonDown
        THEN  BEGIN
                LButtonDown := TRUE;
                SetCapture(HWindow);
                dc := GetDC(HWindow);
                MoveTo(dc, Msg.LParamLo, Msg.LParamHi);
                END;
    END;


PROCEDURE TMyWindow.WMMouseMove(VAR Msg: TMessage);
    BEGIN
        IF LButtonDown
        THEN LineTo(dc, INTEGER(Msg.LParamLo),
                    INTEGER(Msg.LParamHi));
    END;


PROCEDURE TMyWindow.WMLButtonUp(VAR Msg: TMessage);
    BEGIN
        IF LButtonDown
        THEN  BEGIN
```

```
            LButtonDown := False;
            ReleaseCapture;
            ReleaseDC(HWindow, dc);
            END;
    END;

PROCEDURE TMyWindow.NewDraw(VAR Msg: TMessage);
    BEGIN
    END;

PROCEDURE TMyWindow.ChangeColor(VAR Msg: TMessage);
    BEGIN
    END;

PROCEDURE TMyWindow.ChangeStyle(VAR Msg: TMessage);
    BEGIN
    END;

PROCEDURE TMyWindow.ChangeThickness(VAR Msg: TMessage);
    BEGIN
    END;

PROCEDURE TMyWindow.Thin(VAR Msg: TMessage);
    BEGIN
    END;

PROCEDURE TMyWindow.Medium(VAR Msg: TMessage);
    BEGIN
    END;

PROCEDURE TMyWindow.RealThick(VAR Msg: TMessage);
    BEGIN
    END;

PROCEDURE TMyWindow.FullOptions(VAR Msg: TMessage);
    VAR
        MCStatus : WORD;
    BEGIN
        MCStatus := GetMenuState(Attr.Menu, 105,
                        mf_ByCommand);
        IF (MCStatus AND mf_Checked) <> mf_Checked
        THEN  BEGIN
            MCStatus := mf_ByCommand or mf_Checked;
            CheckMenuItem(Attr.Menu, 105, MCStatus);
            { ... additional code for specific tasks ... }
```

```
                MessageBeep(0);
                MessageBox(HWindow, 'Full Menus Now Available',
                      'Event Report', mb_OK);
                END
        ELSE    BEGIN
                MCStatus := mf_ByCommand or mf_UnChecked;
                CheckMenuItem(Attr.Menu, 105, MCStatus);
                { ... additional code for specific tasks ... }
                MessageBeep(0);
                MessageBox(HWindow, 'Short Menus Now Available',
                      'Event Report', mb_OK);
                END
        END;

PROCEDURE TMyWindow.Help(VAR Msg: TMessage);
    BEGIN
    END;
{TMyApp methods}
PROCEDURE TMyApp.InitMainWindow;
    BEGIN
    MainWindow := NEW(PMyWindow, Init(NIL, 'Listing 8.2'));
    END;

{global object variable for application}
VAR
  MyApp : TMyApp;

{main body of program}
BEGIN
    MyApp.Init('Listing8_2');
    MyApp.Run;
    MyApp.Done;
END.
```

In the next chapter, we'll fill out the menu-choice methods by adding another dialog box to the listing: a dialog box with far more power and flexibility than the simple message boxes we've seen so far. We'll also explore more deeply the drawing capabilities you can build into a Windows program with Turbo Pascal for Windows.

Getting User
Input with Dialog Boxes

9

In this chapter, we will show how to create dialog boxes that carry out the commands from the Line menu in Listing 8.1. The first step, however, is to examine precisely what dialog boxes are, how they are created, and how they are executed in a program.

Dialog Resources and Object Types

A dialog box is a special kind of child window that appears inside a main window to receive input from the user. When you plan to implement a dialog box in your Turbo Pascal for Windows program, you need to distinguish between how it appears and what it does:

1. **Appearance:** including the size and location of explanatory text, checkboxes, radio buttons, pushbuttons, and other controls. Except for a few predefined dialog box resources that are included in ObjectWindows (one of which we'll use in this chapter), you'll normally define the appearance of a dialog box in the **Whitewater Resource Toolkit's** *dialog resource editor.* In most cases, therefore, the appearance definition constitues an external Windows resource to be used by your program. As with a menu, each object in the dialog box is assigned a specific identifier through which it is linked with the various procedures and methods in your program.

2. **Function:** How the dialog box works, as opposed to how it looks, is entirely up to your TPW program. By linking various methods and procedures with the objects in the dialog box, you control the circumstances under which the dialog box appears and what results it produces when you select its various buttons, boxes, and controls.

Predefined Dialog Box Types

Turbo Pascal for Windows—specifically, the STDDLGS unit included with the package—defines two standard dialog box types with associated resources, that you do not need to set up in the WRT. These are the *TInputDialog* and *TFileDialog* types, both of which we'll see in this chapter. The *TInputDialog* type provides for structured entry of a short string of text, and the *TFileDialog* type allows the user to select and save disk files.

Because they are a predefined part of ObjectWindows, you neither need to define the appearance of these dialog box types in the WRT nor set up most of the methods they use. Other than these two types, however, you will need to use the WRT to define the dialog box's appearance, as well as to define most of its methods.

Redrawing a Window

The program we developed in Chapter 8 is fine, except for the fact that it doesn't do anything except let the user draw lines. Even those lines disappear as soon as the window is resized. In this section, we'll see how to make the window redraw its contents when it is resized.

To some extent, we're just teaching the window's client area how to do something that the window already knows how to do for itself. When a window is resized, it automatically redraws itself in the new location with the new coordinates. The drawing inside the window disappears, however, because the window has been given no specific instructions about what to do with its client area when it redraws itself; as a result, it redraws the client area as a blank space.

To make the window redraw its client area, we need to store the area's contents in a buffer so that it can be recreated in the new drawing of the window. This sort of operation will be familiar if you've ever set up a buffer under DOS to save and restore a screen from a suspended DOS application, this is exactly the same thing, merely transplanted to the Windows environment. The technique is shown in Listing 9.1.

Listing 9.1

```
PROGRAM Listing9_1;
{  Demonstrates how to redraw a window's client
      area when the window is resized. Specific
      features demonstrated:
      1. Defining an object type to hold the points in
         a drawing.
      2  Initializing a TCollection.
      3. Using a TCollection to store the points in a
         drawing.
```

```
      4. Creating a paint method for the window. }

USES STRINGS, WINTYPES, WINPROCS, WOBJECTS, STDDLGS;

{$R MyRes1.res }

CONST
      cm_New   = 101;
      cm_Color = 102;
      cm_Style = 103;
      cm_Thick = 104;
      cm_Help  = 901;

{=================================================== }
{ ========== TYPE DEFINITION SECTION OF PROGRAM ========= }
{=================================================== }
TYPE
      TMyApp = OBJECT(TApplication)
         PROCEDURE InitMainWindow; VIRTUAL;
         END;

      PMyWindow = ^TMyWindow;
      TMyWindow = OBJECT(TWindow)
         dc: HDC;
         LButtonDown: BOOLEAN;
         Points: PCollection;
         CONSTRUCTOR Init(AParent: PWindowsObject;
            ATitle: PChar);
         DESTRUCTOR Done; VIRTUAL;
         FUNCTION CanClose: BOOLEAN; VIRTUAL;
         PROCEDURE WMLButtonDown(VAR Msg: TMessage);
            VIRTUAL wm_First + wm_LButtonDown;
         PROCEDURE WMLButtonUp(VAR Msg: TMessage);
            VIRTUAL wm_First + wm_LButtonUp;
         PROCEDURE WMMouseMove(VAR Msg: TMessage);
            VIRTUAL wm_First + wm_MouseMove;
         PROCEDURE Paint(PaintDC: HDC;
            VAR PaintInfo: TPaintStruct); VIRTUAL;
         PROCEDURE NewDraw(VAR Msg: TMessage);
            VIRTUAL cm_First + cm_New;
         PROCEDURE ChangeColor(VAR Msg: TMessage);
            VIRTUAL cm_First + cm_Color;
         PROCEDURE ChangeStyle(VAR Msg: TMessage);
            VIRTUAL cm_First + cm_Style;
         PROCEDURE ChangeThickness(VAR Msg: TMessage);
```

```
                VIRTUAL cm_First + cm_Thick;
          PROCEDURE Help(VAR Msg: TMessage);
                VIRTUAL cm_First + cm_Help;
          END;

     {object type to save drawing for repainting}
     PDPoint = ^TDPoint;
     TDPoint = OBJECT(TObject)
        X, Y: INTEGER;
        CONSTRUCTOR Init(AX, AY: INTEGER);
        END;


{═══════════════════}
{TMyWindow methods}
{═══════════════════}


CONSTRUCTOR TMyWindow.Init(AParent: PWindowsObject; ATitle: PChar);
     BEGIN
     TWindow.Init(AParent, ATitle);
     Attr.Menu := LoadMenu(HInstance, PChar(100));
     LButtonDown := FALSE;
     Points := New(PCollection, Init(50, 50));
     END;

DESTRUCTOR TMyWindow.Done;
     BEGIN
     Dispose(Points, Done);
     TWindow.Done;
     END;

FUNCTION TMyWindow.CanClose: BOOLEAN;
     VAR
        Reply: INTEGER;
     BEGIN
        CanClose := TRUE;
        Reply := MessageBox(HWindow,
                  'Do you want to save your work?',
                  'Window content has changed',
                  mb_YesNoCancel or mb_IconQuestion);
        IF (Reply = id_Yes) OR (Reply = id_Cancel)
           THEN CanClose := FALSE;
     END;

PROCEDURE TMyWindow.WMLButtonDown(VAR Msg: TMessage);
     BEGIN
```

```
        Points^.FreeAll;
        InvalidateRect(HWindow, NIL, TRUE);
        IF not LButtonDown
        THEN  BEGIN
                LButtonDown := TRUE;
                SetCapture(HWindow);
                dc := GetDC(HWindow);
                MoveTo(dc, Msg.LParamLo, Msg.LParamHi);
                Points^.Insert(New(PDPoint,
                        Init(Msg.LParamLo, Msg.LParamHi)));
                END;
        END;

PROCEDURE TMyWindow.WMMouseMove(VAR Msg: TMessage);
    BEGIN
    IF LButtonDown
    THEN  BEGIN
            LineTo(dc, INTEGER(Msg.LParamLo),
                    INTEGER(Msg.LParamHi));
            Points^.Insert(New(PDPoint,
                    Init(INTEGER(Msg.LParamLo),
                    INTEGER(Msg.LParamHi))));
            END;
    END;

PROCEDURE TMyWindow.WMLButtonUp(VAR Msg: TMessage);
    BEGIN
    IF LButtonDown
    THEN  BEGIN
            LButtonDown := FALSE;
            ReleaseCapture;
            ReleaseDC(HWindow, dc);
            END;
    END;

PROCEDURE TMyWindow.Paint(PaintDC: HDC;
                VAR PaintInfo: TPaintStruct);
    VAR
        First: BOOLEAN;
    {local procedure under TMyWindow.Paint method}
    PROCEDURE DrawLine(P: PDPoint); far;
        BEGIN
        IF First
        THEN MoveTo(PaintDC, P^.X, P^.Y)
        ELSE LineTo(PaintDC, P^.X, P^.Y);
```

```pascal
        First := FALSE;
        END;

    {main body of TMyWindow.Paint method}
    BEGIN
        First := TRUE;
        Points^.ForEach(@DrawLine);
    END;

PROCEDURE TMyWindow.NewDraw(VAR Msg: TMessage);
    BEGIN
    Points^.FreeAll;
    InvalidateRect(HWindow, NIL, TRUE);
    END;

PROCEDURE TMyWindow.ChangeColor(VAR Msg: TMessage);
    BEGIN
    END;

PROCEDURE TMyWindow.ChangeStyle(VAR Msg: TMessage);
    BEGIN
    END;

PROCEDURE TMyWindow.ChangeThickness(VAR Msg: TMessage);
    BEGIN
    END;

PROCEDURE TMyWindow.Help(VAR Msg: TMessage);
    BEGIN
    MessageBox(HWindow, 'Not yet implemented',
        'Help', mb_Ok or mb_IconExclamation);
    END;

{===================}
{ TDPoint methods}
{===================}
CONSTRUCTOR TDPoint.Init(AX, AY: INTEGER);
    BEGIN
    X := AX;
    Y := AY;
    END;


{================}
{TMyApp methods}
{================}
```

```
PROCEDURE TMyApp.InitMainWindow;
    BEGIN
    MainWindow := New(PMyWindow, Init(NIL, 'Listing 9.1'));
    END;

{=========================================}
{global object variable for application}
{=========================================}
VAR
    MyApp : TMyApp;

{====================}
{main body of program}
{====================}
BEGIN
    MyApp.Init('Listing9_1');
    MyApp.Run;
    MyApp.Done;
END.
```

Defining a Storage Buffer for the Drawing

The first new feature in Listing 9.1 appears in the *TMyWindow* type definition, where we have a new field, *Points*. This field is defined as a *PCollection*, which means that it is a pointer to a variable of type *TCollection*, an object type found in the *WObjects* unit. A collection is something like an object-oriented counterpart of an array, except that it can grow dynamically as needed in increments that you specify. Like an array, it can contain items of pretty much any predefined or user-defined type except file and stream types. Here, we will use it to store the points in a drawing, which we define a little further down in the code as an object type.

The next new wrinkle in the *TMyWindow* object type is the addition of a *Paint* method. This method, which overrides the predefined Paint method that is inherited from the *TWindow* object type, is used automatically when Windows sends a message (*wm_Paint*) that the application window needs to redraw its contents. The first parameter, *PaintDC*, is just a display context used by the Paint method. The second parameter, *PaintInfo*, is a record type (*TPaintStruct*) defined in the *WinTypes* unit; it contains fields with information to redraw the client area. Most of the fields are used by Windows, but three (*hdc* for the display context, *fErase* to indicate if the background has been redrawn, and *rcPaint* to define the rectangle for redrawing) can be changed by the programmer.

Defining an Object Type to Hold Drawing Points

The next step is to define an object type that can hold the points in the drawing.

A drawing can be treated simply as a collection of X,Y coordinate pairs relative to the frame of the window, with each point in the drawing represented by one pair. Thus, and as usual, we define both an object type to hold the points and a corresponding pointer type (*PDPoint*) for the object. The object type (*TDPoint*) has an integer-type field for each coordinate, as well as an Init method to load starting values into the fields of each *TDPoint*-type object variable.

Initializing and Disposing of the Point Collection

Before we can use a TCollection-type variable to hold the points, of course, we have to create it with a call to NEW. In the *TMyWindow.Init* method definition, we add a line to do just that. Here, in

```
Points := New(PCollection, Init(50, 50));
```

we use NEW as a function to create, initialize and load a *TCollection* variable into *Points*. The Init method of *TCollection* takes two integer-type parameters. The first parameter is the starting size of the collection, in terms of the number of items it can hold. The second is the amount by which the collection will grow when it needs to increase in size.

In this case, we are setting up *Points* to start with 50 slots for drawing points and, when the number of points in a drawing exceeds 50, to increase the size of the collection by 50 slots at a time.

The *TMyWindow.Done* method also has to be changed to dispose of the dynamic *Points* variable when the window closes—just as you would dispose of any dynamic variable when it is no longer needed.

Starting a New Drawing

The next difference occurs in the *WMLButtonDown* method. When we start a new drawing, the old contents of the *Points* buffer must be emptied out to make room for the new drawing. A call to the *FreeAll* method of *Points* (which it inherits from

TCollection) does this for us. Next, as the left mouse button is pressed, the final line in the *WMLButtonDown* method inserts a new point into the *Points* collection, with the X and Y coordinates being taken from the current mouse cursor position (contained in the *Msg.LParamLo* and *Msg.LParamHi* parameters).

As the mouse moves with the left button still held down, the *MouseMove* method draws a line in the window, just as before. The difference is that now, each time it draws another point in the line, it inserts the coordinates of that point into the *Points* collection, which grows as needed to hold all the points in the drawing.

The Paint Method

The next step is to set up a *Paint* method to redraw the window's client area from the data stored in the *Points* collection. As noted earlier, this method takes two parameters: a display context on which the redrawing will be performed, and a *PaintInfo* record with information about how the drawing should be carried out. A local variable, *First*, is defined so that the method knows whether or not the point it's currently processing is the first point in the drawing.

A local procedure, *DrawLine*, actually does the work of recreating the drawing. After this procedure runs once, *First* is set to false. The *MoveTo* and *LineTo* methods work just as before, using the *PaintDC* display context and the point fields from each object in the collection.

In the main body of the *Paint* method, we set the *First* variable to true. Then, we call the *ForEach* method of *Points*, which it inherits from the *TCollection* ancestor type. The *ForEach* method takes a pointer to a procedure (@*Drawline*) as its parameter. As it traverses the collection, *ForEach* applies the designated procedure to each of the items in the collection. In this case, it executes the *DrawLine* procedure on each pair of X,Y coordinates. The *ForEach* method must be declared as FAR, because it refers to code in a different memory segment from that of the calling routine.

The rest of the program is similar to what we've already seen in Listing 8.1. If you enter and run the program, draw a line, and then resize the window, you can see the line redrawn in the resized window, as in Figure 9.1.

FIGURE 9.1:

Drawing in a window from Listing 9.1 (top) and the same drawing recreated in a resized window (bottom)

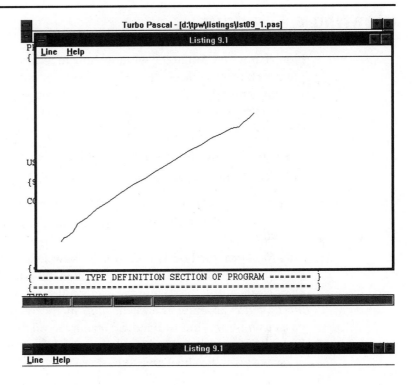

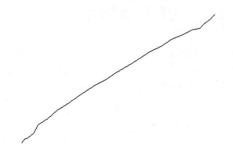

Clearing a Window

Now that we've taught the window how to redraw its client area, we'll how to implement the first choice—"New Drawing"—on the Line menu from the application window created in Listing 9.1. This is a fairly simple operation, and essentially makes explicit what we've already had done for us "behind the scenes" when we start a new drawing.

The relevant code appears in Listing 9.1, and is reproduced below:

```
PROCEDURE TMyWindow.NewDraw(VAR Msg: TMessage);
   BEGIN
   Points^.FreeAll;
   InvalidateRect(HWindow, NIL, TRUE);
   END;
```

This *NewDraw* method is tied to the "New Drawing" menu choice through the *cm_New* command constant that appears in the extension of its heading. First *NewDraw* clears out all the data in the *Points* collection (by calling *FreeAll*). Then, it calls *InvalidateRect* to erase the client area in the window for which the *HWindow* parameter is the window handle. You may recall that the other two parameters are, first, NIL because the window in question has no parent window, and TRUE because we want the client area to be erased.

Creating a Text Input Dialog Box

The other menu items are a little harder to implement because they involve creating a simple dialog box. For our purposes, we will use a *TInputDialog*-type dialog box; this is predefined in the STDDLGS unit, which is named in the USES clause of the program. We will create a different instance of this type of dialog box in response to each menu choice. Each will have its own special properties and require its own special methods.

Changing Line Thickness

The first menu choice we will implement is actually the last choice on the menu: "Change Thickness." We do it first because it's the simplest; so the details of creating the dialog box won't be obscured by too many details of performing the menu choice. The implementation of this menu choice is shown in Listing 9.2.

Listing 9.2

```
PROGRAM Listing9_2;
{  Shows how to change the line thickness for drawing
   in a window. Specific features demonstrated:
   1. Creating a pen object and a handle to the pen.
   2. The three parameters of the CreatePen function.
   3. Executing a TInputDialog dialog box to get text
      input from the user.
   4. Setting up a method to change pen size. }

USES STRINGS, WINTYPES, WINPROCS, WOBJECTS, STDDLGS;

{$R MyRes1.res }
CONST
   cm_New   = 101;
   cm_Color = 102;
   cm_Style = 103;
   cm_Thick = 104;
   cm_Help  = 901;


{=================================================== }
{ ========= TYPE DEFINITION SECTION OF PROGRAM ======= }
{=================================================== }
TYPE
   TMyApp = OBJECT(TApplication)
      PROCEDURE InitMainWindow; VIRTUAL;
      END;

   PMyWindow = ^TMyWindow;
   TMyWindow = OBJECT(TWindow)
      dc: HDC;
      LButtonDown: BOOLEAN;
      MyPen: HPen;
      PenSize: INTEGER;
      Points: PCollection;
      CONSTRUCTOR Init(AParent: PWindowsObject;
         ATitle: PChar);
      DESTRUCTOR Done; VIRTUAL;
      FUNCTION CanClose: BOOLEAN; VIRTUAL;
      PROCEDURE WMLButtonDown(VAR Msg: TMessage);
         VIRTUAL wm_First + wm_LButtonDown;
      PROCEDURE WMLButtonUp(VAR Msg: TMessage);
         VIRTUAL wm_First + wm_LButtonUp;
      PROCEDURE WMMouseMove(VAR Msg: TMessage);
```

```
        VIRTUAL wm_First + wm_MouseMove;
     PROCEDURE SetPenSize(NewSize: INTEGER);
     PROCEDURE Paint(PaintDC: HDC;
        VAR PaintInfo: TPaintStruct); VIRTUAL;
     PROCEDURE NewDraw(VAR Msg: TMessage);
        VIRTUAL cm_First + cm_New;
     PROCEDURE ChangeColor(VAR Msg: TMessage);
        VIRTUAL cm_First + cm_Color;
     PROCEDURE ChangeStyle(VAR Msg: TMessage);
        VIRTUAL cm_First + cm_Style;
     PROCEDURE ChangeThickness(VAR Msg: TMessage);
        VIRTUAL cm_First + cm_Thick;
     PROCEDURE Help(VAR Msg: TMessage);
        VIRTUAL cm_First + cm_Help;
     END;

  {object type to save drawing for repainting}
  PDPoint = ^TDPoint;
  TDPoint = OBJECT(TObject)
     X, Y: INTEGER;
     CONSTRUCTOR Init(AX, AY: INTEGER);
     END;


{==================}
{TMyWindow methods}
{==================}
CONSTRUCTOR TMyWindow.Init(AParent: PWindowsObject;
                           ATitle: PChar);
  BEGIN
  TWindow.Init(AParent, ATitle);
  Attr.Menu := LoadMenu(HInstance, PChar(100));
  LButtonDown := FALSE;
  PenSize := 1;
  MyPen := CreatePen(ps_Solid, PenSize, 0);
  Points := New(PCollection, Init(50, 50));
  END;

DESTRUCTOR TMyWindow.Done;
  BEGIN
  Dispose(Points, Done);
  DeleteObject(MyPen);
  TWindow.Done;
  END;

FUNCTION TMyWindow.CanClose: BOOLEAN;
```

```
VAR
    Reply: INTEGER;
BEGIN
    CanClose := TRUE;
    Reply := MessageBox(HWindow,
                'Do you want to save your work?',
                'Window content has changed',
                mb_YesNoCancel or mb_IconQuestion);
    IF (Reply = id_Yes) OR (Reply = id_Cancel)
        THEN CanClose := FALSE;
END;

PROCEDURE TMyWindow.WMLButtonDown(VAR Msg: TMessage);
    BEGIN
    Points^.FreeAll;
    InvalidateRect(HWindow, NIL, TRUE);
    IF not LButtonDown
    THEN  BEGIN
        LButtonDown := TRUE;
        SetCapture(HWindow);
        dc := GetDC(HWindow);
        SelectObject(dc, MyPen);
        MoveTo(dc, Msg.LParamLo, Msg.LParamHi);
        Points^.Insert(New(PDPoint,
            Init(Msg.LParamLo, Msg.LParamHi)));
        END;
    END;

PROCEDURE TMyWindow.WMMouseMove(VAR Msg: TMessage);
    BEGIN
    IF LButtonDown
    THEN  BEGIN
        LineTo(dc, INTEGER(Msg.LParamLo),
            INTEGER(Msg.LParamHi));
        Points^.Insert(New(PDPoint,
            Init(INTEGER(Msg.LParamLo),
            INTEGER(Msg.LParamHi))));
        END;
    END;

PROCEDURE TMyWindow.WMLButtonUp(VAR Msg: TMessage);
    BEGIN
    IF LButtonDown
    THEN  BEGIN
        LButtonDown := FALSE;
```

```
        ReleaseCapture;
        ReleaseDC(HWindow, dc);
        END;
    END;

PROCEDURE TMyWindow.SetPenSize(NewSize: INTEGER);
    BEGIN
    DeleteObject(MyPen);
    MyPen := CreatePen(ps_Solid, NewSize, 0);
    PenSize := NewSize;
    END;

PROCEDURE TMyWindow.Paint(PaintDC: HDC;
              VAR PaintInfo: TPaintStruct);
    VAR
        First: BOOLEAN;
    {local procedure under TMyWindow.Paint method}
    PROCEDURE DrawLine(P: PDPoint); far;
        BEGIN
        IF First
        THEN MoveTo(PaintDC, P^.X, P^.Y)
        ELSE LineTo(PaintDC, P^.X, P^.Y);
        First := FALSE;
        END;
    {main body of TMyWindow.Paint method}
    BEGIN
        SelectObject(PaintDC, MyPen);
        First := TRUE;
        Points^.ForEach(@DrawLine);
    END;

PROCEDURE TMyWindow.NewDraw(VAR Msg: TMessage);
    BEGIN
    Points^.FreeAll;
    InvalidateRect(HWindow, NIL, TRUE);
    END;

PROCEDURE TMyWindow.ChangeColor(VAR Msg: TMessage);
    BEGIN
    END;

PROCEDURE TMyWindow.ChangeStyle(VAR Msg: TMessage);
    BEGIN
    END;
```

```
PROCEDURE TMyWindow.ChangeThickness(VAR Msg: TMessage);
   VAR
      ThickBuffer: ARRAY[0..5] of CHAR;
      NewSize, ErrorPos: INTEGER;
   BEGIN
      Str(PenSize, ThickBuffer);
      IF Application^.ExecDialog(New(PInputDialog,
         Init(@Self, 'Line Thickness',
         'Enter a new thickness:',
         ThickBuffer, SizeOf(ThickBuffer)))) = id_Ok
       THEN BEGIN
            Val(ThickBuffer, NewSize, ErrorPos);
            IF ErrorPos = 0 THEN SetPenSize(NewSize);
            END;
   END;

PROCEDURE TMyWindow.Help(VAR Msg: TMessage);
   BEGIN
   MessageBox(HWindow, 'Not yet implemented',
      'Help', mb_Ok or mb_IconExclamation);
   END;


{===================}
{ TDPoint methods}
{===================}
CONSTRUCTOR TDPoint.Init(AX, AY: INTEGER);
   BEGIN
   X := AX;
   Y := AY;
   END;
{===================}
{TMyApp methods}
{===================}
PROCEDURE TMyApp.InitMainWindow;
   BEGIN
   MainWindow := New(PMyWindow, Init(NIL, 'Listing 9.2'));
   END;


{=======================================}
{global object variable for application}
{=======================================}
VAR
   MyApp : TMyApp;
```

```
{==========================}
{main body of program}
{==========================}
BEGIN
    MyApp.Init('Listing9_2');
    MyApp.Run;
    MyApp.Done;
END.
```

Setting Up and Using a Pen

One thing that we haven't seen before, and might not have expected, appears in the new definition of the *TMyWindow* type. We've added a field for a "pen" along with another field for the "pen size." What does this have to do with changing the thickness of lines in the window?

The fact is that whenever you draw in a window, you are using a Windows-style "pen" to do it. If you are happy with thin, solid, black lines, then you can use the default pen (which we've been doing) and not worry about creating your own pen object. However, if you want to change any of the characteristics of the lines you draw, then you must define your own pen or other drawing tool. As you might guess, *HPen* is a handle to a predefined *Pen* drawing tool. To change the thickness of the lines, you change the size of the pen you're using. To accomplish this, we have the *PenSize* field and a new method, *SetPenSize*, both of which are used by the *ChangeThickness* method that is invoked when the user selects the "Change Thickness" menu option.

Initializing the Pen

It's in the *TMyWindow.Init* method that we actually set up the pen for use. After setting the *PenSize* variable to 1 (the default line thickness), we call the *CreatePen* function to create a dynamic pen object, which we then attach to the *MyPen* handle. In creating the pen, we must specify three parameters:

- *A line style*, represented by one of several predefined ObjectWindows line style constants.

- *A pen size*, which is an integer denoting the size of the pen. The default value is 1.

- *A line color*, which is a 32-bit value denoting the mix of red, green, and blue that makes up the current line color. The default value is 0 (black).

Thus, although the *TMyWindow.Init* method sets up a pen to draw solid, thin, black lines—which is the default value that we were getting before—we can now change one or more of the pen characteristics.

Disposing of the Pen

Just like the *Points* collection, the pen is a dynamic object that must be disposed of when the window is closed. To do this, we insert a new line in the *TMyWindow.Done* method that calls the API *DeleteObject* method to dispose of the pen. We could simply use DISPOSE, but the pen object is more complicated than most dynamic variables, and using *DeleteObject* saves us the extra work of shutting the pen down.

Selecting the Pen

In a way, using a pen in a Windows program is just like using it in real life. Before you can do anything with a pen, you first have to pick it up. We perform this simple but essential job with an extra line in the *WMLButtonDown* method, where we call the *SelectObject* method to position the pen over the appropriate drawing surface—in this case, the display context denoted by the *dc* variable.

Setting the Pen Size

In a certain sense, it's misleading to call what we do in the *SetPenSize* method "setting the pen size." What we actually do is delete the current pen object and then create a new one with the size that has been passed back from the **Line Thickness** dialog box called from the "Change Thickness" menu option. First, we call *DeleteObject* to delete the current pen object; then we again call *CreatePen* to make a new pen object with the appropriate characteristics and attach it to the *MyPen* handle.

Using a Dialog Box to Get Input

The *TMyWindow.ChangeThickness* method is where things get just a little confusing. The first thing to understand is that to get data out of a dialog box, you must have something to load the data into while the dialog box is still running. Once the dialog box has shut down, the data is gone. That's why we create a local variable *ThickBuffer*: to get the data from the dialog box. Once the user confirms the information in the dialog box by clicking OK, we take the data from *ThickBuffer*, convert it to its numeric representation, and then, if the string is valid, pass it to the *SetPenSize* method, which does the actual work of changing the pen size.

To run the dialog box, we call the *Application.ExecDialog* method. *Application* is a generic identifier that refers to whatever application is currently running. *Exec-Dialog*, a method inherited from the *TApplication* object type, takes a pointer to a dialog object as a parameter and executes the associated dialog. Here, we've embedded a call to NEW in the call to *ExecDialog*. NEW creates a dynamic dialog box object of type *TInputDialog*. The associated *Init* method takes five parameters: a pointer to the object itself, a caption for the frame of the dialog box, a prompt telling the user what to do, a buffer (to get the data out of the dialog box), and the size of the data in the buffer. The dialog box is shown in Figure 9.2.

When the user clicks on OK, the dialog box shuts down and the THEN clause is activated. The character data from *ThickBuffer* is converted to an integer and loaded into the global (to *TMyWindow*) *NewSize* variable, with *ErrorPos* indicating if the operation was successful. If it was (if *ErrorPos* = 0), then *SetPenSize* is called. Presto! The line thickness is changed, as shown in Figure 9.3.

FIGURE 9.2:

The Change Thickness dialog box

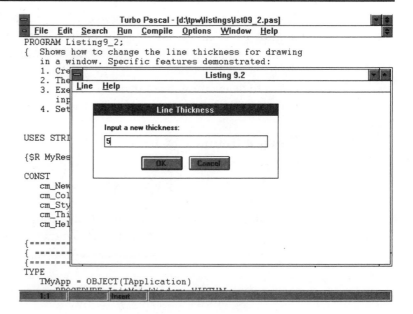

FIGURE 9.3:

The program from Listing 9.2 with a new line thickness

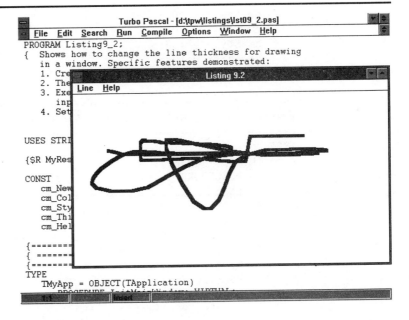

Changing Line Color

Changing line color works essentially the same way as changing line thickness. In Listing 9.3, just as before, we add a new *TMyWindow* field (*PenColor*) to hold the line color, one method (*SetPenColor*) to change the line color, and one method (*Change-Color*) to run the dialog box. The main difference is that because *PenColor* is a *TColor-Ref*-type variable, we use the RGB() function in the *SetPenColor* method to make the code a little easier to understand. A naked 32-bit color value, in hexadecimal, is hard to decipher.

Listing 9.3

```
PROGRAM Listing9_3;
{ Shows how to change the color of a line for drawing
    in a window. Specific features demonstrated:
    1. Pen colors.
    2. How to use the RGB() function.}

USES STRINGS, WINTYPES, WINPROCS, WOBJECTS, STDDLGS;

{$R MyRes1.res }
CONST
```

```
    cm_New   = 101;
    cm_Color = 102;
    cm_Style = 103;
    cm_Thick = 104;
    cm_Help  = 901;


{========================================================== }
{ ========= TYPE DEFINITION SECTION OF PROGRAM ========= }
{========================================================== }
TYPE
    TMyApp = OBJECT(TApplication)
      PROCEDURE InitMainWindow; VIRTUAL;
      END;
    PMyWindow = ^TMyWindow;
    TMyWindow = OBJECT(TWindow)
      dc: HDC;
      ButtonDown: BOOLEAN;
      MyPen: HPen;
      PenSize: INTEGER;
      PenColor : TColorRef;
      Points: PCollection;
      CONSTRUCTOR Init(AParent: PWindowsObject;
          ATitle: PChar);
      DESTRUCTOR Done; VIRTUAL;
      FUNCTION CanClose: BOOLEAN; VIRTUAL;
      PROCEDURE WMLButtonDown(VAR Msg: TMessage);
          VIRTUAL wm_First + wm_LButtonDown;
      PROCEDURE WMLButtonUp(VAR Msg: TMessage);
          VIRTUAL wm_First + wm_LButtonUp;
      PROCEDURE WMMouseMove(VAR Msg: TMessage);
          VIRTUAL wm_First + wm_MouseMove;
      PROCEDURE SetPenColor(NewColor: INTEGER);
      PROCEDURE SetPenSize(NewSize: INTEGER);
      PROCEDURE Paint(PaintDC: HDC;
          VAR PaintInfo: TPaintStruct); VIRTUAL;
      PROCEDURE NewDraw(VAR Msg: TMessage);
          VIRTUAL cm_First + cm_New;
      PROCEDURE ChangeColor(VAR Msg: TMessage);
          VIRTUAL cm_First + cm_Color;
      PROCEDURE ChangeStyle(VAR Msg: TMessage);
          VIRTUAL cm_First + cm_Style;
      PROCEDURE ChangeThickness(VAR Msg: TMessage);
          VIRTUAL cm_First + cm_Thick;
      PROCEDURE Help(VAR Msg: TMessage);
          VIRTUAL cm_First + cm_Help;
```

```
        END;
     {object type to save drawing for repainting}
     PDPoint = ^TDPoint;
     TDPoint = OBJECT(TObject)
        X, Y: INTEGER;
        CONSTRUCTOR Init(AX, AY: INTEGER);
        END;

{=================}
{TMyWindow methods}
{=================}
CONSTRUCTOR TMyWindow.Init(AParent: PWindowsObject; ATitle: PChar);
     BEGIN
     TWindow.Init(AParent, ATitle);
     Attr.Menu := LoadMenu(HInstance, PChar(100));
     ButtonDown := FALSE;
     PenSize := 1;
     PenColor := 0;
     MyPen := CreatePen(ps_Solid, PenSize, PenColor);
     Points := New(PCollection, Init(50, 50));
     END;

DESTRUCTOR TMyWindow.Done;
     BEGIN
     Dispose(Points, Done);
     DeleteObject(MyPen);
     TWindow.Done;
     END;

FUNCTION TMyWindow.CanClose: BOOLEAN;
     VAR
        Reply: INTEGER;
     BEGIN
        CanClose := TRUE;
        Reply := MessageBox(HWindow,
                'Do you want to save your work?',
                'Window content has changed',
                mb_YesNoCancel or mb_IconQuestion);
        IF (Reply = id_Yes) OR (Reply = id_Cancel)
           THEN CanClose := FALSE;
     END;

PROCEDURE TMyWindow.WMLButtonDown(VAR Msg: TMessage);
     BEGIN
     Points^.FreeAll;
```

189

```
       InvalidateRect(HWindow, NIL, TRUE);
       IF not ButtonDown
       THEN  BEGIN
             ButtonDown := TRUE;
             SetCapture(HWindow);
             dc := GetDC(HWindow);
             SelectObject(dc, MyPen);
             MoveTo(dc, Msg.LParamLo, Msg.LParamHi);
             Points^.Insert(New(PDPoint,
                   Init(Msg.LParamLo, Msg.LParamHi)));
             END;
       END;


PROCEDURE TMyWindow.WMMouseMove(VAR Msg: TMessage);
     BEGIN
     IF ButtonDown
     THEN  BEGIN
           LineTo(dc, INTEGER(Msg.LParamLo),
                 INTEGER(Msg.LParamHi));
           Points^.Insert(New(PDPoint,
                 Init(INTEGER(Msg.LParamLo),
                 INTEGER(Msg.LParamHi))));
           END;
     END;


PROCEDURE TMyWindow.WMLButtonUp(VAR Msg: TMessage);
     BEGIN
     IF ButtonDown
     THEN  BEGIN
           ButtonDown := FALSE;
           ReleaseCapture;
           ReleaseDC(HWindow, dc);
           END;
     END;


PROCEDURE TMyWindow.SetPenColor(NewColor: INTEGER);
BEGIN
     DeleteObject(MyPen);
     CASE NewColor OF
     1: BEGIN
        PenColor := RGB(200,0,0);
        MyPen := CreatePen(ps_Solid, PenSize, PenColor);
        END;
     2: BEGIN
        PenColor := RGB(0,200,0);
```

```
            MyPen := CreatePen(ps_Solid, PenSize, PenColor);
            END;
        3: BEGIN
           PenColor := RGB(0,0,200);
           MyPen := CreatePen(ps_Solid, PenSize, PenColor);
           END;
        4: BEGIN
           PenColor := 0;
           MyPen := CreatePen(ps_Solid, PenSize, PenColor);
           END;
        ELSE MyPen := CreatePen(ps_Solid, PenSize, 0)
        END;
END;

PROCEDURE TMyWindow.SetPenSize(NewSize: INTEGER);
    BEGIN
    DeleteObject(MyPen);
    MyPen := CreatePen(ps_Solid, NewSize, PenColor);
    PenSize := NewSize;
    END;

PROCEDURE TMyWindow.Paint(PaintDC: HDC;
               VAR PaintInfo: TPaintStruct);
    VAR
       First: BOOLEAN;
    {local procedure under TMyWindow.Paint method}
    PROCEDURE DrawLine(P: PDPoint); far;
       BEGIN
       IF First
       THEN MoveTo(PaintDC, P^.X, P^.Y)
       else LineTo(PaintDC, P^.X, P^.Y);
       First := FALSE;
       END;
    {main body of TMyWindow.Paint method}
    BEGIN
       SelectObject(PaintDC, MyPen);
       First := TRUE;
       Points^.ForEach(@DrawLine);
    END;

PROCEDURE TMyWindow.NewDraw(VAR Msg: TMessage);
    BEGIN
    Points^.FreeAll;
    InvalidateRect(HWindow, NIL, TRUE);
    END;
```

```
PROCEDURE TMyWindow.ChangeColor(VAR Msg: TMessage);
    VAR
        NewColor,
        ErrorPos: INTEGER;
        ColorBuffer : ARRAY[0..5] OF CHAR;
    BEGIN
        Str(PenColor, ColorBuffer);
        IF Application^.ExecDialog(New(PInputDialog,
            Init(@Self, 'Line Color',
            'Type 1/Red, 2/Green, 3/Blue, 4/Black',
            ColorBuffer, SizeOf(ColorBuffer)))) = id_Ok
        THEN  BEGIN
                Val(ColorBuffer, NewColor, ErrorPos);
                IF ErrorPos = 0 THEN SetPenColor(NewColor);
                END;
    END;


PROCEDURE TMyWindow.ChangeStyle(VAR Msg: TMessage);
    BEGIN
    END;


PROCEDURE TMyWindow.ChangeThickness(VAR Msg: TMessage);
    VAR
        ThickBuffer: ARRAY[0..5] of CHAR;
        NewSize, ErrorPos: INTEGER;
    BEGIN
        Str(PenSize, ThickBuffer);
        IF Application^.ExecDialog(New(PInputDialog,
            Init(@Self, 'Line Thickness',
            'Enter a new thickness:',
            ThickBuffer, SizeOf(ThickBuffer)))) = id_Ok
        THEN BEGIN
                Val(ThickBuffer, NewSize, ErrorPos);
                IF ErrorPos = 0 THEN SetPenSize(NewSize);
                END;
    END;

PROCEDURE TMyWindow.Help(VAR Msg: TMessage);
    BEGIN
    MessageBox(HWindow, 'Not yet implemented',
        'Help', mb_Ok or mb_IconExclamation);
    END;
```

```
{==================}
{ TDPoint methods}
{==================}
CONSTRUCTOR TDPoint.Init(AX, AY: INTEGER);
     BEGIN
     X := AX;
     Y := AY;
     END;


{==================}
{TMyApp methods}
{==================}
PROCEDURE TMyApp.InitMainWindow;
     BEGIN
     MainWindow := New(PMyWindow, Init(NIL, 'Listing 9.3'));
     END;


{==========================================}
{global object variable for application}
{==========================================}
VAR
     MyApp : TMyApp;


{=====================}
{main body of program}
{=====================}
BEGIN
     MyApp.Init('Listing9_3');
     MyApp.Run;
     MyApp.Done;
END.
```

The RGB() function, however, makes it simple. The function takes three parameters, all integers from 0 to 255: first, the intensity of red in the color mix; second, the intensity of green; and third, the intensity of blue. To get pure red, for example, we would use

```
RGB(255,0,0)
```

For pure green, it would be

```
RGB(0,255,0)
```

Unfortunately, the figures in this book are in monochrome, so it's impossible to show here how the colors change. Try it on your own PC, and you'll be impressed with the results. The dialog box is shown in Figure 9.4.

FIGURE 9.4:

The Change Color dialog box

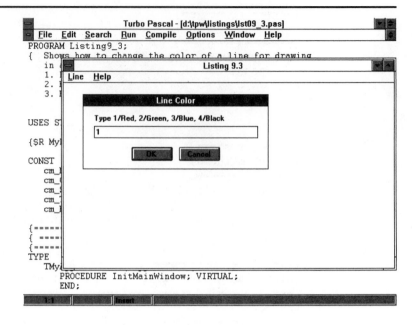

Changing Line Style

The final menu option lets the user change the *style* of the line being drawn in the window. Turbo Pascal for Windows provides several predefined line styles, as listed in Table 9.1.

TABLE 9.1: Line Style Constants

Constant	Line Style
ps_Solid	Solid line
ps_Dash	Dashed line
ps_Dot	Dotted line
ps_DashDot	Alternating dashes and dots
ps_DashDotDot	Alternating dashes and pairs of dots
ps_Null	Invisible line
ps_InsideFrame	Used to draw the inside frame of polygons and polylines

As when we implemented the menu choices to change line thickness and color, in Listing 9.4 we add a new field (*PenStyle*) to *TMyWindow* to hold the line style (actually the pen style). We then add a new method (*SetPenStyle*) to change the line style and another method (*ChangeStyle*) to run the dialog box. All work in the same way as the methods to change line color. The result is shown in Figure 9.5.

Listing 9.4

```
PROGRAM Listing9_4;
{  Shows how to change the style of a line for drawing
      in a window. Specific features demonstrated:
      1. Predefined line styles.
      2. Using a buffer to move data in and out of
         a dialog box. }

USES STRINGS, WINTYPES, WINPROCS, WOBJECTS, STDDLGS;

{$R MyRes1.res }
CONST
      cm_New   = 101;
      cm_Color = 102;
      cm_Style = 103;
      cm_Thick = 104;
      cm_Help  = 901;


{=============================================== }
{ ========= TYPE DEFINITION SECTION OF PROGRAM ========= }
{=============================================== }
TYPE
      TMyApp = OBJECT(TApplication)
         PROCEDURE InitMainWindow; VIRTUAL;
         END;

      PMyWindow = ^TMyWindow;
      TMyWindow = OBJECT(TWindow)
         dc: HDC;
         ButtonDown: BOOLEAN;
         MyPen: HPen;
         PenSize: INTEGER;
         PenColor : TColorRef;
         PenStyle : INTEGER;
         Points: PCollection;
         CONSTRUCTOR Init(AParent: PWindowsObject;
            ATitle: PChar);
```

```
    DESTRUCTOR Done; VIRTUAL;
    FUNCTION CanClose: BOOLEAN; VIRTUAL;
    PROCEDURE WMLButtonDown(VAR Msg: TMessage);
       VIRTUAL wm_First + wm_LButtonDown;
    PROCEDURE WMLButtonUp(VAR Msg: TMessage);
       VIRTUAL wm_First + wm_LButtonUp;
    PROCEDURE WMMouseMove(VAR Msg: TMessage);
       VIRTUAL wm_First + wm_MouseMove;
    PROCEDURE SetPenColor(NewColor: INTEGER);
    PROCEDURE SetPenStyle(NewStyle: INTEGER);
    PROCEDURE SetPenSize(NewSize: INTEGER);
    PROCEDURE Paint(PaintDC: HDC;
       VAR PaintInfo: TPaintStruct); VIRTUAL;
    PROCEDURE NewDraw(VAR Msg: TMessage);
       VIRTUAL cm_First + cm_New;
    PROCEDURE ChangeColor(VAR Msg: TMessage);
       VIRTUAL cm_First + cm_Color;
    PROCEDURE ChangeStyle(VAR Msg: TMessage);
       VIRTUAL cm_First + cm_Style;
    PROCEDURE ChangeThickness(VAR Msg: TMessage);
       VIRTUAL cm_First + cm_Thick;
    PROCEDURE Help(VAR Msg: TMessage);
       VIRTUAL cm_First + cm_Help;
    END;

{object type to save drawing for repainting}
PDPoint = ^TDPoint;
TDPoint = OBJECT(TObject)
    X, Y: INTEGER;
    CONSTRUCTOR Init(AX, AY: INTEGER);
    END;

{====================}
{TMyWindow methods}
{====================}
CONSTRUCTOR TMyWindow.Init(AParent: PWindowsObject; ATitle: PChar);
    BEGIN
    TWindow.Init(AParent, ATitle);
    Attr.Menu := LoadMenu(HInstance, PChar(100));
    ButtonDown := FALSE;
    PenSize := 1;
    PenStyle := ps_Solid;
    PenColor := 0;
    MyPen := CreatePen(PenStyle, PenSize, PenColor);
    Points := New(PCollection, Init(50, 50));
```

```
      END;

DESTRUCTOR TMyWindow.Done;
      BEGIN
      Dispose(Points, Done);
      DeleteObject(MyPen);
      TWindow.Done;
      END;

FUNCTION TMyWindow.CanClose: BOOLEAN;
      VAR
         Reply: INTEGER;
      BEGIN
         CanClose := TRUE;
         Reply := MessageBox(HWindow,
                  'Do you want to save your work?',
                  'Window content has changed',
                  mb_YesNoCancel or mb_IconQuestion);
         IF (Reply = id_Yes) OR (Reply = id_Cancel)
            THEN CanClose := FALSE;
      END;

PROCEDURE TMyWindow.WMLButtonDown(VAR Msg: TMessage);
      BEGIN
      Points^.FreeAll;
      InvalidateRect(HWindow, NIL, TRUE);
      IF not ButtonDown
      THEN  BEGIN
            ButtonDown := TRUE;
            SetCapture(HWindow);
            dc := GetDC(HWindow);
            SelectObject(dc, MyPen);
            MoveTo(dc, Msg.LParamLo, Msg.LParamHi);
            Points^.Insert(New(PDPoint,
                  Init(Msg.LParamLo, Msg.LParamHi)));
            END;
      END;

PROCEDURE TMyWindow.WMMouseMove(VAR Msg: TMessage);
      BEGIN
      IF ButtonDown
      THEN  BEGIN
            LineTo(dc, INTEGER(Msg.LParamLo),
                  INTEGER(Msg.LParamHi));
            Points^.Insert(New(PDPoint,
```

```
                    Init(INTEGER(Msg.LParamLo),
                    INTEGER(Msg.LParamHi))));
        END;
    END;

PROCEDURE TMyWindow.WMLButtonUp(VAR Msg: TMessage);
    BEGIN
    IF ButtonDown
    THEN  BEGIN
        ButtonDown := FALSE;
        ReleaseCapture;
        ReleaseDC(HWindow, dc);
        END;
    END;

PROCEDURE TMyWindow.SetPenColor(NewColor: INTEGER);
BEGIN
    DeleteObject(MyPen);
    CASE NewColor OF
    1: BEGIN
       PenColor := RGB(200,0,0);
       MyPen := CreatePen(PenStyle, PenSize, PenColor);
       END;
    2: BEGIN
       PenColor := RGB(0,200,0);
       MyPen := CreatePen(PenStyle, PenSize, PenColor);
       END;
    3: BEGIN
       PenColor := RGB(0,0,200);
       MyPen := CreatePen(PenStyle, PenSize, PenColor);
       END;
    4: BEGIN
       PenColor := 0;
       MyPen := CreatePen(PenStyle, PenSize, PenColor);
       END;
    ELSE MyPen := CreatePen(PenStyle, PenSize, 0)
    END;
END;

PROCEDURE TMyWindow.SetPenStyle(NewStyle: INTEGER);
    BEGIN
    DeleteObject(MyPen);
    CASE NewStyle OF
    1: BEGIN
       PenStyle := ps_Solid;
```

```
            MyPen := CreatePen(PenStyle, PenSize, PenColor);
            END;
        2: BEGIN
           PenStyle := ps_Dot;
           MyPen := CreatePen(PenStyle, PenSize, PenColor);
           END;
        3: BEGIN
           PenStyle := ps_Dash;
           MyPen := CreatePen(PenStyle, PenSize, PenColor);
           END
        ELSE MyPen := CreatePen(ps_Solid, PenSize, PenColor)
        END;
END;

PROCEDURE TMyWindow.SetPenSize(NewSize: INTEGER);
     BEGIN
     DeleteObject(MyPen);
     MyPen := CreatePen(PenStyle, NewSize, PenColor);
     PenSize := NewSize;
     END;

PROCEDURE TMyWindow.Paint(PaintDC: HDC;
               VAR PaintInfo: TPaintStruct);
     VAR
        First: BOOLEAN;
     {local procedure under TMyWindow.Paint method}
     PROCEDURE DrawLine(P: PDPoint); far;
        BEGIN
        IF First
        THEN MoveTo(PaintDC, P^.X, P^.Y)
        else LineTo(PaintDC, P^.X, P^.Y);
        First := FALSE;
        END;
     {main body of TMyWindow.Paint method}
     BEGIN
        SelectObject(PaintDC, MyPen);
        First := TRUE;
        Points^.ForEach(@DrawLine);
     END;

PROCEDURE TMyWindow.NewDraw(VAR Msg: TMessage);
     BEGIN
     Points^.FreeAll;
     InvalidateRect(HWindow, NIL, TRUE);
     END;
```

```
PROCEDURE TMyWindow.ChangeColor(VAR Msg: TMessage);
    VAR
        NewColor,
        ErrorPos: INTEGER;
        ColorBuffer : ARRAY[0..5] OF CHAR;
    BEGIN
        Str(PenColor, ColorBuffer);
        IF Application^.ExecDialog(New(PInputDialog,
            Init(@Self, 'Line Color',
            'Type 1/Red, 2/Green, 3/Blue, 4/Black',
            ColorBuffer, SizeOf(ColorBuffer)))) = id_Ok
        THEN  BEGIN
            Val(ColorBuffer, NewColor, ErrorPos);
            IF ErrorPos = 0 THEN SetPenColor(NewColor);
            END;
    END;

PROCEDURE TMyWindow.ChangeStyle(VAR Msg: TMessage);
    VAR
        NewStyle,
        ErrorPos: INTEGER;
        StyleBuffer : ARRAY[0..5] OF CHAR;
    BEGIN
        Str(PenStyle, StyleBuffer);
        IF Application^.ExecDialog(New(PInputDialog,
            Init(@Self, 'Line Style',
            'Type 1/Solid, 2/Dotted, 3/Dashed',
            StyleBuffer, SizeOf(StyleBuffer)))) = id_Ok
        THEN  BEGIN
            Val(StyleBuffer, NewStyle, ErrorPos);
            IF ErrorPos = 0 THEN SetPenStyle(NewStyle);
            END;
    END;

PROCEDURE TMyWindow.ChangeThickness(VAR Msg: TMessage);
    VAR
        ThickBuffer: ARRAY[0..5] of CHAR;
        NewSize, ErrorPos: INTEGER;
    BEGIN
        Str(PenSize, ThickBuffer);
        IF Application^.ExecDialog(New(PInputDialog,
            Init(@Self, 'Line Thickness',
            'Input a new thickness:',
            ThickBuffer, SizeOf(ThickBuffer)))) = id_Ok
```

```
            THEN BEGIN
                    Val(ThickBuffer, NewSize, ErrorPos);
                    IF ErrorPos = 0 THEN SetPenSize(NewSize);
                    END;
        END;

PROCEDURE TMyWindow.Help(VAR Msg: TMessage);
    BEGIN
    MessageBox(HWindow, 'Not yet implemented',
        'Help', mb_Ok or mb_IconExclamation);
    END;

{================}
{ TDPoint methods}
{================}
CONSTRUCTOR TDPoint.Init(AX, AY: INTEGER);
    BEGIN
    X := AX;
    Y := AY;
    END;

{================}
{TMyApp methods}
{================}
PROCEDURE TMyApp.InitMainWindow;
    BEGIN
    MainWindow := New(PMyWindow, Init(NIL, 'Listing 9.4'));
    END;

{=========================================}
{global object variable for application}
{=========================================}
VAR
    MyApp : TMyApp;

{===================}
{main body of program}
{===================}
BEGIN
    MyApp.Init('Listing9_4');
    MyApp.Run;
    MyApp.Done;
END.
```

FIGURE 9.5:

A result of changing line style using Listing 9.4

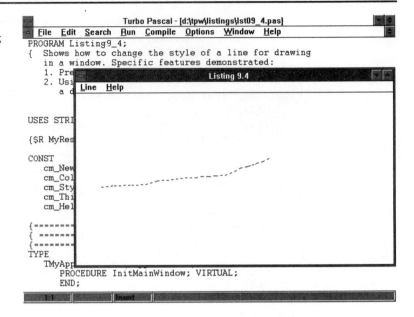

PART III

Intermediate-Level Windows Programming Skills

Creating and Using Dialog Resources

- Types of Resources

- Basic Steps in Creating and Using Dialog Resources

- Creating a Dialog Box in WRT

- Using a Dialog Resource in a Program

- Running the Dialog-Box Program

- " Safe" Dialog Box Execution

In this chapter, we'll show how to create dialog boxes in the **Whitewater Resource Toolkit**—and, what is far more difficult, how to link them into a source program in Turbo Pascal for Windows. First, however, we need to get a better understanding of what Windows resources *are* and what capabilities they make available to the programmer.

What Are Resources?

A Windows resource is an external file that works with your program to define how some of the program's features will appear on screen—including menus, dialog boxes, radio buttons and pushbuttons, checkboxes, icons, and various graphic images. Usually, the resource itself has nothing to do with how these features and devices actually *work:* that part must be defined by you in the source code of your program. There are a few exceptions, where the definition of a resource has a critical impact on how it works, but we'll note those exceptions as we go along.

Like standard program files, a resource file can be in either a source code or a compiled version. The source code version of a menu resource file has the extension .RC and is in plain ASCII text, just like most any other program file. The compiled version often has the extension .RES, (for "resource"), as in the examples we'll be looking at.

In this chapter, we'll create a simple application that does nothing but activate a dialog box resource. To activate this resource, we'll also create (in the same .RES file) a simple menu that calls the dialog box. We won't go into any detail about how to write resource files with a text editor; inasmuch as we have the Whitewater Resource Toolkit, writing resource files in that way would be a tremendous waste of time. (There are also several other excellent resource creation and compilation tools, including the **Borland Resource Workshop**.) However, to give you an idea of what the source code looks like for a simple resource file, Listing 10.1 shows the source code for the resource file we'll create in this chapter:

Listing 10.1

```
NADAMENU MENU
BEGIN
    POPUP "Do &Nothing"
    BEGIN
```

```
    MENUITEM "Run &Dialog Box", 201
    END
END

NOTHING DIALOG 10, 35, 150, 130
CAPTION "The Official Do-Nothing Dialog Box"
STYLE DS_MODALFRAME | WS_POPUP | WS_CAPTION | WS_SYSMENU
BEGIN
    CONTROL "OK",
        1, "BUTTON", BS_PUSHBUTTON | WS_TABSTOP, 107, 34, 32, 12
    CONTROL "Cancel",
        2, "BUTTON", BS_DEFPUSHBUTTON | WS_TABSTOP, 98, 53, 40, 12
    CONTROL "Bupkis",
        101, "BUTTON", BS_AUTORADIOBUTTON, 4, 32, 64, 12
    CONTROL "Nichts",
        102, "BUTTON", BS_AUTORADIOBUTTON, 4, 47, 64, 12
    CONTROL "Nada",
        103, "BUTTON", BS_AUTORADIOBUTTON, 4, 62, 64, 12
    CONTROL "Zip",
        104, "BUTTON", BS_AUTORADIOBUTTON, 4, 80, 64, 12
    CONTROL "Nothing is impossible.",
        -1, "STATIC", SS_LEFT, 35, 8, 74, 9
END
```

This code is surprisingly simple, considering the complex chores that the resource is doing behind the scenes. It defines a menu whose control ID (used to activate this resource in the Turbo Pascal program) is *NADAMENU*, as well as a dialog box whose control ID is *NOTHING*.

Because we won't be writing any source code for Windows resources, we won't pursue this topic further here. However, once we've created the resources that this code represents, as we will do later in the chapter, you'll see the code in action and might want to return to this listing to get a better understanding of how it works.

Types of Resources

There are seven main types of resources that you'll be dealing with in Windows programs. Some are simpler to create and more widely useful than others, but it's a good idea to be familiar with all of them. The seven types are menus, dialogs, accelerators, bitmaps, icons, cursors, and string tables. Bitmaps, icons, and cursors, though functionally different, are created in basically the same way. All seven types of resources can be created, edited, and compiled in the Whitewater Resource Toolkit.

Menus　We've already seen an example of a menu resource in Chapter 9, where we created a menu to change the color, style, and thickness of a line drawn in a window. The choices in a menu can be selected by clicking on them with the mouse, and menu choices can cause submenus to pop open alongside the original menu. Apart from accelerators (discussed below), menus are the easiest resource to create and incorporate into a program.

Dialog Boxes　In its ObjectWindows library and associated resource files, Turbo Pascal for Windows itself defines two simple *dialog box types,* as we discussed in Chapter 9. However, to create more sophisticated dialog boxes, containing a wider variety of control devices such as radio buttons and checkboxes, you need to create an external *dialog resource.*

Each screen object in a dialog box, whether it actually does anything or not, is assigned a control ID through which it can be activated (when appropriate) by the program that is using the dialog resource. Nonfunctional parts of the dialog box, such as "static text," which explains the box to the user but doesn't perform any action in the program, are generally all assigned the control ID of –1.

Dialog box resources are not hard to create, but incorporating them into a program is a fairly complicated process and is virtually undocumented in the Turbo Pascal manuals. That's why we explain the process in excruciating detail later in this chapter.

Accelerators　Accelerators are "speed keys" or "hot keys" that let the user bypass the menus to activate a menu choice. A familiar example of an accelerator is the combination *Ctrl-Insert* to copy a block of text to the Windows clipboard; you could open the Edit menu and select "Copy" instead, but the accelerator saves you keystrokes.

Accelerators are fairly easy to define, and they are entirely optional: it's up to you as the programmer to decide whether you want to associate an accelerator with a menu choice. They are also relatively easy to incorporate into a program, although a couple of special techniques are needed (see Chapter 12 for more details).

Bitmaps   A bitmap, as the name implies, is a binary version of an image. A bitmap can be associated with an action in the program, but need not be so associated. If you associate a bitmap with an action, then when the user clicks on the screen image created by the bitmap, the corresponding action will be initiated.

You create a bitmap in the WRT by using the WRT Bitmap Editor to paint the image, pixel by pixel ("picture elements," the smallest screen elements that can be manipulated by a program), as well as to choose the color(s) and other characteristics.

Icons   An icon is a small bitmap that is used to represent a minimized window for a file, a program, or any Windows task. You create an icon in the WRT by using the WRT Icon Editor, which is quite similar to the Bitmap Editor, except that icons are generally quite small—measuring either 32×32 pixels or 32×16 pixels.

Cursors   Like an icon, a cursor is a small bitmap that shows the current location of the mouse cursor. The WRT Cursor Editor lets you customize the screen appearance of the cursor so that it looks different in different regions of your program's screen window, when it can be expected to perform different operations.

String Tables   A string table, is a resource that can be used to hold text messages for use in your program. Its usefulness is found mainly in situations when you need to change the text displayed by your program without modifying the source code—for example, when you need to produce a foreign-language version.

A Few Observations on the Value of Dialog Resources

In the previous chapter, we saw examples of text-input dialog boxes of the *TInput-Dialog* type, which is predefined in ObjectWindows. This type of dialog box is often useful, but in certain situations it seems a little awkward. For example, in Listing 9.4 we set up a dialog box that let the user choose a line color by typing a number into the input dialog box. This, however, left open two significant questions:

- What happens if the user enters the wrong number?
- Why use text-entry to make a choice from a limited number of alternatives when you could use radio buttons (or some other dialog box device) instead?

There are easy but unsatisfying answers to these questions. The answer to the first question is that if you coded your CASE statement properly, the CASE..ELSE clause will catch any situation in which the user enters the wrong number. The easy answer to the second question, frankly, is that radio buttons and other dialog-box devices can be damn difficult to code—particularly if such features are, ahem, slightly underdocumented in the Turbo Pascal manuals.

But in another sense, difficult or not, radio buttons and the like are what we came here for. If we're just going to set up text-input boxes, we might as well be programming in COBOL for text-only mainframe terminals. There's no point in using a powerful tool like Turbo Pascal for Windows just to create text-input boxes.

Creating radio buttons, checkboxes, and pushbuttons gives you automatic control of the range of user input *and* makes full use of Windows' graphic-interface capabilities. It's a little harder to do, mainly because it involves creating an external Windows resource and then bringing it into your application, but the results are well worth the effort.

Because of the inherent complexity of the topic, however, we'll temporarily part company with the "drawing program" application that we developed in Chapter 9. We'll begin by creating a simple application that does nothing but run a dialog box with some radio buttons and pushbuttons. Then, once the concepts and techniques are clear, we'll return to the drawing application and incorporate our new, more interesting dialog boxes.

The Basic Steps in Creating and Using Dialog Resources

The main steps in creating and using dialog box resources are quite simple, even if the details can get a little hairy. In essence, it all boils down to the following steps:

1. Create a dialog resource in the Whitewater Resource Toolkit (or the Borland Resource Workshop).

2. Include the resource file in your TPW source code using the **$R** compiler directive.

3. Define an object type to "stand in" for the dialog box resource in your program—much the same as you use a file variable to represent a disk file. This object type will usually be a descendant of *TDialog*, an object type defined in ObjectWindows.

4. If you need to get information out of the dialog box, as you normally will, then define a "transfer buffer" record type to hold the information after the dialog box is closed. One field of the parent window (the window from which the dialog box is called) shoud be of this type.

5. Initialize the buffer field of the parent window by passing its address to the *TransferBuffer* field of the dialog box object; this is an inherited field from *TDialog*.

6. Execute the dialog, usually by calling the *Execute* method inherited from *TDialog*.

7. Check the transfer buffer for the dialog's return values, and have the program take action based on those values.

In a certain sense, each of these steps is like comedian Steve Martin's famous advice on how to be a millionaire and not pay taxes: "First, get a million dollars." There are tricks and traps along the way, and they're often either not documented at all or not documented very well. In this chapter, we'll show you how to do it without ending up at the bottom of a pit.

Creating a Dialog Box in the WRT

To begin with, let's get clear on what we will be doing in the Whitewater Resource Toolkit versus what we will be doing in Turbo Pascal itself. As mentioned previously, generally the WRT is used only to design the *appearance* of the dialog box, including the locations and types of controls it contains. Our TPW program, on the other hand, defines what each of the dialog box controls *does*: what happens when you select a radio button, check a checkbox, or click on a pushbutton. There are a few significant exceptions to this rule (such as using the WRT to define the "style" of a radio button, which is a crucial determinant of how it works), but we'll flag each of these exceptions as we get to it.

The other general rule is this: Any dialog box element that you create in the WRT must have a corresponding element in the Turbo Pascal program. Thus, for example, the dialog box itself must have a corresponding object type descended from *TDialog*; this object type must contain fields for the dialog-box controls (except for the *OK* and *Cancel* pushbuttons) and the appropriate methods to process the data in those fields.

Let's start by creating an empty dialog box. Then, we'll add explanatory text, radio buttons, checkboxes, and pushbuttons.

Creating a Dialog Box

To create a dialog box in the WRT, you select the *Dialog* icon button from the WRT main menu. The dialog editor will open, as shown in Figure 10.1. The first thing to do is double-click inside the "Untitled Dialog" box. This will open up the **Dialog Attributes** dialog box, as shown in Figure 10.2.

FIGURE 10.1:
The WRT dialog resource editor

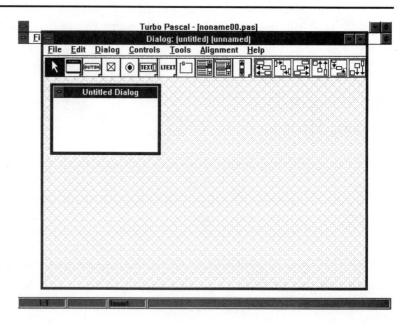

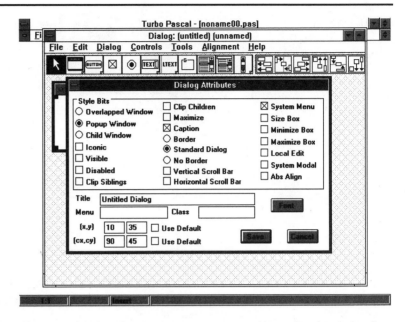

The Dialog Attributes dialog box lets you set various attributes for the dialog box you are creating—such as its title, its resource ID, and its dimensions. As the title for the new dialog box, enter

```
The Official Do-Nothing Dialog Box
```

Below, the *[x,y]* boxes give the X and Y coordinates of the upper left corner of the box, while the *[cx,cy]* boxes give the X and Y coordinates of the lower right corner of the box. Leave the *[x,y]* boxes as they are and change the *[cx,cy]* values to 150 and 130, respectively. When you click on the *Save* button, the new title and the dimensions of the dialog box are displayed, as in Figure 10.3.

Next, we'll add some "static text" to the box. This type of dialog box object doesn't perform any actions, but it provides useful information for the user. First, click on the *LText* (left-justified text) icon button at the top of the WRT dialog box editor; note that it darkens, indicating that this is the particular type of device selected to put in the dialog box. This icon button changes every time you click on it: if you double-click on it, you'll see that it changes to *RText* (right-justified text). Double-click again, and it changes to *CText* (centered text). Double-click one more time and it changes back to *LText*, which is what we wanted in the first place.

FIGURE 10.3:

The new title and dimensions of the dialog box

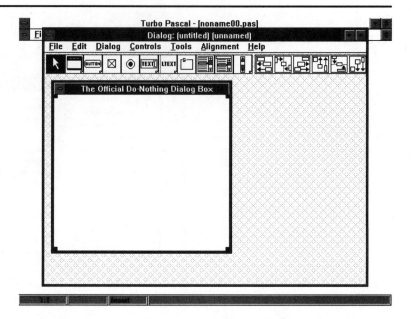

To add static text to the dialog box, now position the mouse cursor in the top center of the dialog box; then click and hold the left mouse button. Drag the mouse just a little, then release the button. The "Left J" text object will appear, as shown in Figure 10.4.

If you double-click inside the rectangle formed by the four dots that delimit the screen object, the **Item Attributes** dialog box appears, as shown in Figure 10.5.

You can use the Item Attributes dialog box to enter the text, the control ID, and the dimensions of the text object you want. In this case, because "nothing" is the purported goal of our official do-nothing dialog box, let's put in a few words of encouragement appropriate to nothingness. In the text box, enter

`Nothing is impossible.`

Then, for the control ID (*Item ID*), enter -1. (A negative number is a good choice for static text; that way, it won't accidentally get mixed up with any other objects that are supposed to *do* things.) In this case, we'll leave the dimensions alone, because it's easier to adjust them with the mouse. When you click on OK, the text will be only partially shown, because we haven't adjusted the dimensions of the text object yet.

FIGURE 10.4:

The left-justified text object appears after you drag the mouse with the LText icon button selected

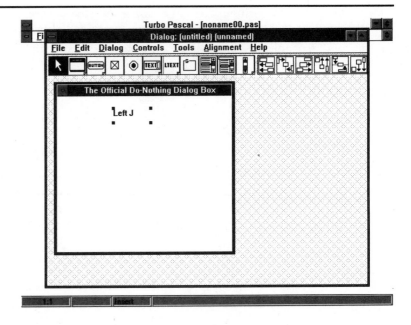

FIGURE 10.5:

The Item Attributes dialog box for static text objects

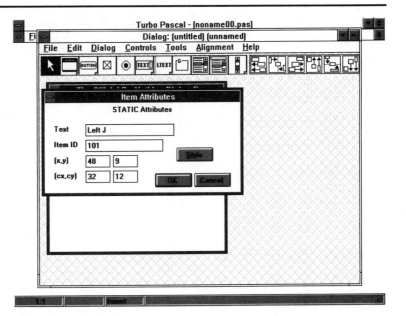

If you position the mouse cursor over the lower right dot in the object, you can see that it changes to a small set of cross-hairs. You can drag the lower right dot to change the dimensions of the object, as shown in Figure 10.6. You can then position the mouse cursor in the middle of the text and drag the object to the desired location in the dialog box.

Creating Radio Buttons

The next step is to add some radio buttons to the dialog box. To add a radio button, you click on the icon that looks like a radio button in the icon palette across the top of the Dialog Attributes dialog box. As before, the button will darken to indicate that it is selected. Position the mouse cursor toward the left of the dialog box, then click and drag it as you did with the text object. The radio button object will appear, as shown in Figure 10.7.

The first thing to do is change the attributes of the radio button. Double-click the radio button object, and the Item Attributes box for buttons will open, as shown in Figure 10.8. For the text, enter Bupkis, and for the control ID (*Item ID*), enter 101.

FIGURE 10.6:

Adjusting the dimensions of the text object

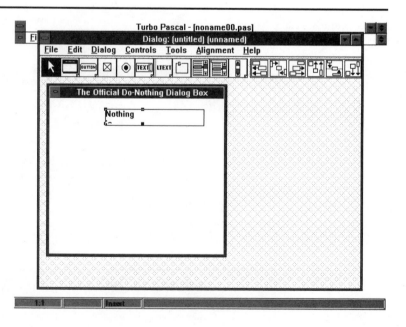

FIGURE 10.7:

The initial appearance of a radio button

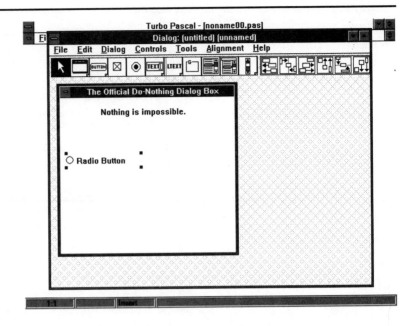

FIGURE 10.8:

The Button Attributes version of the Item Attributes dialog box

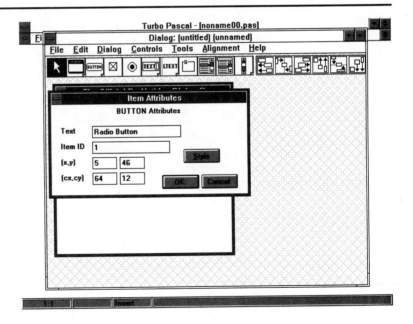

FIGURE 10.9:

The Button Styles dialog box

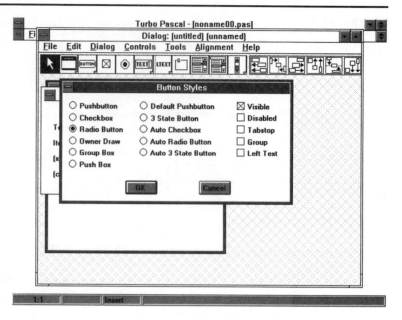

Now, we have to make a very important change in the radio button. Click on the *Style* button to display the **Button Styles** dialog box, shown in Figure 10.9.

The choices in the Button Styles dialog box have a crucial impact on how the currently selected dialog-box control will work. In this case, the default style—*Radio Button*—will not allow the radio button to work as you might expect. Instead, you should click on the button for *Auto Radio Button.*

The significance of this choice is as follows. You use radio buttons to allow the user to select from a number of mutually exclusive alternatives: in our line-drawing program, for example, the user could make the line red, green, blue, or black, but could pick only one color at a time. When the user selects a radio button, you want two things to happen:

1. The selection (called the "focus") should move to that button.

2. All other radio buttons in the same group should be *de*selected.

Unless you make your radio buttons "Auto Radio Buttons," neither of these conditions will be met.

To get back to the "Official Do-Nothing Dialog Box," click on OK in the Button Styles dialog box and again on OK in the Item Attributes dialog box. In the same way that you added the *Bupkis* button, add three more radio buttons on the left side of the box. Don't worry about aligning them precisely; we'll take care of that in a minute. The buttons and values to enter are:

Button Text	Control ID
Nichts	102
Nada	103
Zip	104

When you're finished, the dialog box should look like Figure 10.10.

Grouping Buttons Together

There's one key point we've touched on but haven't explained. Suppose that you have several radio buttons or pushbuttons in the same dialog box, but that they don't all go together. For example, an all-purpose dialog box for our line-drawing program might have one group of radio buttons for color and another group for line

FIGURE 10.10:
Dialog box with radio buttons

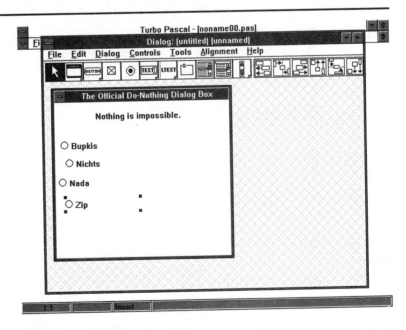

style. When the user selects one color button, all the other color buttons should be deselected, but nothing should happen to the buttons for line style. We need some way to tell the application which buttons go together with which other buttons.

The WRT solves this problem by allowing you to select buttons and then group them together in a single logical group. You can drag the "selection pointer" (the arrow icon) to draw a selection box around all the buttons in the grouping if they are contiguous. To add noncontiguous buttons to a group, press and hold the *Shift* key while clicking on the desired buttons with the mouse. Then, select the "Group Together" option from the Controls menu.

Aligning Buttons

Because the radio buttons are now grouped together, they will work as they should. Moreover, we can now let the WRT position them automatically in the dialog box. To do this, while the four radio buttons are still selected, open the Alignment menu and select "Align Left." The buttons will automatically line up, as shown in Figure 10.11.

FIGURE 10.11:

Automatically aligned radio buttons

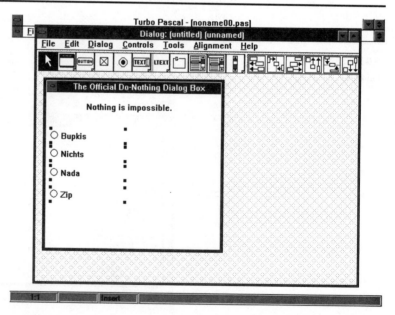

Creating Pushbuttons

Radio buttons, of course, let the user make choices. But they don't perform any *actions*. To do that, we need to include some pushbuttons in the dialog box: an *OK* button and a *Cancel* button should be adequate. To create the first pushbutton, select the "Button" icon from the icon palette, then click and drag the mouse to make a button as shown in Figure 10.12.

Open the **Item Attributes** box in the usual way, by double-clicking on the object to be dealt with (the button you just positioned). For the text of this button, enter OK, and for its ID, enter 1, which is the default Windows control-ID for an OK pushbutton. Don't worry about the button style; in this case, the default values work fine. Click on OK to return to our Official Do-Nothing Dialog Box.

Below the OK button, add a Cancel button in the same way, entering 2 as the control ID (the default control ID for a Cancel button). This time, however, click on the Style button and, in the **Button Styles** dialog box, choose *Default Push Button*. Click on OK twice to return to the Official Do-Nothing Dialog Box. Group the two buttons together as you did the radio buttons, and right-align them using the Alignment menu.

FIGURE 10.12:

Positioning the first pushbutton

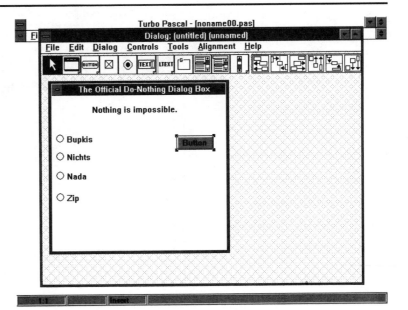

Verifying Groups and IDs

Finally, let's verify that the buttons have the correct control IDs assigned to them and that they are grouped properly. First, display the groups by selecting "Show Item Group" from the Dialog menu; your display should look similar to Figure 10.13. Depending on the type of monitor you have, each group of buttons should have its own characteristic fill-pattern. (The patterns look quite different on different types of monitors.)

As a last step, let's make sure that the buttons have the correct control IDs. Select "Show Item ID" from the Dialog menu. The control ID of each item in the dialog box should be displayed below the item, as shown in Figure 10.14.

Saving the Dialog

Now, you should save the dialog in a resource file. Select "Save" from the File menu and save the dialog in the resource file NOTHING.RES in the same directory that contains your program listings. In the **File/Resource Attributes** dialog box, enter NOTHING as the name for the Official Do-Nothing dialog box.

FIGURE 10.13:

Button groups, viewed by means of the Dialog/Show Item Group command

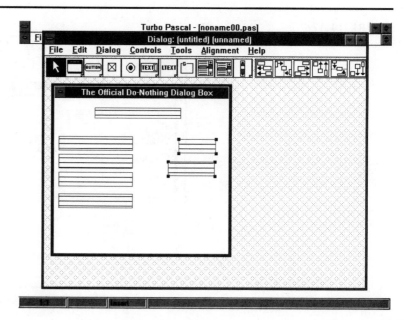

FIGURE 10.14:

Viewing control IDs

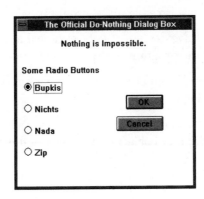

Creating a Do-Nothing Menu

We need to do one more thing before we can use this dialog box in a program: we must create a menu that calls the dialog box. Just as we did in Chapter 9, use the WRT menu editor to create a menu with two lines in it: the menu title,

```
Do &Nothing
```

which should have a value of 0, and one (indented) menu choice,

```
Run &Dialog Box
```

which should have a value of 201. Then save the menu into the same NOTH-ING.RES resource file that contains the Official Do-Nothing dialog box, assigning the menu the name NADAMENU.

Using a Dialog Resource in a Program

Of course, it wouldn't do us much good to create a dialog box—even a "do nothing" dialog box—unless we could use it in a program. This is a pretty tricky job, even though its broad outlines are pretty clear. To use a dialog box in a program, we have to follow the steps mentioned previously:

1. Include the resource file in the program.

2. Define a *TDialog* descendant object type that will "stand in" for the dialog resource in the program code.

3. Set up a transfer buffer to move data back and forth between the program and the dialog box.

4. Initialize the transfer buffer by linking it with the *TransferBuffer* field of the *TDialog* descendant object that represents the dialog box in the program.

5. Execute the dialog box, usually with a call to the *Execute* method inherited from *TDialog*.

6. Check the values returned by the dialog box, and make the program take appropriate actions based on those values.

Our discussion of these points will refer to Listing 10.2, which appears below.

Listing 10.2

```
PROGRAM Listing10_2;
{  Illustrates the overall structure of a program that
   uses an external dialog box resource.
   Associated resource file: NOTHING.RES.
      Dialog resources:
         Menu: NadaMenu
         Dialog Box: Nothing  }

USES STRINGS, WINTYPES, WINPROCS, WOBJECTS;

{$R Nothing.res }

CONST
   {menu choice identifiers}
   cm_Nada  = 201;

   {dialog button identifiers}
   id_bupkis = 101;
   id_nichts = 102;
   id_nada = 103;
   id_zip = 104;
```

```
{============================================================ }
{ ======== TYPE DEFINITION SECTION OF PROGRAM ======== }
{============================================================ }
TYPE
    TMyApp = OBJECT(TApplication)
        PROCEDURE InitMainWindow; VIRTUAL;
        END;

    { Dialog transfer record }
    ItemTransferBuffer = RECORD
        BupkisBtn,
        NichtsBtn,
        NadaBtn,
        ZipBtn   : WORD;
        END;

    PMyWindow = ^TMyWindow;
    TMyWindow = OBJECT(TWindow)
        DDBuffer : ItemTransferBuffer;
        CONSTRUCTOR Init(AParent: PWindowsObject;
            ATitle: PChar);
        FUNCTION CanClose: BOOLEAN; VIRTUAL;
        {methods for menu choices}
        PROCEDURE DoNothingMuch(VAR Msg: TMessage);
            VIRTUAL cm_First + cm_Nada;
        END;

    {dialog box type for doing nothing}
    PMyDialog = ^TMyDialog;
    TMyDialog = OBJECT (TDialog)
        BupkisButton,
        NichtsButton,
        NadaButton,
        ZipButton : PRadioButton;
        CONSTRUCTOR Init(AParent: PWindowsObject;
                         ATitle:PChar);
        END;


{===================}
{TMyWindow methods}
{===================}

CONSTRUCTOR TMyWindow.Init(AParent: PWindowsObject;
                           ATitle: PChar);
```

```
BEGIN
TWindow.Init(AParent, ATitle);
Attr.Menu := LoadMenu(HInstance, 'NadaMenu');
with DDBuffer do
   BEGIN
   BupkisBtn := bf_unchecked;
   NichtsBtn := bf_unchecked;
   NadaBtn := bf_unchecked;
   ZipBtn := bf_unchecked;
   END;
END;

FUNCTION TMyWindow.CanClose: BOOLEAN;
   VAR
      Reply: INTEGER;
   BEGIN
      CanClose := TRUE;
      Reply := MessageBox(HWindow,
               'Do you want to save your work?',
               'Window content has changed',
               mb_YesNoCancel or mb_IconQuestion);
      IF (Reply = id_Yes) OR (Reply = id_Cancel)
         THEN CanClose := FALSE;
   END;

PROCEDURE TMyWindow.DoNothingMuch(VAR Msg: TMessage);
   var  Dlg: TMyDialog;
        Reply, MyResult: Integer;
   BEGIN
   Dlg.Init(@Self, 'Nothing');
   Dlg.TransferBuffer := @DDBuffer;
   Reply := Dlg.Execute;
   Dlg.Done;

   IF Reply = id_Ok THEN
   IF DDBuffer.BupkisBtn = bf_checked
      THEN MyResult := MessageBox(HWindow,
               'You get Bupkis',
               'Event Report',
               mb_OK or mb_IconExclamation)
   ELSE IF DDBuffer.NichtsBtn = bf_checked
      THEN MyResult := MessageBox(HWindow,
               'You get Nichts',
               'Event Report',
               mb_OK or mb_IconExclamation)
```

```
        ELSE IF DDBuffer.NadaBtn = bf_checked
           THEN MyResult := MessageBox(HWindow,
                     'You get Nada',
                     'Event Report',
                     mb_OK or mb_IconExclamation)
        ELSE IF DDBuffer.ZipBtn = bf_checked
           THEN MyResult := MessageBox(HWindow,
                     'You get Zip',
                     'Event Report',
                     mb_OK or mb_IconExclamation)
        ELSE MyResult := MessageBox(HWindow,
                     'You STILL get Zip',
                     'Event Report',
                     mb_OK or mb_IconExclamation);
        END; { of DoNothingMuch routine }


{=====================}
{ TMyDialog methods }
{=====================}

CONSTRUCTOR TMyDialog.init(AParent: PWindowsObject;
                           ATitle: Pchar);
   BEGIN
   TDialog.init(aparent, atitle);
   NEW(BupkisButton, initResource(@Self, id_bupkis));
   NEW(NichtsButton, initResource(@Self, id_nichts));
   NEW(NadaButton, initResource(@Self, id_nada));
   NEW(ZipButton, initResource(@Self, id_zip));
   END;


{================}
{TMyApp methods}
{================}
PROCEDURE TMyApp.InitMainWindow;
   BEGIN
   MainWindow := New(PMyWindow, Init(NIL, 'Listing 10.2'));
   END;


{=================================}
{global object variable for application}
{=================================}
VAR
   MyApp : TMyApp;
```

```
{========================}
{main body of program}
{========================}
BEGIN
    MyApp.Init('Listing10_2');
    MyApp.Run;
    MyApp.Done;
END.
```

Include the Resource

The first step is to include the resource file at the top of the source program. As with the menu in Chapter 9, this is done using the $R compiler directive and the name of the resource file. The resource file named must meet one of the following three criteria:

- It must be in the same directory as the source program, or

- It must have a directory path included in the compiler directive, or

- It must be in one of the Resource directories named in the Options/ **Directories** dialog box in Turbo Pascal for Windows.

Define Identifiers for Dialog-Box Controls

The next step is to define identifiers for the control devices (the buttons, etc.) in the dialog box. As with a menu resource, these identifiers will be used to link the devices in the dialog box resource with the correct methods in the TPW program. Also, as before, we define a command constant identifier to activate the menu choice in the menu resource. This all takes place in the CONST section near the top of the program.

Define a Transfer Buffer

Next, we define a transfer buffer to carry data into and out of the dialog box. When you make a selection in a dialog box, the data that your action creates continues to exist only until the dialog box is destroyed through a call to *TDialog.Done*. Thus, you need this transfer buffer to keep a copy of the data and pass it to the program after the dialog box is closed. This transfer buffer must be a record type with one field (of the appropriate data type) for each control that must pass data out of the dialog box. Here, we define it as *ItemTransferBuffer*, and it has four WORD-type fields (WORD being the appropriate data type for the data created by button and check-box selections).

Note that, just below the definition of *ItemTransferBuffer*, the *TMyWindow* type definition has added a new field of its own: *DDBuffer* a record of type *ItemTransfer-Buffer* to hold the data passed back from the dialog box.

Define a TDialog Descendant Type

The next step is to define a dialog object type to represent the dialog resource in the program itself. Here, the object type is called *TMyDialog*, descended from *TDialog*. It has four fields, one for each of the four radio buttons in the dialog resource. Also, the fields are of type *PRadioButton*, which means each field can hold a pointer to a *TRadioButton*-type object. There's also a new *TMyDialog.Init* constructor method, which overrides the inherited *TDialog.Init* method, because besides constructing the dialog object we also need it to initialize the button fields and link them to the buttons defined in the dialog resource.

Initialize the Buffer

The next point of interest is the *TMyWindow.Init* constructor method. This starts off by doing two things we've seen before: calling *TWindow.Init* and loading the menu resource into the window's menu *Attr* field. (The explicit call is required before you can override *TWindow.Init* in a descendant type.) Next, however, it initializes the window's buffer field (*DDBuffer*) by assigning the value

```
bf_unchecked
```

to each button field of the buffer, indicating that the buttons should be unselected when the dialog box opens. The other value you might assign—to one button field only—is

```
bf_checked
```

indicating that the particular button is selected, by default, when the dialog box opens.

Of course, it's important to note that at this point, the checked/unchecked information has not yet been loaded into the button resources in the dialog box. We've just put the appropriate values into the corresponding fields of the parent window's transfer buffer.

Initialize the Dialog Box

Next, we define how to initialize the dialog box with the *TMyDialog.Init* constructor method. This begins by calling *TDialog.Init*, which takes care of the handle to the parent window and the title of the dialog. Next, we make four calls to NEW to create four dynamic button objects. Each button object is initialized with a call to *InitResource*, which takes two parameters:

- A pointer to the button object being initialized (here, *@Self*).

- The resource ID associated with the button in the external dialog resource. Recall that in the dialog resource, each device had a number assigned to it. In the CONST section of the program, the resource IDs named in *TMyDialog.Init* were defined to match those numbers. Thus, for example, the *BupkisButton* field of *TMyDialog* is associated with the *Bupkis* radio button in the NOTHING dialog resource.

Execute the Dialog

The next step is to define how the dialog box will be executed and shut down. This is done by the *TMyWindow.DoNothingMuch* method. If you look back at the original definition of the *TMyWindow* object type, you will note that the *DoNothingMuch* method has the identifier *cm_nada* in its extension, indicating that it responds to the menu command to "Run Dialog Box."

First, this method creates three local variables: *Dlg*, a variable of the correct type to represent a dialog box, and two integer variables, *Reply* and *MyResult*. It then does the following:

1. It calls the *Dlg* variable's *Init* method, which the variable inherits from *TDialog*. This method takes two parameters: first, a pointer to the dialog variable itself (*@Self*), and second, the resource ID of the dialog box (*Nothing*) created in the resource editor. It is through this call to *Dlg.Init* that the dialog object variable is linked to the external dialog resource.

2. It assigns the values in the parent window's transfer buffer field to the *TransferBuffer* field that the dialog variable inherits from *TDialog*. There's

more to this move than meets the eye: in addition to transferring the data into the dialog box, it sets up a link that transfers the data *out of* the dialog box and into the buffer when the dialog box is shut down. This is all done behind the scenes, by passing a pointer to the parent window's transfer buffer field into the dialog box's *TransferBuffer* field.

3. It executes the dialog variable by calling the *Execute* method that the variable inherits from *TDialog*. The resulting termination code is assigned to the *Reply* variable.

4. It shuts down the dialog with a call to the variable's inherited *Done* method.

Check the Dialog's Return Values

The next step in this method is to inspect the values passed from the dialog box to the parent window's transfer buffer. Different actions can then be taken based on these values. Here, we've simply set up the program to display a message box indicating which radio button was selected in the dialog box. This is a trivial task, of course, but it shows that the data was successfully transferred out of the dialog box and to the parent window.

Running the Dialog-Box Program

The rest of Listing 10.2 is fairly standard. An object variable is declared to represent the application; the variable is initialized, run, and shut down. The results are shown in Figure 10.15.

Adding Checkboxes

You add checkboxes to a dialog box in almost the same way as you create radio buttons. Let's add two checkboxes to the dialog we created and used in Listing 10.2. Use the WRT to open up the NOTHING dialog in the NOTHING.RES resource file. Then select the checkbox button in the dialog editor's icon button palette; the button is a square with an X in it.

FIGURE 10.15:

Message box resulting from choosing the Bupkis radio button once the program in Listing 10.2 is run

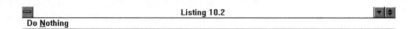

Once you've selected the checkbox button, you're ready to position the checkbox in the dialog box. You do this just as before, by moving the cursor to the approximate place you want to put the control object, then dragging the cursor just a bit. A checkbox object will appear on the screen, as shown in Figure 10.16.

Open the checkbox object as you would a radio button, by double-clicking on it. Then enter Freberg as the checkbox text and use the *Style* button to change the style to Auto Checkbox. Click on *OK* to return to the dialog editor. Put in one more checkbox, making it an Auto Checkbox as well, and label it Rogers. TPW is indifferent to comedians, so you can substitute your own names if you prefer. Select both checkboxes and use the "Group Together" choice from the Controls menu to make the two checkboxes a logical group. Then save the modified dialog box and return to TPW, where we'll make the changes needed in Listing 10.2 so that the program can deal with the checkboxes.

Once back in TPW, we need only make very minor changes to handle the checkboxes. The first step is in the CONST section of the program, where we must add two new identifiers with the same values as the control IDs of the two checkboxes—105 for Freberg and 106 for Rogers. As with other external resources, it's through these identifiers that the checkbox resources are brought into the program.

FIGURE 10.16:

Positioning a checkbox in a
dialog box

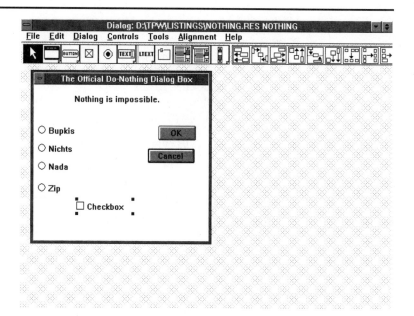

The next step is to add two new fields to the *ItemTransferBuffer* record type—one new field for each checkbox. Like radio buttons, checkboxes have their status indicated by a WORD-type value, so these fields are of the same type as the radio-button fields.

Next, in the definition of the *TMyDialog* object type that stands in for the external resource in the program code, we add two new fields (*Checkbox1* and *Checkbox2*): each field is a pointer to a checkbox object, just as the radio button fields were pointers to radio button objects.

By now, it shouldn't be hard to guess the next step: we need to add two more lines to the *TMyWindow.Init* method to initialize the two new fields in the parent window's transfer buffer record.

We don't intend that these checkboxes have any effect at this time—here, we're just seeing how to set them up. If we did want the program to take some action based on the status of the checkboxes (that is, according to whether they were checked or unchecked), we would write some new code in the *TMyWindow.DoNothingMuch* method to take the actions needed. This, however, is simple Pascal programming, and is left to your own imagination. The complete changes are shown in Listing 10.3.

Listing 10.3

```pascal
PROGRAM Listing10_3;
{ Adds checkboxes to the dialog box in Listing 10.2.
   Associated resource file: NOTHING.RES.
   Dialog resources:
   Menu: NadaMenu
   Dialog Box: Nothing }

USES STRINGS, WINTYPES, WINPROCS, WOBJECTS;

{$R Nothing.res }

CONST
   {menu choice identIFiers}
   cm_Nada  = 202;

   {dialog box identIFiers}
   id_bupkis = 101;
   id_nichts = 102;
   id_nada = 103;
   id_zip = 104;

   id_chkbx1 = 105;
   id_chkbx2 = 106;

{============================================================ }
{ ========= TYPE DEFINITION SECTION OF PROGRAM ========= }
{============================================================ }
TYPE
   TMyApp = OBJECT(TApplication)
      PROCEDURE InitMainWindow; VIRTUAL;
      END;

   { Dialog transfer RECORD }
   ItemTransferBuffer = RECORD
      {radio button fields}
      BupkisBtn,
      NichtsBtn,
      NadaBtn,
      ZipBtn: WORD;

      {checkbox fields}
      ChkBox1,
      ChkBox2  : WORD;
```

```
            END;

        PMyWindow = ^TMyWindow;
        TMyWindow = OBJECT(TWindow)
            DDBuffer : ItemTransferBuffer;
            CONSTRUCTOR Init(AParent: PWindowsObject;
                ATitle: PChar);
            FUNCTION CanClose: BOOLEAN; VIRTUAL;

            {methods for menu choices}
            PROCEDURE DoNothingMuch(VAR Msg: TMessage);
                VIRTUAL cm_First + cm_Nada;
            END;

        {dialog box type for doing nothing}
        PMyDialog = ^TMyDialog;
        TMyDialog = OBJECT (TDialog)
            BupkisButton,
            NichtsButton,
            NadaButton,
            ZipButton : PRadioButton;
            CheckBox1,
            CheckBox2 : PCheckBox;
            CONSTRUCTOR Init(AParent: PWindowsObject;
                ATitle:PChar);
            END;

    {===================}
    {TMyWindow methods}
    {===================}

CONSTRUCTOR TMyWindow.Init(AParent: PWindowsObject;
            ATitle: PChar);
    BEGIN
    TWindow.Init(AParent, ATitle);
    Attr.Menu := LoadMenu(HInstance, 'NadaMenu');
    WITH DDBuffer DO
        BEGIN
        BupkisBtn := bf_unchecked;
        NichtsBtn := bf_unchecked;
        NadaBtn := bf_unchecked;
        ZipBtn := bf_unchecked;
        ChkBox1 := bf_unchecked;
        ChkBox2 := bf_unchecked
        END
```

```
    END;

FUNCTION TMyWindow.CanClose: BOOLEAN;
    VAR
        Reply: INTEGER;
    BEGIN
    CanClose := TRUE;
    Reply := MessageBox(HWindow,
            'Do you want to save your work?',
            'Window content has changed',
            mb_YesNoCancel or mb_IconQuestion);
    IF (Reply = id_Yes) OR (Reply = id_Cancel)
    THEN CanClose := FALSE;
    END;

PROCEDURE TMyWindow.DoNothingMuch(VAR Msg: TMessage);
    VAR
        Dlg: TMyDialog;
        Reply, MyResult: INTEGER;
    BEGIN
    Dlg.Init(@Self, 'Nothing');
    Dlg.TransferBuffer := @DDBuffer;
    Reply := Dlg.Execute;
    Dlg.Done;

    IF Reply = id_Ok THEN
    IF DDBuffer.BupkisBtn = bf_checked
    THEN MyResult := MessageBox(HWindow,
            'You get Bupkis',
            'Event Report',
            mb_OK or mb_IconExclamation)
    ELSE IF DDBuffer.NichtsBtn = bf_checked
    THEN MyResult := MessageBox(HWindow,
            'You get Nichts',
            'Event Report',
            mb_OK or mb_IconExclamation)
    ELSE IF DDBuffer.NadaBtn = bf_checked
    THEN MyResult := MessageBox(HWindow,
            'You get Nada',
            'Event Report',
            mb_OK or mb_IconExclamation)
    ELSE IF DDBuffer.ZipBtn = bf_checked
    THEN MyResult := MessageBox(HWindow,
            'You get Zip',
            'Event Report',
```

```
                  mb_OK or mb_IconExclamation)
        ELSE MyResult := MessageBox(HWindow,
              'You STILL get Zip',
              'Event Report',
              mb_OK or mb_IconExclamation);
        END; { of DoNothingMuch routine }


{=====================}
{ TMyDialog methods }
{=====================}

CONSTRUCTOR TMyDialog.init(AParent: PWindowsObject;
            ATitle: PChar);
    BEGIN
    TDialog.init(aparent, atitle);
    NEW(BupkisButton, initResource(@Self, id_bupkis));
    NEW(NichtsButton, initResource(@Self, id_nichts));
    NEW(NadaButton, initResource(@Self, id_nada));
    NEW(ZipButton, initResource(@Self, id_zip));
    NEW(CheckBox1, initResource(@Self, id_chkbx1));
    NEW(CheckBox2, initResource(@Self, id_chkbx2))
    END;


{===============}
{TMyApp methods}
{===============}
PROCEDURE TMyApp.InitMainWindow;
    BEGIN
    MainWindow := NEW(PMyWindow, Init(NIL, 'Listing 10.3'));
    END;


{===========================================}
{global object variable for application}
{===========================================}
VAR
    MyApp : TMyApp;


{=====================}
{main body of program}
{=====================}
BEGIN
    MyApp.Init('Listing10_3');
    MyApp.Run;
    MyApp.Done;
END.
```

"Safe" Dialog Box Execution

You may have noticed that when we executed the dialog box in Listing 10.2, the technique was different from the one we used in Chapter 9. In the dialog boxes we created there—all of which were based on predefined ObjectWindows types—we used the *ExecDialog* method of the *Application* object. *Application*, as you will recall, is a predefined variable (like *Self*), which always refers to the current application process. With the appropriate changes made for each different dialog box, the code in Listing 9.4 was always something like this:

```
IF Application^.ExecDialog(pointer to dialog) = id_OK THEN
    BEGIN ...
```

Because we were using a predefined object type instead of an external dialog box resource, we didn't need to worry about setting up a transfer buffer and getting the data out of the dialog box: that was all handled for us by TPW.

When we created an external dialog resource, however, we did things a little differently. First, in the method that creates and uses the dialog box, we declared a local variable of the appropriate dialog box object type to correspond to the resource. Then, we passed a pointer to the parent window's transfer buffer into the dialog variable's *TransferBuffer* field, thereby initializing it and setting it up to save the data from the dialog box when the dialog was terminated. Finally, after all that setup, we executed the dialog box with a call to its inherited *TDialog.Execute* method. The code looked like this:

```
VAR
    Dlg: TMyDialog;
    Reply, MyResult: Integer;
BEGIN
    Dlg.Init(@Self, 'Nothing');
    Dlg.TransferBuffer := @DDBuffer;
    Reply := Dlg.Execute;
    Dlg.Done;

    IF Reply = id_Ok THEN
    BEGIN ...
```

This is a more direct way to execute a dialog, and it does have the advantage that setting up the transfer buffer is quite straightforward. However, it has one drawback: it lacks the built-in safety features of executing a dialog box with a call to *ExecDialog*. If you're sure that everything is coded properly, then the direct approach is fine.

If there is any doubt, however—particularly when you're just getting started—it's probably better to stick with using *ExecDialog*. This approach lets *ExecDialog* check to make sure that the dialog box was created successfully and executed without errors. If anything goes wrong, *ExecDialog* simply returns *id_Cancel* to your program. Without this safety feature—that is, if an error occurs in a dialog box that you're running with a bare call to *Dialog.Execute*—your program will probably crash.

Setting up the transfer buffer is a little more complicated with this "safe" method, but it's still not terribly difficult. The approach in Listing 9.4 won't quite do:

```
IF Application^.ExecDialog(New(PInputDialog,
         Init(@Self, 'Line Color',
         'Type 1/Red, 2/Green, 3/Blue, 4/Black',
         ColorBuffer, SizeOf(ColorBuffer)))) = id_Ok
      THEN  BEGIN ...
```

Here, we've embedded the creation and destruction of the dialog box in the middle of the call to *ExecDialog*, so there's nowhere we can link the dialog's transfer buffer to the buffer record of the parent window. This is something that we absolutely *must* do in the program from Listing 10.2, because we're using an external dialog resource. A step-by-step approach to doing the same thing, however, works fine. We just need to make a slight change in the *TMyWindow.DoNothingMuch* method:

```
PROCEDURE TMyWindow.DoNothingMuch(VAR Msg: TMessage);
   VAR
      Dlg: PMyDialog;
      MyResult: Integer;
   BEGIN
      Dlg := New(PMyDialog, Init(@Self, 'Nothing'));
      Dlg^.TransferBuffer := @DDBuffer;
      IF Application^.ExecDialog(Dlg) = id_OK THEN
      ...
```

Instead of trying to do everything in one fell swoop, we take things one at a time. First, we declare a local dialog box variable, just as we did before. The difference is that *this* time, it's not actually a dialog-box variable; instead, it is a *pointer* to that type of dialog box.

Then, using the pointer with a call to NEW, we make it point to a dialog box variable of the appropriate type. We then dereference the pointer (which means that we can now refer to the dialog box variable itself) and, as before, pass the pointer to the parent window's transfer buffer into the dialog variable's *TransferBuffer* field.

After that, the only thing remaining is to execute the dialog, which we can now do either with a (safe) call to *ExecDialog* or a (bold) call to *MyDialog.Execute*. Everything else works the same, and we've bought ourselves a little extra peace of mind.

Integrating Resources into Your Application

- Specifying the Characteristics of Dialog Resources

- Integrating Resources into an Application

- Setting Up Multiple Transfer Buffers

- Creating Multiple Dialog Types

- Initializing Multiple Buffer Fields

- Running Multiple Dialog Resources

In Chapter 10, we saw how to integrate external dialog resources into a Windows application. Because this is such a daunting task, however, the application in Chapter 10 was deliberately simplified in order to clarify only the main points about using a dialog resource in a program. In the process, certain questions were left unasked:

- What happens if you have more than one dialog box? Can you use the same transfer buffer and dialog object types, or do you need one object type for each dialog resource?

- How do you juggle all the command identifiers and dialog resource identifiers in the program?

- Do you need to have different names for the fields of the transfer buffer, the dialog object fields to which they correspond, and the resource identifiers?

In this chapter, we'll look at a more formal and precise way of specifying the contents of dialog boxes. Then, we'll see how to integrate multiple dialog boxes into a "real" application: in the course of doing so, we will answer these and other questions.

Specifying the Characteristics of Dialog Resources

So far, when we've wanted to create a dialog box, it's been a matter of opening the Whitewater Resource Toolkit and then saying "do this, do that, click on that button," and so on. This kind of specification will indeed produce a dialog box, but it depends on two things:

1. You must be using WRT to create the dialog or other resource. If there's a different tool being used, the do- this-then-do-that kind of guidance is extremely unhelpful.

2. You must have time to work with this type of instruction, which is fine for tutorial purposes, but very inefficient for specifying the characteristics of a dialog resource for an experienced Windows application developer.

It will be much more efficient if we give a more-or-less formal specification of the characteristics a dialog box (or other resource) should have. When you are creating multiple resources, you need to have such a specification written down anyway to guide your work. Otherwise, you will spend enormous amounts of time switching back and forth between Turbo Pascal for Windows and the WRT or other resource tool. Did the resource identifier you defined in the program match the resource ID for the appropriate radio button in the dialog box? What was the value of choice X in menu Y? Having a written, formal specification answers these questions for you. Instead of needing to look at the resource itself in the WRT, you can just look at your specification sheet.

Specifying Resources for a Line-Drawing Program

Now, let's specify some resources for the line- drawing program we developed in Chapter 9. You may recall that we used predefined ObjectWindows dialog box types for the dialog boxes in that application. It was simpler than using external dialog resources, but it seemed fairly artificial. Instead of using radio buttons to make a choice of colors, we asked the user to enter a number; likewise for choosing a line style. The only dialog box where "entering a number" seemed natural was in the one to set line thickness, which can vary over a wide range of numeric values.

Therefore, we'll specify three resources for this application:

1. A menu resource identical to the one we created in Chapter 9. This will be shown in Listing 11.1.

2. A dialog resource to change the color of the line being drawn. This will be shown in Listing 11.2.

3. A dialog resource to change the style of the line being drawn. This will be shown in Listing 11.3.

The only thing that might be unfamiliar in the following listings, apart from the formal description technique itself, is the idea of a *group box* in Listing 11.3. You may recall that in a dialog box, we often need to group certain controls together in a single logical group. For example, a group of radio buttons to select line color should function as an integrated unit: if one button is selected, the others must automatically be unselected. To create this kind of group, we use either "Group

Together" in the Control menu of the WRT dialog editor, or (if we haven't already defined the controls) "Start Group" from the same menu.

A group box is related to logical grouping, but is crucially different. A group box is used to *visually* group some related controls together so that the user can see that they work as a unit. It simply draws a rectangle around the controls and displays a line of explanatory text at the top of the rectangle. However, creating a group box has *no effect whatever* on the logical grouping of the controls: it simply puts a rectangle on the screen. You must still put the controls together in a logical group.

To create a group box around radio buttons, use the WRT to set up the resources in Listings 11.1 and 11.2, then, after you've set up the radio buttons in Listing 11.3, click on the "G" *Group Box* icon as shown in Figure 11.1.

Position the cursor above and to the left of the top radio button, then, as usual, drag the mouse just a little to anchor the top left corner of the group box. Next, drag the dot that shows the lower right corner of the group box until all the radio buttons are enclosed in the box, as shown in Figure 11.2.

FIGURE 11.1:

The Group Box icon selected

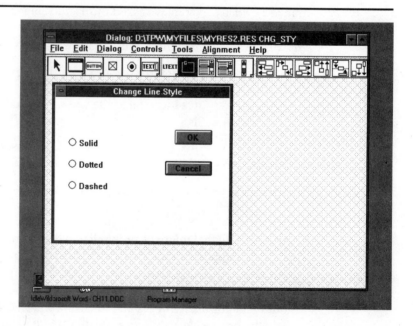

FIGURE 11.2:

The group box enclosing all the radio buttons

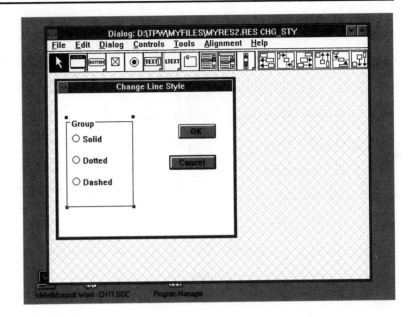

Finally, double-click on the title or border of the group box to bring up its attributes dialog box. Enter the group box's title text and ID: for the title, enter New Line Style, and for the ID, enter -1. Click on *OK* and the completed box will appear, as shown in Figure 11.3.

Listing 11.1

```
{specifying a menu resource}
Menu in file MYRES2.RES: resource name = LINEMENU
Item Text                  Value
&Line                      0
   &New Drawing            100
   Change &Color           200
   Change &Style           300
   Change &Thickness       400
&Help                      901
```

FIGURE 11.3:

The completed group box for the radio buttons

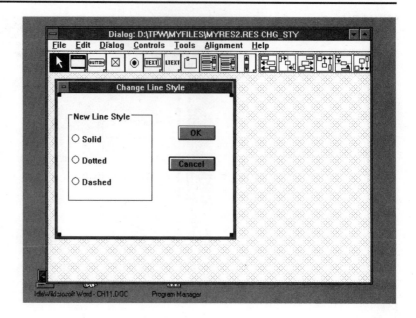

Listing 11.2

```
{specifying a dialog resource to change line color}
Dialog in file MYRES2.RES: resource name = CHG_COL

Dimensions:
x,y = 10,35;
cx,cy = 150,120

Title: Change Line Color
Static text: New Line Color;
ID = -1

Automatic radio buttons --
    left align, space vertically, same size:
ARB text: Red, ID = 201
ARB text: Green, ID = 202
ARB text: Blue, ID = 203
ARB text: Black, ID = 204

Pushbuttons - align right:
PB (pushbutton text): OK, ID = 1
DPB (default pushbutton text): Cancel, ID = 2
```

Listing 11.3

```
{specifying a dialog resource to change line style}
Dialog in file MYRES2.RES: resource name = CHG_STY

Dimensions:
x,y = 10,35
cx,cy = 150, 120

Title: Change Line Style

Radio buttons: left align, space vertically, same size.
ARB text: Solid, ID = 301;
ARB text: Dotted, ID = 302
ARB text: Dashed, ID = 303
Group box to surround radio buttons:
Text for group box: New Line Style
ID = -1
Pushbuttons - right align:
PB text: OK, ID = 1
DPB text: Cancel, ID = 2
```

Integrating Resources into an Application

There are a few tricks in handling multiple dialog boxes; these go beyond what we saw in the simplified example of Chapter 9. The ideas and techniques are illustrated in Listing 11.4.

Listing 11.4

```
PROGRAM Listing11_4;
{  Shows how to incorporate dialog boxes and
   other resources into a non-vacuous program. }

USES STRINGS, WINTYPES, WINPROCS, WOBJECTS, STDDLGS;

{$R MyRes2.res }
CONST
   {menu choice identifiers}
   cm_New   = 100;
   cm_Color = 200;
   cm_Style = 300;
```

```
    cm_Thick = 400;
    cm_Help  = 901;

    {line color dialog button identifiers}
    id_RedBtn   = 201;
    id_GreenBtn = 202;
    id_BlueBtn  = 203;
    id_BlackBtn = 204;

    {line style dialog button identifiers}
    id_SolidBtn  = 301;
    id_DottedBtn = 302;
    id_DashedBtn = 303;

    {color identifiers}
    red = 1;
    green = 2;
    blue = 3;
    black = 4;

    {style identifiers}
    solid = 1;
    dotted = 2;
    dashed = 3;

{========================================================= }
{ ========= TYPE DEFINITION SECTION OF PROGRAM ======= }
{========================================================= }
TYPE
    TMyApp = OBJECT(TApplication)
       PROCEDURE InitMainWindow; VIRTUAL;
       END;

    {Line color dialog transfer record}
    ColorTransferBuffer = RECORD
       RedBtn,
       GreenBtn,
       BlueBtn,
       BlackBtn : WORD;
       END;

    {Line style dialog transfer record}
    StyleTransferBuffer = RECORD
       SolidBtn,
       DottedBtn,
```

```
      DashedBtn   : WORD;
      END;

PMyWindow = ^TMyWindow;
TMyWindow = OBJECT(TWindow)
    ColorBuffer : ColorTransferBuffer;
    StyleBuffer : StyleTransferBuffer;
    dc: HDC;
    LButtonDown: BOOLEAN;
    MyPen: HPen;
    PenSize: INTEGER;
    PenColor : TColorRef;
    PenStyle : INTEGER;
    Points: PCollection;
    CONSTRUCTOR Init(AParent: PWindowsObject;
       ATitle: PChar);
    DESTRUCTOR Done; VIRTUAL;
    FUNCTION CanClose: BOOLEAN; VIRTUAL;
    PROCEDURE WMLButtonDown(VAR Msg: TMessage);
       VIRTUAL wm_First + wm_LButtonDown;
    PROCEDURE WMLButtonUp(VAR Msg: TMessage);
       VIRTUAL wm_First + wm_LButtonUp;
    PROCEDURE WMMouseMove(VAR Msg: TMessage);
       VIRTUAL wm_First + wm_MouseMove;
    PROCEDURE SetPenColor(NewColor: INTEGER);
    PROCEDURE SetPenStyle(NewStyle: INTEGER);
    PROCEDURE SetPenSize(NewSize: INTEGER);
    PROCEDURE Paint(PaintDC: HDC;
       VAR PaintInfo: TPaintStruct); VIRTUAL;
    PROCEDURE NewDraw(VAR Msg: TMessage);
       VIRTUAL cm_First + cm_New;
    PROCEDURE ChangeColor(VAR Msg: TMessage);
       VIRTUAL cm_First + cm_Color;
    PROCEDURE ChangeStyle(VAR Msg: TMessage);
       VIRTUAL cm_First + cm_Style;
    PROCEDURE ChangeThickness(VAR Msg: TMessage);
       VIRTUAL cm_First + cm_Thick;
    PROCEDURE Help(VAR Msg: TMessage);
       VIRTUAL cm_First + cm_Help;
    END;

{dialog box type for changing line color}
PColorDialog = ^TColorDialog;
TColorDialog = OBJECT (TDialog)
    RedBtn,
```

```
         GreenBtn,
         BlueBtn,
         BlackBtn    : PRadioButton;
         CONSTRUCTOR Init(AParent:PWindowsObject;
                          ATitle:PChar);
         END;

    {dialog box type for changing line style}
    PStyleDialog = ^TStyleDialog;
    TStyleDialog = OBJECT (TDialog)
       SolidBtn,
       DottedBtn,
       DashedBtn     : PRadioButton;
       CONSTRUCTOR Init (AParent:PWindowsObject;
                         ATitle:PChar);
       END;

    {object type to save drawing for repainting}
    PDPoint = ^TDPoint;
    TDPoint = OBJECT(TObject)
       X, Y: INTEGER;
       CONSTRUCTOR Init(AX, AY: INTEGER);
       END;

{==================}
{TMyWindow methods}
{==================}
CONSTRUCTOR TMyWindow.Init(AParent: PWindowsObject;
               ATitle: PChar);
    BEGIN
    TWindow.Init(AParent, ATitle);
    Attr.Menu := LoadMenu(HInstance, 'linemenu');
    WITH ColorBuffer DO
       BEGIN
       RedBtn := bf_unchecked;
       GreenBtn := bf_unchecked;
       BlueBtn := bf_unchecked;
       BlackBtn := bf_unchecked;
       END;

    WITH StyleBuffer DO
       BEGIN
       SolidBtn := bf_unchecked;
       DottedBtn := bf_unchecked;
       DashedBtn := bf_unchecked;
```

```
          END;
       LButtonDown := FALSE;
       PenSize := 1;
       PenStyle := ps_Solid;
       PenColor := 0;
       MyPen := CreatePen(PenStyle, PenSize, PenColor);
       Points := New(PCollection, Init(50, 50));
       END;

DESTRUCTOR TMyWindow.Done;
    BEGIN
    Dispose(Points, Done);
    DeleteObject(MyPen);
    TWindow.Done;
    END;

FUNCTION TMyWindow.CanClose: BOOLEAN;
    VAR
        Reply: INTEGER;
    BEGIN
        CanClose := TRUE;
        Reply := MessageBox(HWindow,
                'Do you want to save your work?',
                'Window content has changed',
                mb_YesNoCancel or mb_IconQuestion);
        IF (Reply = id_Yes) OR (Reply = id_Cancel)
            THEN CanClose := FALSE;
    END;

PROCEDURE TMyWindow.WMLButtonDown(VAR Msg: TMessage);
    BEGIN
    Points^.FreeAll;
    InvalidateRect(HWindow, NIL, TRUE);
    IF not LButtonDown
    THEN  BEGIN
            LButtonDown := TRUE;
            SetCapture(HWindow);
            dc := GetDC(HWindow);
            SelectObject(dc, MyPen);
            MoveTo(dc, Msg.LParamLo, Msg.LParamHi);
            Points^.Insert(New(PDPoint,
                Init(Msg.LParamLo, Msg.LParamHi)));
            END;
    END;
```

```
PROCEDURE TMyWindow.WMMouseMove(VAR Msg: TMessage);
   BEGIN
   IF LButtonDown
   THEN   BEGIN
          LineTo(dc, INTEGER(Msg.LParamLo),
               INTEGER(Msg.LParamHi));
          Points^.Insert(New(PDPoint,
               Init(INTEGER(Msg.LParamLo),
               INTEGER(Msg.LParamHi))));
          END;
   END;

PROCEDURE TMyWindow.WMLButtonUp(VAR Msg: TMessage);
   BEGIN
   IF LButtonDown
   THEN   BEGIN
          LButtonDown := FALSE;
          ReleaseCapture;
          ReleaseDC(HWindow, dc);
          END;
   END;

PROCEDURE TMyWindow.SetPenColor(NewColor: INTEGER);
BEGIN
   DeleteObject(MyPen);
   CASE NewColor OF
   1: BEGIN
      PenColor := RGB(200,0,0);
      MyPen := CreatePen(PenStyle, PenSize, PenColor);
      END;
   2: BEGIN
      PenColor := RGB(0,200,0);
      MyPen := CreatePen(PenStyle, PenSize, PenColor);
      END;
   3: BEGIN
      PenColor := RGB(0,0,200);
      MyPen := CreatePen(PenStyle, PenSize, PenColor);
      END;
   4: BEGIN
      PenColor := 0;
      MyPen := CreatePen(PenStyle, PenSize, PenColor);
      END;
   ELSE MyPen := CreatePen(PenStyle, PenSize, 0)
   END;
END;
```

```
PROCEDURE TMyWindow.SetPenStyle(NewStyle: INTEGER);
   BEGIN
   DeleteObject(MyPen);
   CASE NewStyle OF
   1: BEGIN
      PenStyle := ps_Solid;
      MyPen := CreatePen(PenStyle, PenSize, PenColor);
      END;
   2: BEGIN
      PenStyle := ps_Dot;
      MyPen := CreatePen(PenStyle, PenSize, PenColor);
      END;
   3: BEGIN
      PenStyle := ps_Dash;
      MyPen := CreatePen(PenStyle, PenSize, PenColor);
      END
   ELSE MyPen := CreatePen(ps_Solid, PenSize, PenColor)
   END;
END;

PROCEDURE TMyWindow.SetPenSize(NewSize: INTEGER);
   BEGIN
   DeleteObject(MyPen);
   MyPen := CreatePen(PenStyle, NewSize, PenColor);
   PenSize := NewSize;
   END;

PROCEDURE TMyWindow.Paint(PaintDC: HDC;
               VAR PaintInfo: TPaintStruct);
   VAR
      First: BOOLEAN;
   {local procedure under TMyWindow.Paint method}
   PROCEDURE DrawLine(P: PDPoint); far;
      BEGIN
      IF First
      THEN MoveTo(PaintDC, P^.X, P^.Y)
      else LineTo(PaintDC, P^.X, P^.Y);
      First := FALSE;
      END;
   {main body of TMyWindow.Paint method}
   BEGIN
      SelectObject(PaintDC, MyPen);
      First := TRUE;
      Points^.ForEach(@DrawLine);
```

```
        END;

PROCEDURE TMyWindow.NewDraw(VAR Msg: TMessage);
    BEGIN
    Points^.FreeAll;
    InvalidateRect(HWindow, NIL, TRUE);
    END;

PROCEDURE TMyWindow.ChangeColor(VAR Msg: TMessage);
    VAR
        Dlg: TColorDialog;
        Reply : INTEGER;
    BEGIN
        Dlg.Init(@Self, 'chg_col');
        Dlg.TransferBuffer := @ColorBuffer;
        Reply := Dlg.Execute;
        Dlg.Done;
        IF Reply = id_OK THEN
            IF ColorBuffer.RedBtn = bf_checked
            THEN SetPenColor(red)
            ELSE IF ColorBuffer.GreenBtn = bf_checked
            THEN SetPenColor(green)
            ELSE IF ColorBuffer.BlueBtn = bf_checked
            THEN SetPenColor(blue)
            ELSE IF ColorBuffer.BlackBtn = bf_checked
            THEN SetPenColor(black)

            {a line for simple error trapping}
            ELSE SetPenColor(black)
        END;

PROCEDURE TMyWindow.ChangeStyle(VAR Msg: TMessage);
    VAR
        Dlg: TStyleDialog;
        Reply : INTEGER;
    BEGIN
        Dlg.Init(@Self, 'chg_sty');
        Dlg.TransferBuffer := @StyleBuffer;
        Reply := Dlg.Execute;
        Dlg.Done;

        IF Reply = id_OK THEN
            IF StyleBuffer.SolidBtn = bf_checked
            THEN SetPenStyle(solid)
            ELSE IF StyleBuffer.DottedBtn = bf_checked
```

```
            THEN SetPenStyle(dotted)
            ELSE IF StyleBuffer.DashedBtn = bf_checked
            THEN SetPenStyle(dashed)
            {a line for simple error trapping}
            ELSE SetPenStyle(solid)
      END;

PROCEDURE TMyWindow.ChangeThickness(VAR Msg: TMessage);
   VAR
      ThickBuffer: ARRAY[0..5] of CHAR;
      NewSize, ErrorPos: INTEGER;
   BEGIN
      Str(PenSize, ThickBuffer);
      IF Application^.ExecDialog(New(PInputDialog,
         Init(@Self, 'Line Thickness',
         'Input a new thickness:',
         ThickBuffer, SizeOf(ThickBuffer)))) = id_Ok
       THEN BEGIN
            Val(ThickBuffer, NewSize, ErrorPos);
            IF ErrorPos = 0 THEN SetPenSize(NewSize);
            END;
   END;

PROCEDURE TMyWindow.Help(VAR Msg: TMessage);
   BEGIN
   MessageBox(HWindow, 'Not yet implemented',
      'Help', mb_Ok or mb_IconExclamation);
   END;

{==================}
{ TDPoint methods}
{==================}
CONSTRUCTOR TDPoint.Init(AX, AY: INTEGER);
   BEGIN
   X := AX;
   Y := AY;
   END;


{====================}
{Dialog Object Methods}
{====================}
CONSTRUCTOR TColorDialog.Init(AParent:PWindowsObject;
                             ATitle:PChar);

   BEGIN
   TDialog.init(aparent, atitle);
```

```
      NEW(RedBtn, initResource(@Self, id_RedBtn));
      NEW(GreenBtn, initResource(@Self, id_GreenBtn));
      NEW(BlueBtn, initResource(@Self, id_BlueBtn));
      NEW(BlackBtn, initResource(@Self, id_BlackBtn));
      END;

CONSTRUCTOR TStyleDialog.Init(AParent:PWindowsObject;
                             ATitle:PChar);
      BEGIN
      TDialog.init(aparent, atitle);
      NEW(SolidBtn, initResource(@Self, id_SolidBtn));
      NEW(DottedBtn, initResource(@Self, id_DottedBtn));
      NEW(DashedBtn, initResource(@Self, id_DashedBtn));
      END;

{===============}
{TMyApp methods}
{===============}
PROCEDURE TMyApp.InitMainWindow;
      BEGIN
      MainWindow := New(PMyWindow, Init(NIL, 'Listing 11.4'));
      END;

{=========================================}
{global object variable for application}
{=========================================}
VAR
      MyApp : TMyApp;

{==========================}
{main body of program}
{==========================}
BEGIN
      MyApp.Init('Listing11_4');
      MyApp.Run;
      MyApp.Done;
END.
```

Let's take a look at how this works—leaving aside, of course, the points that we've already covered in previous chapters.

The first new wrinkle is that we've separated the different command and resource identifier constants by their type and by what resources they refer to. This has nothing to do with how well the program will work, but has a lot to do with how easily the program code can be understood.

Setting Up Multiple Transfer Buffers

Each menu choice has its own resource ID, as does each button in each dialog box. Because the dialog boxes have different numbers of buttons, we have defined a separate transfer buffer type for each dialog box. The buffer type for the color-change dialog box is called *ColorTransferBuffer*; it has four fields, one for each of the buttons in the dialog. The buffer type for the style-change dialog box is called *Style-TransferBuffer*; it has three fields, one for each button in its corresponding dialog object type and resource. If the two dialogs had exactly the same type, number, and order of buttons, we could in principle use a single buffer type (and a single buffer field in the parent window) to get data in and out of the dialog boxes. This is a tweak that might produce smaller compiled code size at the price of making the source program a little less clear. As before, the fields in the buffer type are WORDs, which is the appropriate type for the checked/unchecked values of the buttons.

As expected, in the parent window type *TMyWindow*, we have two transfer buffer fields: one for the color dialog box, and one for the style dialog box. We don't need to have a field for the dialog box that changes the line's width, because that dialog box isn't associated with an external dialog resource. Everything else in *TMy-Window* is the same as it was before.

Creating Multiple Dialog Types

Next, we create two different dialog box object types, both descended from *TDialog*. The *TColorDialog* type has four fields of type *PRadioButton*, meaning that each field holds a pointer to a radio button. There's also a constructor *TColorDialog.Init* method; this is needed to call NEW, which creates the buttons as dynamic variables that exist while the dialog is open, and to initialize the button variables with a call to *InitResource*, which we'll discuss in a moment.

The structure of the object type for the style dialog box is identical to that of the color dialog box, except that it has three fields instead of four; these correspond to the three buttons in the style dialog resource.

Initializing Multiple Buffer Fields

The next new feature appears in the constructor method for the *TMyWindow* object type. As before, we call the inherited *TWindow.Init* method from the ancestor type. Then, we use separate WITH statements to initialize each transfer buffer field in a window of this type. Remember that this step has nothing to do with the external dialog resource—at least, not yet. At this point, we're just loading the appropriate values into the buffer fields of the parent window. In the second line of this method, we also use *LoadMenu* to activate LINEMENU, the appropriate menu resource for this application.

The procedures and methods to close a window, to set pen color and style, and to respond to mouse clicks, don't change at all from the listing in Chapter 9. This is a good example of modular programming: we can make changes in a few parts of the program (i.e., the dialog boxes and the parts of the program that directly interact with them) and leave the rest of the program as is.

Running Multiple Dialog Resources

The *TMyWindowChangeColor* method, which is invoked in response to a menu choice, has changed quite a bit because it now calls an external dialog resource. It first creates a variable (*Dlg*) of the appropriate dialog object type (*TColorDialog*); this variable will "stand in" for the dialog resource in the program code. We initialize the dialog variable, linking it to the CHG_COL dialog resource in the MyRes2.Res resource file we named at the beginning of the program. As we did in Chapter 10, we then initialize the dialog variable's buttons by loading them with the values from the parent window's transfer buffer; with the same step, we link the transfer buffer to the dialog variable's button fields so that when the dialog is closed, the button values will be copied into the transfer buffer.

The rest of the method is fairly ordinary: the dialog is executed with a call to the variable's *Execute* method, which it inherits from *TDialog*; based on the values in the transfer buffer, the program then executes the *SetPenColor* procedure with the appropriate color parameter. This business of nested IF..THEN..ELSE statements to check the states of radio buttons is a little messy, but there's no straightforward way to use anything that might look neater, such as a CASE statement.

With the expected changes to account for the fact that we're using a different dialog box, the *TMyWindow.ChangeStyle* method is essentially the same as the *ChangeColor* method. The *ChangeThickness* method hasn't changed at all from Listing 9.4, because we're still using a text-input dialog box to prompt the user for a line thickness; this makes sense because of the large number of values that might be entered. In this case, it would be a waste of time and effort to try to cover all the possibilities by using radio buttons.

The *TColorDialog.Init* and *TStyleDialog.Init* methods are, again, essentially the same. Each begins by calling the inherited *Init* method from *TDialog*. Then, each initializes its radio buttons: the first parameter in the NEW statement is the name of the field in the dialog object. The second parameter embeds a call to *InitResource* that links the external button resource (through its resource identifier defined in the CONST section of the program) to the button field in the dialog object type. The rest of the program is identical to Listing 9.4.

Creating and Using Accelerators

- Creating Accelerators in WRT

- Integrating Accelerators into an Application

12

So far, we've seen how to create a Windows application with menus, dialog boxes, and line-drawing capabilities. A very common feature of menus, however, has been missing: the availability of speed keys, or *accelerators*, that allow the user to bypass the menus by using a key combination.

For example, in Turbo Pascal itself, you can copy a selected block of text to the clipboard by opening the Edit menu and selecting "Copy." This is a two-step process that works just fine. However, it's faster simply to press *Ctrl-Insert*, the key combination that automatically executes the "Copy" menu command without any need to open the menu.

Turbo Pascal for Windows makes it very easy to create and use accelerators. In outline, it works like this. First, you use the WRT to create an accelerator table: it consists of the key combinations you want to use and, for each key, the value it should return when pressed. The value of each key combination should be the same as the value returned by selecting the corresponding menu choice. Thus, if the value returned by Line/Change Color is 200, then the accelerator for that menu choice should return a value of 200.

Once you've created the accelerator table, you save it into a resource file that you're using with your program. You then add information about the accelerator keys to the text of the menu choices in your menu resource. Finally, in the source code of your TPW program, you call two methods to load the accelerators into your program. That's all you need.

Creating Accelerators in the WRT

In this section, we'll add accelerators to the menu of the program from Listing 11.4. We'll add three:

Shift-Alt-C to change the line color

Shift-Alt-S to change the line style

Shift-Alt-T to change the line thickness

To activate any of these accelerators, the user will simply hold down the *Shift* and *Alt* keys while pressing the appropriate letter key. There's nothing absolute about using two keys (*Shift-Alt*) and a letter; we could have used the *Control* key (*Ctrl-C, Ctrl-S, Ctrl-T*), the *Alt* key (*Alt-C, Alt-S, Alt-T*), or some combination thereof. We could even have used the *Shift* key (*Shift-C, Shift-S, Shift-T*), though obviously this would be a bad move if the user ever needed to type an uppercase C, S, or T. Likewise, it's a bad idea to assign an accelerator to a function key by itself, because these are almost always used for their own purposes by Windows programs.

The reason for using *Shift-Alt* as the basis for our accelerators is that it's a pretty safe choice. There are a lot of programs that assign special meanings to combinations of the *Control* and *Alt* keys by themselves; Windows programs, for example, commonly use *Alt-F* to open the File menu, and *Ctrl-C* is a very common key combination used to terminate a program process. *Shift-Alt*, on the other hand, isn't likely to interfere with anything.

This spotlights another important point, however: you need to keep track of what key combinations your program is using for different purposes so that you don't end up making the same key combination try to perform two different tasks in the same program context. A formal, written record of the accelerators you use can be just as helpful as the record of your other resource characteristics.

The Accelerator Editor

To set up an accelerator table, you should first make sure that you have the menu choice values that you intend to assign to the accelerator keys. In this case, that means looking at the specification you wrote up for the *LineMenu* resource. The values returned by each menu choice that will get an accelerator are as follows:

Change Color: 200

Change Style: 300

Change Thickness: 400

Each accelerator key combination will return the same value as its corresponding menu choice, so the program won't know (or care) if the user made a menu selection or pressed the accelerator key combination.

Open the WRT accelerator editor by selecting the *Accel* icon button (marked "A") in the icon palette in the WRT main window. It should open as shown in Figure 12.1.

FIGURE 12.1:

The WRT accelerator editor

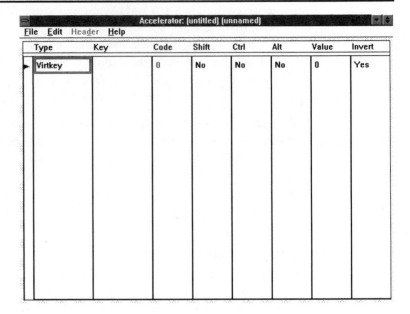

Type	Key	Code	Shift	Ctrl	Alt	Value	Invert
Virtkey		0	No	No	No	0	Yes

At the moment, the accelerator editor has eight columns open. You move from one column to the next in the usual way: by pressing *Tab* or clicking the mouse. Each column contains a different type of information about the accelerator being created, as follows:

Type: This indicates if the accelerator is defined as a "virtual key" (a special kind of key definition kept by Windows) or as an ASCII key. The principal difference between the two is how they are represented in the accelerator table, though there are a few keys that can only be represented in one way: *F5*, for example, must be represented as a virtual key, while the exclamation mark must be represented in ASCII . You can toggle back and forth between the two types by pressing the *spacebar* when the Type column is selected.

Key: This shows the specific key chosen for the accelerator. If you're planning to make *Shift-Alt-C* an accelerator combination (as, indeed, we are), then this column will display an uppercase c if the *Virtkey* type is selected and a lowercase c if the *Ascii* type is selected. Note that this column has nothing to do with what other keys should be pressed (e.g., *Shift* and *Alt*) to activate the accelerator; they are handled in another column further to the right. When we do assign values to those columns, the contents of the Key column may change: if the *Ascii* type is selected, for instance, and we change the *Ctrl* column to indicate Yes, it will change from c to ^c.

Code: This column is automatically filled in with the accelerator's *keyboard scan code*. The keyboard scan code is different from the ASCII code for the key, but you generally should not have to worry about it. One warning: some older, off-brand PC clones with nonstandard BIOSes used idiosyncratic keyboard scan codes, especially for special keys such as the *Scroll Lock* key. In the unlikely event that a user runs your program on one of these older clones, the accelerators might not work.

Shift: This indicates whether or not the *Shift* key should be held down to activate the accelerator. This column can only be used if the *Virtkey* type is selected.

Ctrl: Similar to the Shift column, this column determines if the *Control* key must be held down to activate the accelerator. This column can only be used if the *Virtkey* type is selected.

Alt: Similar to the Shift and Ctrl columns, this column determines if the *Alt* key must be held down to activate the accelerator. This column can only be used if the *Virtkey* type is selected.

Value: This column contains the control ID number for the accelerator in the current row of the table. For example, when we define an accelerator for the "Change Color" choice in the Line menu, this column will contain the number 200, because (1) that is the value we assigned to the corresponding menu choice when we created it in the menu editor, and (2) that is the value assigned to the corresponding command constant in the source code of the program. This ID number, by the way, does not need to be different from the ID numbers used to identify entities in other resources: just like a local variable in a procedure, its scope is restricted to the accelerator table and won't clash with other identifiers in, for example, dialog boxes.

Invert: This column determines whether or not the menu item associated with the accelerator will be highlighted when the user presses the accelerator key combination. It toggles between yes and no, but has no effect on how the accelerator works.

One other column, the Symbol column, is displayed if you are editing a header file for an accelerator table. You usually won't need to worry about this, so we won't pursue the topic here.

Defining an Accelerator Table

To define the accelerators for our line-drawing application, enter the following values in the accelerator table:

	Accelerator 1	Accelerator 2	Accelerator 3
Type	Virtkey	Virtkey	Virtkey
Key	C	S	T
Shift	Yes	Yes	Yes
Ctrl	No	No	No
Alt	Yes	Yes	Yes
Value	200	300	400

When you're finished, the accelerator editor should look like Figure 12.2. Save it into the MYRES2.RES file under the resource ID `linekeys`.

FIGURE 12.2: The accelerator editor with values loaded

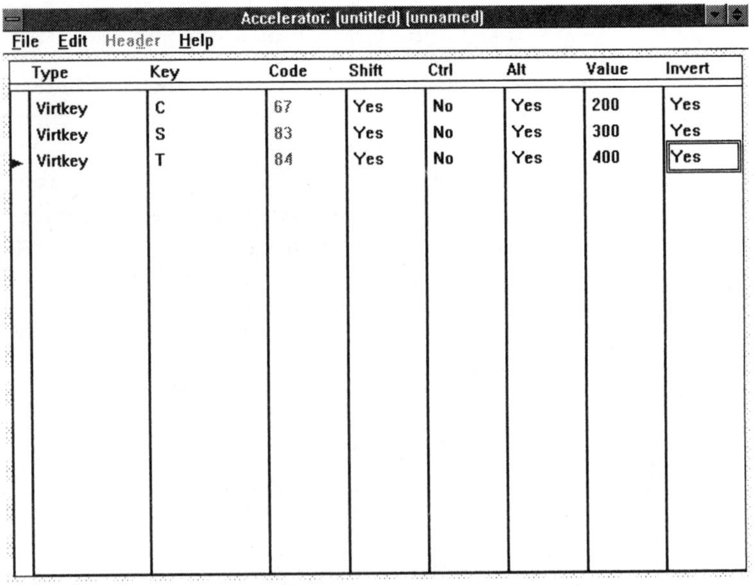
Accelerator: (untitled) (unnamed)
File Edit Header Help
Type Key Code Shift Ctrl Alt Value Invert
Virtkey C 67 Yes No Yes 200 Yes
Virtkey S 83 Yes No Yes 300 Yes
Virtkey T 84 Yes No Yes 400 Yes

Integrating Accelerators into an Application

Now that the accelerator table has been created, there are two more steps to take. First, we must modify the menu resource so that the menu-choice text alerts the user to the existence of the accelerator key combinations. Second, we must load the accelerator resource into the program by making a slight addition to the source code.

Changing the Menu Resource

To change the menu resource, we simply call up the menu in MYRES2.RES from the WRT menu editor. We want the key combinations for the accelerators to be displayed next to their corresponding menu choices. Thus, we'll go into the menu and, on the same line as each menu choice with an accelerator, insert a tab and then the keys for the accelerator.

However, you can't just press the *Tab* key to insert a tab. The code to insert a tab in a menu resource is \t (backslash+t). This code, familiar if you're also a C programmer, contains a backslash to tell the WRT that a special character is coming, and then a *t* to indicate that it's a tab.

When you're finished, the menu editor should look like Figure 12.3. Save it to MYRES2.RES under the same resource name (linemenu). You should test the menu before leaving the menu editor, and it should look like Figure 12.4.

Loading the Accelerator Table

The final step is to load the accelerator table resource into the program. Because we've already included the MYRES2.RES resource file with the *$R* compiler directive, the only additional step is to add one line to the *TMyApp.InitMainWindow* method from Listing 11.4, as shown below:

```
PROCEDURE TMyApp.InitMainWindow;
    BEGIN
    MainWindow := New(PMyWindow, Init(NIL, 'Listing 11.4'));
    HAccTable := LoadAccelerators(HInstance, 'linekeys');
    END;
```

FIGURE 12.3:

The menu resource with accelerator text added

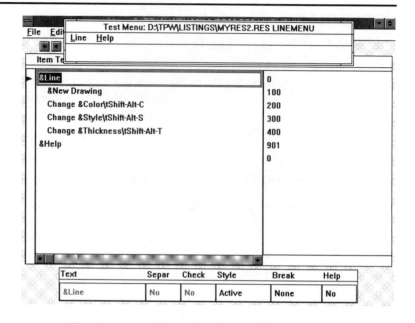

FIGURE 12.4:

The menu resource with test menu displayed

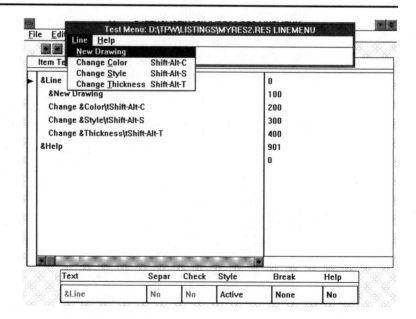

Here, *HAccTable* is a handle to an accelerator table that is associated with the calling application. *LoadAccelerators* is a function that takes two parameters: a handle to the calling application, and the resource ID of the accelerator table. Because this is a one-line change in Listing 11.4, we won't print the entire listing, but you should save the new version as `Listing 12.1`.

Opening and Saving
Files and Streams

- **Collections and Streams**

- **File I/O with Streams**

- **Opening and Saving Files**

- **Modifying the Object Types**

- **Initializing and Using Streams**

Fite handling in Turbo Pascal for Windows is not terribly difficult, but it is both different and slightly more complex than file handling in standard DOS Turbo Pascal programs. Some of these differences have to do with the fact that TPW programs must operate in the Windows environment. Others, such as working with files of objects, have nothing much to do with Windows, but come from the nature of object-oriented programming.

In this chapter, we'll look first at files of objects and then at standard text files. The first is inherently a little more complicated than the second, and requires more preparatory discussion of *collections* and *streams*—which are roughly the object-oriented equivalents of arrays and typed files. We'll illustrate the concepts by modifying the program in Listing 12.1, adding the ability to create, save, and load files of objects.

Collections and Streams

The starting point for understanding collections and streams is to see how they differ from their non-object-oriented counterparts.

Understanding Collections

The best way to understand collections is to contrast them with *arrays*, to which they bear a few similarities. Although arrays are fast, they are inflexible. An array has to be fully defined at compile time, both in terms of the size of the array and in terms of what each array slot will contain; this is necessitated by the requirement that array elements be stored contiguously in main memory. If you need to add items later, or would like to store items of various sizes in an array, you are generally out of luck.

A TPW collection is designed to sidestep these limitations. Just as you can have an array of pointers (for example, to linked lists in a hash table), you can have an object that *includes* an array of (untyped) pointers to other objects. This is what is meant by "collection."

Of course, using untyped pointers is tricky regardless of whether you're in TPW or doing object-oriented programming. You can't simply use the traditional NEW and

DISPOSE routines, because you and the compiler can't be sure how much memory to allocate or deallocate for the referent of an untyped pointer.

To handle such problems, TPW provides the abstract object type called *TCollection*, which serves as an ancestor for other object types. The *TCollection* type has four fields:

Count: This field holds the number of items currently in the collection, up to the current maximum size of the collection.

Delta: If needed, a collection can increase in size at run time. The delta field specifies the size of the increments. For example, you could specify that if the collection needs to expand beyond its initial size, it will grow by 50 slots at a time (i.e., delta = 50). Although increasing the size of a collection at run time slows down your program, it can be important to have the possibility to do so. Setting delta to zero means that the collection cannot expand at run time.

Items: This holds a pointer to the array of pointers that is the backbone of the *TCollection* object.

Limit: This is the maximum number of elements that can be contained in the collection. Because of the performance penalty from increasing the size of the collection at run time, it's not a bad idea, when setting the initial limit, to think of the collection as an array that must have enough slots to accommodate any probable number of items.

TCollection also has a large number of methods to manipulate the data in its fields. The most important are:

Init: This is the *TCollection* constructor field. It takes two integer parameters: one for the initial size of the collection (to set an initial value for the *Limit* field) and one for the amount by which the size can change (to set the value for the *Delta* field). If you're still new to collections, the obvious question is: why doesn't the *Init* routine have anything in it about the nature of the objects in the collection? The answer is that the array in the collection holds only *untyped pointers* to the objects that the collection "contains." No matter what those objects are or how big they are, the size of the pointers will always be the same. Thus, the *Init* routine doesn't have to worry about the actual items—and it knows how big the pointers will be, since they all occupy the same amount of memory.

Load: This loads items into a collection from a *stream*, which is roughly the object-oriented counterpart of a standard, non-OOP file (see the section on streams later in this chapter). It assumes that the items are descendants of *TObject*, and must be overridden if they are not.

ForEach: This applies a particular procedure (a pointer to which is passed to the method, as its only parameter) to each item in the collection. The items are processed in the order they appear in the collection. The procedure cannot be an object method.

FirstThat and **LastThat:** These methods find an element in the collection based on criteria specified by the user. Each method, if used, returns a pointer to the location of the "found" item matching the criteria, or returns nil if all items fail to match the criteria.

FreeAll: This deletes all items in the collection and de-allocates the memory they occupied. Like *Load*, it assumes that it is dealing with descendants of *TObject*.

Done: This not only deletes all items and de-allocates the memory (by calling *TCollection.FreeAll*), but it also sets the *Limit* field to zero.

Store: This stores the collection and its constituent items in a stream. This method takes the stream as its only parameter.

Predefined Collection Types

As mentioned earlier, *TCollection* is an abstract type, and is not meant to be used as is. It serves as an ancestor type for both ObjectWindows and user-defined collection types.

Two important *TCollection* descendant types are predefined in ObjectWindows: *TSortedCollection* and *TStrCollection*.

TSortedCollection, which is itself an abstract type, automatically keeps its items sorted. How the items are sorted, and on what field, is determined by the specifics of the descendant type derived from *TSortedCollection*. It includes a *Compare* method that checks the key field (the sort field) of new items as they are added to the collection and inserts them in the correct order. *TSortedCollection* also includes a method for binary search (a *lg n* searching algorithm) to find items in the collection. Duplicate keys are not allowed.

TStrCollection, a descendant of *TSortedCollection*, sets up a sorted list of ASCII text strings.

Understanding Streams

A stream is the file I/O counterpart of a collection; it is simply a collection of objects that is en route to some destination. The destination could be a serial port, expanded memory, or—most likely—a disk file. However, Turbo Pascal will not allow you to simply create a typed file of objects. Using a stream solves this problem because the stream itself (that is, the object based on and descended from a *TStream* type) knows that it's dealing with objects and includes *within itself* all the data and methods needed to save and load disk files; the file part itself can still be as "dumb" as ever. In shorthand, you might think of a stream as the sum of

1. a collection of objects

2. information on how to store and load them

3. a disk file

Registering an Object Type for Streaming

Because a stream may have to handle widely different kinds of objects, you have to provide TPW with information about the type of the objects involved before you can send them to a disk file or other device. This is called *registering* the object type with the stream, and uses a predefined TPW procedure, *RegisterType*.

Registering an object type for use with a stream takes a number of steps. The first is the most involved: you need to declare a "stream registration record" that contains information about the stream. Perhaps the most important information contained in this record is the location in memory of the stream's *Load* and *Store* methods, which do much of the hard work associated with opening and saving streams with disk files.

The stream registration record is a predefined TPW type called *TStreamRec*, structured as follows:

```
PStreamRec = ^TStreamRec;
TStreamRec = RECORD
     ObjType: WORD; { an identifier for the type of the object }
     VMTLink : WORD;
     Load : Pointer;   { untyped pointer to the object's LOAD
                         method }
```

```
Store: Pointer;    { untyped pointer to the object's STORE
                          method }
Next: WORD
END;
```

It's conventional to name a stream registration record after the object type it registers, substituting an initial "R" for the initial "T." Thus, in Listing 13.1 (later in this chapter), the *TDPoint* object type is registered with a stream registration record named *RDPoint*.

There are really only three fields in the stream registration record that you need to worry about: the *ObjType* field, the *Load* field, and the *Store* field. *ObjType* gets an integer identifier between 0 and 65,535, but TPW reserves the numbers 0..999 for itself, so you shouldn't use numbers in that range. This field is really little more than a placeholder, because the number you use in this field does not need to be referenced anywhere else in your program, nor does it need to be referenced or defined in any of the units or resources that your program uses. All you need to worry about are two things:

- The number you put in the *ObjType* field of a particular stream registration record must be unique; it must not occur elsewhere in your program.

- This number identifies the type of objects that are saved and loaded by reference to this stream registration record. If you change the number and then attempt to load a stream that you saved under a different *ObjType* number, you'll get an unrecoverable application error because TPW won't have any idea of what it's trying to load.

The *Load* and *Store* fields are set up in basically the same way. When you declare an object type that you plan to use in a stream, you must declare *Load* and *Store* methods for that object type. Because the *Load* and *Store* fields contain pointers to those methods, you simply put the pointer addresses in the fields, as in

```
Load : @TDPoint.Load;
Store: @TDPoint.Store;
```

After creating the stream registration record, the second major step to registering an object type for use with a stream is to ensure that your object type contains appropriate *Load* and *Store* methods. *Load* is a constructor method; *Store* is a standard procedure-type method. We'll look at an example in Listing 13.1 later in this chapter.

The third and final step is to make use of the information you provided in the first step, by setting up a procedure that will actually register the stream. This would be something like

```
PROCEDURE RegisterStream;
    BEGIN
    RegisterType(RCollection);
    RegisterType(RDPoint)
    END;
```

This is, in fact, the procedure we'll use in Listing 13.1 to register a stream for saving line drawings. The first line in the BEGIN..END part of the procedure calls the TPW *RegisterType* routine to register the collection that stores the points, while the second line calls the same routine to register the object type of the points themselves.

File I/O with Streams

Let's proceed with an example. Earlier, we created a line-drawing program that could create drawings as well as change line color, style, and thickness. What it could not do was save a drawing to a file and then reload it when needed. Listing 13.1 adds this capability.

Listing 13.1

```
PROGRAM Listing13_1;
{ Shows how to set up the framework for opening
    and saving line drawings to files. Features
    demonstrated:
        1. Modifying an object type for use in
            a stream.
        2. Setting up a stream registration record.
        3. Registering a stream.
        4. Using standard ObjectWindows FileSave
            and FileLoad dialog boxes.  }

USES STRINGS, WINTYPES, WINPROCS, WOBJECTS, STDDLGS, WINDOS;

{$R MyRes3.res }
CONST
    {menu choice identifiers}
    cm_New     = 101;
    cm_Open    = 102;
```

```
      cm_Save    = 103;
      cm_SaveAs  = 104;

      cm_NewDraw = 100;
      cm_Color = 200;
      cm_Style = 300;
      cm_Thick = 400;
      cm_Help        = 901;

      {line color dialog button identifiers}
      id_RedBtn    = 201;
      id_GreenBtn = 202;
      id_BlueBtn  = 203;
      id_BlackBtn = 204;

      {line style dialog button identifiers}
      id_SolidBtn  = 301;
      id_DottedBtn = 302;
      id_DashedBtn = 303;

      {color identifiers}
      red = 1;
      green = 2;
      blue = 3;
      black = 4;

      {style identifiers}
      solid = 1;
      dotted = 2;
      dashed = 3;

{================================================================ }
{ ========= TYPE DEFINITION SECTION OF PROGRAM ========= }
{================================================================ }
TYPE
      TMyApp = OBJECT(TApplication)
         PROCEDURE InitMainWindow; VIRTUAL;
         END;

      {Line color dialog transfer record}
      ColorTransferBuffer = RECORD
         RedBtn,
         GreenBtn,
         BlueBtn,
         BlackBtn : WORD;
```

```
   END;

{Line style dialog transfer record}
StyleTransferBuffer = RECORD
   SolidBtn,
   DottedBtn,
   DashedBtn   : WORD;
   END;


PMyWindow = ^TMyWindow;
TMyWindow = OBJECT(TWindow)
   ColorBuffer : ColorTransferBuffer;
   StyleBuffer : StyleTransferBuffer;
   dc: HDC;
   LButtonDown: BOOLEAN;
   MyPen: HPen;
   PenSize: INTEGER;
   PenColor : TColorRef;
   PenStyle : INTEGER;
   Points: PCollection;

   { NEW }
   FileName: ARRAY[0..fsPathName] OF CHAR;
   NotSaved, IsNewFile : BOOLEAN;

   CONSTRUCTOR Init(AParent: PWindowsObject;
      ATitle: PChar);
   DESTRUCTOR Done; VIRTUAL;
   FUNCTION CanClose: BOOLEAN; VIRTUAL;
   PROCEDURE WMLButtonDown(VAR Msg: TMessage);
      VIRTUAL wm_First + wm_LButtonDown;
   PROCEDURE WMLButtonUp(VAR Msg: TMessage);
      VIRTUAL wm_First + wm_LButtonUp;
   PROCEDURE WMMouseMove(VAR Msg: TMessage);
      VIRTUAL wm_First + wm_MouseMove;
   PROCEDURE SetPenColor(NewColor: INTEGER);
   PROCEDURE SetPenStyle(NewStyle: INTEGER);
   PROCEDURE SetPenSize(NewSize: INTEGER);
   PROCEDURE Paint(PaintDC: HDC;
      VAR PaintInfo: TPaintStruct); VIRTUAL;

   { NEW }
   PROCEDURE FileNew(VAR Msg: TMessage);
      VIRTUAL cm_First + cm_New;
   PROCEDURE FileOpen(VAR Msg: TMessage);
```

```
          VIRTUAL cm_First + cm_Open;
      PROCEDURE FileSave(VAR Msg: TMessage);
          VIRTUAL cm_First + cm_Save;
      PROCEDURE FileSaveAs(VAR Msg: TMessage);
          VIRTUAL cm_First + cm_SaveAs;
      PROCEDURE LoadFile;
      PROCEDURE SaveFile;

      PROCEDURE NewDraw(VAR Msg: TMessage);
          VIRTUAL cm_First + cm_NewDraw;
      PROCEDURE ChangeColor(VAR Msg: TMessage);
          VIRTUAL cm_First + cm_Color;
      PROCEDURE ChangeStyle(VAR Msg: TMessage);
          VIRTUAL cm_First + cm_Style;
      PROCEDURE ChangeThickness(VAR Msg: TMessage);
          VIRTUAL cm_First + cm_Thick;
      PROCEDURE Help(VAR Msg: TMessage);
          VIRTUAL cm_First + cm_Help;
      END;

{dialog box type for changing line color}
PColorDialog = ^TColorDialog;
TColorDialog = OBJECT (TDialog)
    RedBtn,
    GreenBtn,
    BlueBtn,
    BlackBtn    : PRadioButton;
    CONSTRUCTOR Init(AParent:PWindowsObject;
                     ATitle:PChar);
    END;

{dialog box type for changing line style}
PStyleDialog = ^TStyleDialog;
TStyleDialog = OBJECT (TDialog)
    SolidBtn,
    DottedBtn,
    DashedBtn   : PRadioButton;
    CONSTRUCTOR Init (AParent:PWindowsObject;
                      ATitle:PChar);
    END;

{object type to save drawing for repainting}
PDPoint = ^TDPoint;
TDPoint = OBJECT(TObject)
    X, Y: INTEGER;
```

```
        CONSTRUCTOR Init(AX, AY: INTEGER);

        { NEW }
        CONSTRUCTOR Load(VAR S: TStream);
        PROCEDURE Store(VAR S: TStream);
        END;

{ NEW }
CONST
    RDPoint : TStreamRec
    = (ObjType : 1111;
       VMTLink :OFS(TypeOf(TDPoint)^);
       Load : @TDPoint.Load;
       Store: @TDPoint.Store);

    PROCEDURE RegisterStream;
        BEGIN
        RegisterType(RCollection);
        RegisterType(RDPoint)
        END;

{==================}
{TMyWindow methods}
{==================}
CONSTRUCTOR TMyWindow.Init(AParent: PWindowsObject; ATitle:
PChar);
    BEGIN
    TWindow.Init(AParent, ATitle);
    Attr.Menu := LoadMenu(HInstance, 'linemenu');
    WITH ColorBuffer DO
        BEGIN
        RedBtn := bf_unchecked;
        GreenBtn := bf_unchecked;
        BlueBtn := bf_unchecked;
        BlackBtn := bf_unchecked;
        END;
    WITH StyleBuffer DO
        BEGIN
        SolidBtn := bf_unchecked;
        DottedBtn := bf_unchecked;
        DashedBtn := bf_unchecked;
        END;
    LButtonDown := FALSE;
    PenSize := 1;
    PenStyle := ps_Solid;
```

281

```
    PenColor := 0;
    MyPen := CreatePen(PenStyle, PenSize, PenColor);
    Points := New(PCollection, Init(50, 50));

    { NEW }
    NotSaved := False;
    IsNewFile := True;
    RegisterStream;
    END;

DESTRUCTOR TMyWindow.Done;
    BEGIN
    Dispose(Points, Done);
    DeleteObject(MyPen);
    TWindow.Done;
    END;

FUNCTION TMyWindow.CanClose: BOOLEAN;
    VAR
        Reply: INTEGER;
    BEGIN
        CanClose := TRUE;

        { NEW }
        IF NotSaved
        THEN  BEGIN
                Reply := MessageBox(HWindow,
                    'Do you want to save your work?',
                    'Window content has changed',
                    mb_YesNoCancel or mb_IconQuestion);
                IF (Reply = id_Yes) OR (Reply = id_Cancel)
                THEN CanClose := FALSE;
                END
    END;

PROCEDURE TMyWindow.WMLButtonDown(VAR Msg: TMessage);
    BEGIN
    Points^.FreeAll;
    InvalidateRect(HWindow, NIL, TRUE);
    IF not LButtonDown
    THEN  BEGIN
            LButtonDown := TRUE;
            SetCapture(HWindow);
            dc := GetDC(HWindow);
            SelectObject(dc, MyPen);
```

```
                    MoveTo(dc, Msg.LParamLo, Msg.LParamHi);
                    Points^.Insert(New(PDPoint,
                            Init(Msg.LParamLo, Msg.LParamHi)));
                    END;
            END;

PROCEDURE TMyWindow.WMMouseMove(VAR Msg: TMessage);
        BEGIN
        IF LButtonDown
        THEN  BEGIN
                LineTo(dc, INTEGER(Msg.LParamLo),
                        INTEGER(Msg.LParamHi));
                Points^.Insert(New(PDPoint,
                        Init(INTEGER(Msg.LParamLo),
                        INTEGER(Msg.LParamHi))));
                END;
        END;

PROCEDURE TMyWindow.WMLButtonUp(VAR Msg: TMessage);
        BEGIN
        IF LButtonDown
        THEN  BEGIN
                LButtonDown := FALSE;
                ReleaseCapture;
                ReleaseDC(HWindow, dc);
                END;
        END;

PROCEDURE TMyWindow.SetPenColor(NewColor: INTEGER);
BEGIN
        DeleteObject(MyPen);
        CASE NewColor OF
        1: BEGIN
           PenColor := RGB(200,0,0);
           MyPen := CreatePen(PenStyle, PenSize, PenColor);
           END;
        2: BEGIN
           PenColor := RGB(0,200,0);
           MyPen := CreatePen(PenStyle, PenSize, PenColor);
           END;
        3: BEGIN
           PenColor := RGB(0,0,200);
           MyPen := CreatePen(PenStyle, PenSize, PenColor);
           END;
        4: BEGIN
```

```
            PenColor := 0;
            MyPen := CreatePen(PenStyle, PenSize, PenColor);
            END;
        ELSE MyPen := CreatePen(PenStyle, PenSize, 0)
        END;
END;


PROCEDURE TMyWindow.SetPenStyle(NewStyle: INTEGER);
    BEGIN
    DeleteObject(MyPen);
    CASE NewStyle OF
    1: BEGIN
        PenStyle := ps_Solid;
        MyPen := CreatePen(PenStyle, PenSize, PenColor);
        END;
    2: BEGIN
        PenStyle := ps_Dot;
        MyPen := CreatePen(PenStyle, PenSize, PenColor);
        END;
    3: BEGIN
        PenStyle := ps_Dash;
        MyPen := CreatePen(PenStyle, PenSize, PenColor);
        END
    ELSE MyPen := CreatePen(ps_Solid, PenSize, PenColor)
    END;
END;


PROCEDURE TMyWindow.SetPenSize(NewSize: INTEGER);
    BEGIN
    DeleteObject(MyPen);
    MyPen := CreatePen(PenStyle, NewSize, PenColor);
    PenSize := NewSize;
    END;


PROCEDURE TMyWindow.Paint(PaintDC: HDC;
                VAR PaintInfo: TPaintStruct);
    VAR
        First: BOOLEAN;

    {local procedure under TMyWindow.Paint method}
    PROCEDURE DrawLine(P: PDPoint); far;
        BEGIN
        IF First
        THEN MoveTo(PaintDC, P^.X, P^.Y)
        else LineTo(PaintDC, P^.X, P^.Y);
```

```
            First := FALSE;
            END;

        {main body of TMyWindow.Paint method}
        BEGIN
            SelectObject(PaintDC, MyPen);
            First := TRUE;
            Points^.ForEach(@DrawLine);
        END;

{ NEW METHODS }
PROCEDURE TMyWindow.FileNew(VAR Msg: TMessage);
    BEGIN
        Points^.FreeAll;
        InvalidateRect(HWindow, NIL, TRUE);
        NotSaved := FALSE;
        IsNewFile := TRUE
    END;

PROCEDURE TMyWindow.FileOpen(VAR Msg: TMessage);
    BEGIN
        IF CanClose
        THEN
            IF Application^.ExecDialog(
                NEW(PFileDialog,
                Init(@Self, PChar(sd_FileOpen),
                StrCopy(FileName, '*.*')))) = id_OK
            THEN LoadFile;
    END;

PROCEDURE TMyWindow.FileSave(VAR Msg: TMessage);
    BEGIN
        IF IsNewFile
        THEN FileSaveAs(Msg)
        ELSE SaveFile
    END;

PROCEDURE TMyWindow.FileSaveAs(VAR Msg: TMessage);
    VAR Dlg: PFileDialog;
    BEGIN
        IF IsNewFile
        THEN StrCopy(FileName, '');
```

```
      IF Application^.ExecDialog(New(PFileDialog,
          Init(@Self, PChar(sd_FileSave), FileName))) = id_Ok
      THEN SaveFile
   END;

PROCEDURE TMyWindow.LoadFile;
   VAR
      TempCollection: PCollection;
      FileToLoad: TDosStream;
   BEGIN
      FileToLoad.Init(FileName, stOpen);
      TempCollection := PCollection(FileToLoad.Get);
      FileToLoad.Done;
      IF TempCollection <> NIL
      THEN  BEGIN
            Dispose(Points, Done);
            Points := TempCollection;
            InvalidateRect(HWindow, NIL, TRUE);
            END;
      NotSaved := False;
      IsNewFile := False;
   END;

PROCEDURE TMyWindow.SaveFile;
   VAR
      FileToSave: TDosStream;
   BEGIN
      FileToSave.Init(FileName, stCreate);
      FileToSave.Put(Points);
      FileToSave.Done;
      IsNewFile := False;
      NotSaved := False;
   END;

PROCEDURE TMyWindow.NewDraw(VAR Msg: TMessage);
   BEGIN
   Points^.FreeAll;
   InvalidateRect(HWindow, NIL, TRUE);
   END;

PROCEDURE TMyWindow.ChangeColor(VAR Msg: TMessage);
   VAR
      Dlg: TColorDialog;
```

```
            Reply : INTEGER;
        BEGIN
           Dlg.Init(@Self, 'chg_col');
           Dlg.TransferBuffer := @ColorBuffer;
           Reply := Dlg.Execute;
           Dlg.Done;

           IF Reply = id_OK THEN
               IF ColorBuffer.RedBtn = bf_checked
               THEN SetPenColor(red)
               ELSE IF ColorBuffer.GreenBtn = bf_checked
               THEN SetPenColor(green)
               ELSE IF ColorBuffer.BlueBtn = bf_checked
               THEN SetPenColor(blue)
               ELSE IF ColorBuffer.BlackBtn = bf_checked
               THEN SetPenColor(black)
               ELSE SetPenColor(black)
        END;

    PROCEDURE TMyWindow.ChangeStyle(VAR Msg: TMessage);
        VAR
            Dlg: TStyleDialog;
            Reply : INTEGER;
        BEGIN
           Dlg.Init(@Self, 'chg_sty');
           Dlg.TransferBuffer := @StyleBuffer;
           Reply := Dlg.Execute;
           Dlg.Done;

           IF Reply = id_OK THEN
               IF StyleBuffer.SolidBtn = bf_checked
               THEN SetPenStyle(solid)
               ELSE IF StyleBuffer.DottedBtn = bf_checked
               THEN SetPenStyle(dotted)
               ELSE IF StyleBuffer.DashedBtn = bf_checked
               THEN SetPenStyle(dashed)
               ELSE SetPenStyle(solid)
        END;

    PROCEDURE TMyWindow.ChangeThickness(VAR Msg: TMessage);
        VAR
            ThickBuffer: ARRAY[0..5] of CHAR;
            NewSize, ErrorPos: INTEGER;
        BEGIN
           Str(PenSize, ThickBuffer);
```

```
        IF Application^.ExecDialog(New(PInputDialog,
            Init(@Self, 'Line Thickness',
            'Input a new thickness:',
            ThickBuffer, SizeOf(ThickBuffer)))) = id_Ok
          THEN BEGIN
              Val(ThickBuffer, NewSize, ErrorPos);
              IF ErrorPos = 0 THEN SetPenSize(NewSize);
              END;
      END;

PROCEDURE TMyWindow.Help(VAR Msg: TMessage);
    BEGIN
    MessageBox(HWindow, 'Not yet implemented',
        'Help', mb_Ok or mb_IconExclamation);
    END;


{================}
{ TDPoint methods}
{================}
CONSTRUCTOR TDPoint.Init(AX, AY: INTEGER);
    BEGIN
    X := AX;
    Y := AY;
    END;

{ NEW }
CONSTRUCTOR TDPoint.Load(VAR S: TStream);
    BEGIN
        S.Read(X, SizeOf(X));
        S.Read(Y, SizeOf(Y))
    END;

PROCEDURE TDPoint.Store(VAR S: TStream);
    BEGIN
        S.Write(X, SizeOf(X));
        S.Write(Y, SizeOf(Y))
    END;


{======================}
{Dialog Object Methods}
{======================}
CONSTRUCTOR TColorDialog.Init(AParent:PWindowsObject;
                              ATitle:PChar);
```

```
    BEGIN
    TDialog.init(aparent, atitle);
    NEW(RedBtn, initResource(@Self, id_RedBtn));
    NEW(GreenBtn, initResource(@Self, id_GreenBtn));
    NEW(BlueBtn, initResource(@Self, id_BlueBtn));
    NEW(BlackBtn, initResource(@Self, id_BlackBtn));
    END;

CONSTRUCTOR TStyleDialog.Init(AParent:PWindowsObject;
                              ATitle:PChar);
    BEGIN
    TDialog.init(aparent, atitle);
    NEW(SolidBtn, initResource(@Self, id_SolidBtn));
    NEW(DottedBtn, initResource(@Self, id_DottedBtn));
    NEW(DashedBtn, initResource(@Self, id_DashedBtn));
    END;

{===============}
{TMyApp methods}
{===============}
PROCEDURE TMyApp.InitMainWindow;
    BEGIN
    MainWindow := New(PMyWindow, Init(NIL, 'Listing 13.1'));
    HAccTable := LoadAccelerators(HInstance, 'linekeys');
    END;

{=========================================}
{global object variable for application}
{=========================================}
VAR
    MyApp : TMyApp;

{=====================}
{main body of program}
{=====================}
BEGIN
    MyApp.Init('Listing13_1');
    MyApp.Run;
    MyApp.Done;
END.
```

Before you can run Listing 13.1, you need to modify the menu resource in *MYRES2.RES* so that it includes a File menu and appropriate menu choices. The

easiest thing to do in WRT is simply to open up some new lines at the top of the
LINEMENU menu resource after &Help, then add the following:

Item Text	Value
&File	0
New	101
Open	102
Save	103
Save As...	104

Then save the modified resource as MYRES3.RES, the resource file named in Listing 13.1.

> **NOTE**
>
> To add blank lines within a menu resource when using the WRT, select the
> last value in the resource (in this case, 901) and press *Enter*. This creates a
> new blank line. Now click repeatedly on the up-arrow icon button to move
> the blank line where you want it in the list. Repeat the process to create
> more blank lines, or copy the blank line into the clipboard and paste it into the
> list as many times as you need.

There are quite a few new features in Listing 13.1, so let's look at them one at a time.
We'll start with the easiest: using TPW and ObjectWindows standard routines and
types to open and close files.

Opening and Saving Files

TPW makes it fairly easy to open and close files. The parts of the job that require
interaction with MS-DOS are handled by the WinDOS unit, which you can see is included in Listing 13.1's USES clause at the top of the program. The fancier parts—
setting up a file-open or file-save dialog box, displaying the contents of the current
directory, and letting the user enter a file name—are handled by the predefined
ObjectWindows type *TFileDialog*, provided in the unit STDDLGS and the resource
file STDDLGS.RES.

You might wonder why, if we are using a dialog box whose appearance is defined
in STDDLGS.RES, this resource file is not named in Listing 13.1 with a {$R} compiler

directive. The reason is that the resource file *is* named by the unit STDDLGS, and we named the unit in the USES clause. This makes STDDLGS.RES available, if indirectly, to the program.

The place where the file-open dialog box puts in an appearance is in the *TMyWindow.FileOpen* method. In that method, we first test the Boolean variable *CanClose* to determine if the current window contents have been changed without having been saved to disk. If the haven't been saved, then we call *Application^.ExecDialog* with a call to NEW and the predefined pointer type *PFileDialog*, which points to a *TFileDialog*-type object. The *Init* method is called in the usual way, and takes three parameters:

@Self (which we've seen before—in Chapter 10 under "Execute the Dialog")

PChar(sd_FileOpen) delivers a PCHAR representation of the predefined identifier for the standard dialog box type to open files

StrCopy(FileName, '*.*') copies the file specification `*.*` into the dialog box's *File Name* field for the list of files to select from. (The `*.*` means that all files will be displayed. We could just as easily have made it `*.PAS`, which would have displayed all Pascal source code files, or `S*.*`, which would have displayed all files whose names begin with the letter *S*.)

If the dialog box executes successfully and returns a value of *id_OK*, this method calls the *TMyWindow.LoadFile* method, which is just a little more complicated. This method first creates two local variables: a pointer to a *TCollection* object to hold the file contents when loaded, and a *TDosStream* object to provide the conduit through which the file will be loaded into the collection. It then initializes the stream variable by calling the predefined method *TDosStream.Init*, which takes two parameters: first, a file name, and second, an "access mode," which denotes the way the stream is being used. Different access mode identifiers are defined for different operations:

Access Mode	Operation
stCreate	Creates file
stOpenRead	Opens read-only file
stOpenWrite	Opens file for writing
stOpen	Opens file for reading and writing

The *TempCollection* variable then gets a pointer to the data loaded from the file, after which the *FileToLoad* variable's inherited *Done* method (from *TDosStream*) is called. The method then checks to see if the file was empty; if it isn't, it disposes of the data in the parent window's *Points* field and then passes the pointer in *TempCollection* to *Points*, from which the file's contents are recreated in the window. In order to do this, the predefined *InvalidateRect* routine is called. This routine takes three parameters:

- *HWindow*, a handle to the parent window.

- A *TRect*-type object indicating the region to be updated in the parent window's client area. (Use NIL to indicate the entire client area.)

- A Boolean value indicating whether the region should be erased (true) or not (false) prior to updating.

Finally, the *NotSaved* and *IsNewFile* Boolean variables are set to false to indicate that no changes have (yet) been made in this window's contents.

Saving a file works pretty much the same, and in fact, is a bit less complicated. The only major difference is that it works through three methods instead of two. If the file has already been saved and the user doesn't wish to change the file name, then there's no need to open a dialog box to name the file and specify its directory. Thus, the menu command-response method *TMyWindow.FileSave* first checks to see if the file is a new file that has not been named or saved previously; if so, it calls *TMyWindow.FileSaveAs*, which opens a file-save dialog box (denoted by the standard identifier *sd_FileSave*) so that the user can name the file and specify its location. If the file has already been named or saved, the *FileSave* method calls *TMyWindow.SaveFile*, which simply saves the file under its current name and in its current directory.

Modifying the Object Types

Because we plan to save the contents of the parent window to a disk file, it will be helpful if the parent window has fields to hold the name of the currently loaded file and its status as a not-saved or a new file. We add these fields to *TMyWindow*, which also happens to be the application's main window. The *NotSaved* and *IsNewFile* fields are standard Boolean fields indicating the status of the window contents. When a new file is loaded, when a change is made in an existing drawing, or when a drawing is saved, the methods that carry out these tasks make the appropriate changes in the values of these fields. The *FileName* field is simply a null-terminated array of characters; *fsPathName* is a constant defined in the WinDOS unit and is equal to 79.

Also added to the parent window are all the methods it needs to create, open, and save files.

The parent window isn't the only thing that needs to be modified. The type definition of *TDPoint* also needs new *Load* and *Store* methods so that it knows how to load itself from a file and store itself to a file when called upon to do so. These new methods are actually quite simple:

```
CONSTRUCTOR TDPoint.Load(VAR S: TStream);
    BEGIN
        S.Read(X, SizeOf(X));
        S.Read(Y, SizeOf(Y))
    END;

PROCEDURE TDPoint.Store(VAR S: TStream);
    BEGIN
        S.Write(X, SizeOf(X));
        S.Write(Y, SizeOf(Y))
    END;
```

The *Load* constructor calls the *Read* method of the stream from which the point is being loaded to get the X and Y coordinates that constitute the point. The *Store* method does just the reverse, calling the stream's *Write* method to write the coordinates into the stream.

Initializing and Using Streams

The stream in Listing 13.1 is registered and initialized just as we discussed earlier. First, the program declares a *TStreamRec* to keep track of the object types in the stream, and then a *RegisterStream* method registers both the collection and point types for use with a stream. *RegisterStream* itself is actually called (as opposed to merely being defined) in the parent window's *Init* method, *TMyWindow.Init*.

The result of running the program is shown in Figure 13.1.

FIGURE 13.1:

Running the line-drawing program with file open/save capabilities

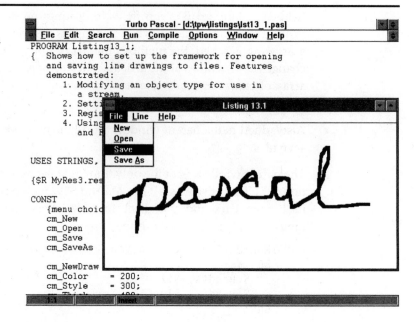

Working with Text-Input Resources and Combo Boxes

- The TInputDialog Object Type

- Steps in Setting Up Edit Fields in a Dialog Box

- Creating Combo Boxes

So far, we've seen how to define dialog resources in the WRT and link those resources into a Turbo Pascal for Windows program. In this chapter, we'll take a closer look at how to extend the usefulness of dialog boxes with *edit controls* and *combo boxes,* enabling the program to get a greater variety of information from the user.

Getting Text Input

The ancestor of all standard dialog box types in TPW is *TDialog,* on which we based the dialog object types we created earlier. ObjectWindows, however, provides two other predefined dialog box types that are descended from *TDialog,* each designed for a specific purpose: *TInputDialog,* which lets you prompt the user to enter a single line of text, and *TFileDialog,* which lets the user open and save files. We've seen both in action already. Now, we'll take a closer look at *TInputDialog* to see how it prompts the user to enter a single-line text string. After that, we'll apply that information to creating our own dialog box that lets the user enter text-string information.

The TInputDialog Object Type

The actual definition of the *TInputDialog* object type is given in the STDDLGS unit, as shown in Listing 14.1.

Listing 14.1

```
CONST
    id_Prompt = 100;
    id_Input  = 101;

PInputDialog = ^TInputDialog;
TInputDialog = OBJECT(TDialog)
    Caption: PChar;
    Prompt: PChar;
    Buffer: PChar;
    BufferSize: WORD;
    CONSTRUCTOR Init(AParent: PWindowsObject;
        ACaption, APrompt, ABuffer: PChar; ABufferSize: WORD);
    FUNCTION CanClose: BOOLEAN; VIRTUAL;
    PROCEDURE SetupWindow; VIRTUAL;
    end;
```

```
CONSTRUCTOR TInputDialog.Init(AParent: PWindowsObject;
    ACaption, APrompt, ABuffer: PChar; ABufferSize: Word);
  BEGIN
  TDialog.Init(AParent, PChar(sd_InputDialog));
  Caption := ACaption;
  Prompt := APrompt;
  Buffer := ABuffer;
  BufferSize := ABufferSize;
  END;

FUNCTION TInputDialog.CanClose: BOOLEAN;
  BEGIN
  GetDlgItemText(HWindow, id_Input, Buffer, BufferSize);
  CanClose := TRUE;
  END;

PROCEDURE TInputDialog.SetupWindow;
  BEGIN
  TDialog.SetupWindow;
  SetWindowText(HWindow, Caption);
  SetDlgItemText(HWindow, id_Prompt, Prompt);
  SetDlgItemText(HWindow, id_Input, Buffer);
  SendDlgItemMessage(HWindow, id_Input, em_LimitText,
      BufferSize - 1, 0);
  END;
```

The TInputDialog Resource Definition

The appearance of the dialog box created with *TInputDialog*, as shown in Figure 14.1, is defined as an external resource that can be viewed or modified in the WRT. This dialog box resource introduces a new type of dialog control device—an *edit field*, which is simply a box in which the user can type text or other printable information.

Notice that there isn't any text displayed in the resource itself: all the text that normally appears in the *TInputDialog* dialog box is provided by the TPW program or, in this case, by the STDDLGS unit. The empty boxes labeled 100 and 101 are both edit fields. The edit field positioned on top of *100* gets the prompt text (*APrompt*) from the program that uses the resource. The edit field on top of label *101* gets text from the user, and the TPW program then retrieves that text from the dialog box. The window caption (*ATitle*) is also passed to *TInputDialog*, and thence to the dialog box on the screen, from the calling program.

FIGURE 14.1:

The TInputDialog resource displayed in the WRT

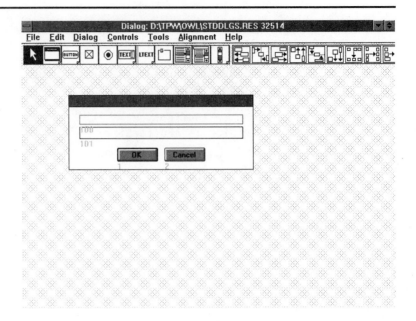

TInputDialog Fields

The *TInputDialog* object type (descended from *TDialog*) has four fields, three of which have to do with either displaying text for the user or getting text from the user. The fourth field sets the size of the text that the user can enter into the dialog box. The fields are:

Field	Purpose
Caption	Sets caption for dialog box frame (*PChar* type)
Prompt	Sets prompt inside dialog box, telling user what to do (*PChar* type)
Buffer	Gets text input from the user (*PChar* type)
BufferSize	Sets the maximum length of the text string the user can enter (*WORD* type)

The SetUpWindow Method

The *SetUpWindow* method of *TInputDialog* has three new features that merit our attention: the *SetWindowText* method, the *SetDlgItemText* method, and the *SendDlgItemMessage* method.

The *SetWindowText* method sets the caption for the frame of a window. It takes two parameters: a handle to the window for which text is being set, and the text (a null-terminated string) that contains the caption for the window.

The *SetDlgItemText* method provides a more flexible way of setting up static-text captions and other prompts in a dialog box. Previously, we've seen how to set up static text in a dialog resource itself. The disadvantage of this method is that the text can't be changed. If you wanted to use the same dialog resource for a variety of different purposes, you'd be out of luck. *SetDlgItemText* provides a solution. Instead of putting a static-text object at the desired position in your dialog resource, you simply put an edit field. To load the field with the text you want, you call *SetDlgItemText*, passing to it the edit field's control ID (parameter #2), along with the handle to the dialog (parameter #1) and the text you want to use (a null-terminated string, parameter #3).

The *SendDlgItemMessage* method is a very versatile routine that can be used to send several different kinds of information to a control in a dialog box. Here, it's used to set a limit to the number of characters that can be entered into the edit field by sending the Windows message *em_LimitText* (parameter #3) along with the desired maximum length of the text string that can be entered by the user (parameter #4). The specific code is:

```
SendDlgItemMessage(HWindow, id_Input,
    em_LimitText, BufferSize - 1, 0);
```

Here, *HWindow* just identifies the dialog box, *id_Input* is the edit field's control ID, *em_LimitText* identifies the kind of message that is being sent to the control, *BufferSize - 1* is the maximum allowable length of a text string that the user can enter, and *0* stands in for a final parameter that isn't being used here.

The CanClose Method

The new wrinkle in the *CanClose* method (a function) is its call to *GetDlgItemText*, which retrieves the user-entered text from the edit field. Here, the code is

```
GetDlgItemText(HWindow, id_Input, Buffer, BufferSize)
```

where *id_Input* is the control ID of the edit field, *Buffer* is the place the text will be copied into, and *BufferSize* is the size of the buffer. Using this method embedded in the *CanClose* function allows you to "automate" the retrieval of the text from the edit field when the dialog box is closed.

Steps in Setting Up Edit Fields in a Dialog Box

Based on what we've seen, there are several distinct steps involved in setting up edit fields in a dialog box—even if these steps are often obscured by the details of particular programs:

1. Define the dialog resource with the edit fields.

2. For each edit field, define a corresponding object type in the TPW program; the object type should be descended from *TEdit*.

3. Make sure that there's an appropriate transfer buffer record outside the dialog box to get the text from the edit field.

4. When the dialog box is closed, pass the text from the edit field to the transfer buffer.

An Example of Text-Input Dialog Fields

Let's look at another example of setting up edit fields in a dialog box—one that is more ambitious yet still simple enough to see the outlines of what is going on. Listing 14.2 shows a program that prompts the user to enter data for student records: name, grade point average (GPA), and class status. This could be the front end for a more complete program that would copy each new student record to a linked list, then save the entire list to a file for a student database. The dialog box that results from running Listing 14.2 is shown in Figure 14.2; your screen may look slightly different, depending on how you laid out the dialog resource.

Listing 14.2

```
PROGRAM Listing14_2;
{  Shows how to set up edit fields in a dialog
   box. Specific features demonstrated:
   1. Creating edit field objects in the program.
   2. Setting up a transfer buffer record.
   3. Setting the dimensions of the application window.
   4. Initializing the transfer buffer with FillChar.
   5. Copying formatted data from the transfer buffer
      to an array with WVSPrintf, and formatting it in
      the process. }

{$R SDataApp.RES}
```

FIGURE 14.2:

Dialog box from Listing 14.2

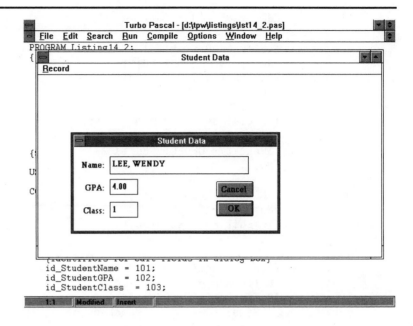

```
USES WOBJECTS, WINTYPES, WINPROCS, STRINGS, WINDOS;

CONST
    {menu command identifiers}
    cm_AddRec   = 201;
    cm_EditRec  = 202;
    cm_SaveRecs = 203;
    cm_Quit     = 204;

    {identifiers for edit fields in dialog box}
    id_StudentName  = 101;
    id_StudentGPA   = 102;
    id_StudentClass = 103;

    SNameLen  = 25;
    SGPALen   = 5;
    SClassLen = 1;

TYPE

    { Main application object }
    TStudentDataApp = OBJECT(TApplication)
    PROCEDURE InitMainWindow; VIRTUAL;
```

```
   END;

   { Name input field }
   PNameEdit = ^TNameEdit;
   TNameEdit = OBJECT(TEdit)
   END;

   { Social security number input field }
   PGPAEdit = ^TGPAEdit;
   TGPAEdit = OBJECT(TEdit)
   END;

   { Numeric input field }
   PNumEdit = ^TNumEdit;
   TNumEdit = OBJECT(TEdit)
   END;

   { Data transfer record for employee data dialog }
   PBufferRec = ^TBufferRec;
   TBufferRec = RECORD
      Name: ARRAY [0..SNameLen] of CHAR;
      GPA: ARRAY[0..SGPALen] of CHAR;
      Class: ARRAY[0..SClassLen] OF CHAR;
      END;

   { Application main window }
   PDataWindow = ^TDataWindow;
   TDataWindow = OBJECT(TWindow)
      BufferRec: TBufferRec;
      CONSTRUCTOR Init(AParent: PWindowsObject;
         ATitle: PChar);
      PROCEDURE AddRec(VAR Msg: TMessage);
         VIRTUAL cm_First + cm_AddRec;
      PROCEDURE EditRec(VAR Msg: TMessage);
         VIRTUAL cm_First + cm_EditRec;
      PROCEDURE SaveRecs(VAR Msg: TMessage);
         VIRTUAL cm_First + cm_SaveRecs;
      PROCEDURE Quit(VAR Msg: TMessage);
         VIRTUAL cm_First + cm_Quit;
   END;

{ TDataWindow }
CONSTRUCTOR TDataWindow.Init(AParent: PWindowsObject; ATitle:
PChar);
   BEGIN
```

```
    TWindow.Init(AParent, ATitle);
    Attr.Menu := LoadMenu(HInstance, 'RecMenu');
    Attr.X := 20;
    Attr.Y := 50;
    Attr.W := 600;
    Attr.H := 350;
    FillChar(BufferRec, SizeOf(BufferRec), 0);
    END;

PROCEDURE TDataWindow.AddRec(VAR Msg: TMessage);
    VAR
        Dlg: PDialog;
        TempPtr: PWindowsObject;
        SFldPtrs: ARRAY[0..2] of Longint;
        Result: ARRAY [0..255] of CHAR;
    BEGIN
        Dlg := NEW(PDialog, Init(@Self, 'StudentRecs'));
        Dlg^.TransferBuffer := @BufferRec;
        TempPtr := NEW(PNameEdit,
            InitResource(Dlg, id_StudentName,
            SNameLen + 1));
        TempPtr := NEW(PGPAEdit,
            InitResource(Dlg, id_StudentGPA,
            SGPALen + 1 ));
        TempPtr := NEW(PNumEdit,
            InitResource(Dlg, id_StudentClass,
            SClassLen + 1));
        IF Application^.ExecDialog(Dlg) = id_OK
        THEN  BEGIN
                SFldPtrs[0] := Longint(@BufferRec.Name);
                SFldPtrs[1] := Longint(@BufferRec.GPA);
                SFldPtrs[2] := Longint(@BufferRec.Class);
                WVSPrintF(Result,
                    'Name:'#9'%s'#13#10'GPA:'#9'%s'#13#10'Class:'#9'%s',
                    SFldPtrs);
                MessageBox(HWindow, Result,
                    'Student Data Entered', mb_OK);
        END;
    END;

PROCEDURE TDataWindow.EditRec(VAR Msg: TMessage);
    BEGIN
    MessageBeep(0);
    MessageBox(HWindow, 'Not yet implemented.',
        'Edit Records', mb_OK);
```

```
    END;

PROCEDURE TDataWindow.SaveRecs(VAR Msg: TMessage);
    BEGIN
    MessageBeep(0);
    MessageBox(HWindow, 'Not yet implemented.',
          'Save Records', mb_OK);
    END;

PROCEDURE TDataWindow.Quit(VAR Msg: TMessage);
    BEGIN
    CloseWindow
    END;

{ TStudentDataApp }
PROCEDURE TStudentDataApp.InitMainWindow;
    BEGIN
    MainWindow := NEW(PDataWindow, Init(NIL, 'Student Data'));
    END;

{global application object variable}
VAR
    StDataApp: TStudentDataApp;

{main body of program}
BEGIN
    StDataApp.Init('Student Data Application');
    StDataApp.Run;
    StDataApp.Done;
END.
```

In order to run this listing, you should create a resource called *SDataApp.Res* with a menu and a dialog box in it. These resources should have the following characteristics:

Listing 14.3

```
Menu:
Popup menu name: Record; value: 0
    Menu item: &Add Record; value: 201
    Menu item: &Edit Record; value: 202
    Menu item: &Save Record; value: 203
    Menu item: &Quit; value: 204
    Control Name: RecMenu

Dialog Box:
```

```
Box Title: Student Data
Edit Field #1:
   Caption (static text) = Name: ; Control ID = -1
   Text (edit text) = Name: ; Control ID = 101
Edit Field #2:
   Caption (static text) = GPA: ; Control ID = -1
   Text (edit text) = GPA: ; Control ID = 102
Edit Field #3:
   Caption (static text) = Class: ; Control ID = -1
   Text (edit text) = Class: ; Control ID = 103
Pushbutton #1:
   Text: OK
   Control ID: 1
Pushbutton #2:
   Text: Cancel
   Control ID: 2
Control Name: StudentRecs
```

There's quite a bit in Listing 14.2. The first step, of course, is to include the resource file *SDataApp.Res* and define the constant identifiers for the menu choices and the dialog box's edit fields. We then specify a maximum length for each edit field: this is the maximum number of characters that the user will be allowed to enter. Because each edit field will correspond to an array [0..maxlength], this means that there will always be an extra array slot to hold the null character needed to terminate the string.

Each edit field in the dialog resource gets a corresponding *TEdit*-descendant object type in the program. If we wanted to, we could build more into these object types, including data validation and other features. Here, however, we're focusing on the broad outlines of setting up the edit fields, and don't want to complicate things with unnecessary details.

As usual, there is a transfer buffer record type, *TBufferRec*, a variable of which will catch the data from the edit fields when the dialog box is closed. This data type is instantiated as a field of the parent window (*TDataWindow*) that calls the dialog box. The parent window itself has all the usual methods, including methods to respond to each of the menu choices.

The *TDataWindow.Init* method has a couple of new tricks in it. First, we use the predefined *Attr* record inherited from *TWindow* to set the location and dimensions of the parent window. Here, X and Y denote the coordinates of the upper left corner of the parent window, while W and H denote its width and height, respectively. Finally, we call the predefined *FillChar* method to initialize the transfer buffer, padding it with null characters.

It's in *TDataWindow.AddRec* where things really get subtle and interesting. This is, of course, the method that calls the dialog box and, when the dialog box closes, retrieves the text data that the user typed in. First, the method declares four local variables:

> **Dlg**, which is a pointer that will be used to create the dialog object variable.

> **TempPtr**, a generic pointer that will be used three times. Each time, the pointer will be used to create a different edit-field variable that is then linked to the corresponding edit field in the dialog box.

> **SFldPtrs**, an array of three pointers. After the dialog box is closed, each of the pointers will point to a different field of the transfer buffer record—meaning, each one will point to a different text data item entered by the user into the dialog box.

> **Result**, an array of characters that will hold the data from all three edit fields of the dialog box. By inserting some formatting characters (tab, carriage return/line feed) into the array, we can simply "print" the contents of the array to the screen and it will be preformatted.

In the main body of the method, the first step is to create a dynamic dialog box object with a call to NEW; in the process, we initialize the object and link it to the *StudentRecs* dialog resource from the *SDataApp.Res* resource file. After creating and initializing the dialog object, we take a pointer to the parent window's transfer buffer and pass it to the dialog object's *TransferBuffer* field, just as we would do with any other dialog box.

We then use the local pointer variable *TempPtr* to create and initialize three dynamic edit field objects, one for each of the edit fields in the dialog box. In the course of doing so, we link each with the appropriate dialog box edit field and specify the maximum allowable length of user-entered text strings. In each case, the length is *maxlen + 1*, allowing an extra slot for the null terminator.

The dialog box is called in the standard "safe" way, by using *Application^.Exec-Dialog*. Then, after the dialog box is closed, each slot in the local variable array of pointers gets a pointer to one of the fields in the transfer buffer record. This array of pointers is then passed as the last parameter to the *WVSPrintf* method, which writes the data from the transfer buffer into the local array of characters, *Result*.

When *WVSPrintf* writes the data to the *Result* array, however, it doesn't just write the data. It inserts formatting characters as well. For the *Name* field, for example, it writes the prefix Name:, along with a #9 character (tab) and a format specifier %s, which says that the data should be formatted as a text string. It then appends two more characters, #13#10 (CR/LF, or carriage return/line feed), so that when the data is displayed, a line break and new line will be inserted at that point. The same technique is used with the data from the other transfer buffer fields.

Finally, the routine calls the *MessageBox* method to display the data. The result is shown in Figure 14.3.

The only other new feature in Listing 14.2 is in the *TDataWindow.Quit* method, which responds to the "Quit" menu choice. This method calls the inherited *Close-Window* method; when *CloseWindow* is applied to the main window of an application, the application is terminated.

FIGURE 14.3:

Displaying a student data record

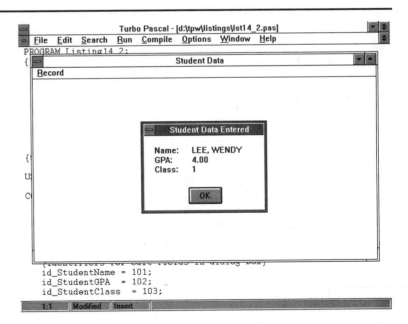

Creating Combo Boxes

Apart from edit fields, one of the most useful control objects you can put into a dialog box is a *combo box,* which comes in several different flavors. Combo boxes let the user select from a list of options. The most familiar example of a combo box is one that we've already seen in the predefined *TFileDialog* dialog box type; in a file dialog, the box that contains the list of files in the current directory is a combo box. If the dialog is to open a file, the user selects one of the items in the combo box by clicking on it with the mouse, and can then open the corresponding file by clicking on *OK.*

Combo boxes (and list boxes, which are merely a simpler version of combo boxes) are fairly easy to set up and use. As usual, however, it's also easy to get lost in the details of a particular program that have nothing to do with the combo boxes themselves. Here, we'll show how to create four different types of combo box, each time leaving out any details not relevant to the combo box at hand.

List Boxes

The simplest type of combo box is called a *list box.* As the name implies, it is pretty much just a box with a list in it. The user can select any of the items in the box by clicking on it with the mouse. A program that sets up a list box is shown in Listing 14.4, and the result of running the program is shown in Figure 14.4.

Listing 14.4

```
PROGRAM Listing14_4;
{  Demonstrates a simple list box. }

USES WOBJECTS, WINTYPES, WINPROCS;

CONST
   id_LBox = 100;
   id_StatText = 101;

type
   ComboBoxApplication = OBJECT(TApplication)
      PROCEDURE InitMainWindow; VIRTUAL;
   END;

   PComboBoxWindow = ^ComboBoxWindow;
```

```
ComboBoxWindow = OBJECT(TWindow)
   LBox: PListBox;
   CONSTRUCTOR Init(AParent: PWindowsObject;
      ATitle: PChar);
   PROCEDURE SetupWindow; VIRTUAL;
END;

CONSTRUCTOR ComboBoxWindow.Init(AParent: PWindowsObject;
            ATitle: PChar);
   VAR
      AStat : PStatic;
   BEGIN
      TWindow.Init(AParent, ATitle);
      Attr.X := 150;
      Attr.Y := 80;
      Attr.W := 300;
      Attr.H := 200;
      LBox := New(PListBox, Init(@Self, id_LBox,
               70, 40, 150, 100));
      AStat := New(PStatic, Init(@Self, id_StatText,
               'Simple List Box',
               70, 18, 150, 20, 0));
   END;

PROCEDURE ComboBoxWindow.SetupWindow;
   BEGIN
      TWindow.SetupWindow;
      LBox^.AddString('Frank');
      LBox^.AddString('Eddie');
      LBox^.AddString('David');
      LBox^.AddString('Charles');
      LBox^.AddString('Bill');
      LBox^.AddString('Andy');
   END;

PROCEDURE ComboBoxApplication.InitMainWindow;
   BEGIN
   MainWindow := New(PComboBoxWindow,
            Init(nil, 'Listing 14.4'));
   END;

{global object variable for application}
VAR
   CBoxApp : ComboBoxApplication;
```

```
{main body of program}
BEGIN
    CBoxApp.Init('Listing 14.4');
    CBoxApp.Run;
    CBoxApp.Done;
END.
```

In Listing 14.4, we first declare identifiers for the list box itself and for the static text we want to display inside the parent window to explain what the list box is. These can pretty much be anything you like: they don't refer to anything outside the TPW program. We then declare the parent window type, including a field that holds a pointer to the list box. We also include a call to the inherited *SetUpWindow* method, which does some behind-the-scenes work for us.

In the *ComboBoxWindow.Init* method, we first declare a local pointer variable to point to the static text in the window that will explain the list box. Next, we call *TWindow.Init,* and then reset the dimensions of the parent window. We then call *NEW* to create a dynamic list box object; in the embedded call to Init, we specify the dimensions of the list box. We do the same sort of thing with *NEW* to create the static text object.

FIGURE 14.4:

List box created by Listing 14.4

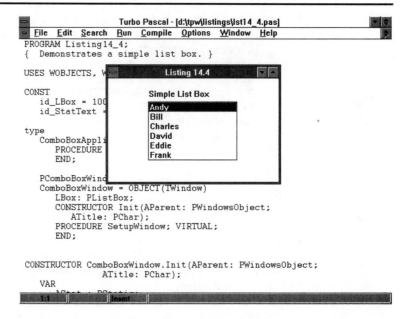

In the *ComboBox.SetupWindow* method, we first call the inherited *SetupWindow* method from *TWindow*. Then, we use the list box object type's predefined *AddString* method to load the list box with the names of several students. Notice an interesting thing: although the students' names are loaded in reverse alphabetical order, the list box in Figure 14.4 displays them in standard alphabetical order. List boxes (and combo boxes) automatically display their contents in standard sorted order, regardless of the order in which they are loaded.

The rest of Listing 14.4 is fairly standard.

Simple Combo Boxes

A simple combo box is very much like a plain list box, except that it has a separate subwindow at the top, which displays the currently selected item. A program to set up a simple combo box is shown in Listing 14.5; the result of running the program is shown in Figure 14.5.

Listing 14.5

```
PROGRAM Listing14_5;
{  Demonstrates a simple combo box. }

USES WOBJECTS, WINTYPES, WINPROCS;

CONST
    id_CBox = 100;
    id_StatText = 101;

type
    ComboBoxApplication = OBJECT(TApplication)
        PROCEDURE InitMainWindow; VIRTUAL;
        END;

    PComboBoxWindow = ^ComboBoxWindow;
    ComboBoxWindow = OBJECT(TWindow)
        CBox: PComboBox;
        CONSTRUCTOR Init(AParent: PWindowsObject;
            ATitle: PChar);
        PROCEDURE SetupWindow; VIRTUAL;
        END;

CONSTRUCTOR ComboBoxWindow.Init(AParent: PWindowsObject;
                                ATitle: PChar);
```

FIGURE 14.5:

A simple combo box created by
Listing 14.5

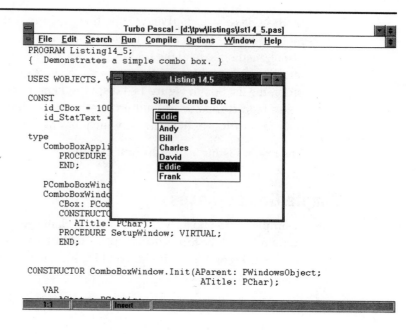

```
                    Turbo Pascal - [d:\tpw\listings\lst14_5.pas]
  File   Edit   Search   Run   Compile   Options   Window   Help
PROGRAM Listing14_5;
{  Demonstrates a simple combo box. }

USES WOBJECTS, W              Listing 14.5

CONST                      Simple Combo Box
    id_CBox = 100
    id_StatText =           Eddie
                            Andy
type                        Bill
    ComboBoxAppli           Charles
        PROCEDURE           David
        END;                Eddie
                            Frank
    PComboBoxWin
    ComboBoxWind
        CBox: PCom
        CONSTRUCTO
          ATitle: PChar);
        PROCEDURE SetupWindow; VIRTUAL;
        END;

CONSTRUCTOR ComboBoxWindow.Init(AParent: PWindowsObject;
                                    ATitle: PChar);
        VAR
        1:1              Insert
```

```
VAR
    AStat : PStatic;
BEGIN
    TWindow.Init(AParent, ATitle);
    Attr.X := 150;
    Attr.Y := 80;
    Attr.W := 300;
    Attr.H := 250;
    CBox := New(PComboBox,
        Init(@Self, id_CBox,
        70, 40, 150, 130,
        cbs_Simple, 0));
    CBox^.Attr.Style := CBox^.Attr.Style
            and not ws_VScroll;
    AStat := New(PStatic,
        Init(@Self, id_StatText,
        'Simple Combo Box',
        70, 18, 150, 20, 0));
    END;

PROCEDURE ComboBoxWindow.SetupWindow;
```

```
    BEGIN
        TWindow.SetupWindow;
        CBox^.AddString('Frank');
        CBox^.AddString('Eddie');
        CBox^.AddString('David');
        CBox^.AddString('Charles');
        CBox^.AddString('Bill');
        CBox^.AddString('Andy');
    END;

PROCEDURE ComboBoxApplication.InitMainWindow;
    BEGIN
    MainWindow := New(PComboBoxWindow,
        Init(nil, 'Listing 14.5'));
    END;

{global object variable for application}
VAR
    CBoxApp : ComboBoxApplication;

{main body of program}
BEGIN
    CBoxApp.Init('Listing 14.5');
    CBoxApp.Run;
    CBoxApp.Done;
END.
```

For the most part, Listing 14.5 proceeds in the same way as Listing 14.4. In the *ComboBoxWindow.Init* method, *cbs_simple* (the next-to-last parameter of the *Init* routine in the NEW statement for generating a combo box) passes a combo box object to *CBox* to tell TPW that we're creating a simple combo box. The next statement sets the style attribute inherited from *TWindow*, and adds that this combo box isn't scrollable.

Drop-Down Combo Boxes

A bit fancier than a simple combo box is a drop-down combo box. The list associated with this box is not shown at all until the user clicks on a down-arrow button to the right of the "item selected" field. This arrow opens and closes the list window. This type of combo box is demonstrated in Listing 14.6; the result is shown in Figure 14.6. Note that in the *ComboBoxWindow.Init* method, where we create a dynamic combo box object and load its pointer into *CBox*, the next-to-last

FIGURE 14.6:

Drop-down combo box created by Listing 14.6

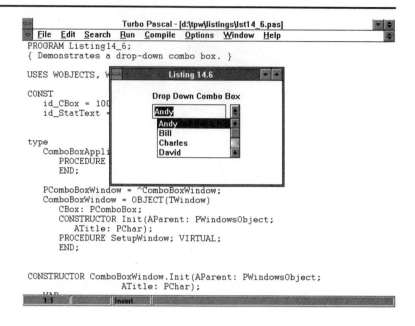

parameter in the call to *NEW* is *cbs_DropDown*, which indicates that this is a drop-down combo box.

Listing 14.6

```
PROGRAM Listing14_6;
{ Demonstrates a drop-down combo box. }

USES WOBJECTS, WINTYPES, WINPROCS;

CONST
    id_CBox = 100;
    id_StatText = 101;

type
    ComboBoxApplication = OBJECT(TApplication)
        PROCEDURE InitMainWindow; VIRTUAL;
        END;

    PComboBoxWindow = ^ComboBoxWindow;
    ComboBoxWindow = OBJECT(TWindow)
```

```
      CBox: PComboBox;
      CONSTRUCTOR Init(AParent: PWindowsObject;
         ATitle: PChar);
      PROCEDURE SetupWindow; VIRTUAL;
      END;

CONSTRUCTOR ComboBoxWindow.Init(AParent: PWindowsObject;
                   ATitle: PChar);
   VAR
      AStat : PStatic;
   BEGIN
      TWindow.Init(AParent, ATitle);
      Attr.X := 150;
      Attr.Y := 80;
      Attr.W := 300;
      Attr.H := 200;
      CBox := New(PComboBox,
                  Init(@Self, id_CBox,
                  70, 40, 150, 100,
                  cbs_DropDown, 0));
      AStat := New(PStatic,
                  Init(@Self, id_StatText,
                  'Drop Down Combo Box',
                  70, 18, 150, 20, 0));
   END;

PROCEDURE ComboBoxWindow.SetupWindow;
   BEGIN
      TWindow.SetupWindow;
      CBox^.AddString('Frank');
      CBox^.AddString('Eddie');
      CBox^.AddString('David');
      CBox^.AddString('Charles');
      CBox^.AddString('Bill');
      CBox^.AddString('Andy');
   END;

PROCEDURE ComboBoxApplication.InitMainWindow;
   BEGIN
   MainWindow := New(PComboBoxWindow,
         Init(nil, 'Listing 14.6'));
   END;
```

```
{global object variable for application}
VAR
    CBoxApp : ComboBoxApplication;

{main body of program}
BEGIN
    CBoxApp.Init('Listing 14.6');
    CBoxApp.Run;
    CBoxApp.Done;
END.
```

Combo Boxes with Drop-Down Lists

Even fancier than the drop-down combo box is a combo box with a drop-down list. Apart from looking slightly different, this type of combo box can use inherited *Show* and *Hide* methods, associated with pushbuttons, to open and close its associated list box on the screen. In Listing 14.7 we've included the *Show* and *Hide* buttons with a drop-down combo box so you can compare the two different methods of displaying and hiding the combo box's list—either by clicking on the down-arrow button next to the list box or by clicking on the *Show* or *Hide* buttons. Normally you would use only one of these methods. The result of Listing 14.7 is shown in Figure 14.7.

FIGURE 14.7:

A combo box with drop-down list

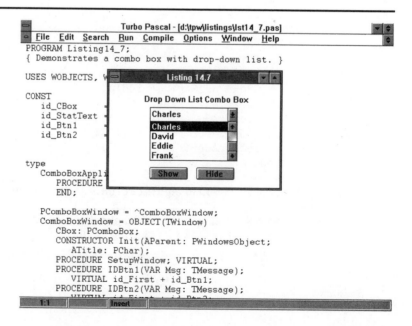

Listing 14.7

```
PROGRAM Listing14_7;
{ Demonstrates a combo box with drop-down list. }

USES WOBJECTS, WINTYPES, WINPROCS;

CONST
   id_CBox     = 100;
   id_StatText = 101;
   id_Btn1     = 102;
   id_Btn2     = 103;

type
   ComboBoxApplication = OBJECT(TApplication)
      PROCEDURE InitMainWindow; VIRTUAL;
      END;

   PComboBoxWindow = ^ComboBoxWindow;
   ComboBoxWindow = OBJECT(TWindow)
      CBox: PComboBox;
      CONSTRUCTOR Init(AParent: PWindowsObject;
         ATitle: PChar);
      PROCEDURE SetupWindow; VIRTUAL;
      PROCEDURE IDBtn1(VAR Msg: TMessage);
         VIRTUAL id_First + id_Btn1;
      PROCEDURE IDBtn2(VAR Msg: TMessage);
         VIRTUAL id_First + id_Btn2;
      END;

CONSTRUCTOR ComboBoxWindow.Init(AParent: PWindowsObject;
                                ATitle: PChar);
   VAR
      ABtn : PButton;
      AStat : PStatic;
   BEGIN
      TWindow.Init(AParent, ATitle);
      Attr.X := 150;
      Attr.Y := 80;
      Attr.W := 300;
      Attr.H := 200;
      CBox := New(PComboBox,
               Init(@Self, id_CBox,
```

```
                70, 40, 150, 100,
                cbs_DropDownList, 0));
        ABtn := New(PButton,
                Init(@Self, id_Btn1, 'Show',
                70, 140, 65, 20,
                False));
        ABtn := New(PButton,
                Init(@Self, id_Btn2, 'Hide',
                150, 140, 65, 20,
                False));
        AStat := New(PStatic,
                Init(@Self, id_StatText,
                'Drop Down List Combo Box',
                60, 18, 190, 20, 0));
    END;

PROCEDURE ComboBoxWindow.SetupWindow;
    BEGIN
        TWindow.SetupWindow;
        CBox^.AddString('Frank');
        CBox^.AddString('Eddie');
        CBox^.AddString('David');
        CBox^.AddString('Charles');
        CBox^.AddString('Bill');
        CBox^.AddString('Andy');
    END;

PROCEDURE ComboBoxWindow.IDBtn1(VAR Msg: TMessage);
    BEGIN
        CBox^.ShowList;
    END;

PROCEDURE ComboBoxWindow.IDBtn2(VAR Msg: TMessage);
    BEGIN
        CBox^.HideList;
    END;

PROCEDURE ComboBoxApplication.InitMainWindow;
    BEGIN
    MainWindow := New(PComboBoxWindow,
            Init(nil, 'Listing 14.7'));
    END;
```

```
{global object variable for application}
VAR
    CBoxApp : ComboBoxApplication;

{main body of program}
BEGIN
    CBoxApp.Init('Listing 14.7');
    CBoxApp.Run;
    CBoxApp.Done;
END.
```

Creating and Using Bitmaps, Icons, and Cursors

- Using the WRT Bitmap Editor

- Using a Bitmap in a TPW Program

- Moving and Enlarging Bitmaps

- Using the WRT Icon Editor

- Displaying an Icon for a Minimized Program

- Creating and Using Cursors

- Creating and Using String Tables

In this chapter, we'll look at four other parts of the **Whitewater Resource Toolkit**, each of which enables you to create a different kind of Windows resource. The first three—bitmaps, icons, and cursors—are created in much the same way, although there are a few minor differences. All three are on-screen images that you draw in a WRT paint editor.

The fourth resource type we'll look at in this chapter, the string table, keeps text used by your program in a separate resource file, instead of embedded in the source code of your program. This makes it easier and safer to change text messages to the user, inasmuch as you no longer have to make changes in the source code file.

Creating Bitmaps

Bit-mapped graphics images to be displayed by a Windows program are usually stored in a .RES resource file along with the other resources used by a program. They can also be stored by themselves as bitmap (.BMP) files.

Creating bitmaps is a very simple process; you can use the WRT's bitmap editor, the **Borland Resource Workshop**, the Windows **Paint** accessory program, or any other painting program to create and store the image, though it's generally best to have it in a .RES resource file to use it in a program. Using bitmaps in a program is also fairly straightforward, although there are a lot of "additional" details that you can pursue to improve your program's bitmap-handling performance.

In this section, our first task will be to create a bitmap with the WRT bitmap editor. After that, we'll show how to integrate the bitmap into a program. Finally, we'll look at some tricks for using bitmaps more efficiently in your programs.

Bitmaps, icons, and cursors are all created in essentially the same way, so many points in our discussion will help prepare for these topics later in the chapter.

Using the WRT Bitmap Editor

The first step in creating a bitmap is to open the WRT's bitmap editor by selecting the Bitmap button from the WRT main control screen. The bitmap editor will open, as shown in Figure 15.1.

FIGURE 15.1:

The WRT bitmap editor

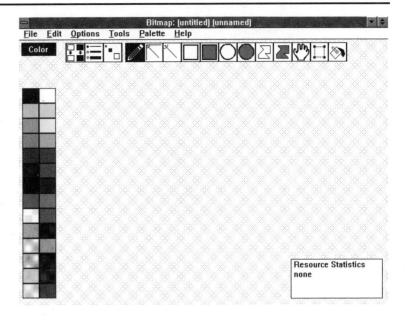

To create a new bitmap, select "New" from the File menu. The **New Bitmap Dimensions** dialog box will open, displaying the default values for a 72-by-72-pixel bitmap that can use up to 16 colors. Simply click on *OK* to accept the default values. A blank drawing surface will open, as shown in Figure 15.2.

The title bar of the bitmap editor window displays the usual information about the resource being created or edited: first, the resource file it resides in, and second, its resource name or ID. In the case of Figures 15.1 and 15.2, of course, this line shows "untitled/unnamed" because we haven't yet named the bitmap or saved it to a resource file.

The next line is the menu bar, from which you can select the usual file and editing operations, as well as choose various options for drawing a bitmap, such as the drawing tool you want to use and the thickness of lines that will be drawn. Each of the menu options in the Options, Tools, and Palette menus has a corresponding tool button in the row of icon buttons under the menu bar. It's generally easier to click on one of the tool buttons than use the menus, so we'll explain the features offered

FIGURE 15.2:

The WRT bitmap editor with a blank drawing surface

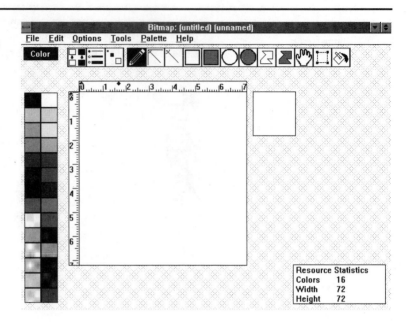

by each button; just remember that the same features are available through the corresponding menu choices. The drawing tools are as follows:

The Toggle tool lets you "reverse" the current background color when you're drawing with the pencil drawing tool. Thus, if the background color is white, you'll be drawing a black line; if the background is black, you'll be drawing with a white line.

The Line Width tool lets you change the thickness of the line that will be drawn with the pencil or other drawing tools. There are three settings, shown on the tool itself: thin, medium, and thick.

The Magnifying tool enables you to "zoom in" the drawing surface so that a small part of the bitmap is displayed in the same screen area. This is useful for doing detailed drawings that would otherwise be difficult for anyone without a very, very steady mouse hand. The three settings are actual size, 4× actual size, and 8× actual size.

The Pencil tool is the main freehand drawing tool, and works just like a normal pencil. It draws with the currently selected line color and thickness.

The Constrained Line tool lets you draw straight lines that "snap" to some multiple of a 45-degree angle. Thus, you can draw lines that are perfectly horizontal, vertical, or diagonal.

The Line tool enables you to draw perfectly straight lines. With this tool selected, a straight line is drawn between the point where you first press the mouse button and the point where you release it, no matter how many twists and turns you take along the way.

The Hollow Rectangle tool lets you draw a hollow rectangle. Press the left mouse button at the point you want one corner of a rectangle and release it at the point you want the opposite corner.

The Filled Rectangle tool lets you draw a filled rectangle in the same way you would draw a hollow rectangle (see above). The border and fill use whatever color is currently selected.

The Hollow Ellipse tool (which shows something that looks more like a circle than an ellipse) allows you to draw circles and ellipses in much the same way you use the rectangle tools. The "flatness" or "thickness" of the ellipse is determined by the angle along which you drag the mouse.

The Filled Ellipse tool works just like the hollow ellipse tool, except that it draws an ellipse filled with the currently selected color.

The Hollow Polygon tool   I think we all get the idea by now, don't we?

The Filled Polygon tool   Ditto.

The Dragging Hand tool enables you to drag the bitmap box around the editing area.

The Region Selector tool enables you to select a region in the bitmap to cut or copy to the Windows Clipboard.

The Fill tool lets you "pour" the currently selected color into a closed region of the bitmap, or into the entire background.

To create a bitmap, you simply draw the image you want in the editing area, using the drawing tools provided. Figure 15.3 shows a bitmap with a magnification factor of 4; near the top right corner of the editing area is the pencil drawing tool. Draw a bitmap on your own; it doesn't have to look like the one in the figure. In the next section, we'll see how to use the bitmap in a TPW program.

FIGURE 15.3:

A bitmap created in the WRT bitmap editor

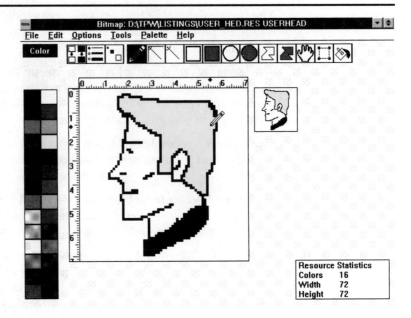

Using a Bitmap in a TPW Program

There are several basic steps to loading and using a bitmap in a TPW program:

1. Set up a field in the parent window to hold a handle to the bitmap.

2. In the parent window's *Init* method, use *LoadBitMap* to load a handle to the bitmap into the parent window's bitmap handle field.

3. Override the parent window's *Paint* method with a new version that will display and dispose of the bitmap.

4. In the new *Paint* method, create two local variables: one for a display context, and one to hold a handle to a bitmap.

5. In the new *Paint* method, use *CreateCompatibleDC* to get an appropriate display context onto which you can paint the bitmap. Load this display context into the local display context variable.

6. In the new *Paint* method, use the *SelectObject* function to pass the handle to the bitmap (the handle of the bitmap you want to display) to the local display context variable. Assign the result of *SelectObject* to the local handle variable.

7. Use the *BitBlt* routine to draw the bitmap into the display context passed to the *Paint* routine as a parameter.

8. To shut down the bitmap operation, use *SelectObject* again to reload the local bitmap-handle variable into the local display context variable. Then call *DeleteDC* to delete the display context and release the bitmap.

That, in a nutshell, is how it works. Let's look at how these steps are applied in a real TPW program, shown in Listing 15.1.

Listing 15.1

```
PROGRAM Listing15_1;
{ Shows how to use a bitmap resource in a program.
  Specific features demonstrated:
  1. Defining a bitmap-handle field in the parent window.
  2. Using LoadBitMap to load the bitmap resource.
  3. Modifying the Paint routine to display the bitmap.
  4. Disposing of the bitmap and display context. }

{$r user_hed.res}

USES WOBJECTS, WINTYPES, WINPROCS;

TYPE
    BitmapApplication = object (TApplication)
        PROCEDURE InitMainWindow; VIRTUAL;
    END;

    PBitmapWindow = ^BitmapWindow;
    BitmapWindow = OBJECT (TWindow)
        HImage : Hbitmap;
        CONSTRUCTOR init(aparent:PWindowsObject;
            ATitle:PChar);
        DESTRUCTOR Done; VIRTUAL;
        PROCEDURE Paint(PaintDC:HDC;
            VAR PaintInfo:TPaintStruct);
            VIRTUAL;
    END;

PROCEDURE BitmapApplication.InitMainWindow;
    BEGIN
    MainWindow := NEW(PBitmapWindow,
        init(NIL, 'Listing 15.1: Loading and Displaying a Bitmap'));
```

```
    END;

CONSTRUCTOR BitmapWindow.init(aparent:PWindowsObject;
        atitle:PChar);
    BEGIN
    TWindow.init(aparent, atitle);
    Attr.X := 50;
    Attr.Y := 50;
    Attr.W := 500;
    Attr.H := 400;
    HImage := loadbitmap(hinstance, 'userhead');
    END;

DESTRUCTOR BitmapWindow.done;
    BEGIN
    DeleteObject(HImage);
    TWindow.done;
    END;

PROCEDURE BitmapWindow.Paint(paintdc:hdc;
            VAR paintinfo:tpaintstruct);
    VAR
        OldObject : THandle;
        MemDC: HDC;
    BEGIN
        MemDC := createcompatibleDC(PaintDC);
        OldObject := SelectObject(MemDC, HImage);
        BitBlt(PaintDC, 200, 100, 72, 72, MemDC,
            0, 0, srcCopy);
        SelectObject(MemDC, OldObject);
        DeleteDC(MemDC);
    END;

{global object variable for application}
VAR
    BitmapApp : BitmapApplication;

{main body of program}
BEGIN
    BitmapApp.init('Listing 15.1');
    BitmapApp.run;
    BitmapApp.done
END.
```

The first step in Listing 15.1 is, as usual, to include the appropriate resource file in the program. Here, it's USER_HED.RES. We then declare the main application type *BitmapApplication* in the usual way.

The declaration of the main window type *BitmapWindow* includes a field to hold a handle to a bitmap; this field will get the handle to the image in the resource file and pass it to the appropriate methods when needed. There are three methods: a constructor method and a destructor method, needed for setup and shutdown tasks, and a *Paint* method that overrides the *Paint* method inherited from *TWindow*.

The main reason we needed to declare a constructor *BitmapWindow.Init* method was to load the bitmap. In this method, however, we also succumb to the temptation to add a cosmetic touch by specifying the dimensions of the application's main window. After calling *TWindow.Init* (never forget this step!) and specifying the window dimensions, we call the *loadbitmap* function.

Loadbitmap takes two parameters: first, a handle to the current application instance, and, second, the *PChar*-type string that identifies the bitmap. If the bitmap's resource ID is an integer, you can use *PChar()* to recast it as a null-terminated string, for example, as in `PChar(100)`. Because *loadbitmap* is a function, it returns a value—in this case, a handle to the bitmap, which we load into the bitmap-handle field of the application's main window.

The main reason for declaring a new destructor method is to call *DeleteObject* with the handle to the bitmap. This is a very important step. Bitmaps take up a big chunk of memory, and if you forget to delete the bitmap before terminating your program, it will remain in memory until you end your Windows session. After deleting the bitmap, we call the *TWindow.Done* method to handle all the other shutdown tasks for us.

The key player in Listing 15.1 is the *BitmapWindow.Paint* method. This overrides the inherited *Paint* method from *TWindow* and takes two parameters: a handle to a display context on which the *Paint* method will do its work, and a *tpaintstruct*-type variable that contains behind-the-scenes information used by the *Paint* method.

The new *Paint* method declares two local variables: first, *OldObject*, a generic handle variable that we'll use to catch a bitmap handle passed from *SelectObject*; and *MemDC*, a handle to a display context. (HDC itself is a generic handle type, but is used for clarity.)

In the main body of the method, the first task is to create a new display context that is compatible with the one that was passed as a parameter to the *Paint* method. This display context will hold the bitmap image in memory (hence the name, *MemDC*) so that we can copy the image to the display context that we're *really* interested in: the *PaintDC* display context that will make the image appear in the application's main window. To do this, we use the *createcompatibleDC* function, which takes a handle to a display context as a parameter and returns a handle to a display context that is compatible with the parameter—that is, *if* the operation was successful. If something went wrong, it returns a value of zero, which gives you a way to test the result in situations where you might be in doubt.

Next, we call the *SelectObject* function to associate the handle to the bitmap with the local display-context variable. Because *SelectObject* is a function, it returns a value—whatever handle (actual or null) was in the local display-context variable before the function was called. In this case, we're not going to do anything with it, but it's generally a good practice to save this handle in a variable in case you need it; so we've saved it to the local *OldObject* variable. The first parameter of *SelectObject* is the handle to the display context. The second parameter, in this case, is the handle to the bitmap, but it can also be a handle to a brush, font, pen, or region. As with *createcompatibleDC*, the *SelectObject* function returns a value of *0* if an error occurs.

The next step is to call the *BitBlt* routine to copy the image from the local display context *MemDC* to the *PaintDC* parameter used by *Paint*. This will actually make the image appear in the application window. *BitBlt* (for "bit blasting") takes nine parameters, but six of them are for coordinates in the window, so it's less complicated than it sounds. The parameters, in order, are:

- The "destination" display context—in this case, *PaintDC*
- The X and Y coordinates of the upper left corner of the region in which the image should be drawn
- The width and height of the rectangular region in which the image is to be drawn
- The "source" display context—in this case, *MemDC*
- The X and Y coordinates of the upper left corner of the source display context
- An identifier for a ternary raster operation—in this case, *srcCopy*, indicating that the call to *BitBlt* should copy a bitmap from one display context to another

Here, we want to locate the image at an X coordinate of 200 (relative to the window's upper left corner) and a Y coordinate of 100. The bitmap is a 72×72 image, and we're copying it from the local *MemDC* display context. Because *MemDC* is not actually in the window, we specify the values 0,0 for its upper left corner, and finally use the ternary raster operation identifier *srcCopy*.

After drawing the image with *BitBlt*, we prepare to shut down the *Paint* operation by calling *SelectObject* again, this time to re-associate the old handle with the *MemDC* display context. Having done this, we finally call *DeleteDC* to delete the display context; this automatically releases the associated handle and anything associated with it. The rest of Listing 15.1 is standard stuff. The result of running it is shown in Figure 15.4.

Moving and Enlarging Bitmaps

Loading a bitmap and displaying it in a program seems easy enough once you know how to do it. But suppose that you want to move it around in a window, or make it bigger (or smaller)? Both of those tasks are fairly straight-forward, though each has its own tricks that need to be mastered. Taking things one at a time,

FIGURE 15.4: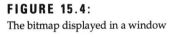

The bitmap displayed in a window

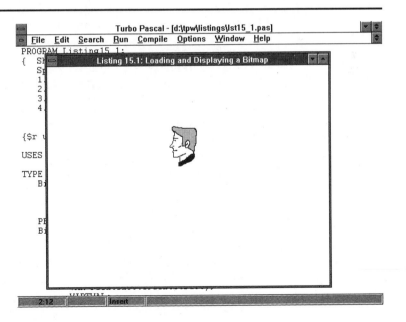

Listing 15.2 shows how to move a bitmap image from one location to another within a window.

Listing 15.2

```
PROGRAM Listing15_2;
{  Using the StretchBlt routine to move a bitmap
   to a new position in a window. Specific features
   demonstrated:
   1. How to use StretchBlt to copy a bitmap
      image to a new location.
   2. How to use BitBlt to "erase" the old image
      by drawing a new white-on-white image in the
      same location. }

{$r user_hed.res}

USES WOBJECTS, WINTYPES, WINPROCS;

TYPE
    BitmapApplication = object (TApplication)
    PROCEDURE InitMainWindow; VIRTUAL;
    END;

    PBitmapWindow = ^BitmapWindow;
    BitmapWindow = OBJECT (TWindow)
       HImage : Hbitmap;
       CONSTRUCTOR init(aparent:PWindowsObject;
          ATitle:PChar);
       DESTRUCTOR Done; VIRTUAL;
       PROCEDURE Paint(PaintDC:HDC;
          VAR PaintInfo:TPaintStruct);
          VIRTUAL;
       END;

PROCEDURE BitmapApplication.InitMainWindow;
    BEGIN
    MainWindow := NEW(PBitmapWindow,
       init(NIL, 'Listing 15.2: Moving a Bitmap'));
    END;

CONSTRUCTOR BitmapWindow.init(aparent:PWindowsObject;
         atitle:PChar);
    BEGIN
    TWindow.init(aparent, atitle);
```

```
      Attr.X := 50;
      Attr.Y := 50;
      Attr.W := 500;
      Attr.H := 400;
      HImage := loadbitmap(hinstance, 'userhead');
      END;

DESTRUCTOR BitmapWindow.done;
    BEGIN
    DeleteObject(HImage);
    TWindow.done;
    END;

PROCEDURE BitmapWindow.Paint(paintdc:hdc;
                VAR paintinfo:tpaintstruct);
    VAR
        OldObject : THandle;
        MemDC: HDC;
        counter : longint;
    BEGIN
        MemDC := createcompatibleDC(PaintDC);
        OldObject := SelectObject(MemDC, HImage);

        {Draw the initial image}
        BitBlt(PaintDC, 50, 50, 72, 72, MemDC,
            0, 0, srcCopy);

        {  This is an empty FOR loop to delay drawing
           the new image long enough that the process
           can be seen. Depending on your PC, you may
           need to use a larger or smaller number for
           the number of loops.}
        FOR counter := 1 TO 200000 DO BEGIN END;

        {Draw a new image in a different location.}
        StretchBlt(paintdc, 200, 200, 72, 72, MemDC,
            0, 0, 72, 72, srcCopy);

        {"Erase" the old image by redrawing it in the
          same location, but making it completely white.}
          BitBlt(paintDC, 50, 50, 72, 72, MemDC,
          0, 0, Whiteness);

        SelectObject(MemDC, OldObject);
        DeleteDC(MemDC);
```

```
    END;

{global object variable for application}
VAR
    BitmapApp : BitmapApplication;

{main body of program}
BEGIN
    BitmapApp.init('Listing 15.2');
    BitmapApp.run;
    BitmapApp.done
END.
```

Listing 15.2 is like Listing 15.1, except for the addition of three new steps in the *BitmapWindow.Paint* routine. All three steps occur after the initial call to *BitBlt*, which draws the original image in the window. (I've changed the image coordinates to make the move more noticeable.)

The first new step is simple and familiar to any experienced programmer: an empty FOR loop that does nothing but kill some time. This allows the original image to stay on the screen long enough that you can see it before it's moved to its new location. I used 200,000 loops, which is about right for a 33MHz 80386-based PC; depending on your PC, you may need more or fewer loops.

Next, we call *StretchBlt* to draw the same image in a different location in the window. *StretchBlt* takes 11 parameters, and like *BitBlt*, most of them are coordinates:

- The "destination" display context—here, *paintDC*
- The X and Y coordinates of the upper left corner of the region where the new image is to be drawn
- The width and height of the new image to be drawn
- The "source" display context—here, *MemDC*
- The X and Y coordinates of the upper left corner of the image region in the source display context
- The width and height of the image region in the source display context
- A ternary raster operation identifier indicating the operation to be performed

Here, because we're simply moving the image, we use the same width and height dimensions, changing only the coordinates for the upper left corner of the image region—from 50, 50 (the coordinates used in the call to *BitBlt*) to 200, 200.

There's just one other problem. The call to *StretchBlt* makes a new image at the desired location, but it does nothing to erase the old image at the old location. To do this, we call *BitBlt* again and redraw the image in the original location. This time, however, we use the ternary raster operation identifier *Whiteness* as the last parameter in the call to *BitBlt*. This makes *BitBlt* draw an image identical to the original one, in the same location—except that this time, because it's white-on-white, it effectively erases the old image.

Enlarging a bitmap image is also done with a call to *StretchBlt*, as shown in Listing 15.3. There are a couple of differences, however, that need to be explained.

Listing 15.3

```
PROGRAM Listing15_3;
{  Using the StretchBlt routine to enlarge a bitmap. }

{$r user_hed.res}

USES WOBJECTS, WINTYPES, WINPROCS;

TYPE
    BitmapApplication = object (TApplication)
        PROCEDURE InitMainWindow; VIRTUAL;
        END;

    PBitmapWindow = ^BitmapWindow;
    BitmapWindow = OBJECT (TWindow)
        HImage : Hbitmap;
        CONSTRUCTOR init(aparent:PWindowsObject;
            ATitle:PChar);
        DESTRUCTOR Done; VIRTUAL;
        PROCEDURE Paint(PaintDC:HDC;
            VAR PaintInfo:TPaintStruct);
            VIRTUAL;
        END;

PROCEDURE BitmapApplication.InitMainWindow;
    BEGIN
    MainWindow := NEW(PBitmapWindow,
        init(NIL, 'Listing 15.3: Enlarging a Bitmap'));
    END;

CONSTRUCTOR BitmapWindow.init(aparent:PWindowsObject;
        atitle:PChar);
```

```
BEGIN
TWindow.init(aparent, atitle);
Attr.X := 50;
Attr.Y := 50;
Attr.W := 500;
Attr.H := 400;
HImage := loadbitmap(hinstance, 'userhead');
END;

DESTRUCTOR BitmapWindow.done;
   BEGIN
   DeleteObject(HImage);
   TWindow.done;
   END;

PROCEDURE BitmapWindow.Paint(paintdc:hdc;
               VAR paintinfo:tpaintstruct);
   VAR
      OldObject : THandle;
      MemDC: HDC;
      counter : longint;
   BEGIN
      MemDC := createcompatibleDC(PaintDC);
      OldObject := SelectObject(MemDC, HImage);

      {Draw the initial image}
      BitBlt(PaintDC, 50, 50, 72, 72, MemDC,
            0, 0, srcCopy);

      {  This is an empty FOR loop to delay drawing
         the new image long enough that the process
         can be seen. Depending on your PC, you may
         need to use a larger or smaller number for
         the number of loops.}
      FOR counter := 1 TO 200000 DO BEGIN END;

      {  Draw a new, larger image in the same location.
         There's no need to erase the old image. The
         new image is drawn over it, automatically
         erasing it. The new image is four times the
         size of the old image.}
      StretchBlt(paintdc, 50, 50, 288, 288, MemDC,
         0, 0, 72, 72, srcCopy);

      SelectObject(MemDC, OldObject);
```

```
        DeleteDC(MemDC);
    END;

{global object variable for application}
VAR
    BitmapApp : BitmapApplication;

{main body of program}
BEGIN
    BitmapApp.init('Listing 15.3');
    BitmapApp.run;
    BitmapApp.done
END.
```

This time, we call *StretchBlt*, but use the same X and Y coordinates for the upper left corner of the image region. What changes are the width and height parameters: each of these is four times the original size of the 72×72 bitmap.

Because the new, larger image is being drawn directly over the old image, it automatically erases the old image. The result of running Listing 15.3 is shown in Figure 15.5.

FIGURE 15.5:

Enlarging a bitmap image in a window

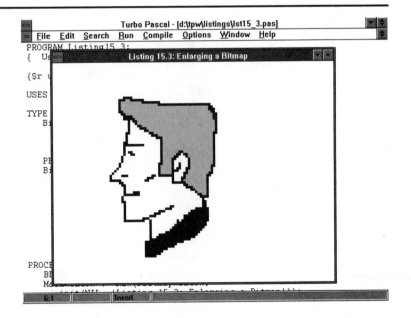

Creating and Using Icons

Icons are also bitmaps, but they are a special kind of bitmap. You can create an icon to provide the user with a custom-made selectable object—for example, to represent a minimized program on the Windows desktop (just like the Turbo Pascal for Windows icon, the Windows Write icon, and so on).

Using the WRT Icon Editor

The first step in creating an icon is to open the WRT icon editor or another icon editor, such as the one in the Borland Resource Workshop. You draw the icon in the same way you do any other bitmap. A sample icon is shown in Figure 15.6.

This icon is saved in a resource file called STARFIRE.RES. You can save an icon either in a .RES resource file or by itself as a .ICO icon file. The resource name for this icon may seem a little puzzling: *SF4P16C*. That's because it's designed to contain information about the particular icon resource. The "SF" is for StarFire—that's the mnemonic name of the icon. "4P16C" indicates that the icon format is four-planes, 16-colors.

FIGURE 15.6:

An icon created in the WRT icon editor

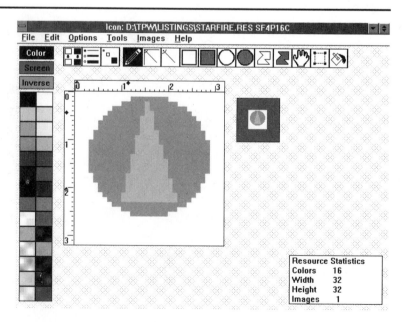

You can create and store an icon image in four different formats in the same .RES file. Depending on which type of display device (i.e., monitor) is used, the correct format will be selected by Windows—but *only* if you've included it. These formats are listed in a drop-down combo box when you first create the icon, as shown in Figure 15.7, so you simply pick the format you want to use. You should create a separate version of the icon for each format to give your icon maximum device independence.

Displaying an Icon for a Minimized Program

Loading and displaying an icon is actually pretty simple—TPW and Windows do most of the work for you behind the scenes. Listing 15.4 shows how to load and display an icon.

Listing 15.4

```
PROGRAM Listing15_4;
{ Shows how to use an icon (stored in an .RES resource
   file) to represent a minimized program on the Windows
```

FIGURE 15.7:

Choosing an icon format in the WRT icon editor

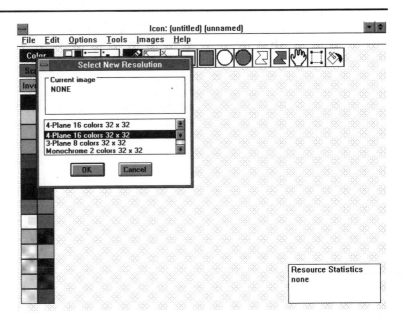

```
desktop. Specific features demonstrated:
1. Overriding the inherited TWindow.GetWindowClass
   method in order to load the icon resource.
2. Using the LoadIcon function.
3. Loading the icon handle into the window's
   inherited HIcon field. }

{$r starfire.res}

USES WOBJECTS, WINTYPES, WINPROCS;

TYPE
    StarFireApplication = OBJECT (TApplication)
        PROCEDURE InitMainWindow; VIRTUAL;
        END;

    PStarFireWindow = ^StarFireWindow;
    StarFireWindow = OBJECT(TWindow)
        PROCEDURE GetWindowClass(
            VAR AWndClass:TWndClass);
            VIRTUAL;
        END;

PROCEDURE StarFireApplication.InitMainWindow;
    BEGIN
    MainWindow := NEW(PStarFireWindow,
        Init(NIL, 'Listing 15.4: Icon Demonstration'))
    END;

PROCEDURE StarFireWindow.GetWindowClass(
            VAR AWndClass:TWndClass);
    BEGIN
    TWindow.GetWindowClass(AWndClass);
    AWndClass.HIcon := LoadIcon(HInstance, 'sf4p16c')
    END;

VAR
    StarFireApp : StarFireApplication;

BEGIN
    StarFireApp.Init('StarFire');
    StarFireApp.Run;
    StarFireApp.Done
END.
```

There are just a few new tricks in this listing. The first step, as usual, is to include the appropriate .RES file in the program. Then, we define the main application type and the main window type. The only method in the main window type *StarFire-Window* is a new version of the *GetWindowClass* method, overriding the version that *StarFireWindow* inherits from *TWindow*.

GetWindowClass does a lot of setup work behind the scenes, setting various attributes for the window. Therefore, the first thing we do in the new version of the method is to call the inherited version from *TWindow*. That way, we don't have to worry about anything but the specific task for which we created the new version: to load a handle to the icon into the window class's inherited *HIcon* field. We do this in a way that by now is familiar: on the left, the field, and on the right, a call to a function (*LoadIcon*) that takes a handle to the current application instance and the resource name of the icon. The result of the call to *LoadIcon* is the handle to the icon, which is passed to the *HIcon* field.

And that's all we need to do! Everything else in the listing is routine. If you run the program, then minimize it, the icon will appear on the Windows desktop as in Figure 15.8.

FIGURE 15.8:

The StarFire icon displayed on the Windows desktop

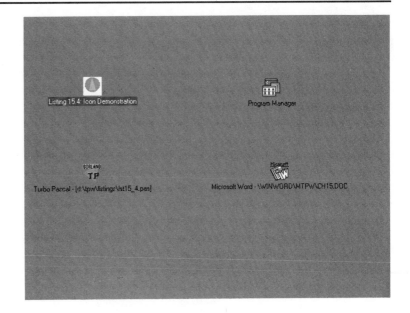

Creating and Using Cursors

Creating and using a custom-designed cursor is very similar to creating and using an icon. In both cases, you use the WRT to create the image and then load it into the application's main window attributes with a new *GetWindowClass* method. The big difference between cursors and icons, apart from the obvious differences in their use, is that a cursor must have a "hot spot" to indicate the operational part of the cursor.

With the standard Windows arrow cursor, the hot spot is the tip of the arrow. To select something and click on it with the mouse, you must position this hot spot over the thing you want to select. The tail end of the arrow won't work: it has to be the tip, the hot spot.

The WRT cursor editor therefore has one additional tool that isn't needed in the bitmap and icon editors: the cross-hairs tool at the far right of the row of tool buttons. To use this tool, you first create the cursor image, then select the hot-spot cross-hairs tool, and then click on the part of the image that you want to function as the hot spot. A sample cursor that we'll demonstrate in Listing 15.5 is shown in Figure 15.9.

FIGURE 15.9:

A cursor created in the WRT cursor editor

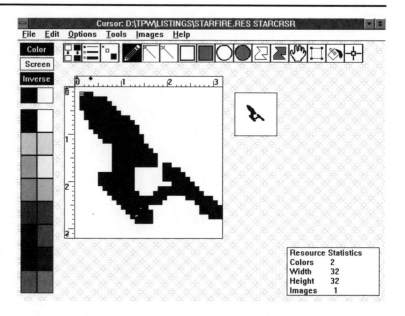

Note the hot spot tool at the far right of the row of tool buttons. The cursor we've created, called *Starcrsr*, will be displayed any time the cursor is located inside Listing 15.5's main window.

To run the program in Listing 15.5, create your own cursor in the WRT cursor editor. Save it to the STARFIRE.RES resource file, and give it the resource name of Starcrsr.

Now, let's take a look at how to use this cursor in a program. Listing 15.5 shows how to do it.

Listing 15.5

```
PROGRAM Listing15_5;
{  Shows how to use a customized cursor (stored in a
   .RES resource file). Specific features demonstrated:
   1. The window class's inherited HCursor field.
   2. Using the LoadCursor function. }

{$r starfire.res}

USES WOBJECTS, WINTYPES, WINPROCS;

TYPE
    StarFireApplication = OBJECT (TApplication)
    PROCEDURE InitMainWindow; VIRTUAL;
    END;

    PStarFireWindow = ^StarFireWindow;
    StarFireWindow = OBJECT(TWindow)
       PROCEDURE GetWindowClass(
          VAR AWndClass:TWndClass);
       VIRTUAL;
    END;

PROCEDURE StarFireApplication.InitMainWindow;
    BEGIN
    MainWindow := NEW(PStarFireWindow,
        Init(NIL, 'Listing 15.5: Custom Cursor Demonstration'))
    END;

PROCEDURE StarFireWindow.GetWindowClass(
             VAR AWndClass:TWndClass);
    BEGIN
```

```
    TWindow.GetWindowClass(AWndClass);
    AWndClass.HIcon := LoadIcon(HInstance, 'sf4p16c');
    AWndClass.HCursor := LoadCursor(HInstance, 'starcrsr');
    END;

VAR
    StarFireApp : StarFireApplication;

BEGIN
    StarFireApp.Init('StarCursor');
    StarFireApp.Run;
    StarFireApp.Done
END.
```

This is actually pretty easy stuff. All you really need to do is add one more line to the *GetWindowClass* method to load the cursor resource handle into the window's *HCursor* field. Just like *LoadIcon*, *LoadCursor* takes two parameters: a handle to the current application instance and the PChar-type string that identifies the cursor resource. Beyond that, it's all automatic: whenever the cursor location is in the application's main window, the cursor's appearance will change to the design you created.

Creating and Using String Tables

One of the most sophisticated capabilities offered by Windows is support for *string tables*. String tables allow you, as the programmer, to keep up to 64K of the text messages used by the program in a resource file separate from the program code.

The primary argument for using string tables is the same as for keeping other program elements in a separate resource file. By doing so, you can change the items in the resource without having to recode parts of your Windows application program. In the case of string tables, this means that you can change the messages and other text items that your program displays without going back into the source code. If, for example, you need to produce a foreign-language version of your program, you need only change the string table and make very minor alterations in your source code.

Another benefit of using string tables is that you reduce your program's memory requirements by loading text strings on an "as needed" basis instead of keeping them in memory all the time.

Using the WRT String Table Editor

The WRT string table editor works in a way very similar to the menu editor. On the left is a column of integer values for each string in the table. These values are assigned by the editor itself and you can't change them. On the right is the actual text of each string; the maximum length is 255 characters. The maximum size of a string table is 64K, and text in a string table should not have quote marks around it. Figure 15.10 shows the string editor with three strings entered, in response to a restaurant server's question, "What do you want?"

You save a string table in the same way as any other resource, with one exception. Only one string table is allowed in any resource file, so the WRT automatically assigns the resource name STRINGTABLE, which you can't change. This is shown in Figure 15.11.

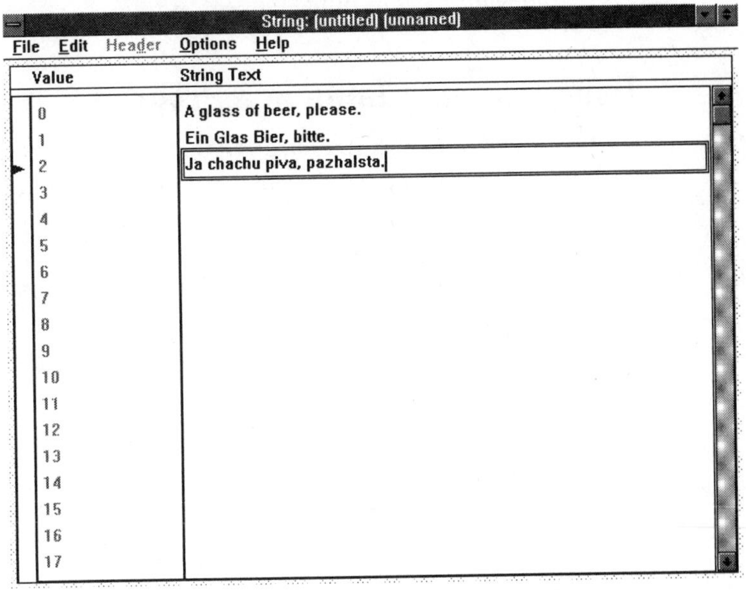

FIGURE 15.10:

The WRT string table editor with values entered

Value	String Text
0	A glass of beer, please.
1	Ein Glas Bier, bitte.
2	Ja chachu piva, pazhalsta.
3	
4	
5	
6	
7	
8	
9	
10	
11	
12	
13	
14	
15	
16	
17	

FIGURE 15.11:
The WRT automatically assigns the
name "STRINGTABLE"

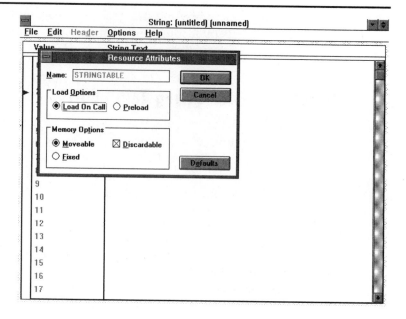

Create this string table for use with Listing 15.6 in the next section, and save it into
the *Starfire.Res* resource file.

Using a String Table in a Program

As with any resource, creating the string table is only half the battle. The other half
is incorporating it into your TPW program—but with string tables that part is easy.
The technique is shown in Listing 15.6, below.

Listing 15.6

```
PROGRAM Listing15_6;
{ Demonstrates how to use a string table. }

{$r starfire.res}

USES WOBJECTS, WINTYPES, WINPROCS;

TYPE
```

```
MyStringApplication = OBJECT (TApplication)
PROCEDURE InitMainWindow; VIRTUAL;
END;

PMyStringWindow = ^TMyStringWindow;
TMyStringWindow = OBJECT (TWindow)
    CONSTRUCTOR Init(AParent:PWindowsObject;
        ATitle:PChar);
    PROCEDURE WMRButtonDown(VAR Msg:TMessage);
        VIRTUAL wm_First + wm_RButtonDown;
    END;

PROCEDURE MyStringApplication.InitMainWindow;
    BEGIN
    MainWindow :=
        NEW(PMyStringWindow,
            Init(NIL, 'Listing 15.6: String Table Demo'))
    END;

CONSTRUCTOR TMyStringWindow.Init(AParent:PWindowsObject;
                    ATitle:PChar);
    BEGIN
    TWindow.Init(AParent, ATitle);
    WITH Attr DO
        BEGIN
        x := 50;
        y := 50;
        w := 550;
        h := 400
        END
    END;

PROCEDURE TMyStringWindow.WMRButtonDown(VAR Msg:TMessage);
    VAR
        OrderString : ARRAY[0..35] OF CHAR;
    BEGIN
        IF LoadString(HInstance, 0, OrderString, 35) > 0
        THEN MessageBox(HWindow, OrderString,
                'What would you like?',
                mb_OK OR mb_IconQuestion)
    END;

VAR
    MyStringApp : MyStringApplication;
```

```
BEGIN
   MyStringApp.Init('Listing 15.6');
   MyStringApp.Run;
   MyStringApp.Done
END.
```

We've set up this program to be as simple as possible so that nothing obscures what's going on with the string table and its contents. In fact, the program is completely ordinary except for the internal details of the *WMRButtonDown* method, which responds to a right mouse button click by displaying a message box.

In the *WMRButtonDown* method, we first declare a local character-array variable to hold the null-terminated string that we'll get from the string table. Then, we use the *LoadString* function in an IF statement. *LoadString* is a function in the Windows API that our TPW program calls in order to get the string from the string table. The function takes four parameters, which in this case are as follows:

HInstance, which is a handle to the compiled module whose file contains the string being loaded

0, which here tells the function to get the string in row #0 of the string table

OrderString, which is the TPW program's buffer variable into which the string is loaded from the string table

35, which is the maximum length of the string that can be loaded into the buffer—i.e., the size of the buffer minus 1 (for the null terminator)

If the operation fails, the *LoadString* function returns a value of 0. Here, we make a nod in the direction of error-checking by setting up the whole thing in an IF statement, but we don't do anything more.

To see how the program in Listing 15.6 works, enter it in the TPW program editor, compile it, and run it. The message box will appear when you click on the right mouse button inside the program's main window, and should look like Figure 15.12. Changing the text displayed by the program to a different language is as simple as changing the second parameter in the call to *LoadString*. If you change it from 0 to 1, you'll get the message displayed in Figure 15.13; if you change it to 2, you'll get the message displayed in Figure 15.14.

FIGURE 15.12:

An English-language string loaded
from the string table

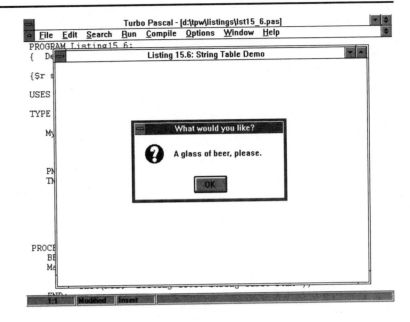

FIGURE 15.13:

A German-language string loaded
from the string table

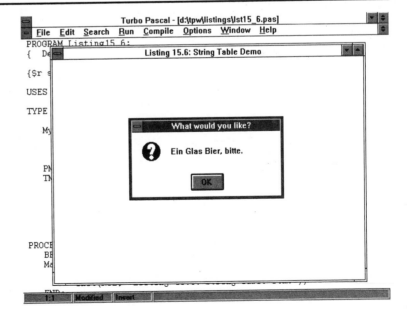

FIGURE 15.14:

A Russian-language string loaded from the string table

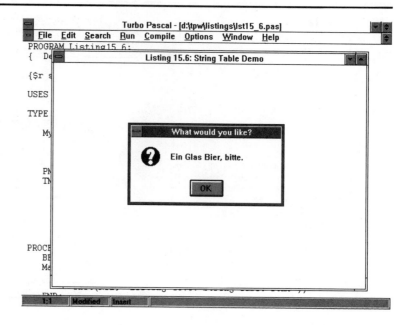

CHAPTER
SIXTEEN

Using Turbo
Debugger for Windows

- **Tips for Debugging Windows Applications**

- **Putting a Watch on a Variable**

- **Stepping through a Program**

- **Setting Breakpoints**

- **Inspecting Values**

- **Creating Macros**

Turbo Debugger for Windows, included with Turbo Pascal for Windows, provides both high-level and low-level features for debugging your TPW applications. Many of the features, such as stepping through source code one line at a time, correspond to features in the DOS version of Turbo Pascal itself; others correspond to features found in the DOS version of Turbo Debugger; and others are new in Turbo Debugger for Windows.

Tips for Debugging Windows Applications

Throughout this book, we've seen how TPW insulates the programmer from many of the complexities of Windows programming. There's no denying, however, that Windows programming—even with Turbo Pascal for Windows—is an intricate and sometimes intimidating business. There are two factors that make writing and debugging Windows applications especially challenging:

- Windows programming, even with TPW, involves learning a completely new set of procedures, functions, data types, and the like—amounting to a specialized I/O language built on top of standard Turbo Pascal. This means that, beyond ordinary bugs, you can have problems arising from unfamiliarity with the new specialized I/O language.

- Unlike traditional structured programming, Windows programming with TPW is object-oriented. By now, most programmers are pretty good at debugging standard structured programs. Object-oriented programs, however, don't work in the same way as standard structured programs and, hence, require some new approaches to debugging. Many design and debugging principles stay the same, but many change, too.

The bad news is that Turbo Debugger for Windows can't help you deal with either of these challenges: you'll have to learn TPW and object-oriented debugging techniques on your own (with a little assistance from this book). The good news is that even while you're learning, TDW can be a tremendous help in identifying and isolating bugs.

A few basic principles from standard structured programming apply to object-oriented Windows applications as well.

1. *Design the program before you start coding.* This is particularly important in object-oriented applications, in which the panoply of object types and messages can easily get out of hand unless you begin with a very clear "bird's-eye view" of how the program should be structured. In a TPW program, this means identifying the windows, dialog boxes, and other resource types that will be used in the program; deciding what ObjectWindows elements each part of the program should use; and deciding how the different parts of the program fit together (for example, a dialog's transfer buffer record will be a field in a particular window).

2. *Code the main program framework first.* This means setting up the application's main window and the other objects that will be called by the main window, but leaving other details of the implementation for later. This enables you to create a "runnable" version that doesn't do anything. As you code the details of the various methods, one at a time, you can test each to make sure it works properly before coding the next.

3. *To the extent possible, code and test each method and object type separately.* This can get pretty difficult when methods call other methods that reside in other objects (and so on), but if you code the different parts of the program in the proper sequence, it is at least possible.

Introducing Turbo Debugger for Windows

You can activate Turbo Debugger for Windows in two ways. Normally, you'll start it by selecting "Debugger" from the Run menu of TPW. However, you can also start it from the Windows desktop by clicking on the TDW icon.

In order to use Turbo Debugger with a TPW application, you must first compile the application with full debugging information turned on. You can do this from the TPW Options menu. In the **Compiler Options** dialog box, check the box for *Debug Information,* as shown in Figure 16.1. Then, in the **Linker Options** dialog box, check the boxes for a *Detailed* map file and *Debug Info in EXE,* as shown in Figure 16.2. (If you prefer, you can set these options for one program only by embedding the appropriate compiler directives at the top of your source code.)

FIGURE 16.1:

Turning on debug information in the Compiler Options box

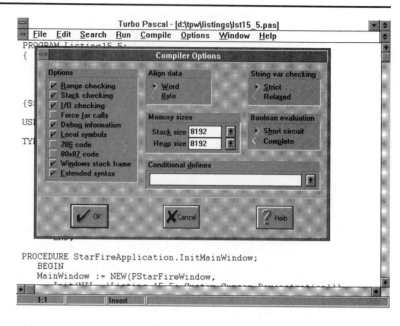

FIGURE 16.2:

Setting linker options for detailed map file and debug information in the .EXE file

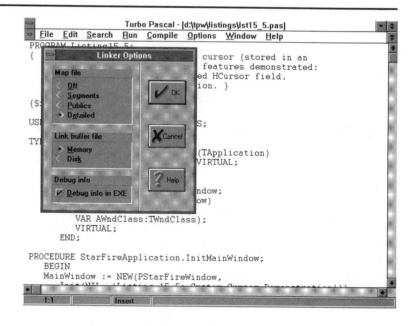

Turbo Debugger for Windows provides seven main features to help debug your applications, as well as a wide variety of options that you can choose from the TDW menus. With Turbo Debugger for Windows, you can search for bugs in a program using the following techniques:

Tracing allows you to step through the source code of your program one line at a time, as well as stepping into any subroutines that are called by the various parts of your program. This allows you to monitor the values of variables and follow the flow of the program one line at a time. This can uncover many common bugs: for example, a variable whose value never changes or an object that is calling the wrong version of a method.

Back tracing works the same as tracing except that, as you might guess, you work backwards through the program code.

Stepping is similar to tracing, except that you "step over" subroutine calls. In tracing, if an object calls a certain method, you "trace into" that method and view its operation line by line. In stepping, if an object calls a certain method, you "step over" the internal details of the method—simply executing it and moving on to the next line of code. Tracing and stepping are not mutually exclusive: in the same run through a program, you can trace into some subroutines and step over others.

Viewing is a tremendously powerful feature that lets you view the contents of almost anything connected with your program—values in variables, the stack, processor registers, and so on. This information appears in a special window in Turbo Debugger.

Inspecting allows you to take a "snapshot" of your program's state at a particular point in its execution, and then examine the values of various program elements at that point. For example, you might want to look at the values of the first, last, and middle slots of an array, or at the values of some dereferenced pointers. This feature is usually used in combination with a breakpoint (where your program executes to a desired point in the code and then stops).

Changing values lets you change the value of a variable in the middle of a program run, enabling you to see the effects of various values.

Watching values allows you to observe how the value of a variable changes as the program executes line by line. This feature is used in conjunction with tracing or stepping.

TDW Windows

Turbo Debugger provides a variety of different windows in which you can view different aspects of your program in the debugging process. The windows are as follows:

Module displays the source code for the current program module that you're debugging—whether it's in the main source file of your program or in a unit. In this window, you can set breakpoints in the code or follow the program execution as you step through line by line.

Watches displays the values of selected variables as the program runs.

Breakpoints displays the breakpoints in your program. In case you're unfamiliar with the idea, a breakpoint is a location you specify in the source code of your program. When you run the program in Turbo Debugger for Windows, the program will run up to the breakpoint and then stop. Then, you can inspect the values of variables, processor registers, and other program entities to determine if there's a problem. When you're finished, you can either restart the program from the breakpoint or return to the beginning of the program to run the whole thing again.

Stack displays the current contents of the stack, where subroutine calls are stored while the subroutines are active. Like a stack data structure, the first-called routine is at the bottom of the stack, the last-called routine is at the top, and the calls are popped off by your program in reverse order.

Log displays the "message log," which consists of the messages TDW generates about your program during the debugging session.

Variables displays all the variables that are accessible from the current position in your program's source code. The upper part of the window displays global variables, while the lower part of the window displays local variables in the current method or subroutine (if there are any).

File displays the contents of a disk file. The file can be viewed either in ASCII characters or in hexadecimal notation. In the File window, you can also search for specific sequences of text or bytes, and can correct or otherwise change the contents of the file.

CPU displays the current contents of the central processor and its registers and flags, including disassembled machine instructions. This is useful for finding very subtle, low-level bugs, but isn't needed for most garden-variety programs. There are five sections in the CPU window: for disassembled machine instructions, for hex bytes, for hex words, for CPU registers, and for CPU flags.

Dump "dumps" the data in an area of memory to the screen so that you can inspect the data. The data can be viewed as ASCII characters, hexadecimal bytes, words, double-words, or in any floating-point format. (This is the same as the data section of the CPU window.)

Registers displays the contents of the processor registers and flags. (This is the same as the registers and flags sections of the CPU window.)

Numeric Coprocessor displays the current contents of a numeric coprocessor if one is present.

Execution History displays the lines of assembly and source code that have been executed so far in the current run of your program.

Hierarchy shows the ancestry of all object types used in the current program module; the object type is displayed on the left, the hierarchy tree is shown on the right.

Windows Messages displays a list of the messages that have been passed back and forth between the windows in your application.

Operations with Turbo Debugger for Windows

There are several important operations that you'll perform again and again with Turbo Debugger for Windows: putting a watch on a variable, stepping through a program, setting breakpoints, inspecting values, and creating macros. Let's look at each of these in turn.

Putting a Watch on a Variable

The most efficient way to put a watch on a variable is to position the text cursor (not the mouse cursor) on the first letter of the variable expression that you want to watch, then press *Ctrl-F7* or select "Add watch" from the Data menu. This will open a dialog box asking you for the name of the variable to watch, with the variable you've selected already entered into the box. To put a watch on the variable, you simply press *Enter*.

Sometimes, of course, you want to watch a variable that isn't spelled out per se in the source code of your program—such as, for example, the *n*th slot of an array. In that case, you can simply press *Ctrl-F7* or select "Add watch" and then type in the expression whose referent you want to watch, such as

```
Listhead.next^.next^.next^.name
```

or

```
ThisArray[n]
```

Whenever the variable is accessible from the current point in the program, its value will be displayed in the Watch window. You can put a watch on as many variables as you like, though it gets kind of cumbersome if you have more than four or five watches at the same time.

Stepping Through a Program

The operation that goes naturally with watching a variable is stepping through a program. To execute your source code one line at a time, you simply press *F8*, and the program will start executing at the beginning. If you want to trace into subroutines and method calls, you can press *F7* instead of *F8*, and of course, you can mix the two modes in stepping through a single program—tracing into some subroutines but not others.

As you step (or trace) through the program, the values of the watched variables will appear in the Watch window.

Setting Breakpoints

There are times when stepping all the way through a program doesn't make much sense. You may only be interested in what happens to a variable at a certain point in the program, and if that point is toward the end of the program, stepping is an inefficient way to get there. On the other hand, you may be less interested in watching the value of the variable *change* than in simply finding out what it *is* at a certain point in the program. For these purposes, setting breakpoints is the ideal solution.

You set a breakpoint by positioning the text cursor immediately above the line of code where you want the program to stop. Then, either press *F2* or select "Toggle" from the Breakpoints menu. A horizontal red bar will appear, indicating that a breakpoint has been inserted at the desired location. When you run the program in Turbo Debugger, it will stop just before the line of code under the breakpoint.

To remove a breakpoint, you simply position the text cursor on the breakpoint and again press *F2* or select "Toggle" from the Breakpoints menu. You can insert as many breakpoints as you like; though, as with watches, it gets "bunglesome" (as Charles Hobbs so memorably puts it) if you have too many.

Inspecting Values

The way you'll usually use breakpoints is with the Evaluate/Modify feature, which you activate either by pressing *Ctrl-F4* or by selecting "Evaluate/Modify" from the Data menu. This opens a window in which you can type the expression whose value you want to inspect.

Creating Macros

To automate your work in TDW, simply open the Macros submenu and select "Create." The speed key for this operation, if you want to avoid the menu, is *Alt-=* (the *Alt* key together with the equals sign). This prompts you for the key combination that will be used to activate the macro once it is recorded. It then puts TDW in "recording" mode, and all the strokes you type will be recorded in a macro associated with the key combination you specified.

To stop recording, you simply select "Stop Recording" from the Macros submenu or press *Alt- -* (the *Alt* key together with the hyphen key).

If you decide that you'll no longer need a particular macro, you can select "Remove" from the Macros submenu. TDW then prompts you for the key combination associated with the macro you want to remove, and deletes only that macro. On the other hand, if you want to delete all the macros currently in use, you can select "Delete All" from the Macros submenu, and all current macros will be deleted.

Other TDW Features

There are many other TDW features that can help you debug your Windows programs, but which are beyond the scope of this book. Some of these features are highly specialized, such as inspecting processor registers, while others are more general, such as customized windows to inspect scalars, pointers, and the like. The best way to learn TDW is to use it in debugging real-life TPW programs.

PART IV

Advanced Windows Programming Skills

Using the Windows Multiple-Document Interface (MDI)

17

- **A Simple MDI Application**

- **An Enhanced MDI Application**

One thing that almost all Windows applications can do is open multiple windows within the application. This feature is implemented by means of the Windows *Multiple-Document Interface (MDI)*.

Writing an MDI application—i.e., an application that can manage multiple child windows—is much easier in TPW than you might imagine. All that's really needed is a type of window that can serve as a containing "frame" to keep track of the different windows inside it and allow the user to perform operations on those windows. ObjectWindows provides this in the *TMDIWindow* type, a descendant of *TWindow*. A *TMDIWindow*-type window keeps pointers to the windows it contains (its child windows) in a linked list that is one of its object fields.

The child windows are not created directly in their parent window (the *TMDIWindow* object) itself. They are actually created in the parent window's client area, which must be a *TMDIClient*-type object, and which the parent window keeps in its *ClientWnd* object field. The client area is very much like the Windows desktop itself. It is in the client area that windows are opened, closed, moved, minimized, rearranged, and so forth.

There is also a variety of standard operations supported by MDI parent windows, such as creating new child windows, cascading or tiling those windows inside the parent's client area, and arranging the icons that represent minimized child windows. Although an MDI window supports these operations, they must be provided with the help of an associated menu resource.

A Simple MDI Application

The preceding gives some of the conceptual background of MDI applications, but there's no substitute for seeing an example. To set up an MDI application, we must first create an appropriate menu resource. Using the WRT (or any other resource editor), create the menu and accelerator resources specified in Listing 17.1. Then, enter the TPW program shown in Listing 17.2.

Listing 17.1

```
Menu resource
&Child Windows;  value = 0
     &New Window\tF3;  value = 24339
     &Cascade Windows\tShift+F5; value = 24337
```

```
        &Tile Windows\tShift+F4;  value = 24336
        Arrange &Icons\tShift+F3;  value = 24335
        Close &All Windows;  value = 24338
Resource file name: MDI_DEMO.RES
name = MDI_MENU
Accelerator resource
Acc #1: Virtkey; key = F3; Shift = yes; Ctrl = no; Alt = no;
        value = 24335; Invert = yes
Acc #2: Virtkey; key = F3; Shift = no; Ctrl = no; Alt = no;
        value = 24339; Invert = yes
Acc #3: Virtkey; key = F4; Shift = yes; Ctrl = no; Alt = no;
        value = 24336; Invert = yes
Acc #4: Virtkey; key = F5; Shift = yes; Ctrl = no; Alt = no;
        value = 24337; Invert = yes
Resource file name: MDI_DEMO.RES
name = MDI_ACCS
```

Listing 17.2

```
PROGRAM Listing17_2;
{Shows a simple MDI application that can open multiple
windows, cascade and tile the windows, arrange icons,
and close all the windows. These features are all pre-
defined in ObjectWindows. }

{$R MDI_Demo.Res}

USES WOBJECTS, WINTYPES, WINPROCS;

TYPE
    TMDIApplication = OBJECT(TApplication)
        PROCEDURE InitMainWindow; VIRTUAL;
        END;

{This next type declaration is not strictly needed,
and is included because we are going to extend the
TMDI_FrameWindow type in Listing 17.3. If we wanted
to skip this declaration, we could simply use NEW
with TPW's predefined PMDIWindow pointer type in
the InitMainWindow method.
------------------------------------ }
PMDI_FrameWindow = ^TMDI_FrameWindow;
TMDI_FrameWindow = OBJECT(TMDIWindow)
    END;
```

```
PROCEDURE TMDIApplication.InitMainWindow;
    BEGIN
        MainWindow := New(PMDI_FrameWindow,
        Init('Listing 17.2: Simple MDI Demonstration',
            LoadMenu(HInstance, 'MDI_Menu')));
        HAccTable := LoadAccelerators(HInstance,
            'MDI_Accs');
    END;

{global object variable for application}
VAR
    MDI_DemoApp: TMDIApplication;

{main body of program}
BEGIN
    MDI_DemoApp.Init('Listing 17.2');
    MDI_DemoApp.Run;
    MDI_DemoApp.Done;
END.
```

The results of running Listing 17.2 are shown in Figures 17.1 through 17.3. With remarkably few lines of TPW code, we've set up a window that can open and close

FIGURE 17.1:

Cascading multiple child windows from Listing 17.2

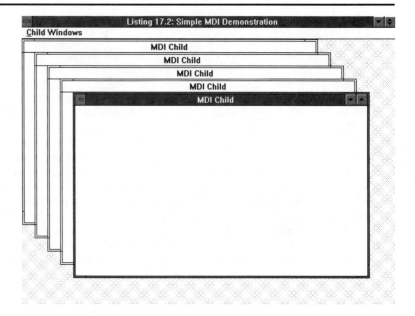

FIGURE 17.2:

Tiled multiple child windows from Listing 17.2

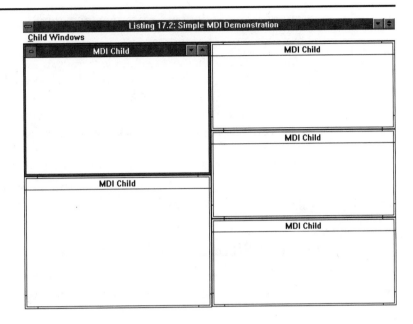

FIGURE 17.3:

Minimized multiple child windows (with menu open) from Listing 17.2

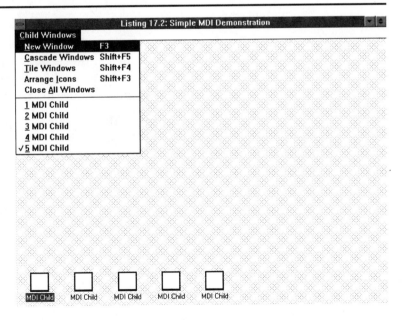

multiple child windows, rearrange them, and display their icons when they are minimized.

You may notice that all the child windows in the program from Listing 17.2 have the same window title: "MDI Child." Of course you can modify the TPW program so that each MDI child window gets its own title (often the name of a disk file that the window contains) and exhibits other unique characteristics, but MDI child windows do have certain limitations compared to the parent window:

- They can never extend outside the borders of their parent window.

- They cannot have their own menus—all the operations done on them must be done from the parent window's menu.

Parts of a Simple MDI Application

Let's go through Listings 17.1 and 17.2 step by step. Listing 17.1—the resource specification—will be familiar in some respects, but odd in others. In the menu resource, each menu item gets menu text, then a tab ($\backslash t$), then the "speed key" (accelerator) for that menu item. The values of the menu items, however, are so different from what we've used up to now that you may suspect they're not just random choices.

In fact, the values aren't random choices. These are the values preassigned in ObjectWindows to these particular predefined menu operations. ObjectWindows will do all the work for you in setting up the methods to perform these operations, but only if you know these integer values to include in the menu resource.

These values are documented, after a fashion, on page 457 of the *Windows Reference Guide* that is included with TPW. There are only two problems with the documentation: Some of the values given are incorrect, and they're all in hexadecimal notation, which isn't what you need even if they were correct. Table 17.1, below, gives the *correct* values (in decimal notation) to use for these and related menu choices when you set up menus in the WRT (or other resource editor).

As for the program in Listing 17.2 itself, it begins in the usual way by using the {$R ..} compiler directive to include the resource file, then sets up the main object variable for the application itself. The application itself, in spite of the name TMDIApplication, is to be a standard-issue *TApplication*-type object, with nothing at all special about it.

TABLE 17.1: Predefined constants for standard menu choices

	Name	"Official" Value	Decimal Value
Offset Values	cm_First	$A000	40960
	cm_Internal	$FF00	65280
	cm_Reserved	cm_Internal - cm_First	24320
Edit Commands	cm_EditCut	cm_Reserved + 0	24320
	cm_EditCopy	cm_Reserved + 1	24321
	cm_EditPaste	cm_Reserved + 2	24322
	cm_EditDelete	cm_Reserved + 3	24323
	cm_EditClear	cm_Reserved + 4	24324
	cm_EditUndo	cm_Reserved + 5	24325
	cm_EditFind	cm_Reserved + 6	24326
	cm_EditReplace	cm_Reserved + 7	24327
	cm_EditFindNext	cm_Reserved + 8	24328
File and MDI Commands	cm_FileNew	cm_Reserved + 9	24329
	cm_FileOpen	cm_Reserved + 10	24330
	cm_MDIFileNew	cm_Reserved + 11	24331
	cm_MDIFileOpen	cm_Reserved + 12	24332
	cm_FileSave	cm_Reserved + 13	24333
	cm_FileSaveAs	cm_Reserved + 14	24334
	cm_ArrangeIcons	cm_Reserved + 15	24335
	cm_TileChildren	cm_Reserved + 16	24336
	cm_CascadeChildren	cm_Reserved + 17	24337
	cm_CloseChildren	cm_Reserved + 18	24338
	cm_CreateChild	cm_Reserved + 19	24339
	cm_Exit	cm_Reserved + 20	24340

Note that these values could be changed in future versions of TPW and ObjectWindows; if so, your resource specifications might need to be changed as well. Check these out when upgrading to later versions.

The next step is to define a type for the application's main window. This one *does* need to be special, because it must be an MDI window. Ordinarily, in an application this simple, we could omit this step and just make the main window of type *TMDIWindow*, which is all we're really doing anyway. However, this type definition sets the stage for Listing 17.3, where we'll give each child window its own unique window title. The program would work equally well, however, if we omitted the *TMDI_FrameWindow* declaration and, in the *TMDIApplication.InitMainWindow* method, used the predefined *TMDIWindow* as the type for the main application window.

In the *InitMainWindow* method, another difference shows up. Initializing an MDI window is just a little more complicated than initializing a plain *TWindow*-type window. That's because it is known in advance that an MDI window is going to have a menu, so the menu-loading step is included in the call to the window's *Init* constructor method. This method takes two parameters: a null-terminated string, which will be the window title, and a handle to a menu resource, which in this case is returned by the call to *LoadMenu*.

Normally, the child window menu is displayed at the top left of the menu bar. However, if you have other menu popups that you want to appear first, you can change the position of the child window menu by overriding the inherited *TMDIWindow.Init* constructor and explicitly setting the child menu position to something else—for example, so that it will be the third menu in the menu bar, as in

```
CONSTRUCTOR TMDI_FrameWindow.Init(ATitle: PChar; AMenu: HMenu);
    BEGIN
    TMDIWindow.Init(ATitle, AMenu);
    ChildMenuPos := 3
    END;
```

Getting back to Listing 17.2, the next step in *InitMainWindow* is to load the accelerator resource, which is done the same way we've done it before. Then we declare an object variable for the application and run it. That's all there is to it. Most of the work is done for us by TPW and ObjectWindows.

An Enhanced MDI Application

There's so much in TPW's MDI features that a whole book could be devoted to the subject. Let's look at just one more example to show how you can add new features to an MDI application. Listing 17.3 shows an application that sets up each child window with its own unique window title. It also gives a hint of just how much work is going on behind the scenes even in a simple MDI application. The results of running the program are shown in Figures 17.4 through 17.6.

Listing 17.3

```
PROGRAM Listing17_3;
{Shows a slightly more sophisticated MDI application
in which each child window gets a unique title. }

{$R MDI_Demo.Res}

USES WOBJECTS, WINTYPES, WINPROCS, STRINGS;

TYPE
    TMDIApplication = OBJECT(TApplication)
        PROCEDURE InitMainWindow; VIRTUAL;
        END;

    PMDI_DemoChild = ^TMDI_DemoChild;
    TMDI_DemoChild = OBJECT(TWindow)
        Number: INTEGER;
        CONSTRUCTOR Init(AParent: PWindowsObject;
            ChildNumber: INTEGER);
        END;

    PMDI_FrameWindow = ^TMDI_FrameWindow;
    TMDI_FrameWindow = OBJECT(TMDIWindow)
        FUNCTION CreateChild: PWindowsObject; VIRTUAL;
        END;

CONSTRUCTOR TMDI_DemoChild.Init(AParent:PWindowsObject;
                    ChildNumber: INTEGER);
    VAR
        TitleStr: ARRAY[0..15] of CHAR;
        ChildNumberStr: ARRAY[0..5] of CHAR;
    BEGIN
        Str(ChildNumber, ChildNumberStr);
        StrCat(StrECopy(TitleStr, 'Window #'), ChildNumberStr);
        TWindow.Init(AParent, TitleStr);
        Number := ChildNumber;
    END;

FUNCTION TMDI_FrameWindow.CreateChild: PWindowsObject;
    VAR
        ChildNumber: INTEGER;
```

```
        {local function under CreateChild method}
        FUNCTION NumberMade(WinPtr:PMDI_DemoChild): BOOLEAN; FAR;
            BEGIN
            NumberMade := ChildNumber = WinPtr^.Number;
            END;

        {main body of CreateChild method}
        BEGIN
            ChildNumber := 1;
            WHILE FirstThat(@NumberMade) <> NIL DO
                    INC(ChildNumber);
            CreateChild := Application^.MakeWindow(NEW(
                    PMDI_DemoChild, Init(@Self,
                    ChildNumber)));
        END;

PROCEDURE TMDIApplication.InitMainWindow;
        BEGIN
            MainWindow := New(PMDI_FrameWindow,
            Init('Listing 17.3: Enhanced MDI Demonstration',
                    LoadMenu(HInstance, 'MDI_Menu')));
            HAccTable := LoadAccelerators(HInstance,
                    'MDI_Accs');
        END;

{global object variable for application}
VAR
        MDI_DemoApp: TMDIApplication;

{main body of program}
BEGIN
        MDI_DemoApp.Init('Listing 17.3');
        MDI_DemoApp.Run;
        MDI_DemoApp.Done;
END.
```

This is still a simple application by Windows standards, but it is significantly more complex than the program in Listing 17.2. The first thing to notice is that we've added the STRINGS unit to the program's USES clause; that's because we're going to need string-manipulation routines to set up the window titles.

The next new feature is the declaration of a window type (*TMDI_DemoChild*) for the child windows. In this type, we include a field for the window number (because

FIGURE 17.4:

An enhanced MDI application with cascading windows

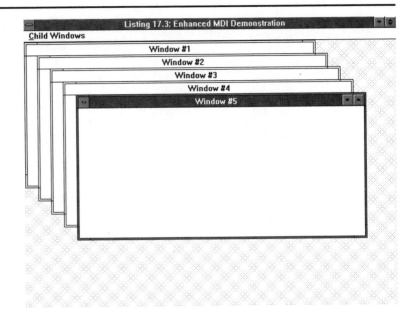

FIGURE 17.5:

An enhanced MDI application with tiled windows

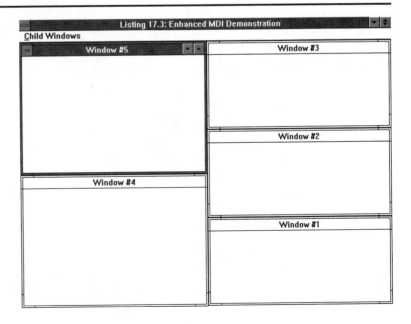

FIGURE 17.6:
An enhanced MDI application with minimized windows

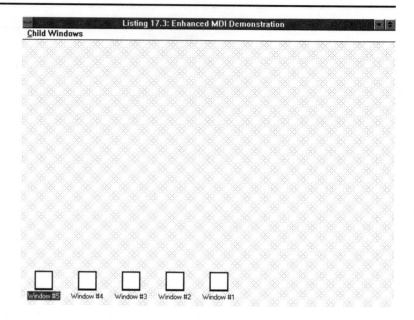

there may be more than one window open in the application) and override the inherited *Init* constructor to include the window number in the title.

Because the child windows will no longer be plain, generic MDI windows, the parent window type *TMDI_FrameWindow* must now have a method to create its child windows. This overrides the *CreateChild* method inherited from the predefined *TMDIWindow* type, which we didn't need to define in Listing 17.2, because we were using it—as well as the MDI child windows—"as is." Here, however, we override it because we're adding a new feature to it. *CreateChild* is a function, and it returns a pointer to the newly created child window. This pointer is added to the parent window's linked list of pointers to child windows.

In the specification of the *TMDI_DemoChild* type's *Init* constructor, we use several routines from the STRINGS unit to concatenate a boilerplate text item with the number of the window. After declaring two local variables to hold the window title and window number, respectively, we call the predefined *Str* routine to convert the window number (passed to *Init* as a parameter) to a string and copy it to the null-terminated string variable *ChildNumberStr*. We then call the *StrCat* routine to concatenate null-terminated strings, using the *StrECopy* routine to copy the desired text into the first eight slots of the *TitleStr* array. *StrCat* then adds the content of

ChildNumberStr to the end of the value returned by *StrECopy*, and we have our window title. The rest is standard, as we call the *TWindow.Init* routine with the parent-window handle and the child-window title, then assigning the appropriate number to the child window's *Number* field.

Next, we define the details of the parent window's *CreateChild* function. After defining a local variable to hold the number of the child window, we set up a function to get the appropriate window number for us. *NumberMade* takes a pointer to a child window as its argument and returns TRUE if the child window's number field is the same as the current value of the local *ChildNumber* variable. This is actually a pretty tricky move for which the tricky programmers at Borland deserve the credit, and its significance (as well as the reason why the function must be FAR) becomes clear when we get to the main body of the method.

In the main body of the method, we call the *FirstThat* method inherited from the *TWindowsObject* abstract type. This method traverses the child-window linked list of the parent window. At each node in the list, it calls the *NumberMade* function. To the function, it passes the pointer to the current node's corresponding child window as an argument. If the pointer is not NIL, then the end of the list has not yet been reached, and the window number is incremented by 1. The end result is that when the end of the child window list is reached, the window number has been set to the appropriate value.

The function passed to *FirstThat*, however, must be FAR, so that it can access data in another segment. (This is why the *NumberMade* function had the FAR directive in its heading.)

After incrementing the window number, we call the *CreateChild* method with the predefined *Application^.MakeWindow* method to create the child window. The rest of Listing 17.3 should be fairly familiar.

Memory Management with Turbo Pascal and Windows

- **Windows Operating Modes**

- **Memory Addressing Schemes**

- **How Windows Organizes PC Memory**

- **Turbo Pascal and Memory Management**

Most discussions of Windows tend to focus on its graphic-interface characteristics: how to set up windows and dialog boxes, how to work with bitmaps, and the like. In a way, this is unfortunate, because many of Windows' most impressive and important features never appear on the PC's screen. Windows' memory management capabilities fall into this category.

Turbo Pascal for Windows' ability to work with Windows' memory management is equally impressive, even though most of it goes on behind the scenes and doesn't need to concern the programmer. There are times, however, when you'll want to work directly with the Windows memory manager, and TPW provides several ways for you to do that. It also helps a great deal to understand just how Windows does manage memory, so we'll begin this chapter by covering the basics of Windows memory management. Then, we'll look at how TPW helps you work with the Windows memory manager, both directly and indirectly.

Windows Operating Modes

Windows manages memory in one of three different modes, depending on the hardware that the user has available. Each mode is designed to make maximum use of the memory and processor resources that are available. *Real mode*, the least ambitious, will run on any Windows-capable PC, *standard mode* requires at least an 80286-class PC and a minimum one megabyte of RAM, and *enhanced mode* requires an 80386-class PC and at least two megabytes of RAM.

Memory Addressing Schemes

In order to understand some of the key differences between real, standard, and enhanced modes, it's necessary to take a brief look at the addressing methods used by different PC processors and how Windows works with these processors.

The most primitive addressing mode was introduced with the original IBM PC and its 8086-class (actually an 8088) processor. This was called *segmented addressing*. Because the 8086 is a 16-bit processor, it was automatically capable of addressing 2 to the 16th power (64K) different memory locations. However, the PC was intended to be able to address a full megabyte of RAM, which meant that some trick would be needed to extend the addressable memory capabilities of the 16-bit processor.

The trick was segmented addressing, which combines two 16-bit logical addresses to give a single 20-bit physical address—enough to cover a full megabyte of RAM. The total address space is divided into 64K segments. The address of any particular item in RAM is given in *segment:offset* form. The first number (usually given in hexadecimal) is the address of the particular 64K memory segment in which the item resides; the second (the offset) is the item's address relative to the beginning of the segment.

A program can get the fastest performance when it keeps the segment address constant and all that changes is the offset address. An address in the same segment (using only the offset address) is called "near," while an address in a different segment is called "far." Within a segment, the offset address can vary up to 64K: from $0000 to $FFFF. We've seen a few examples of near and far method calls in our TPW program listings.

An 8086-class or higher processor has registers to keep track of all the different segments it uses. Segment addresses are kept in the code segment register, the data segment register, the stack segment register, and the extra segment register.

With the introduction of the 80286-class processor came *protected mode.* In protected mode, the segment address no longer refers to a physical memory address where the segment begins, but instead to an address in a "descriptor table" of 24-bit memory addresses in physical memory. The offset address is used with the descriptor table address to derive a 24-bit address in physical memory. This meant, among other things, that the 80286 could directly address up to 16 megabytes (2 to the 24th power) of RAM.

In the 80386-class and later processors, segments were no longer limited to 64K in size; in fact, a segment could now be as large as 4 gigabytes. Descriptor tables were also made more sophisticated so that the 80386 could use virtual memory, up to an almost unimaginable memory size of 64 terabytes.

Real Mode

Real mode is the simplest operating mode of Windows (it was available in versions prior to 3.0) and requires at least an 8086 processor and 640K of RAM. It handles memory in a way that is quite similar to the method used by MS-DOS—one reason that programs developed for Windows real mode can have a hard time adapting to the more sophisticated standard and enhanced modes.

Real mode's segmented-addressing scheme gives it a maximum address space of one megabyte, 640K of which is available for DOS applications. As with the other operating modes, real mode sees code and data segments as *fixed* (cannot be moved), *moveable* (can be moved), and *discardable* (can be released when not in use).

In real mode, Windows sets up its global heap as a contiguous area in memory containing both code and data segments, with discardable code segments stacked on top of moveable code and data segments, which in turn are on top of non-moveable code and data segments.

Standard Mode

Standard mode is somewhat more sophisticated than real mode, and is used automatically by Windows 3.0 when the PC has at least an 80286-class processor and from one to two megabytes of RAM. The big advance in standard mode is that Windows uses the protected-mode capabilities of the 80286 (and later) processors. As we saw earlier in the discussion of addressing schemes, a key benefit is that this makes a larger memory space (16 megabytes) available for use by Windows. Windows in standard mode can use both *extended memory* (RAM above one megabyte) and *high memory* (which is the first segment in extended memory, normally reserved for other functions) for the *Windows global heap.* To take advantage of high memory, Windows uses HIMEM.SYS or a similar device driver installed in the PC's CONFIG.SYS file.

Enhanced Mode

Enhanced mode is the most advanced operating mode offered in Windows 3.0, and requires at least an 80386-class processor and at least two megabytes of RAM. This mode uses the most advanced features of the 80386-class processor, *e.g.,* virtual memory addressing and demand paging; the result is that even programs too large to fit into physical memory can be run in this mode.

In addition, enhanced mode uses the "virtual 8086" capabilities of the 80386-class processor to run each multitasked application on its own imaginary 8088 processor. This not only provides extra protection against collisions between separate multitasked applications, but also allows Windows to run as many as 16 standard MS-DOS applications at the same time, with each application getting its own dedicated address space of 680k in memory. (In spite of this, some MS-DOS applications are so ill-behaved that even Windows 3.0 running in enhanced mode can't cope with the mischief they create; Microsoft Word for DOS, surprisingly, is one of them.)

Even in enhanced mode, Windows 3.0 has trouble containing the trouble when a multitasked application crashes, and the way in which applications are multitasked is itself not foolproof.

How Windows Organizes PC Memory

Windows really is a major advance over ordinary MS-DOS, particularly in the area of memory management. Under MS-DOS, PC memory is organized in a hierarchical fashion that is relatively inflexible. At the bottom of PC memory are the BIOS, interrupt vector table, and MS-DOS itself. Above that are device drivers and memory-resident (TSR) programs. Finally, at the top, is the currently loaded application program, which normally takes all remaining memory for itself. The program code segment, the stack, and the heap are restricted to the size initially allocated within the application's allocated memory space; in addition, their locations in memory are fixed (unmoveable).

The practical outcome is relatively inefficient use of memory. In the overall DOS environment, it means that device drivers and TSR programs cannot be unloaded unless all the memory locations above them have been unloaded first; thus, even when they are not being used and are no longer needed, the memory they occupy is still unavailable for other uses. Furthermore, because the dynamic variables on the heap can be unloaded in random order from within an application program's memory space, the heap space that is available will seldom be in a single contiguous segment, and thus may be inadequate for a new large dynamic variable such as an array.

Under Windows, virtually all of these restrictions and inefficiencies disappear. Windows manages all the memory from the point at which MS-DOS loads it into RAM to the end of physical memory; all of this memory is what is called the "Windows global heap." In most cases, Windows can rearrange code and data segments for different applications, and discard what is not currently needed, so that available memory is used with maximum efficiency.

No Need for MaxAvail

The way in which Windows dynamically reorganizes available PC memory (and uses virtual memory) reduces the need for some routines from the DOS version of Turbo Pascal, such as *MaxAvail*, which determines the size of the largest contiguous memory block on the heap. Because Windows automatically compacts heap memory (apart from the exceptions noted earlier), the amount of free heap memory will often be very close to or the same as the amount of contiguous free heap memory.

Fixed versus Moveable Segments

Any Windows application has at least one code segment and at least one data segment, but it can have more if needed. These segments can be either *fixed*, which means that they must stay in the same physical memory location no matter what, or *moveable*, which means that Windows can move them to a different location if needed to make more efficient use of memory. The idea of moveable segments is alien to MS-DOS, which must pretty much leave things wherever they are in RAM as long as they are needed. Because pointers in DOS programs refer to physical memory locations, if a segment belonging to a DOS program were moved, any pointer references to data or instructions in that segment would immediately become invalid.

A Windows application, however, can generally depend on Windows itself to keep pointer references up to date as it moves data and code segments around in memory—because most pointers will be "near pointers," i.e., pointers that refer to an offset address relative to the beginning of the segment. As long as Windows keeps track of where the beginning of the segment is, any near-pointer references will still be valid. "Far pointers," however—pointers that include both a physical segment address and an offset address—will become invalid even under Windows; this is why standard DOS applications must be treated by Windows as fixed rather than moveable. However, the vast majority of segments used in Windows applications are moveable. If you see a resource script for a menu, for example, it will normally be specified as moveable, as in the script for the MDI demonstration menu in Chapter 17 (repeated below):

```
MDI_MENU  MENU LOADONCALL MOVEABLE PURE DISCARDABLE
BEGIN
POPUP "&Child Windows"
   BEGIN
   MenuItem  "&New Window\tF3", 24339
```

```
        MenuItem  "&Cascade Windows\tShift+F5", 24337
        MenuItem  "&Tile Windows\tShift+F4", 24336
        MenuItem  "Arrange &Icons\tShift+F3", 24335
        MenuItem  "Close &All Windows", 24338
        END
END
```

> **NOTE**
>
> Unless there is a compelling reason to do otherwise, all windows applications and resources should be made moveable. Applications that require fixed segments interfere with Windows' ability to manage memory efficiently.

Discardable Segments

Another characteristic of Windows memory segments is that they are often *discardable*, meaning that Windows can free up the memory they occupy if they haven't been used for a while. (The data or instructions they contain, of course, can always be reloaded from disk.) To determine which segments to discard, Windows uses an algorithm called "least recently used," which boils down to, "If it hasn't been used for a while, then maybe it's not needed anymore or not needed very often, so let's dump it." Normally, discardable segments will be ones that don't change after being loaded—such as code segments but not data segments.

Also, a discardable segment is *ipso facto* a moveable segment (though a moveable segment is not necessarily a discardable segment). Windows resource specifications will normally be discardable unless you specifically say otherwise.

Turbo Pascal and Memory Management

Most of the time, Turbo Pascal for Windows will handle all the memory-management chores for you. Once in a while, however, you'll need to work with Windows' memory manager directly; TPW makes it easy to do so. For example, you might have a large bitmap or an extremely large array that won't fit into the data segment allocated to the program itself. In such a case, TPW provides functions that let you store the large data item in Windows' global heap.

This spotlights, in fact, the main division that you'll encounter in making your applications manage memory: there's the application's local memory, allocated to it by Windows when the program is loaded (the "local heap," set up in the application's data segment) and the global heap, which is all the free memory not being used by Windows or another Windows application.

In general, using local memory results in faster program performance, but is limited to 64K in size. Using global memory, on the other hand, is slower but can provide virtually limitless memory for large data items.

Using the Application's Local Memory

Memory that can only be accessed by a particular application (or a particular instance of an application) is called the application instance's *local heap,* and resides in the application instance's data segment along with the stack and global variables used by the program. Any space in the data segment not used for the stack or global variables is available to the local heap. However, the space is *not* automatically allocated to the local heap by Windows; for that, you must either use the *$M* compiler directive or just set the default heap size in the dialog box called up by the TPW Options/Compiler menu choice. (The default heap size is 8,192 bytes.)

If the data segment is fixed, then only the amount of heap memory specified during compilation of the program will be available. However, if the data segment is moveable—certainly the more common situation—then Windows will automatically allocate more heap space if needed, as long as the 64K size limit for local heap memory will not be exceeded. In this situation, Windows might also move the data segment, invalidating far pointers to data in the segment—a reason for careful defensive programming.

An important TPW function for working with local heap memory is *LocalAlloc,* a Windows API function that allocates a block of memory from the local heap. It takes one or more flag values as parameters; these flags tell it what characteristics should be assigned to the memory block being allocated—for example, whether or not it is fixed, discardable, etc. In addition to the flags, the final parameter is the size, in bytes, of the memory block to be allocated. The flag identifiers used with *LocalAlloc* are shown in Table 18.1.

TABLE 18.1: Local memory flags used with the LocalAlloc function

Identifier	Meaning
lmem_Discardable	Block is discardable. (It must also be moveable.)
lmem_Fixed	Block cannot be moved from its initial memory location.
lmem_Moveable	Block can be moved to a new memory location.
lmem_NoCompact	No other memory blocks should be compacted or discarded in allocating space for this memory block.
lmem_NoDiscard	No other memory blocks should be discarded in allocating space for this memory block.
lmem_ZeroInit	The memory block's contents will be initialized to zero.

In as much as it is a function, *LocalAlloc* returns a value. This value is a handle to the memory block allocated; however, if the allocation attempt was unsuccessful, it returns a value of 0.

The memory block allocated by *LocalAlloc* will be at least as large as the size in bytes passed to the function as a parameter, and it can be larger. To find the exact size of the memory block, you need to use *LocalSize*, a Windows API function that takes the handle to the memory block as a parameter and returns the size in bytes of the memory block (or 0 if the handle is invalid).

Before you can gain access to the data in a local block, however, you must use *Local-Lock*, another Windows API function. This function temporarily makes the block become fixed at its current location in the local heap. *LocalLock* takes a handle to the memory block as its only parameter, and returns a pointer to the block's current location (or NIL if the operation did not succeed). The flip side of *LocalLock* is *Local-Unlock*, which restores the locked (fixed) memory block to its previous status.

When TPW takes care of memory allocation for you, you generally don't have to do anything to clean up afterwards: TPW will do it for you. But when you directly allocate memory, you need to clean up after yourself before shutting down the application. You do this—freeing local memory blocks—by using *LocalFree*, another Windows API function, which can be used not only to de-allocate memory blocks at the close of an application, but also to de-allocate memory blocks during an application's run if they are no longer needed. *LocalFree* is something like *Dispose* in standard Pascal: it takes a handle to a memory block as a parameter, frees up the memory in the block, and invalidates the handle, which cannot be reused.

Using Windows' Global Memory

Just as TPW allows you to work with an application's local heap memory, it also allows you to work directly with Windows' *global heap memory,* which is shared with other applications. Using global memory is trickier than using local memory, and depending on how much memory is available on the user's machine, it could have a serious impact on the performance of your own and other Windows programs that are running at the same time. For that reason, among others, you need to be extra careful if and when you dip into Windows' global memory. One principle to remember is that global memory blocks should be freed up as soon as they are no longer needed.

The global cousin of *LocalAlloc* is, sensibly enough, *GlobalAlloc,* which takes one or more flags as parameters plus the size of the desired block in bytes. However, because global memory is inherently more complex than local memory (inasmuch as it must be shared with Windows and other applications), there are more flags than there are for *LocalAlloc*. The most important of these flags are shown in Table 18.2.

Like *LocalAlloc, GlobalAlloc* returns a handle to the memory block if the allocation was successful, or 0 if it was not successful. Any time a block is directly allocated in the global heap, no other block is allowed to be moved or discarded; you can use *gmem_No-Discard* and *gmem_NoCompact* to achieve this result. Also, as with *LocalAlloc, GlobalAlloc*

TABLE 18.2:   Important global memory flags used with the GlobalAlloc function

Identifier	Meaning
gmem_DDEShare	The block can be shared by multiple Windows applications by using dynamic data exchange (DDE). However, the block is discarded when the application that allocated it is closed.
gmem_Discardable	The block can be discarded. This requires that the block also be specified as moveable.
gmem_Fixed	The block cannot be moved to a different memory location.
gmem_Moveable	The block can be moved to a different memory location.
gmem_NoCompact	No other memory blocks should be compacted or discarded in allocating space for this memory block.
gmem_NoDiscard	No other memory blocks should be discarded in allocating space for this memory block.
gmem_ZeroInit	The memory block's contents will be initialized to 0.

will allocate a memory block that is at least the size specified in the final, number-of-bytes parameter. To determine the actual size of the block, you can use the *Global-Size* function, which works in the same way as the *LocalSize* function.

Before working with a global memory block, you should first call *GlobalLock* to fix it at a particular physical memory location. *GlobalLock* takes the handle to the memory block and returns a pointer to its physical location. When they are no longer needed, the memory blocks should be de-allocated with a call to *GlobalFree* or *GlobalDiscard*, which work in the same way as the corresponding local-memory functions.

Using the Clipboard and Dynamic Data Exchange (DDE)

- **Copying to the Clipboard**

- **Pasting from the Clipboard**

- **Dynamic Data Exchange**

In this chapter, we'll see how to exchange data between different Windows applications. There are two ways of accomplishing this task. The first method, in which the data exchange is under the user's direct control, employs the Windows clipboard to *paste* data—including text, bitmaps, and other formats—from one window to another. The second, which two cooperating applications manage in the background, is called *dynamic data exchange* (*DDE*), and requires considerable programming sophistication.

Both approaches use some of the memory-management routines that we saw in Chapter 18.

TPW and the Windows Clipboard

If you've worked with Windows programs much at all, you're already intimately familiar with the Windows clipboard. It allows the user to highlight a block of text, copy it into a buffer area in memory, and then copy from that buffer to another window or another location in the same window.

How it all works, however, is a little more complex, even in a TPW program. First, your application must get a pointer to the data that needs to be copied to the clipboard. Then, it gets a handle to a moveable, global memory block, locks the block in position, and copies the data into the block. It then checks to see if the clipboard is available; if it is, the application empties the current contents of the clipboard and copies the data (along with a format identifier) to the clipboard. Finally, it closes the clipboard, making the data available for pasting into other windows or other locations in the same window. Retrieving data from the clipboard is essentially the same process, simply in reverse.

Let's take a look at how to copy data to the clipboard. Listing 19.1 shows a simple example in which a text string gets copied. The results of running Listing 19.1 are shown in Figures 19.1 through 19.3.

Listing 19.1

```
PROGRAM Listing19_1;
{ Shows how to copy text to the Windows clipboard. }

USES WOBJECTS, WINPROCS, WINTYPES, STRINGS;
```

```
CONST
   id_EdFld = 100;

TYPE
   PClipApplication = ^TClipApplication;
   TClipApplication = OBJECT (TApplication)
      PROCEDURE InitMainWindow; VIRTUAL;
      END;

   PMyClipWindow = ^TMyClipWindow;
   TMyClipWindow = OBJECT (TWindow)
      Editor : PEdit;
      CONSTRUCTOR Init(AParent:PWindowsObject;
         ATitle:PChar);
      PROCEDURE GetPtrToText;
      FUNCTION TextToCB(CopiedText:PChar): BOOLEAN;
      PROCEDURE CTTCB(VAR Msg:TMessage);
         VIRTUAL wm_First + wm_RButtonDown;
      END;

VAR
   PtrToText : PChar;
   TheText: ARRAY[0..30] OF CHAR;

CONSTRUCTOR TMyClipWindow.Init(AParent:PWindowsObject;
         ATitle:PChar);
   BEGIN
   TWindow.Init(AParent, ATitle);
   Attr.X := 100;
   Attr.Y := 50;
   Attr.W := 400;
   Attr.H := 250;
   Editor := NEW(PEdit,
      Init(@Self, id_EdFld, 'Some text to copy',
      100, 100, 200, 25, 30, FALSE))
   END;

PROCEDURE TMyClipWindow.GetPtrToText;
   BEGIN
   IF Editor^.GetText(@TheText, 30) <> 0
   THEN PtrToText := @TheText
   ELSE PtrToText := NIL
   END;

FUNCTION TMyClipWindow.TextToCB(CopiedText:PChar): BOOLEAN;
```

```
        VAR
            TextGlobalHandle : THandle;
            TextGlobalPtr  : PChar;
        BEGIN
        TextToCB := FALSE;
        IF (CopiedText <> NIL)
        AND (StrLen(CopiedText) > 0) THEN
            BEGIN
            TextGlobalHandle := GlobalAlloc(
                gmem_Moveable, StrLen(CopiedText) + 1);
            IF TextGlobalHandle <> 0 THEN
                BEGIN
                TextGlobalPtr := GlobalLock(TextGlobalHandle);
                IF TextGlobalPtr <> NIL THEN
                    BEGIN
                    StrCopy(TextGlobalPtr, CopiedText);
                    GlobalUnlock(TextGlobalHandle);
                    IF OpenClipboard(HWindow) THEN
                        BEGIN
                        EmptyClipboard;
                        SetClipboardData(cf_Text,
                        TextGlobalHandle);
                        CloseClipboard;
                        TextToCB := TRUE
                        END
                    ELSE GlobalFree(TextGlobalHandle)
                    END
                ELSE GlobalFree(TextGlobalHandle)
                END
            END
        END;

PROCEDURE TMyClipWindow.CTTCB(VAR Msg:TMessage);
        BEGIN
        GetPtrToText;
        IF TextToCB(PtrToText)
        THEN Editor^.SetText('Text copied to clipboard')
        ELSE Editor^.SetText('Clipboard copy failed.')
        END;

PROCEDURE TClipApplication.InitMainWindow;
        BEGIN
        MainWindow :=
            NEW(PMyClipWindow,
            Init(NIL, 'Listing 19.1: Clipboard Demo'))
```

```
        END;

VAR
    MyCBApp : TClipApplication;

{main body of program}
BEGIN
    MyCBApp.Init('Listing 19.1');
    MyCBApp.Run;
    MyCBApp.Done
END.
```

FIGURE 19.1:

Ready to copy text to the clipboard

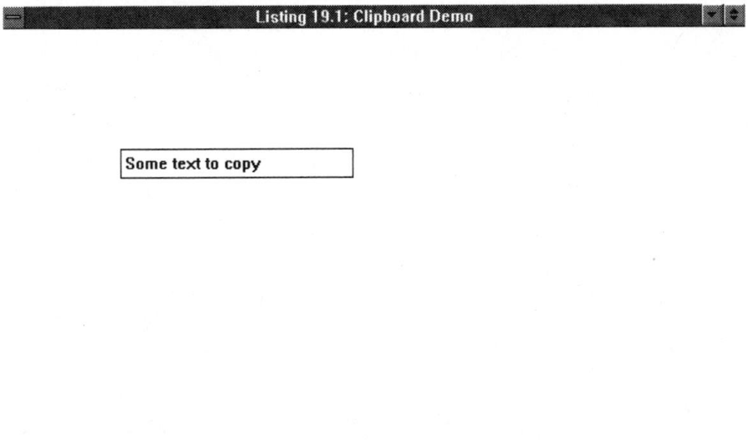

Listing 19.1: Clipboard Demo

Some text to copy

FIGURE 19.2:

Text successfully copied to the clipboard

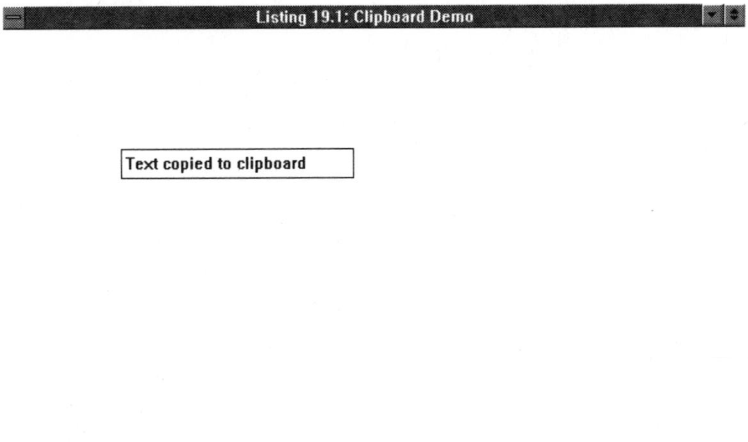

Listing 19.1: Clipboard Demo

Text copied to clipboard

FIGURE 19.3:

Text successfully pasted back from the clipboard

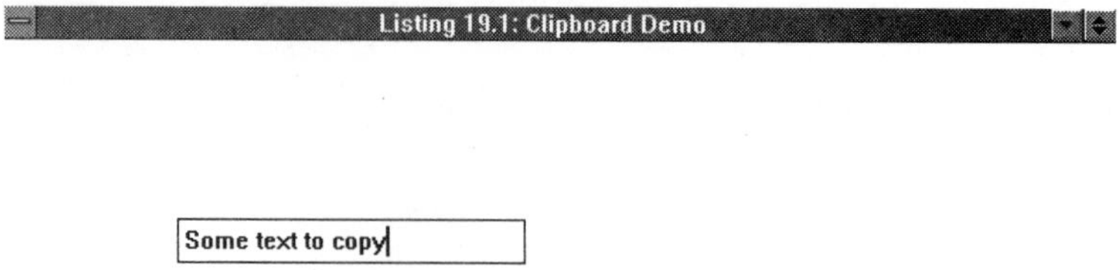

Before we get into the details of Listing 19.1, let's zoom in on one specific line in the *TMyClipWindow.TextToCB* function. In the fifth indented BEGIN..END block (the one farthest to the right), the program actually opens the Windows clipboard and copies the data into it. In doing so, it must inform the clipboard about the type of data that is going to be copied. That's what is done by the following line of code, which occurs in the middle of the block:

```
SetClipboardData(cf_Text, TextGlobalHandle);
```

This line actually does two things. First, it takes a global Windows handle to the data and passes that handle to the clipboard. Second—and this is the point we want to focus on—it passes an identifier to the clipboard showing what kind of data the clipboard is getting. There are several predefined Windows identifiers indicating the different formats in which the clipboard can receive data. They are listed in Table 19.1.

Steps in Copying to the Clipboard

The essential steps in copying to the clipboard are somewhat simpler than Listing 19.1 might lead you to believe. First, you must get a pointer to a null-terminated string: i.e. a *PChar*-type variable, because like C, TPW treats a pointer to an array of characters the same as it does an array of characters. Thus, a *PChar*-type variable can be thought of as either an array of characters or as a pointer to an array of characters—whichever is more convenient in the current situation.

At any rate, once you have such a pointer, you pass it to a function as a parameter. This function gets a handle to a Windows global memory block and copies the

TABLE 19.1: Clipboard data format identifiers

Format Identifier	Meaning
cf_Text	Standard text data—i.e., a null terminated ASCII string, each line of which is deliminated by a carriage return/linefeed character
cf_Bitmap	A Windows-compatible bitmap, such as the ones we created in the earlier chapter on icons and bitmaps.
cf_MetaFilePict	A metafile picture. This is a file containing Windows Graphics Device Interface (GDI) functions together with a data item of type *MetaFilePict*.
cf_SYLK	Data in the Microsoft Symbolic Link format, used for data exchange between Microsoft's Excel, Chart, and Multiplan application packages. This is similar to the *cf_Text* format, except that the data need not be null-terminated.
cf_DIF	Data in the Data Interchange Format used by the old VisiCalc spreadsheet program. This is also similar to *cf_Text* but need not be null-terminated.
cf_TIFF	Data in the Tag Image File Format, a popular format for storing graphic images.
cf_OEMText	Text data. This is similar to *cf_Text*, but instead of ASCII, the data uses the OEM character set.
cf_DIB	A device-independent bitmap beginning with information about the bitmap and then data in the bitmap.
cf_Palette	A Windows handle attached to a color palette, usually used together with *cf_DIB* to define the palette used by the bitmap.

pointer's referenced data into the memory block. It then checks to see if the clipboard is available. If it is, then the function empties the current contents of the clipboard, takes the handle to the global memory block, and passes it to the clipboard. It then closes the clipboard and, presto, the data is available for pasting.

Inside Listing 19.1

Let's see how these steps apply in Listing 19.1. The first step, as usual, is to declare the relevant TPW units. Then, we define a constant identifier for the edit field that we want to place in the middle of the application window. We'll use this edit field to get the initial text for copying to the clipboard, then to display a message indicating whether or not the copy operation was successful, and finally to display text pasted back from the clipboard. This isn't the only way to do it, of course, but it's probably the simplest that's a real ObjectWindows application.

Let's first go down to the *TMyClipWindow.CTTCB* method, in the bottom third of the listing, to see the overall structure of what's going on. First, the *CTTCB* method calls the *GetPtrToText* method to get a pointer to the text that we want to copy to the clipboard. Then, it passes that pointer to the *TextToCB* function, which attempts to do the actual copying process. If the process is successful, then it returns a value of TRUE, and the edit field gets a new text string, "Text copied to clipboard". If the process is unsuccessful (which can happen for a wide variety of reasons), then the new text in the edit field is "Clipboard copy failed."

Now let's go back to the top and look at the details. The definition of the overall application object type is standard stuff. Then, in the object definition of the application's main window, we include a field for the edit object that will contain the text to be pasted to and from the clipboard. In order to perform the copying and pasting operations, we include three methods: a procedure that gets a pointer to the text in the edit field, a function that actually copies the text to the clipboard, and a "shell" routine that manipulates both of those methods in response to a right-button mouse click.

Because the pointer to the text and the text-string array are shared by multiple routines, they are declared as global variables.

The *TClipWindow.Init* routine takes care of some basic housekeeping chores. First, it calls the inherited *TWindow.Init* routine to handle all the initialization details that we don't want to bother with. Then, as a cosmetic touch, it sets the position and dimensions of the application's main window. Finally, it initializes the editor field of the main window, creating a new single-line edit object and inserting the phrase "Some text to copy" into it.

The *TClipWindow.GetPtrToText* method calls the *GetText* function that the edit field inherits from its ancestor object type, *TStatic*. The *GetText* function takes two parameters: a pointer to a null-terminated string (in this case, a pointer to the global *TheText* variable) and an integer that denotes the maximum number of characters allowed in that null-terminated string. It copies the text from the edit field into the null-terminated string, and returns as a value the actual number of characters copied. This allows us to test whether the copy was successful by seeing if the return value was zero. If the copy was successful—that is, if the return value of *GetText* is not zero—then we assign the address of the null-terminated string to the global *PtrToText* variable. If not, then we set the pointer to NIL.

The Heart of the Operation: The *TextToCB* Function

The *TMyClipWindow.TextToCB* function is where things really get intricate. It first declares two local variables: one as a handle to pass to the clipboard, and one as a pointer to manipulate the text string inside the method.

In the main body of the routine, the function first sets itself to FALSE. Then it checks to see if it's received as a parameter a pointer to some actual data. If the *GetPtrToText* operation was successful, this pointer will not be NIL and the length of the text it points to will be greater than zero. If these conditions are both satisfied, it gives us a "green light" to go ahead and try to copy the text to the clipboard.

The first step is to get a handle to a global memory block, using the *GlobalAlloc* API function that we discussed in Chapter 18. The memory block must be moveable but not discardable, so we simply use the *gmem_Moveable* identifier with *GlobalAlloc* and specify the size as the length of the copied text plus one byte (to allow for the null terminator). If this operation was successful—that is, if we did get a global memory block and assign its handle to *TextGlobalHandle*—then the value of *Text-GlobalHandle* will be non-zero.

If it is non-zero, then we lock the global memory block in position so that it doesn't get moved during the copy operation. (If it moved, then our copied text could end up almost anywhere, with unpredictable results.) We pass the result—a pointer to the memory block—to *TextGlobalPtr*, which will automatically be set to NIL if the operation doesn't succeed.

If the operation was a success, then we call the *StrCopy* routine from the STRINGS unit to copy the text from the *CopiedText* parameter into the global memory block. Once that is done, we can then unlock the memory block in preparation for the final step of passing its handle to the clipboard.

Before we can pass anything to the clipboard, however, we must first check to see if the clipboard is available. If it is in use by another program, the call to *Open-Clipboard* on behalf of this particular application window (*HWindow*) will return a value of FALSE. If not—if the clipboard is available—then the function calls the Windows API function *EmptyClipboard* to clear the clipboard of any data it contains from previous copy operations. Then, the *TextToCB* function calls *SetClipboardData* to pass the global memory block's handle to the clipboard, using one of the data format identifiers we saw earlier in Table 19.1.

Finally, the function closes the clipboard so that it can be used to copy data to other windows or locations in the same window. This also frees it for use with other Windows applications.

Buried at the end of these IF code blocks are two vital ELSE clauses. What they amount to is this:

- If you don't have a valid pointer to some data, then you can't copy any data to the clipboard, so you should call *GlobalFree* to release the global memory block and invalidate its handle.

- If (for whatever reason) you can't open the clipboard, then you can't copy any data to it. Therefore, you should call *GlobalFree* to release the global memory block and invalidate its handle.

Running Listing 19.1

To run Listing 19.1, simply wait for the application main window to open and the text message "Some text to copy" to appear. Then, click the right mouse button with the mouse cursor inside the window border, and the new message "Text copied to clipboard" should appear. To verify that the text was copied, highlight and delete the text in the edit field. Then, with the text cursor in the edit field, press *Shift-Ins* to paste the original text back from the clipboard into the edit field.

Pasting Data from the Clipboard

Pasting data from the clipboard, if you're implementing it in source code, essentially just reverses the process of copying data to the clipboard. You open the clipboard with a call to *OpenClipboard*, check the format of the data it contains with *IsClipboardFormatAvailable*, retrieve the data by calling *GetClipboardData*, and close the clipboard with a call to *CloseClipboard*.

Dynamic Data Exchange

Dynamic data exchange is a very sophisticated Windows capability that allows two applications to exchange data "behind the scenes," without direct intervention or control by the user. DDE is so advanced, in fact, that there aren't yet very many PC applications for it, and the specifics of implementing DDE are beyond the scope of this book.

However, in outline, DDE is not that hard to understand. DDE is a "protocol"—a convention that tells two cooperating applications what they can expect from each other and how to interpret certain types of messages. In fact, DDE uses a group of Windows messages, all of which begin with the prefix *wm_DDE_*. Through these messages, one application can send data to or request data from another application. The topic will receive further treatment in a later edition of this book.

Using the Windows Graphics Device Interface (GDI)

- Basics of Using the GDI

- Important Windows GDI Functions: Rectangle, Pie, Ellipse, Brushes, and Fill Styles

- Creating Business Graphics

- Including Text with Graphics

- Using Windows Fonts

The Windows *Graphics Device Interface* (*GDI*) is one of the most important features of Microsoft Windows. Because computer hardware and peripherals (such as monitors, printers, plotters, and so forth) have been developed over the years by many different companies using different techniques, it's a considerable problem to make sure that a program supports at least most of the devices it's likely to meet on a user's desk.

If you've developed graphics programs under the DOS version of Turbo Pascal, then you're already intimately familiar with the problem. In order to make your program work with most of the PC video adapters and monitors available, you had to include all the relevant *BGI* (*Borland Graphics Interface*) drivers on the disk along with your program.

What makes the Windows GDI such a great advance is that you no longer have to worry about what equipment your program will run on. Instead of making your program try to detect the installed graphics hardware and then use the appropriate driver, which must be included, your program simply writes to the Windows GDI. Windows itself then takes care of translating your program's graphics output into the appropriate form—regardless of whether it's being sent to the video monitor, the printer, or some other device. Any device supported by Windows is automatically supported by your program.

This has implications beyond merely saving you the trouble of including drivers with your program for CGA, Hercules, EGA, VGA, and other video modes, and reflects the whole philosophy of Windows. In theory—though not yet in practice, of course—you can develop a Windows program on a PC that will run on any other hardware platform that is capable of running Windows. It could be a PC, a mainframe or minicomputer terminal, a Unix workstation, or even (John Sculley's worst nightmare!) an Apple Macintosh.

In previous chapters, we've already seen some features of the GDI, such as its line drawing features, pens, line styles, and color support. In this chapter, we'll extend that discussion by looking at some of the most important GDI techniques and features for creating business graphics instead of simply drawing lines in a window.

Basics of Using the GDI

The key element in displaying graphics in a Windows application (as well as for many other Windows tasks) is a *display context,* also referred to as a *device context.* This is the destination to which your program sends its graphics output. Windows itself then takes the graphics output from the display context, translates it, and sends it in the appropriate format to the desired output device.

In earlier chapters, we've discussed three important points about display contexts that are worth reiterating here:

1. Display contexts are a global resource that must be shared by all concurrently running Windows applications. Windows 3.0 provides a total of five display or device contexts.

2. You can obtain a display context from Windows by calling the Windows API function *GetDC(),* where the parameter of *GetDC()* is the handle to the window that needs the display context. You then load the handle to the display context into a variable of type HDC, which is a special TPW type for holding display contexts.

3. As soon as the display context is no longer needed, it must, *must* be released with a call to the Windows API function ReleaseDC. Failure to release a display context means that it will not be available to other programs that need it, or indeed, to other uses of the *GetDC* function in the same program. Once you've used up the five display contexts, your programs can crash if they need any more.

Using the TWindow.Paint Method

One trick that can make drawing graphics somewhat simpler is to use TPW's *TWindow.Paint* method. This method, which you will normally override so that you can customize it to draw the graphics you want, responds to a *Windows wm_Paint* message and automatically gets and releases a display context when it is called. This display context is automatically passed to the *Paint* method as one of its two parameters: *PaintDC,* which is a handle to a display context, and *PaintInfo,* which is a record of type *TPaintStruct* that contains information needed by the application for using the *Paint* method. Normally, you can ignore the *PaintInfo* parameter and let the ancestor method handle the details.

There's no absolute reason why you need to use the *Paint* method to display your graphics, as long as you remember to do the housekeeping work (e.g., getting and releasing display contexts) yourself. In general, however, it's just easier to bundle your graphics routines inside *Paint* unless there's a specific reason to do otherwise. Using the *Paint* method is illustrated in Listing 20.1, below. The result of running the program from Listing 20.1 is shown in Figure 20.1.

Listing 20.1

```
PROGRAM Listing20_1;
{ Shows some of the most important Windows GDI functions
  and how they work. Specific features demonstrated:
    1.    Using a Paint method to draw graphics.
    2.    The Windows GDI functions Rectangle, Pie,
          and Ellipse.
    3.    The Windows GDI function TextOut. }

USES WOBJECTS, WINTYPES, WINPROCS;

TYPE
    Grafapplication = object (tapplication)
        PROCEDURE InitMainWindow; VIRTUAL;
        END;

    PGrafWindow = ^TGrafWindow;
    TGrafWindow = OBJECT(TWindow)
    CONSTRUCTOR Init(AParent:PWindowsObject;
            ATitle:PChar);
        PROCEDURE Paint(PaintDC:HDC;
            VAR Paintinfo:TPaintStruct); VIRTUAL;
        END;

PROCEDURE Grafapplication.InitMainWindow;
    BEGIN
    MainWindow :=
        new(PGrafwindow, Init(
            NIL, 'Listing 20.1: Windows GDI Functions Demo'));
    END;

CONSTRUCTOR TGrafwindow.Init(AParent:PWindowsObject;
                                        ATitle:PChar);
    BEGIN
    TWindow.Init(AParent, ATitle);
    attr.x := 50;
```

404

```
        attr.y := 50;
        attr.w := 500;
        attr.h := 400;
        END;

PROCEDURE TGrafwindow.Paint(PaintDC:HDC;
        VAR Paintinfo: TPaintStruct);

        BEGIN
        Rectangle(PaintDC, 40,40,150,150);
        TextOut(PaintDC, 70,160, 'Square', 6);

        Pie(PaintDC, 180,40,400,120, 375,95,350,60);
        TextOut(PaintDC, 300, 120, 'Pie Slice', 9);

        Ellipse(PaintDC, 40,200,150,310);
        TextOut(PaintDC, 80,320, 'Circle', 6);

        Ellipse(PaintDC, 220,180,450,235);
        TextOut(PaintDC, 320,245, 'Ellipse', 7);

        {draw a line as a "flat" rectangle}
        Rectangle(PaintDC,220,300,450,302);
        TextOut(PaintDC, 325,312, 'Line', 4);

        END;

VAR
    GrafApp : GrafApplication;

BEGIN
    GrafApp.Init('Listing 20.1');
    GrafApp.Run;
    GrafApp.Done
END.
```

The features of Listing 20.1 that are relevant to our discussion of the *Paint* method are as follows. First, *TWindow.Paint* is automatically inherited by our application's main window from its ancestor *TWindow*. However, the inherited method is a generic Paint method that won't display customized graphics. That's why normally you will override the inherited Paint method with your own version which incorporates the graphics you want to create.

FIGURE 20.1:

The graphics generated by the program in Listing 20.1

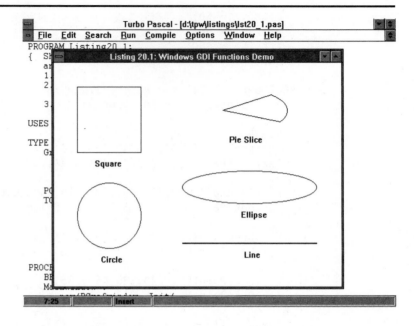

Accordingly, the first step is to declare an explicit *Paint* method in the definition of the application's main window type. To work in the same way as the inherited method (but do different things), the method declaration must have the same header as the inherited method: the two parameters *PaintDC* and *PaintInfo*. It must also be virtual so that the right versions of any *Paint*-related methods get called.

The rest is quite simple. Because the *Paint* method automatically takes care of getting and releasing a display context for its window, you as the programmer are freed to concentrate on the details of generating the graphics you want. Listing 20.1 uses several of the most important predefined graphics routines in the Windows GDI, so let's take a look at each. These routines are provided by Windows itself, not ObjectWindows, but TPW is set up so that you can easily take advantage of them.

Important
Windows GDI Functions

Windows has so many functions for the programmer—even just functions related to graphics—that documenting all of them would fill another entire book. Here, we'll just look at some of the most important ones. By using these functions creatively, it's easy to create attractive business graphics in your programs. The specific functions we will look at here are *Rectangle, Pie, Ellipse,* and *TextOut.* We'll postpone our discussion of TextOut until after we've seen how to use Windows fill styles ("hatch styles") to fill in the graphic images.

Rectangle

Rectangle, the first Windows GDI function called in Listing 20.1's Paint method, allows you to draw a rectangle by specifying a display context and the coordinates of the rectangle's upper left and lower right corners relative to the upper left corner of the parent window. We've made our rectangle a square by giving it equal height and width dimensions, but it doesn't have to be a square. The syntax of the function is:

```
Rectangle(DC: HDC; x1, y1, x2, y2: INTEGER): BOOLEAN
```

In this case, the display context parameter is *PaintDC,* automatically used by the *Paint* method. The upper left corner is at 40,40 and the lower right corner is 150,150; thus, the dimensions of the rectangle are 110 by 110. These aren't pixels; they're logical units Windows uses to map your graphics into whatever output device is being used.

Just as we saw in the earlier line-drawing program, *Rectangle* uses the currently selected pen to do its drawing, so you can change line style, thickness, and color in any way you want. It also uses the currently selected Windows *fill style* to fill the rectangle, a feature we'll use in the next program listing. If you don't explicitly set up a pen or a brush with a fill style, Windows uses the default pen (which produces a thin black line) and the default fill style (no fill pattern). Also, as a function, *Rectangle* returns a value that you can use to test whether or not the function was called successfully. If the operation failed, then the function returns a value of 0 (FALSE).

Near the bottom of the source code, we call *Rectangle* one more time. Now, however, we use it to draw a rectangle that is 230 units wide and 2 units high—resulting in a "flat rectangle" that is the same thing as a straight line.

Pie

The next Windows GDI function used in Listing 20.1 is *Pie,* which draws a pie slice with the coordinates you specify. This function is a bit more complicated than *Rectangle,* because it takes more parameters and applies them in a slightly odd way. The declaration syntax of the function is

```
FUNCTION Pie(DC: HDC; x1, y1, x2, y2, x3, y3, x4, y4: Integer):
   BOOLEAN;
```

The first parameter of *Pie* is, as usual, a display context to which the graphics output of the function will be sent. The next four parameters (*x1, y1, x2, y2*) are the coordinates of the bounding rectangle, which determines the overall size, shape, and position of the pie slice. The next two parameters (*x3, y3*) are the coordinates of the starting point of the pie's arc—its "crust," so to speak. The final two parameters are the ending point of the pie's arc, counterclockwise from the starting point. Here, the ending point is above and to the left of the starting point, so the pie slice appears as a single slice. If the ending point were below and to the left of the starting point, the graphic image would look like a whole pie with just a slice cut out of it.

Like the *Rectangle* function, *Pie* draws with the currently selected pen and fills the slice with the currently selected fill style. It returns a value of 0 (FALSE) if the operation fails for any reason.

Ellipse

The *Ellipse* function works in a way that is a little less obvious than the *Rectangle* function. With *Ellipse*, you specify the display context, then the coordinates of the upper left and lower right corners of the ellipse's bounding rectangle. The function will then draw the biggest ellipse that will fit in the bounding rectangle. If the rectangle is a square, then you'll get a circle for the ellipse; if it's higher than it is wide or wider than it is high, you'll get a corresponding ellipse. The declaration syntax of the function is:

```
FUNCTION Ellipse(DC: HDC; x1, y1, x2, y2: INTEGER): BOOLEAN;
```

Just like the *Rectangle* function, *Ellipse* is drawn with the currently selected pen and filled with the currently selected fill style. Also, it returns a value of 0 if the function call was not successful for any reason.

In Listing 20.1, we used *Ellipse* twice: once with a square bounding rectangle to produce a circle, and once with a non-square bounding rectangle to produce what would more often be referred to as an actual "ellipse."

Using Brushes and Fill Styles

The graphic images in Figure 20.1 look fine, but they would be more striking if they were filled in. That little trick is demonstrated by the program in Listing 20.2, which uses Windows brushes and fill styles to fill in the images with different fill patterns. The result of running the program from Listing 20.2 is shown in Figure 20.2.

Listing 20.2

```
PROGRAM Listing20_2;
{  Shows how to use fill styles to fill in Windows
   graphics. Specific features demonstrated:
   1.     Using handles to brushes.
   2.     Using Windows fill styles for graphic drawings.
   3.     Deleting brushes when finished with them. }

USES WOBJECTS, WINTYPES, WINPROCS;

TYPE
     Grafapplication = object (tapplication)
         PROCEDURE InitMainWindow; VIRTUAL;
         END;

     PGrafWindow = ^TGrafWindow;
     TGrafWindow = OBJECT(TWindow)
     CONSTRUCTOR Init(AParent:PWindowsObject;
             ATitle:PChar);
         PROCEDURE Paint(PaintDC:HDC;
             VAR Paintinfo:TPaintStruct); VIRTUAL;
         END;

PROCEDURE Grafapplication.InitMainWindow;
   BEGIN
   MainWindow :=
       new(PGrafwindow, Init(
           NIL, 'Listing 20.2: Windows GDI Fill Styles Demo'));
   END;

constructor TGrafwindow.Init(AParent:PWindowsObject;
                                              ATitle:PChar);
   BEGIN
   TWindow.Init(AParent, ATitle);
   attr.x := 50;
   attr.y := 50;
```

```
    attr.w := 500;
    attr.h := 400;
    END;

PROCEDURE TGrafwindow.Paint(PaintDC:HDC;
                            VAR Paintinfo:
TPaintStruct);
    VAR
        NewBrush,
        OldBrush : HBrush;

    {local procedure under Paint method}
    PROCEDURE DrawBar(x1, y1, x2, y2,
        BarFillStyle: INTEGER);
        BEGIN
        NewBrush := CreateHatchBrush(BarFillStyle, 0);
        OldBrush := SelectObject(PaintDC, NewBrush);
        Rectangle(PaintDC, x1, y1, x2, y2);
        SelectObject(PaintDC, OldBrush);
        DeleteObject(NewBrush);
        END;

    {local procedure under Paint method}
    PROCEDURE DrawPieSlice(x1,y1,x2,y2,
        x3,y3,x4,y4, PieFillStyle: INTEGER);
        BEGIN
        NewBrush := CreateHatchBrush(PieFillStyle, 0);
        OldBrush := SelectObject(PaintDC, NewBrush);
        Pie(PaintDC, x1, y1, x2, y2, x3, y3, x4, y4);
        SelectObject(PaintDC, OldBrush);
        DeleteObject(NewBrush);
        END;

      {local procedure under Paint method}
      PROCEDURE DrawEllipse(x1,y1,x2,y2, EFillStyle: INTEGER);
        BEGIN
        NewBrush := CreateHatchBrush(EFillStyle, 0);
        OldBrush := SelectObject(PaintDC, NewBrush);
        Ellipse(PaintDC, x1, y1, x2, y2);
        SelectObject(PaintDC, OldBrush);
        DeleteObject(NewBrush);
        END;

    {main body of paint method}
    BEGIN
```

```
DrawBar(40,40,150,150, hs_Cross);
TextOut(PaintDC, 70,160, 'Square', 6);

DrawPieSlice(180,40,400,120,
    375,95,350,60, hs_DiagCross);
TextOut(PaintDC, 300, 120, 'Pie Slice', 9);

DrawEllipse(40,200,150,310, hs_BDiagonal);
TextOut(PaintDC, 80,320, 'Circle', 6);

DrawEllipse(220,180,450,235, hs_FDiagonal);
TextOut(PaintDC, 320,245, 'Ellipse', 7);

{draw a line as a "flat" rectangle}
Rectangle(PaintDC,220,300,450,302);
TextOut(PaintDC, 325,312, 'Line', 4);

END;

VAR
    GrafApp : GrafApplication;

BEGIN
    GrafApp.Init('Listing 20.2');
    GrafApp.Run;
    GrafApp.Done
END.
```

The program in Listing 20.2 works the same as the one in Listing 20.1, except that we've added brushes with fill styles to fill in the drawings. This means a slightly more involved *Paint* method, so let's look at it step by step.

The first thing to notice is that, overall, we've created three local procedures inside the *Paint* method. Each local procedure handles drawing one of the different types of figures. This step merely simplifies the overall structure of the *Paint* method, making it easier to see what's going on and less likely to have hidden bugs.

As local variables, we declare two handles to fill styles. The use of these two variables becomes apparent in the first local procedure, *DrawBar*. This procedure takes five parameters:

x1 and **y1**, the coordinates of the upper left corner of the rectangle being drawn

FIGURE 20.2:

Output from running Listing 20.2

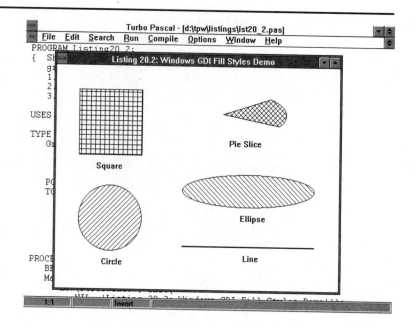

FIGURE 20.2:

Output from running Listing 20.2

x2 and **y2**, the coordinates of the lower right corner of the rectangle being drawn

BarFillStyle, an integer type that can be represented by a predefined fill style identifier

The last parameter is the new twist here. Windows defines a number of different fill styles that you can use. To use a fill style, you have to set up a brush. The fill styles available are listed in Table 20.1.

TABLE 20.1: Hatch-style fill identifiers

Identifier	Fill Style
hs_BDiagonal	Backward-slanted (downward to the right) diagonal lines
hs_Cross	Crosses resembling plus signs
hs_DiagCross	Crosses resembling the letter 'x'
hs_FDiagonal	Forward-slanted (upward to the right) diagonal lines
hs_Horizontal	Horizontal lines
hs_Vertical	Vertical lines

The main body of the *DrawBar* procedure consists of variations on what we saw in our earlier line-drawing program when we substituted one pen drawing tool for another. First, we call the Windows GDI function *CreateHatchBrush* to get a handle to a new brush tool that uses the fill style specified in the *BarFillStyle* parameter. The second parameter in the call to *CreateHatchBrush* is a *TColorRef*-type number that denotes the color of the fill pattern; here, we've simply let it be 0, making the lines in the fill pattern black. As a function, *CreateHatchBrush* returns a handle to a brush tool; we assign the handle to the local *NewBrush* variable.

We then call *SelectObject* just as we did in the line-drawing program to substitute one pen tool for another. You may recall that *SelectObject* takes two parameters: a display context, which here is *PaintDC*, and an object, which here is the handle to the new brush tool. It sets up the new brush tool to work in the display context and, simultaneously, kicks out whatever corresponding tool was there before, returning it as the *SelectObject* function's return value. We assign the return value to the local *OldBrush* variable, and we're ready to draw with the new fill style.

The next step is simply to call the *Rectangle* function with the *PaintDC* display context and the appropriate coordinates. Because *NewBrush* is now selected as the "official" drawing tool for *PaintDC*, the *Rectangle* function automatically draws a filled-in figure with the chosen fill style.

Having done our drawing, we immediately switch back to the old brush and, to conserve system resources, dispose of the newly created dynamic brush object with a call to *DeleteObject*.

The other local procedures in the *Paint* method work in exactly the same way as the *DrawBar* procedure, though the parameters vary slightly. In the main body of the *Paint* method, we draw the figures exactly as before, but this time using our local procedures and an assortment of fill styles.

Creating Business Graphics

Turbo Pascal for Windows and Windows itself lack some of the more mature capabilities for creating business graphics found in the DOS version of Turbo Pascal. However, by using some fairly simple tricks, you can turn out attractive business graphics with surprisingly little effort. For more sophisticated graphics, you might consider buying a package of predefined TPW graphics units, such as the excellent **ObjectGraphics** package from the Whitewater Group, the same company that makes the Whitewater Resource Toolkit. (No, I don't get paid for mentioning them.)

Here, we'll simply show how to do the graphics. In a real graphics program, of course, you'd provide a front-end part that would get the data for the graphics from the user. Listing 20.3 shows how to use the *Rectangle* and *TextOut* functions to create a simple bar chart. Figure 20.3 shows the result of running the program in Listing 20.3.

Listing 20.3

```
PROGRAM Listing20_3;
{  Shows how to create a simple bar chart with Windows
   GDI functions. Specific features demonstrated:
   1.     Storing bar dimensions in an array.
   2.     Creating simple routines to draw and label the
          chart. }

USES WOBJECTS, WINTYPES, WINPROCS;

TYPE
    BarChartapplication = object (tapplication)
        PROCEDURE InitMainWindow; VIRTUAL;
        END;

    grafdims = RECORD
                x1, y1, x2, y2: INTEGER
                END;

    PBarChartWindow = ^TBarChartWindow;
    TBarChartWindow = OBJECT(TWindow)
        grafbars : ARRAY[0..3] OF grafdims;
        CONSTRUCTOR Init(AParent:PWindowsObject;
            ATitle:PChar);
        PROCEDURE Paint(PaintDC:HDC;
            VAR Paintinfo:TPaintStruct); VIRTUAL;
        END;

PROCEDURE BarChartapplication.InitMainWindow;
    BEGIN
    MainWindow :=
        new(PBarChartwindow, Init(
            NIL, 'Listing 20.3: Bar Chart Demo'));
```

```
    END;

constructor TBarChartwindow.Init(AParent:PWindowsObject;
                                           ATitle:PChar);
    BEGIN
    TWindow.Init(AParent, ATitle);
    attr.x := 50;
    attr.y := 50;
    attr.w := 500;
    attr.h := 400;

    grafbars[0].x1 := 65;
    grafbars[0].y1 := 250;
    grafbars[0].x2 := 385;
    grafbars[0].y2 := 252;

    grafbars[1].x1 := 75;
    grafbars[1].y1 := 130;
    grafbars[1].x2 := 175;
    grafbars[1].y2 := 250;

    grafbars[2].x1 := 175;
    grafbars[2].y1 := 110;
    grafbars[2].x2 := 275;
    grafbars[2].y2 := 250;

    grafbars[3].x1 := 275;
    grafbars[3].y1 := 90;
    grafbars[3].x2 := 375;
    grafbars[3].y2 := 250;
    END;

PROCEDURE TBarChartwindow.Paint(PaintDC:HDC;
    VAR Paintinfo: TPaintStruct);
    VAR
        NewBrush,
        OldBrush : HBrush;

    PROCEDURE DrawBar(x1, y1, x2, y2,
                                    BarFillStyle:
INTEGER);
        BEGIN
        NewBrush := CreateHatchBrush(BarFillStyle, 0);
        OldBrush := SelectObject(PaintDC, NewBrush);
        Rectangle(PaintDC, x1, y1, x2, y2);
```

```
          SelectObject(PaintDC, OldBrush);
          DeleteObject(NewBrush);
          END;

{main body of paint method}
BEGIN
Rectangle(PaintDC, grafbars[0].x1, grafbars[0].y1,
               grafbars[0].x2, grafbars[0].y2);
DrawBar(grafbars[1].x1, grafbars[1].y1,
               grafbars[1].x2, grafbars[1].y2,
               hs_BDiagonal);
DrawBar(grafbars[2].x1, grafbars[2].y1,
               grafbars[2].x2, grafbars[2].y2,
               hs_Cross);
DrawBar(grafbars[3].x1, grafbars[3].y1,
               grafbars[3].x2, grafbars[3].y2,
               hs_FDiagonal);

TextOut(PaintDC, 120, 260, 'Jun', 3);
TextOut(PaintDC, 220, 260, 'Jul', 3);
TextOut(PaintDC, 320, 260, 'Aug', 3);
TextOut(PaintDC, 150, 40, 'Third-Quarter Results', 21);
END;

VAR
    BarChartApp : BarChartApplication;

BEGIN
    BarChartApp.Init('Listing 20.3');
    BarChartApp.run;
    BarChartApp.done
END.
```

Including Text with Graphics

The program in Listing 20.3, for the most part, simply applies the features we saw in this chapter's first two listings, adding a minor trick here and there just to make the code simpler. We declare a record type to hold the dimensions of each bar in a multi-bar chart, then use that type in an array for one of the fields in the parent window. We call a local *DrawBar* routine, just as before, inside the *Paint* method to draw the bars, and then label the bars and the chart as a whole with the Windows GDI *TextOut* function.

FIGURE 20.3:

The bar chart created by the program in Listing 20.3

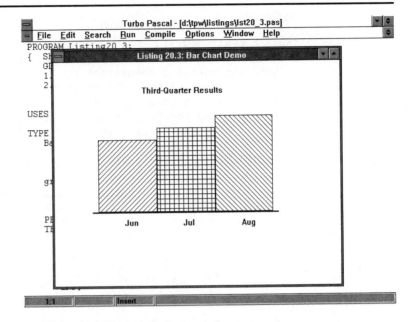

The *TextOut* function is not complicated, and it is quite useful. It takes five parameters:

- A handle to a display context (here, *PaintDC*)
- The x and y coordinates where the text string should begin
- The text string itself
- The number of characters in the text string

Using Windows Fonts

One thing we didn't include in the program from Listing 20.3 is very interesting type faces, or fonts, in the text that goes with the bar chart. Frankly, dealing with Windows fonts can be a fairly complex business. Fortunately, there are a few shortcuts. One such shortcut is to avoid using the *CreateFont* function, which takes 14 parameters, and use instead the *CreateFontIndirect* function, which takes only 1 parameter. This technique for using fonts is shown in Listing 20.4. The result of running the program is shown in Figure 20.4.

Listing 20.4

```
PROGRAM Listing20_4;
{  Shows how to use predefined Windows fonts.
   Specific features demonstrated:
   1.     Using a TLogFont-type record.
   2.     Using handles to fonts.
   3.     Using the CreateFontIndirect function.
   4.     Deleting fonts when finished with them. }

USES WOBJECTS, WINTYPES, WINPROCS, STRINGS;

TYPE
    FontDemoapplication = object (tapplication)
        PROCEDURE InitMainWindow; VIRTUAL;
        END;

    grafdims = RECORD
                x1, y1, x2, y2: INTEGER
                END;

    PFontDemoWindow = ^TFontDemoWindow;
    TFontDemoWindow = OBJECT(TWindow)
        grafbars : ARRAY[0..3] OF grafdims;
    CONSTRUCTOR Init(AParent:PWindowsObject;
            ATitle:PChar);
        PROCEDURE Paint(PaintDC:HDC;
            VAR Paintinfo:TPaintStruct); VIRTUAL;
        END;

PROCEDURE FontDemoapplication.InitMainWindow;
    BEGIN
    MainWindow :=
        new(PFontDemowindow, Init(
            NIL, 'Listing 20.4: Font Demonstration'));
    END;

constructor TFontDemowindow.Init(AParent:PWindowsObject;
                                                ATitle:PChar);
    BEGIN
    TWindow.Init(AParent, ATitle);
    attr.x := 50;
    attr.y := 50;
    attr.w := 500;
    attr.h := 400;
```

```
            grafbars[0].x1 := 65;
            grafbars[0].y1 := 250;
            grafbars[0].x2 := 385;
            grafbars[0].y2 := 252;

            grafbars[1].x1 := 75;
            grafbars[1].y1 := 130;
            grafbars[1].x2 := 175;
            grafbars[1].y2 := 250;

            grafbars[2].x1 := 175;
            grafbars[2].y1 := 110;
            grafbars[2].x2 := 275;
            grafbars[2].y2 := 250;

            grafbars[3].x1 := 275;
            grafbars[3].y1 := 90;
            grafbars[3].x2 := 375;
            grafbars[3].y2 := 250;
            END;

PROCEDURE TFontDemowindow.Paint(PaintDC:HDC;
    VAR Paintinfo: TPaintStruct);
    VAR
        NewBrush,
        OldBrush : HBrush;
        FontInfo    : TLogFont;
        OldFont,
        NewFont    : HFont;

PROCEDURE SetUpFont(FStyle, FWeight, FHeight, FWidth: INTEGER);
        BEGIN
        WITH FontInfo DO
            BEGIN
            lfHeight := FHeight;
            lfWidth := FWidth;
            lfWeight := FWeight;
            lfItalic := FStyle;
            lfUnderLine := 0;
            lfStrikeOut := 0;
            lfQuality := Proof_Quality;
            strPcopy(lfFaceName, 'Tms Rmn');
            END
        END;
```

```
PROCEDURE DrawBar(x1, y1, x2, y2, BarFillStyle: INTEGER);
        BEGIN
        NewBrush := CreateHatchBrush(BarFillStyle, 0);
        OldBrush := SelectObject(PaintDC, NewBrush);
        Rectangle(PaintDC, x1, y1, x2, y2);
        SelectObject(PaintDC, OldBrush);
        DeleteObject(NewBrush);
        END;

    {main body of paint method}
    BEGIN
    Rectangle(PaintDC, grafbars[0].x1, grafbars[0].y1,
                grafbars[0].x2, grafbars[0].y2);
    DrawBar(grafbars[1].x1, grafbars[1].y1,
                grafbars[1].x2, grafbars[1].y2,
                hs_BDiagonal);
    DrawBar(grafbars[2].x1, grafbars[2].y1,
                grafbars[2].x2, grafbars[2].y2,
                hs_Cross);
    DrawBar(grafbars[3].x1, grafbars[3].y1,
                grafbars[3].x2, grafbars[3].y2,
                hs_FDiagonal);

    SetUpFont(0,700,10,0);
    NewFont := CreateFontIndirect(FontInfo);
    OldFont := SelectObject(PaintDC, NewFont);
    TextOut(PaintDC, 100, 260, 'Jun', 3);
    TextOut(PaintDC, 200, 260, 'Jul', 3);
    TextOut(PaintDC, 300, 260, 'Aug', 3);
    SelectObject(PaintDC, OldFont);
    DeleteObject(newFont);

    SetUpFont(0,1000,50,0);
    NewFont := CreateFontIndirect(FontInfo);
    OldFont := SelectObject(PaintDC, NewFont);
    TextOut(PaintDC, 80, 40, 'Third-Quarter Results', 21);
    SelectObject(PaintDC, oldFont);
    DeleteObject(newFont);
    END;

VAR
    FontDemoApp : FontDemoApplication;

BEGIN
```

FIGURE 20.4:

The bar chart with new fonts

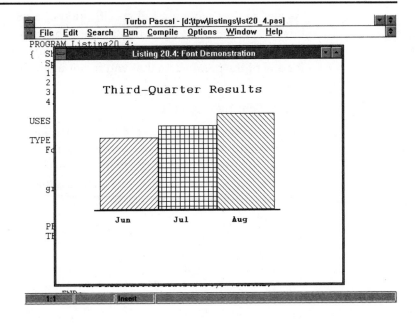

```
        FontDemoApp.Init('Listing 20.4: Font Demo');
        FontDemoApp.run;
        FontDemoApp.done
END.
```

Depending on your monitor, you may need to use smaller values for the darkness and size parameters of *SetUpFont* and/or change the coordinates to accommodate the text string in *TextOut*.

A font is like any other Windows object. As mentioned previously, you can load a font into your program in one of two ways: with the Windows GDI function *CreateFont* or with the Windows GDI function *CreateFontIndirect*. The syntax for *CreateFont* is

```
CreateFont(Height, Width, Escapement,
    Orientation, Weight: INTEGER;

    Italic, Underline, StrikeOut, CharSet,
    OutputPrecision, ClipPrecision, Quality,
    PitchAndFamily:BYTE;

    FaceName;: PChar): HFont
```

As you can see, giving a full specification of a font's characteristics is no simple business. Fortunately, if you don't want to have to be an expert on fonts, there's an easy way out: use *CreateFontIndirect* instead, and let Windows supply default values for any of the parameters that you're not interested in. The syntax for *CreateFont-Indirect* is

```
CreateFontIndirect(LogFont);
```

This is certainly a lot simpler. But, as Nobel laureate economist Milton Friedman often reminds us, there's no such thing as a free lunch (…unless you're a politician). Using *CreateFontIndirect* means that you must declare a variable of type *TLogFont* to hold the font's characteristics, and then pass that variable as a parameter when you call the *CreateFontIndirect* function. *TLogFont* is a predefined record type that's set up as follows:

```
TLogFont = RECORD
    lfHeight: INTEGER;
    lfWidth: INTEGER;
    lfEscapement: INTEGER;
    lfOrientation: INTEGER;
    lfWeight: INTEGER;
    lfItalic: BYTE;
    lfUnderline: BYTE;
    lfStrikeOut: BYTE;
    lfCharSet: BYTE;
    lfOutPrecision: BYTE;
    lfClipPrecision: BYTE;
    lfQuality: BYTE;
    lfPitchAndFamily: BYTE;
    lfFaceName: ARRAY[0..lf_FaceSize - 1] OF CHAR;
END;
```

You can see that we really didn't "eliminate" any information about the font by using *CreateFontIndirect*. What's the payoff, then? It's simply this: instead of having to specify values for all the different font characteristics by passing each as a parameter to *CreateFont*, you can simply change the fields you want in the *TLogFont* record variable and accept the defaults for all the rest. This not only makes your life easier, but it simplifies your code.

Many of the font characteristics are almost incomprehensible unless you're already familiar with fonts. The ones you're most likely to use are listed in Table 20.2.

The first step in using fonts is to set up (here, in the *Paint* method) a local variable to hold the *TLogFont* information, and two other local variables to hold handles to fonts. We then set up a local procedure which takes as parameters the font characteristics we want to change, and load the values we want into the appropriate fields of the *TLogFont*-type variable *FontInfo*.

TABLE 20.2: Important font-characteristic fields of TLogFont

Field	Meaning
lfHeight and *lfWidth*	Average height and width of the font
lfWeight	The "weight" of the font—i.e., its boldness—in inked pixels per 1000. The value can be from 0..1000. Normal boldness is 400.
lfItalic, lfUnderline, and *lfStrikeOut*	If non-zero, these fields mean that the text should use italic, underlined, or strikeout fonts, respectively
lfCharSet	Denotes one of three predefined Windows font character sets: *ANSI_CharSet, OEM_CharSet,* or *Symbol_CharSet*
lfQuality	Denotes the display quality of the font: *Default_Quality, Draft_Quality,* or *Proof_Quality*
lfFaceName	Contains the name of the font in a null-terminated string. If this field is NIL, Windows will use the default font.

A little farther down, we make our first call to the local *SetUpFont* procedure, loading the values we want into *FontInfo*. We then pass the variable as a parameter to *CreateFontIndirect*, which returns a handle to the font. Using *SelectObject* just as we did for pens and brushes, we associate the new font handle with the *PaintDC* display context and "kick out" whatever font was already there into the *OldFont* variable. We then use *TextOut* to display the text we want (the names of months in the quarter), reselect the old font back into the *PaintDC* display context, and dispose of the dynamically created new font by calling *DeleteObject*. As usual, this last step is important so as not to waste system resources.

We then repeat the process to display the title of the bar chart, because we want the title to be larger than the month names; therefore, we have to load different values into *FontInfo*. The rest of the program is standard stuff.

Creating and Using Dynamic Link Libraries (DLL)

How to Set Up a Dynamic Link Library

Importing DLL Routines into a Unit

Using DLL Routines in a Program

21

A *dynamic link library (DLL)* is an executable module of code and/or data which can be linked to a program at run time. This is a fairly advanced Windows feature, and one that is not needed for many applications. However, it's important to know the basics of what DLLs are and how they are applied, and that's what we will look at in this chapter.

Why Dynamic Link Libraries?

The point of creating dynamic link libraries is that different Windows applications can share the code and data that they contain, thereby economizing on system resources and making it possible to create "standard" libraries that all application programs can use. Windows itself makes use of DLLs to provide Windows functions and resources that need to be available to all Windows applications. Windows fonts, which we saw in Chapter 20, are an example of what DLLs can contain; all libraries used by Windows itself are DLLs.

In some ways, DLLs are a lot like Turbo Pascal units, except that they can be shared by all Windows programs (no matter what language they were written in) and can include data as well as subroutines. The benefits are the same: standardized features do not need to be recreated or retyped into each program's source code. The big difference between DLLs and Turbo Pascal units is that DLLs are not linked to the program when it is compiled; instead, they are linked as needed at run time. In Windows terminology, a Turbo Pascal unit (such as the WinDOS or the WObjects unit) is a "static" rather than a "dynamic" link library.

Another point about DLLs is that they can be written in any source language and used by a TPW program. In a certain sense, of course, this is an obvious point, but it's worth remembering. You can create DLLs in Turbo Pascal for use by TPW programs and any other Windows programs; in your TPW programs, you can use DLLs created with Turbo Pascal, Borland C++, Microsoft C, or any other Windows-capable programming platform.

How to Set Up a Dynamic Link Library

The best way to understand how DLLs work is to set up a simple one. Listing 21.1 shows a simple dynamic link library that contains a single procedure: *FlipFlop*, a routine that exchanges the values of two character-type variables. Note that Listing 21.1 should be saved under the name FLIPDLL.PAS instead of the usual "listing-filename."

Listing 21.1

```
LIBRARY FlipDLL;
{Listing 21.1: Demonstrates setting up a simple
dynamic link library. }

{Any units used would be named here. In this case,
none is needed. }

PROCEDURE FlipFlop(VAR vbl1, vbl2: CHAR); EXPORT;
    VAR
        TempVbl: CHAR;
    BEGIN
        TempVbl := vbl1;
        vbl1 := vbl2;
        vbl2 := TempVbl
    END;

EXPORTS FlipFlop  INDEX 1;

BEGIN
END.
```

There's nothing essentially very complex about this listing. At the top is the header, which uses the reserved word *Library* to indicate that this is going to be a dynamic link library instead of a regular TPW program or unit. Then comes the descriptive name of the DLL, which in this case is *FlipDLL*. If any TPW units were needed by the routines in the DLL, the units would be named on the next line.

The details of the routines in the DLL are then spelled out. The headers of the routines end with the directive EXPORT, indicating that they will be exported to another module.

The next part of the DLL specifies the exported routines and gives each an index value. This index value is used in the unit that calls the routine from the DLL; the index identifies the exported routine.

Finally, there is an empty BEGIN..END initialization section, just as you might have with a regular Turbo Pascal unit.

You should compile the dynamic link library in Listing 21.1 in preparation for the next step, which is creating a unit to import the DLL routine into a TPW program.

Importing DLL Routines into a Unit

To use a DLL in a TPW program, you must first create a unit that imports the routine from the DLL. This unit is then, in turn, used by your TPW program to gain access to the routines in the DLL. Listing 21.2 shows how to set up a unit that works with the DLL in Listing 21.1.

Listing 21.2

```
UNIT Flip;
INTERFACE
PROCEDURE FlipFlop(VAR vbl1, vbl2: CHAR);
IMPLEMENTATION
PROCEDURE FlipFlop; EXTERNAL 'FlipDLL' INDEX 1;
END.
```

This unit looks almost exactly like any other Turbo Pascal unit, but with one key exception. Instead of spelling out the details of FlipFlop in the IMPLEMENTATION section, the unit refers the compiler to an external module which it identifies as *FlipDLL*—the name of our dynamic link library from Listing 21.1. Within that DLL, the unit identifies the appropriate routine by referring to its index value, which in this case is *1*.

In preparation for the final step of running the program that uses the DLL, save the unit under the name FLIP.PAS and compile it.

Using DLL Routines in a Program

The rest of the process is remarkably easy. You don't even need to know, for this step, that the routine you want is in a dynamic link library. All you need to do is name the appropriate unit in a USES clause. Listing 21.3 shows how to use a DLL in a program, and Figure 21.1 shows the result of running the program.

Listing 21.3

```
PROGRAM Listing21_3;
{Demonstrates how a program can use a DLL. }

USES WinCRT, Flip;

VAR
    letter1, letter2: CHAR;

BEGIN
    letter1 := 'a';
    letter2 := 'b';
    WRITELN('Letter #1 is ', letter1, '.');
    WRITELN('Letter #2 is ', letter2, '.');
```

FIGURE 21.1:

Output from running the program in Listing 21.3

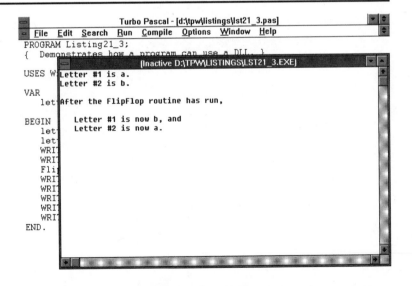

```
    FlipFlop(letter1, letter2);
    WRITELN;
    WRITELN('After the FlipFlop routine has run,');
    WRITELN;
    WRITELN('   Letter #1 is now ', letter1, ', and');
    WRITELN('   Letter #2 is now ', letter2, '.')
END.
```

APPENDICES

APPENDIX
A

Using the Borland Resource Workshop

The initial release of Turbo Pascal for Windows (version 1.0) contained the **Whitewater Resource Toolkit** as a tool for creating and editing Windows resources. Borland, however, has created its own resource editor, the **Borland Resource Workshop**, and this is scheduled to replace the WRT in future releases of the TPW package. This appendix documents the basic differences between the Borland Resource Workshop and the WRT.

If you've already worked your way through this book, it should be quite easy to learn the ins and outs of the Borland Resource Workshop. You already understand what the types of resources are and how they are incorporated into your Windows programs. Here, we'll just take a quick guided tour to get you started with the BRW.

Installing the Borland Resource Workshop

Installing the Borland Resource Workshop is as easy as installing Turbo Pascal for Windows itself. Insert the BRW installation disk into one of your floppy drives; here, we'll assume that it's the *a:* drive. Then, from the Windows Program Manager, choose "Run" from the File menu. In the dialog box that opens up, enter

```
a:install.exe
```

and press *Enter*. The installation program will then offer some default choices for the directory in which the BRW should be installed and some other options. Simply make any changes you want in the default choices and follow the prompts. The installation program does the rest.

Using the Borland Resource Workshop

The BRW is organized differently than the Whitewater Resource Toolkit. In the WRT, you load each resource editor separately, then you load the resource file into that editor. This limits your ability to work with a variety of different resource types in the same resource file. The BRW has managed to sidestep this difficulty.

Instead of viewing a resource itself as the basic item it deals with, the BRW views the resource file as its primary focus. This means that instead of loading a resource from a resource file, you load information from the file itself into the BRW, and can then pick and choose the resources you want to work on.

When you first start the BRW, a blank screen appears with only File and Help menus displayed along the menu bar. The File menu, as shown in Figure A.1, allows you to create a new project or open an existing project. ("Project," in this context, means a whole resource file with all of its included resources.)

When you choose "Open Project" from the File menu, the **Open Project** dialog box opens, as shown in Figure A.2. When you first open the dialog box, the *File Type* list is not open, but when you click on the arrow button to the right of the *File Type* box, the whole list opens up, as shown in the figure. (As you might guess, the *File Type* box is a Windows combo box, as discussed in Chapter 14.)

For now, let's just stick with opening a .RES-type resource file, which is the default. Switching to the appropriate directory, open a .RES resource file. The BRW will pop open a window that shows all the resources in the file and the type of each, as

FIGURE A.1:

The File menu in the Borland Resource Workshop

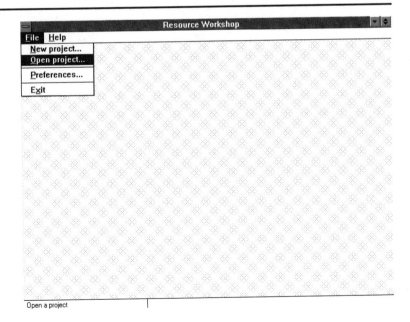

FIGURE A.2:
The Open Project dialog box with the File Type combo box open

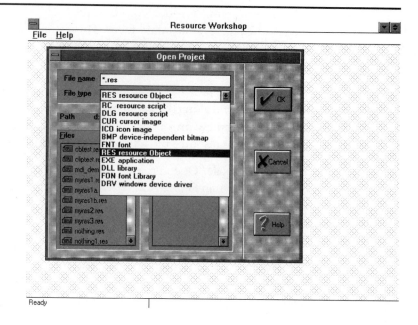

shown in Figure A.3. (In this example, I've opened STARFIRE.RES, which we created in Chapter 15.) To open a particular resource, just double-click on its resource name in the list, or highlight it and press *Enter*. The appropriate resource editor will automatically be opened and the resource will be loaded into it.

Notice one other thing about Figure A.3: four new menu titles have appeared in the menu bar. We'll look at how to use each of these menus as we work through the different resource editors in the BRW.

The Menu Editor

To demonstrate the BRW menu editor, let's add a new menu resource to our resource file. You start a new resource by selecting "New" from the Resource menu. The **New Resource** dialog box opens as shown in Figure A.4.

In Figure A.4, the STRINGTABLE resource type is automatically highlighted in the *Resource Type* combo box because that's the type that is highlighted in the loaded

FIGURE A.3:

A window pops open showing the available resources in the file

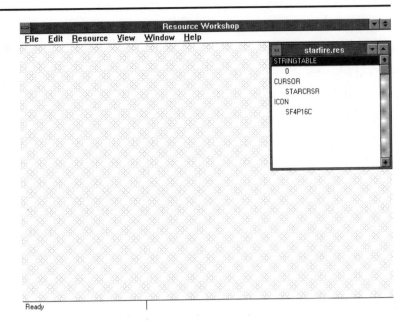

FIGURE A.4:

The New Resource dialog box

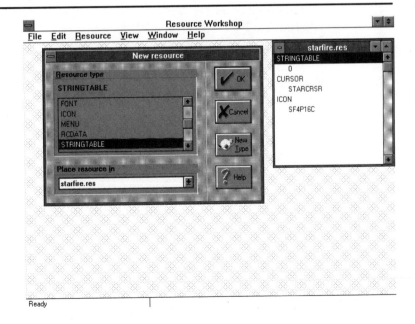

FIGURE A.5:

The BRW menu editor

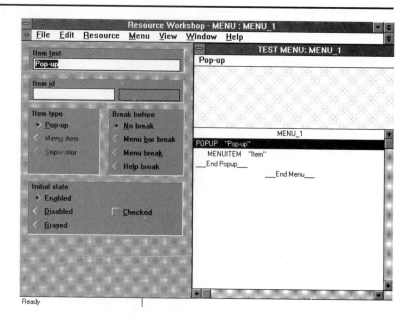

resource file. Here, however, we're more interested in using the menu editor, so double-click on the MENU resource type. The BRW menu editor will open, as shown in Figure A.5.

The tasks to be accomplished in the BRW menu editor are very similar to those in the WRT menu editor; the only things that really differ are the buttons you push on screen. To add a new menu item (called a "statement" in the BRW), you position the highlight in the "outline window" (the one with the scroll bars, at the lower right of the menu editor). Move the highlight bar to the item *above* the position at which you want the new item to appear, then either choose "New menu item" from the Menu menu or simply press the *Ins* key on your keyboard. A new item will be inserted just below the line you had highlighted, at the same level of indentation as the highlighted line. To insert a new menu pop-up, simply press *Ctrl-P* or choose "Insert Pop-up" from the Menu menu; a new pop-up will be inserted below the highlighted line.

One "shortcut" feature of the BRW menu editor is that its Menu menu offers choices that will insert a complete, predefined File, Edit, or Help menu into your menu bar.

FIGURE A.6:

The Menu menu

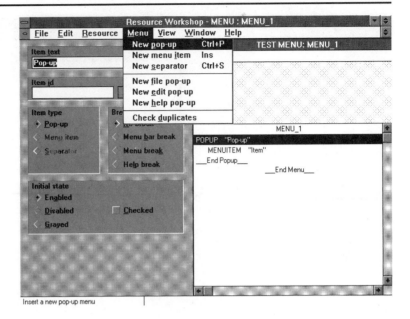

(The Menu menu is shown in Figure A.6.) To insert a new File menu, you position the highlight where you want the new pop-up menu to appear and then select "New File Pop-up" from the Menu menu. The same procedure is used to insert new Edit or Help pop-up menus.

The Dialog Editor

Because this is only a guided tour—we're not going to create any new resources at this point in the book—close the menu editor by clicking on the system window-control button at the top left of the menu editor window. (Be careful not to get the BRW's button by mistake.) Open the dialog editor by choosing "New" from the Resource menu and selecting the dialog resource type from the combo box. The dialog editor will open, as shown in Figure A.7.

Most of the features in the BRW dialog editor are familiar from the WRT. The tools at the right side of the window have the same functions as in the WRT; the menu choices in the BRW's control menu correspond as well. The BRW adds some extra cosmetic features, such as a "Black Box" feature that you can select from the control

FIGURE A.7:

The BRW dialog editor

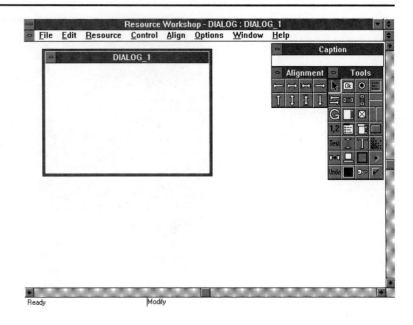

menu—this inserts a box drawn with thick, dark lines into your dialog box, as shown in Figure A.8.

The Accelerator Editor

Close the dialog editor and, through the Resource menu, start up a new accelerator resource just as we did with the other resources. The accelerator editor will open as shown in Figure A.9.

The BRW accelerator editor works exactly the same as the corresponding WRT accelerator editor. In the *Command* box on the left is shown the command value returned by the accelerator being created; this value is the same as the value returned by the corresponding menu choice in the menu resource. Underneath the *Command* box is the *Key* box, which displays the key that activates the accelerator; further down are radio buttons and checkboxes to show if the key is ASCII or a Virtkey, and if the *Alt, Shift,* or *Ctrl* buttons need to be held down to activate the accelerator.

FIGURE A.8:

Adding a "black box" to a dialog box

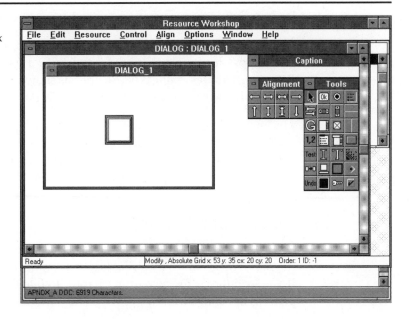

FIGURE A.9:

The BRW accelerator editor

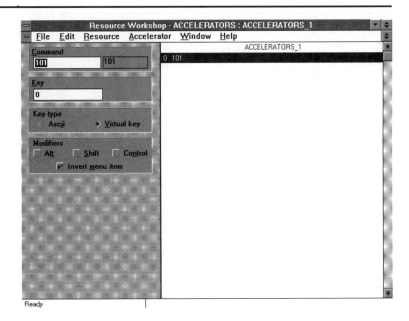

The Paint Editor

The BRW paint editor is used to create and edit bitmaps, icons, cursors, and fonts. If you close the accelerator editor and open a new "bitmap" resource, the **New Bitmap Attributes** dialog box will open as shown in Figure A.10, and then the paint editor will open as shown in Figure A.11.

The tools in the BRW paint editor correspond with few exceptions to the tools in the WRT bitmap editor (indeed, in any standard Windows paint program). The BRW paint editor also offers a few new cosmetic features to "pretty up" bitmaps and other images, such as the ability to choose the shape of the brush (or "airbrush").

The String Table Editor

As in the other BRW resource editors, the BRW string table editor works in largely the same way as the WRT string table editor, with a few minor variations in detail. If you load the string table from Chapter 15 into the BRW string table editor, it appears as in Figure A.12.

FIGURE A.10:

The New Bitmap Attributes dialog box

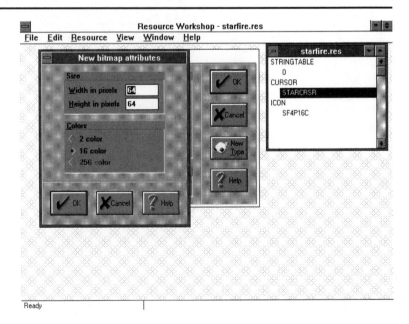

FIGURE A.11:

The BRW paint editor

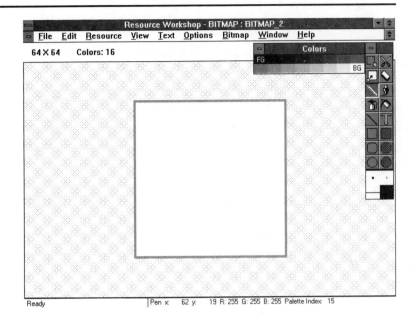

FIGURE A.12:

The BRW string table editor

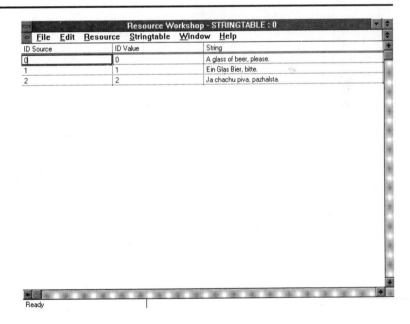

Other Windows Programming Tools

Particularly since the release of Windows 3.0, there has been a rapid growth in the availability and sophistication of tools for programming Windows applications. The tools now available vary greatly in their power, flexibility, sophistication, and ease of use. Most are intended for professional programmers, but some even let nontechnical end users write Windows programs.

It would be impossible to cover all these tools in a short appendix, particularly since they continue to be introduced at such a rapid rate. However, we will take a look here at some of the most important—those that are best established and those that are likely to be the most influential in the next few years. They are not discussed in order of merit or importance, so don't read anything into the sequencing of the following discussions.

Microsoft C with the Windows Software Developers' Kit (SDK)

This is the granddaddy of Windows programming tools and is still the most widely used. When companies advertise for Windows programmers, this is usually what they mean, unless they specify a different tool such as Borland C++ or Turbo Pascal for Windows. Unlike some of the other tools discussed here, Microsoft C (at least as this book was being written) would run under Windows but was not a Windows program like TPW.

Until recently, you had to buy the Windows Software Developers' Kit separate from the Microsoft C compiler/development environment. Now, however—probably in response to the extensive SDK-like features offered in Borland's C++ package— Microsoft is including a copy of Microsoft C with the Windows SDK package. (The reverse isn't true: you don't automatically get a copy of the SDK when you buy Microsoft C.)

The advantage of the Microsoft C/Windows SDK combination is that, particularly if you're already a whiz at Microsoft C, it's a sophisticated and powerful Windows programming tool designed by the same company that sells Windows. The SDK itself includes Windows libraries; a debugging version of the Windows kernel; resource editors for fonts, dialogs, and icons; a resource compiler; a help compiler; and several debugging tools, including Microsoft's CodeView debugger and an execution profiler. In Microsoft C, you get the integrated development environment that started in QuickC and was then moved into Microsoft C.

QuickC for Windows

This is Microsoft's entry-level C programming package for Windows, shown in Figure B.1. It includes not only the QuickC for Windows compiler and integrated development environment (similar to the integrated development environment in Turbo Pascal for Windows), but also separate modules for program design, dialog box creation/editing, and image (bitmap, etc.) creation/editing.

The principal advantage of QuickC for Windows is that it's a good entry platform for developing C-language Windows programs in a way that is maximally compatible with the high-end Microsoft C/Windows SDK combination. It also has the added tutorial and cosmetic touches that have distinguished the DOS line of "Quick" language products and is, therefore, a good vehicle to learn C programming for Windows. What it does not have, of course, is support for C++, which is even more ideally suited for Windows programming than C.

Borland C++

This is the C++ development environment created by Borland for heavy-duty Windows programming. Unlike Microsoft C, it is actually a Windows-based program, and provides the full ObjectWindows libraries found in Turbo Pascal for Windows.

FIGURE B.1:

QuickC for Windows

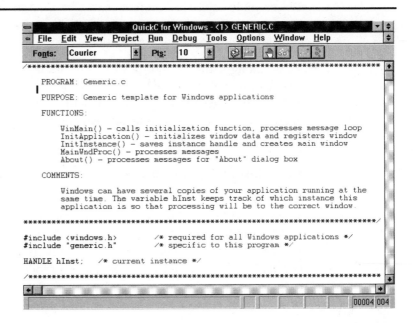

It also includes Turbo Debugger for Windows, an execution profiler, and the complete "Turbo Vision" application framework for creating standard-interface non-Windows programs under MS-DOS.

The principal advantage of Borland C++ is that it is the most powerful and widely-used platform for C++ Windows programming. The ObjectWindows library, as we've seen in this book, saves the programmer a great deal of work that would be necessary if he/she were using Microsoft C and the Windows SDK.

Turbo C++ for Windows

This is Borland's entry-level C++ Windows programming product. It includes the ObjectWindows library, is a Windows-based program, and has many of the features found in the high-end Borland C++. However, it lacks the most advanced features as well as some compiler optimizations to create smaller and faster .EXE files.

Actor

Actor (shown in Figure B.2) is a Windows-based development environment that supports pure object-oriented programming and includes the ObjectWindows library found in Turbo Pascal for Windows and Borland C++. (The Whitewater Group, which created Actor, provided consulting support to Borland in developing ObjectWindows.) In its "Professional" edition, Actor also includes the Whitewater Resource Toolkit and ObjectGraphics, which makes it easier to incorporate graphics and clip art into Windows applications.

Actor, though still a minority platform, has been catching on for rapid and no-headaches development of Windows applications. A key feature of Actor is *multiple inheritance*, which allows an object type to derive features from more than one line of ancestor types. This is done indirectly by making such features "classless"—i.e., by making them standalone methods outside of an object type.

Smalltalk/V for Windows

Smalltalk/V for Windows (shown in Figure B.3) is like Actor in the sense that it is a pure object-oriented programming language and development environment for Windows. Also like Actor, Smalltalk started out as a little-known language which, though still in no danger of losing its minority status, has steadily grown in popularity and acquired an almost fanatical following among programmers who use it.

FIGURE B.2:

Actor 4.0 with Class Browser open

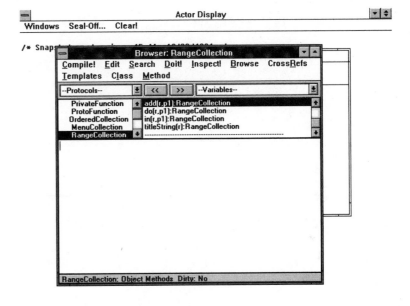

FIGURE B.3:

Smalltalk/V for Windows

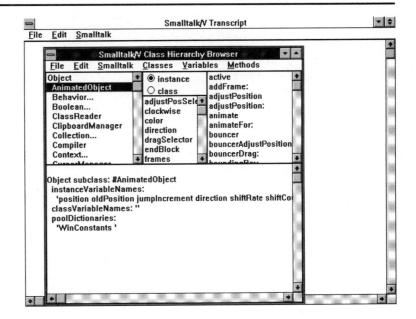

APPENDIX

C

ObjectWindows Reference

This appendix contains information about ObjectWindows taken from the interface section of TPW's WOBJECTS unit, along with comments supplied by the author. This section, which is not in the TPW manuals (it's available only in a disk file), lists all the basic TPW OBJECT types and their method headers, as well as constants and other identifiers used by Turbo Pascal for Windows. Material from the WOBJECTS unit is copyright 1991 by Borland International and is reprinted with permission.

```
UNIT WObjects;

{$S-}

INTERFACE

USES WINTYPES, WINPROCS, STRINGS;

CONST

{ Application message constants }
wm_First    = $0000;
id_First    = $8000;
id_Internal = $8F00;
nf_First    = $9000;
nf_Internal = $9F00;
cm_First    = $A000;
cm_Internal = $FF00;
wm_Count    = $8000;
id_Count    = $1000;
nf_Count    = $1000;
cm_Count    = $6000;

{ Standard child ID messages }
id_Reserved     = id_Internal - id_First;
id_FirstMDIChild = id_Reserved + 1;
id_MDIClient    = id_Reserved + 2;

{ Standard command messages }
cm_Reserved  = cm_Internal - cm_First;
cm_EditCut   = cm_Reserved + 0;
cm_EditCopy  = cm_Reserved + 1;
cm_EditPaste = cm_Reserved + 2;
cm_EditDelete = cm_Reserved + 3;
cm_EditClear = cm_Reserved + 4;
cm_EditUndo  = cm_Reserved + 5;
```

```
cm_EditFind   = cm_Reserved + 6;
cm_EditReplace  = cm_Reserved + 7;
cm_EditFindNext = cm_Reserved + 8;

cm_FileNew    = cm_Reserved + 9;
cm_FileOpen   = cm_Reserved + 10;
cm_MDIFileNew  = cm_Reserved + 11;
cm_MDIFileOpen  = cm_Reserved + 12;
cm_FileSave   = cm_Reserved + 13;
cm_FileSaveAs  = cm_Reserved + 14;
cm_ArrangeIcons = cm_Reserved + 15;
cm_TileChildren = cm_Reserved + 16;
cm_CascadeChildren = cm_Reserved + 17;
cm_CloseChildren = cm_Reserved + 18;
cm_CreateChild  = cm_Reserved + 19;
cm_Exit    = cm_Reserved + 20;

{ TWindowsObject Flags masks }
wb_KBHandler = $01;
wb_FromResource = $02;
wb_AutoCreate = $04;
wb_MDIChild  = $08;
wb_Transfer  = $10;

{ TWindowsObject Status codes }
em_InvalidWindow  = -1;
em_OutOfMemory   = -2;
em_InvalidClient  = -3;
em_InvalidChild  = -4;
em_InvalidMainWindow = -5;

{ TWindowsObject Transfer codes }
tf_SizeData = 0;
tf_GetData = 1;
tf_SetData = 2;

{ TCheckBox check states }
bf_Unchecked = 0;
bf_Checked = 1;
bf_Grayed = 2;

{ TStream access modes }
stCreate = $3C00;   { Create new file }
stOpenRead = $3D00;   { Read access only }
stOpenWrite = $3D01;   { Write access only }
```

```
stOpen  = $3D02;    { Read and write access }

{ TStream error codes }
stOk  = 0;    { No error }
stError = -1;    { Access error }
stInitError = -2;    { Cannot initialize stream }
stReadError = -3;    { Read beyond END of stream }
stWriteError = -4;    { Cannot expand stream }
stGetError = -5;    { Get of unregistered OBJECT type }
stPutError = -6;    { Put of unregistered OBJECT type }

{ Maximum TCollection size }
MaxCollectionSize = 65520 DIV SizeOf(Pointer);

{ TCollection error codes }
coIndexError = -1;    { Index out of range }
coOverflow = -2;    { Overflow }

TYPE
{ String pointer }
PString = ^String;

{ Type conversion records }
WordRec = RECORD Lo, Hi: BYTE END;
LongRec = RECORD Lo, Hi: WORD END;
PtrRec = RECORD Ofs, Seg: WORD END;

{ General arrays }
PByteArray = ^TByteArray;
TByteArray = ARRAY[0..32767] of BYTE;
PWordArray = ^TWordArray;
TWordArray = ARRAY[0..16383] of WORD;

{ TObject base OBJECT }
PObject = ^TObject;
TObject = OBJECT
CONSTRUCTOR Init;
PROCEDURE Free;
DESTRUCTOR Done;
P| VIRTUAL;
END;

{ TStreamRec }
PStreamRec = ^TStreamRec;
TStreamRec = RECORD
```

```
ObjType: WORD;
VmtLink: WORD;
Load: Pointer;
Store: Pointer;
Next: WORD;
END;

{ TStream }
PStream = ^TStream;
TStream = OBJECT(TObject)
Status: INTEGER;
ErrorInfo: INTEGER;
CONSTRUCTOR Init;
PROCEDURE CopyFrom(VAR S: TStream; Count: Longint);
PROCEDURE Error(Code, Info: INTEGER);
   VIRTUAL;
PROCEDURE Flush;
   VIRTUAL;
FUNCTION Get: PObject;
FUNCTION GetPos: Longint;
   VIRTUAL;
FUNCTION GetSize: Longint;
   VIRTUAL;
PROCEDURE Put(P: PObject);
PROCEDURE Read(VAR Buf; Count: WORD);
   VIRTUAL;
FUNCTION ReadStr: PString;
PROCEDURE Reset;
PROCEDURE Seek(Pos: Longint);
   VIRTUAL;
FUNCTION StrRead: PChar;
PROCEDURE StrWrite(P: PChar);
PROCEDURE Truncate;
   VIRTUAL;
PROCEDURE Write(VAR Buf; Count: WORD);
   VIRTUAL;
PROCEDURE WriteStr(P: PString);
END;

{ TDosStream }
PDosStream = ^TDosStream;
TDosStream = OBJECT(TStream)
Handle: WORD;
CONSTRUCTOR Init(FileName: PChar; Mode: WORD);
DESTRUCTOR Done;
```

```
      VIRTUAL;
FUNCTION GetPos: Longint;
   VIRTUAL;
FUNCTION GetSize: Longint;
   VIRTUAL;
PROCEDURE Read(VAR Buf; Count: WORD);
   VIRTUAL;
PROCEDURE Seek(Pos: Longint);
   VIRTUAL;
PROCEDURE Truncate;
   VIRTUAL;
PROCEDURE Write(VAR Buf; Count: WORD);
   VIRTUAL;
END;

{ TBufStream }
PBufStream = ^TBufStream;
TBufStream = OBJECT(TDosStream)
Buffer: Pointer;
BufSize: WORD;
BufPtr: WORD;
BufEnd: WORD;
CONSTRUCTOR Init(FileName: PChar; Mode, Size: WORD);
DESTRUCTOR Done;
   VIRTUAL;
PROCEDURE Flush;
   VIRTUAL;
FUNCTION GetPos: Longint;
   VIRTUAL;
FUNCTION GetSize: Longint;
   VIRTUAL;
PROCEDURE Read(VAR Buf; Count: WORD);
   VIRTUAL;
PROCEDURE Seek(Pos: Longint);
   VIRTUAL;
PROCEDURE Truncate;
   VIRTUAL;
PROCEDURE Write(VAR Buf; Count: WORD);
   VIRTUAL;
END;

{ TEmsStream }
PEmsStream = ^TEmsStream;
TEmsStream = OBJECT(TStream)
Handle: WORD;
```

```
PageCount: WORD;
Size: Longint;
Position: Longint;
CONSTRUCTOR Init(MinSize, MaxSize: Longint);
DESTRUCTOR Done;
    VIRTUAL;
FUNCTION GetPos: Longint;
    VIRTUAL;
FUNCTION GetSize: Longint;
    VIRTUAL;
PROCEDURE Read(VAR Buf; Count: WORD);
    VIRTUAL;
PROCEDURE Seek(Pos: Longint);
    VIRTUAL;
PROCEDURE Truncate;
    VIRTUAL;
PROCEDURE Write(VAR Buf; Count: WORD);
    VIRTUAL;
END;

{ TCollection types }
PItemList = ^TItemList;
TItemList = ARRAY[0..MaxCollectionSize - 1] of Pointer;

{ TCollection OBJECT }
PCollection = ^TCollection;
TCollection = OBJECT(TObject)
Items: PItemList;
Count: INTEGER;
Limit: INTEGER;
Delta: INTEGER;
CONSTRUCTOR Init(ALimit, ADelta: INTEGER);
CONSTRUCTOR Load(VAR S: TStream);
DESTRUCTOR Done;
    VIRTUAL;
FUNCTION At(Index: INTEGER): Pointer;
PROCEDURE AtDelete(Index: INTEGER);
PROCEDURE AtFree(Index: INTEGER);
PROCEDURE AtInsert(Index: INTEGER; Item: Pointer);
PROCEDURE AtPut(Index: INTEGER; Item: Pointer);
PROCEDURE Delete(Item: Pointer);
PROCEDURE DeleteAll;
PROCEDURE Error(Code, Info: INTEGER);
    VIRTUAL;
FUNCTION FirstThat(Test: Pointer): Pointer;
```

```
PROCEDURE ForEach(Action: Pointer);
PROCEDURE Free(Item: Pointer);
PROCEDURE FreeAll;
PROCEDURE FreeItem(Item: Pointer);
   VIRTUAL;
FUNCTION GetItem(VAR S: TStream): Pointer;
   VIRTUAL;
FUNCTION IndexOf(Item: Pointer): INTEGER;
   VIRTUAL;
PROCEDURE Insert(Item: Pointer);
   VIRTUAL;
FUNCTION LastThat(Test: Pointer): Pointer;
PROCEDURE Pack;
PROCEDURE PutItem(VAR S: TStream; Item: Pointer);
   VIRTUAL;
PROCEDURE SetLimit(ALimit: INTEGER);
   VIRTUAL;
PROCEDURE Store(VAR S: TStream);
END;

{ TSortedCollection OBJECT }
PSortedCollection = ^TSortedCollection;
TSortedCollection = OBJECT(TCollection)
Duplicates: BOOLEAN;
CONSTRUCTOR Init(ALimit, ADelta: INTEGER);
CONSTRUCTOR Load(VAR S: TStream);
FUNCTION Compare(Key1, Key2: Pointer): INTEGER;
   VIRTUAL;
FUNCTION IndexOf(Item: Pointer): INTEGER;
   VIRTUAL;
PROCEDURE Insert(Item: Pointer);
   VIRTUAL;
FUNCTION KeyOf(Item: Pointer): Pointer;
   VIRTUAL;
FUNCTION Search(Key: Pointer; VAR Index: INTEGER): BOOLEAN;
   VIRTUAL;
PROCEDURE Store(VAR S: TStream);
END;

{ TStringCollection OBJECT }
PStringCollection = ^TStringCollection;
TStringCollection = OBJECT(TSortedCollection)
FUNCTION Compare(Key1, Key2: Pointer): INTEGER;
   VIRTUAL;
PROCEDURE FreeItem(Item: Pointer);
```

```
   VIRTUAL;
FUNCTION GetItem(VAR S: TStream): Pointer;
   VIRTUAL;
PROCEDURE PutItem(VAR S: TStream; Item: Pointer);
   VIRTUAL;
END;


{ TStrCollection OBJECT }
PStrCollection = ^TStrCollection;
TStrCollection = OBJECT(TSortedCollection)
FUNCTION Compare(Key1, Key2: Pointer): INTEGER;
   VIRTUAL;
PROCEDURE FreeItem(Item: Pointer);
   VIRTUAL;
FUNCTION GetItem(VAR S: TStream): Pointer;
   VIRTUAL;
PROCEDURE PutItem(VAR S: T
Stream; Item: Pointer);
VIRTUAL;
END;


{ TMessage windows message RECORD }
PMessage = ^TMessage;
TMessage = RECORD
Receiver: HWnd;
Message: WORD;
CASE INTEGER OF
0: (
WParam: WORD;
LParam: Longint;
Result: Longint);
1: (
WParamLo: BYTE;
WParamHi: BYTE;
LParamLo: WORD;
LParamHi: WORD;
ResultLo: WORD;
ResultHi: WORD);
END;


{ ObjectWindows pointer types }
PWindowsObject = ^TWindowsObject;
PWindow  = ^TWindow;
PDialog  = ^TDialog;
PDlgWindow  = ^TDlgWindow;
```

```
PMDIWindow  = ^TMDIWindow;
PControl    = ^TControl;
PButton     = ^TButton;
PCheckBox   = ^TCheckBox;
PRadioButton = ^TRadioButton;
PGroupBox   = ^TGroupBox;
PStatic     = ^TStatic;
PEdit       = ^TEdit;
PListBox    = ^TListBox;
PComboBox   = ^TComboBox;
PScrollBar  = ^TScrollBar;
PMDIClient  = ^TMDIClient;
PScroller   = ^TScroller;
PApplication = ^TApplication;

{ TWindowsObject OBJECT }
TWindowsObject = OBJECT(TObject)
Status: INTEGER;
HWindow: HWnd;
Parent, ChildList: PWindowsObject;
TransferBuffer: Pointer;
Instance: TFarProc;
Flags: BYTE;
CONSTRUCTOR Init(AParent: PWindowsObject);
CONSTRUCTOR Load(VAR S: TStream);
DESTRUCTOR Done;
    VIRTUAL;
PROCEDURE Store(VAR S: TStream);
PROCEDURE DefWndProc(VAR Msg: TMessage);
    VIRTUAL {index 8};
PROCEDURE DefCommandProc(VAR Msg: TMessage);
    VIRTUAL {index 12};
PROCEDURE DefChildProc(VAR Msg: TMessage);
    VIRTUAL {index 16};
PROCEDURE DefNotificationProc(VAR Msg: TMessage);
    VIRTUAL {index 20};
PROCEDURE SetFlags(Mask: BYTE; OnOff: BOOLEAN);
FUNCTION IsFlagSet(Mask: BYTE): BOOLEAN;
FUNCTION FirstThat(Test: Pointer): PWindowsObject;
PROCEDURE ForEach(Action: Pointer);
FUNCTION Next: PWindowsObject;
FUNCTION Previous: PWindowsObject;
PROCEDURE EnableKBHandler;
PROCEDURE EnableAutoCreate;
PROCEDURE DisableAutoCreate;
```

```
PROCEDURE EnableTransfer;
PROCEDURE DisableTransfer;
FUNCTION Register: BOOLEAN;
    VIRTUAL;
FUNCTION Create: BOOLEAN;
    VIRTUAL;
PROCEDURE Destroy;
    VIRTUAL;
FUNCTION GetId: INTEGER;
    VIRTUAL;
FUNCTION ChildWithId(Id: INTEGER): PWindowsObject;
FUNCTION GetClassName: PChar;
    VIRTUAL;
FUNCTION GetClient: PMDIClient;
    VIRTUAL;
PROCEDURE GetChildPtr(VAR S: TStream; VAR P);
PROCEDURE PutChildPtr(VAR S: TStream; P: PWindowsObject);
PROCEDURE GetSiblingPtr(VAR S: TStream; VAR P);
PROCEDURE PutSiblingPtr(VAR S: TStream; P: PWindowsObject);
PROCEDURE GetWindowClass(VAR AWndClass: TWndClass);
    VIRTUAL;
PROCEDURE SetupWindow;
    VIRTUAL;
PROCEDURE Show(ShowCmd: INTEGER);
FUNCTION CanClose: BOOLEAN;
    VIRTUAL;
FUNCTION Transfer(DataPtr: Pointer; TransferFlag: WORD): WORD;
    VIRTUAL;
PROCEDURE TransferData(Direction: WORD);
    VIRTUAL;
PROCEDURE DispatchScroll(VAR Msg: TMessage);
    VIRTUAL;
PROCEDURE CloseWindow;
PROCEDURE GetChildren(VAR S: TStream);
PROCEDURE PutChildren(VAR S: TStream);
FUNCTION CreateChildren: BOOLEAN;
PROCEDURE WMVScroll(VAR Msg: TMessage);
    VIRTUAL wm_First + wm_VScroll;
PROCEDURE WMHScroll(VAR Msg: TMessage);
    VIRTUAL wm_First + wm_HScroll;
PROCEDURE WMCommand(VAR Msg: TMessage);
    VIRTUAL wm_First + wm_Command;
PROCEDURE WMClose(VAR Msg: TMessage);
    VIRTUAL wm_First + wm_Close;
PROCEDURE WMDestroy(VAR Msg: TMessage);
```

```
        VIRTUAL wm_First + wm_Destroy;
PROCEDURE WMNCDestroy(VAR Msg: TMessage);
        VIRTUAL wm_First + wm_NCDestroy;
PROCEDURE WMActivate(VAR Msg: TMessage);
        VIRTUAL wm_First + wm_Activate;
PROCEDURE WMQueryEndSession(VAR Msg: TMessage);
        VIRTUAL wm_First + wm_QueryEndSession;
PROCEDURE CMExit(VAR Msg: TMessage);
        VIRTUAL cm_First + cm_Exit;
END;

{ TWindow creation attributes }
TWindowAttr = RECORD
Title: PChar;
Style: LongInt;
ExStyle: LongInt;
X, Y, W, H: INTEGER;
Param: Pointer;
CASE INTEGER OF
0: (Menu: HMenu);     { Menu handle }
1: (Id: INTEGER);     { Child identifier }
END;

{ TWindow OBJECT }
TWindow = OBJECT(TWindowsObject)
Attr: TWindowAttr;
DefaultProc: TFarProc;
Scroller: PScroller;
FocusChildHandle: THandle;
CONSTRUCTOR Init(AParent: PWindowsObject; ATitle: PChar);
CONSTRUCTOR InitResource(AParent: PWindowsObject;
    ResourceID: WORD);
CONSTRUCTOR Load(VAR S: TStream);
DESTRUCTOR Done;
    VIRTUAL;
PROCEDURE Store(VAR S: TStream);
PROCEDURE SetCaption(ATitle: PChar);
PROCEDURE GetWindowClass(VAR AWndClass: TWndClass);
    VIRTUAL;
FUNCTION GetId: INTEGER;
    VIRTUAL;
FUNCTION Create: BOOLEAN;
    VIRTUAL;
PROCEDURE DefWndProc(VAR Msg: TMessage);
    VIRTUAL;
```

```
PROCEDURE WMActivate(VAR Msg: TMessage);
   VIRTUAL wm_First + wm_Activate;
PROCEDURE SetupWindow;
   VIRTUAL;
PROCEDURE WMCreate(VAR Msg: TMessage);
   VIRTUAL wm_First + wm_Create;
PROCEDURE WMHScroll(VAR Msg: TMessage);
   VIRTUAL wm_First + wm_HScroll;
PROCEDURE WMVScroll(VAR Msg: TMessage);
   VIRTUAL wm_First + wm_VScroll;
PROCEDURE WMPaint(VAR Msg: TMessage);
   VIRTUAL wm_First + wm_Paint;
PROCEDURE Paint(PaintDC: HDC; VAR PaintInfo: TPaintStruct);
   VIRTUAL;
PROCEDURE WMSize(VAR Msg: TMessage);
   VIRTUAL wm_First + wm_Size;
PROCEDURE WMMove(VAR Msg: TMessage);
   VIRTUAL wm_First + wm_Move;
PROCEDURE WMLButtonDown(VAR Msg: TMessage);
   VIRTUAL wm_First + wm_LButtonDown;
END;

{ TDialog creation attributes }
TDialogAttr = RECORD
Name: PChar;
Param: LongInt;
END;

{ TDialog OBJECT }
TDialog = OBJECT(TWindowsObject)
Attr: TDialogAttr;
IsModal: BOOLEAN;
CONSTRUCTOR Init(AParent: PWindowsObject; AName: PChar);
CONSTRUCTOR Load(VAR S: TStream);
DESTRUCTOR Done;
   VIRTUAL;
PROCEDURE Store(VAR S: TStream);
FUNCTION Create: BOOLEAN;
   VIRTUAL;
FUNCTION Execute: INTEGER;
   VIRTUAL;
PROCEDURE EndDlg(ARetValue: INTEGER);
   VIRTUAL;
PROCEDURE Destroy;
   VIRTUAL;
```

```
FUNCTION GetItemHandle(DlgItemID: INTEGER): HWnd;
FUNCTION SendDlgItemMsg(DlgItemID: INTEGER;
   AMsg, WParam: WORD;   LParam: LongInt): LongInt;
PROCEDURE Ok(VAR Msg: TMessage);
   VIRTUAL id_First + id_Ok;
PROCEDURE EnterOk(VAR Msg: TMessage);
   VIRTUAL cm_First + id_Ok;
PROCEDURE Cancel(VAR Msg: TMessage);
   VIRTUAL id_First + id_Cancel;
PROCEDURE EnterCancel(VAR Msg: TMessage);
   VIRTUAL cm_First + id_Cancel;
PROCEDURE WMInitDialog(VAR Msg: TMessage);
   VIRTUAL wm_First + wm_InitDialog;
PROCEDURE WMClose(VAR Msg: TMessage);
   VIRTUAL wm_First + wm_Close;
PROCEDURE DefWndProc(VAR Msg: TMessage);
   VIRTUAL;
END;

{ TDlgWindow OBJECT }
TDlgWindow = OBJECT(TDialog)
CONSTRUCTOR Init(AParent: PWindowsObject; AName: PChar);
PROCEDURE GetWindowClass(VAR AWndClass: TWndClass);
   VIRTUAL;
FUNCTION Create: BOOLEAN;
   VIRTUAL;
PROCEDURE Ok(VAR Msg: TMessage);
   VIRTUAL id_First + id_OK;
PROCEDURE Cancel(VAR Msg: TMessage);
   VIRTUAL id_First + id_Cancel;
END;

{ TMDIWindow OBJECT }
TMDIWindow = OBJECT(TWindow)
 ClientWnd: PMDIClient;
 ChildMenuPos: INTEGER;
CONSTRUCTOR Init(ATitle: PChar; AMenu: HMenu);
DESTRUCTOR Done;
   VIRTUAL;
CONSTRUCTOR Load(VAR S: TStream);
PROCEDURE Store(VAR S: TStream);
PROCEDURE SetupWindow;
   VIRTUAL;
PROCEDURE InitClientWindow;
   VIRTUAL;
```

```
FUNCTION GetClassName: PChar;
   VIRTUAL;
FUNCTION GetClient: PMDIClient;
   VIRTUAL;
PROCEDURE GetWindowClass(VAR AWndClass: TWndClass);
   VIRTUAL;
PROCEDURE DefWndProc(VAR Msg: TMessage);
   VIRTUAL;
FUNCTION InitChild: PWindowsObject;
   VIRTUAL;
FUNCTION CreateChild: PWindowsObject;
   VIRTUAL;
PROCEDURE CMCreateChild(VAR Msg: TMessage);
   VIRTUAL cm_First + cm_CreateChild;
PROCEDURE TileChildren;
   VIRTUAL;
PROCEDURE CascadeChildren;
   VIRTUAL;
PROCEDURE ArrangeIcons;
   VIRTUAL;
PROCEDURE CloseChildren;
   VIRTUAL;
PROCEDURE CMTileChildren(VAR Msg: TMessage);
   VIRTUAL cm_First + cm_TileChildren;
PROCEDURE CMCascadeChildren(VAR Msg: TMessage);
   VIRTUAL cm_First + cm_CascadeChildren;
PROCEDURE CMArrangeIcons(VAR Msg: TMessage);
   VIRTUAL cm_First + cm_ArrangeIcons;
PROCEDURE CMCloseChildren(VAR Msg: TMessage);
   VIRTUAL cm_First + cm_CloseChildren;
END;

{ TControl OBJECT }
TControl = OBJECT(TWindow)
CONSTRUCTOR Init(AParent: PWindowsObject;
   AnId: INTEGER;  ATitle: PChar; X, Y, W, H: INTEGER);
CONSTRUCTOR InitResource(AParent: PWindowsObject; ResourceID:
WORD);
FUNCTION Register: BOOLEAN;
   VIRTUAL;
FUNCTION GetClassName: PChar;
   VIRTUAL;
PROCEDURE WMPaint(VAR Msg: TMessage);
   VIRTUAL wm_First + wm_Paint;
END;
```

```
{ TButton OBJECT }
TButton = OBJECT(TControl)
CONSTRUCTOR Init(AParent: PWindowsObject;
    AnId: INTEGER;  AText: PChar; X, Y, W, H: INTEGER;
    IsDefault: BOOLEAN);
CONSTRUCTOR InitResource(AParent: PWindowsObject; ResourceID:
WORD);
FUNCTION GetClassName: PChar;
    VIRTUAL;
END;

{ TCheckBox OBJECT }
TCheckBox = OBJECT(TButton)
Group: PGroupBox;
CONSTRUCTOR Init(AParent: PWindowsObject;
    AnID: INTEGER; ATitle: PChar; X, Y, W, H: INTEGER;
    AGroup: PGroupBox);
CONSTRUCTOR InitResource(AParent: PWindowsObject;
    ResourceID: WORD);
CONSTRUCTOR Load(VAR S: TStream);
PROCEDURE Store(VAR S: TStream);
PROCEDURE Check;
PROCEDURE Uncheck;
PROCEDURE Toggle;
FUNCTION GetCheck: WORD;
PROCEDURE SetCheck(CheckFlag: WORD);
FUNCTION Transfer(DataPtr: Pointer; TransferFlag: WORD): WORD;
    VIRTUAL;
PROCEDURE BNClicked(VAR Msg: TMessage);
    VIRTUAL nf_First + bn_Clicked;
END;

{ TRadioButton OBJECT }
TRadioButton = OBJECT(TCheckBox)
CONSTRUCTOR Init(AParent: PWindowsObject;
    AnID: INTEGER; ATitle: PChar; X, Y, W, H:
    INTEGER; AGroup: PGroupBox);
END;

{ TGroupBox OBJECT }
TGroupBox = OBJECT(TControl)
NotifyParent: BOOLEAN;
CONSTRUCTOR Init(AParent: PWindowsObject;
    AnID: INTEGER; AText: PChar; X, Y, W, H: INTEGER);
```

```
CONSTRUCTOR InitResource(AParent: PWindowsObject;
    ResourceID: WORD);
CONSTRUCTOR Load(VAR S: TStream);
PROCEDURE Store(VAR S: TStream);
FUNCTION GetClassName: PChar;
    VIRTUAL;
PROCEDURE SelectionChanged(ControlId: INTEGER);
    VIRTUAL;
END;

{ TStatic OBJECT }
TStatic = OBJECT(TControl)
TextLen: WORD;
CONSTRUCTOR Init(AParent: PWindowsObject;
    AnId: INTEGER;  ATitle: PChar; X, Y, W, H: INTEGER;
    ATextLen: WORD);
CONSTRUCTOR InitResource(AParent: PWindowsObject;
    ResourceID: WORD;  ATextLen: WORD);
CONSTRUCTOR Load(VAR S: TStream);
PROCEDURE Store(VAR S: TStream);
FUNCTION GetClassName: PChar;
    VIRTUAL;
FUNCTION GetText(ATextString: PChar;
    MaxChars: INTEGER): INTEGER;
PROCEDURE SetText(ATextString: PChar);
PROCEDURE Clear;
FUNCTION Transfer(DataPtr: Pointer; TransferFlag: WORD): WORD;
    VIRTUAL;
END;

{ TEdit OBJECT }
TEdit = OBJECT(TStatic)
CONSTRUCTOR Init(AParent: PWindowsObject;
    AnId: INTEGER; ATitle: PChar;  X, Y, W, H: INTEGER;
    ATextLen: WORD; Multiline: BOOLEAN);
FUNCTION GetClassName: PChar;
    VIRTUAL;
PROCEDURE Undo;
FUNCTION CanUndo: BOOLEAN;
PROCEDURE Paste;
PROCEDURE Copy;
PROCEDURE Cut;
FUNCTION GetNumLines: INTEGER;
FUNCTION GetLineLength(LineNumber: INTEGER): INTEGER;
FUNCTION GetLine(ATextString: PChar;
```

```
    StrSize, LineNumber: INTEGER): BOOLEAN;
PROCEDURE GetSubText(ATextString: PChar;
    StartPos, EndPos: INTEGER);
FUNCTION DeleteSubText(StartPos, EndPos: INTEGER): BOOLEAN;
FUNCTION DeleteLine(LineNumber: INTEGER): BOOLEAN;
PROCEDURE GetSelection(VAR StartPos, EndPos: INTEGER);
FUNCTION DeleteSelection: BOOLEAN;
FUNCTION IsModified: BOOLEAN;
PROCEDURE ClearModify;
FUNCTION GetLineFromPos(CharPos: INTEGER): INTEGER;
FUNCTION GetLineIndex(LineNumber: INTEGER): INTEGER;
PROCEDURE Scroll(HorizontalUnit, VerticalUnit: INTEGER);
FUNCTION SetSelection(StartPos, EndPos: INTEGER): BOOLEAN;
PROCEDURE Insert(ATextString: PChar);
FUNCTION Search(StartPos: INTEGER;
    AText: PChar; CaseSensitive: BOOLEAN): INTEGER;
PROCEDURE SetupWindow;
    VIRTUAL;
PROCEDURE CMEditCut(VAR Msg: TMessage);
    VIRTUAL cm_First + cm_EditCut;
PROCEDURE CMEditCopy(VAR Msg: TMessage);
    VIRTUAL cm_First + cm_EditCopy;
PROCEDURE CMEditPaste(VAR Msg: TMessage);
    VIRTUAL cm_First + cm_EditPaste;
PROCEDURE CMEditDelete(VAR Msg: TMessage);
    VIRTUAL cm_First + cm_EditDelete;
PROCEDURE CMEditClear(VAR Msg: TMessage);
    VIRTUAL cm_First + cm_EditClear;
PROCEDURE CMEditUndo(VAR Msg: TMessage);
    VIRTUAL cm_First + cm_EditUndo;
END;

{ TListBox message name type }
TMsgName = (
mn_AddString, mn_InsertString, mn_DeleteString,
mn_ResetContent, mn_GetCount, mn_GetText,
mn_GetTextLen, mn_SelectString, mn_SetCurSel,
mn_GetCurSel);

{ Multiple selection transfer RECORD }
PMultiSelRec = ^TMultiSelRec;
TMultiSelRec = RECORD
Count: INTEGER;
Selections: ARRAY[0..32760] OF INTEGER;
END;
```

```
{ TListBox OBJECT }
TListBox = OBJECT(TControl)
CONSTRUCTOR Init(AParent: PWindowsObject;
   AnId: INTEGER;  X, Y, W, H: INTEGER);
FUNCTION GetClassName: PChar;
   VIRTUAL;
FUNCTION AddString(AString: PChar): INTEGER;
FUNCTION InsertString(AString: PChar; Index: INTEGER): INTEGER;
FUNCTION DeleteString(Index: INTEGER): INTEGER;
PROCEDURE ClearList;
FUNCTION Transfer(DataPtr: Pointer; TransferFlag: WORD): WORD;
   VIRTUAL;
FUNCTION GetCount: INTEGER;
FUNCTION GetString(AString: PChar; Index: INTEGER): INTEGER;
FUNCTION GetStringLen(Index: INTEGER): INTEGER;
FUNCTION GetSelString(AString: PChar;
   MaxChars: INTEGER): INTEGER;
FUNCTION SetSelString(AString: PChar; Index: INTEGER): INTEGER;
FUNCTION GetSelIndex: INTEGER;
FUNCTION SetSelIndex(Index: INTEGER): INTEGER;
END;

{ TComboBox OBJECT }
TComboBox = OBJECT(TListBox)
TextLen: WORD;
CONSTRUCTOR Init(AParent: PWindowsObject;
   AnID: INTEGER;  X, Y, W, H: INTEGER;
   AStyle: WORD; ATextLen: WORD);
CONSTRUCTOR InitResource(AParent: PWindowsObject;
   ResourceID: INTEGER; ATextLen: WORD);
CONSTRUCTOR Load(VAR S: TStream);
PROCEDURE Store(VAR S: TStream);
FUNCTION GetClassName: PChar;
   VIRTUAL;
PROCEDURE ShowList;
PROCEDURE HideList;
FUNCTION Transfer(DataPtr: Pointer; TransferFlag: WORD):
   WORD; VIRTUAL;
PROCEDURE SetupWindow;
   VIRTUAL;
END;

{ TScrollBar transfer RECORD }
TScrollBarTransferRec = RECORD
```

469

```
LowValue: INTEGER;
HighValue: INTEGER;
Position: INTEGER;
END;

{ TScrollBar OBJECT }
TScrollBar = OBJECT(TControl)
LineMagnitude, PageMagnitude: INTEGER;
CONSTRUCTOR Init(AParent: PWindowsObject;
    AnID: INTEGER; X, Y, W, H: INTEGER;
    IsHScrollBar: BOOLEAN);
CONSTRUCTOR InitResource(AParent: PWindowsObject;
    ResourceID: WORD);
CONSTRUCTOR Load(VAR S: TStream);
PROCEDURE Store(VAR S: TStream);
FUNCTION GetClassName: PChar;
    VIRTUAL;
PROCEDURE SetupWindow;
    VIRTUAL;
PROCEDURE GetRange(VAR LoVal, HiVal: INTEGER);
FUNCTION GetPosition: INTEGER;
PROCEDURE SetRange(LoVal, HiVal: INTEGER);
PROCEDURE SetPosition(ThumbPos: INTEGER);
FUNCTION DeltaPos(Delta: INTEGER): INTEGER;
FUNCTION Transfer(DataPtr: Pointer; TransferFlag: WORD): WORD;
    VIRTUAL;
PROCEDURE SBLineUp(VAR Msg: TMessage);
    VIRTUAL nf_First + sb_LineUp;
PROCEDURE SBLineDown(VAR Msg: TMessage);
    VIRTUAL nf_First + sb_LineDown;
PROCEDURE SBPageUp(VAR Msg: TMessage);
    VIRTUAL nf_First + sb_PageUp;
PROCEDURE SBPageDown(VAR Msg: TMessage);
    VIRTUAL nf_First + sb_PageDown;
PROCEDURE SBThumbPosition(VAR Msg: TMessage);
    VIRTUAL nf_First + sb_ThumbPosition;
PROCEDURE SBThumbTrack(VAR Msg: TMessage);
    VIRTUAL nf_First + sb_ThumbTrack;
PROCEDURE SBTop(VAR Msg: TMessage);
    VIRTUAL nf_First + sb_Top;
PROCEDURE SBBottom(VAR Msg: TMessage);
    VIRTUAL nf_First + sb_Bottom;
END;

{ TMDIClient OBJECT }
```

```
TMDIClient = OBJECT(TControl)
ClientAttr: TClientCreateStruct;
CONSTRUCTOR Init(AParent: PMDIWindow);
CONSTRUCTOR Load(VAR S: TStream);
PROCEDURE Store(VAR S: TStream);
FUNCTION GetClassName: PChar;
   VIRTUAL;
PROCEDURE TileChildren;
   VIRTUAL;
PROCEDURE CascadeChildren;
   VIRTUAL;
PROCEDURE ArrangeIcons;
   VIRTUAL;
END;

{ TScroller OBJECT }
TScroller = OBJECT(TObject)
Window: PWindow;
XPos: LongInt;
   { current horizontal pos in horz scroll units }
YPos: LongInt;
   { current vertical pos in vert scroll units }
XUnit: INTEGER;
   { logical device units per horz scroll unit }
YUnit: INTEGER;
   { logical device units per vert scroll unit }
XRange: LongInt;
   { # OF scrollable horz scroll units }
YRange: LongInt;
   { # OF scrollable vert scroll units }
XLine: INTEGER;
   { # OF horz scroll units per line }
YLine: INTEGER;
   { # OF vert scroll units per line }
XPage: INTEGER;
   { # OF horz scroll units per page }
YPage: INTEGER;
   { # OF vert scroll units per page }
AutoMode: BOOLEAN;
   { auto scrolling mode }
TrackMode: BOOLEAN;
   { track scroll mode }
AutoOrg: BOOLEAN;
   { AutoOrg indicates Scroller offsets origin }
HasHScrollBar: BOOLEAN;
```

```
HasVScrollBar: BOOLEAN;
CONSTRUCTOR Init(TheWindow: PWindow;
    TheXUnit, TheYUnit: INTEGER;
    TheXRange, TheYRange: LongInt);
CONSTRUCTOR Load(VAR S: TStream);
PROCEDURE Store(VAR S: TStream);
PROCEDURE SetUnits(TheXUnit, TheYUnit: LongInt);
PROCEDURE SetPageSize;
    VIRTUAL;
PROCEDURE SetSBarRange;
    VIRTUAL;
PROCEDURE SetRange(TheXRange, TheYRange: LongInt);
PROCEDURE BeginView(PaintDC: HDC;
    VAR PaintInfo: TPaintStruct); VIRTUAL;
PROCEDURE EndView;
    VIRTUAL;
PROCEDURE VScroll(ScrollRequest: WORD; ThumbPos: INTEGER);
    VIRTUAL;
PROCEDURE HScroll(ScrollRequest: WORD; ThumbPos: INTEGER);
    VIRTUAL;
PROCEDURE ScrollTo(X, Y: LongInt);
PROCEDURE ScrollBy(Dx, Dy: LongInt);
PROCEDURE AutoScroll;
    VIRTUAL;
FUNCTION IsVisibleRect(X, Y: LongInt; XExt, YExt: INTEGER):
BOOLEAN;
END;

{ TApplication OBJECT }
TApplication = OBJECT(TObject)
Status: INTEGER;
Name: PChar;
MainWindow: PWindowsObject;
HAccTable: THandle;
KBHandlerWnd: PWindowsObject;
CONSTRUCTOR Init(AName: PChar);
PROCEDURE InitApplication;
    VIRTUAL;
PROCEDURE InitInstance;
    VIRTUAL;
PROCEDURE InitMainWindow;
    VIRTUAL;
PROCEDURE Run;
    VIRTUAL;
```

```
PROCEDURE SetKBHandler(AWindowsObject: PWindowsObject);
PROCEDURE MessageLoop;
   VIRTUAL;
FUNCTION ProcessAppMsg(VAR Message: TMsg): BOOLEAN;
   VIRTUAL;
FUNCTION ProcessDlgMsg(VAR Message: TMsg): BOOLEAN;
   VIRTUAL;
FUNCTION ProcessAccels(VAR Message: TMsg): BOOLEAN;
   VIRTUAL;
FUNCTION ProcessMDIAccels(VAR Message: TMsg): BOOLEAN;
   VIRTUAL;
FUNCTION MakeWindow(AWindowsObject: PWindowsObject):
   PWindowsObject; VIRTUAL;
FUNCTION ExecDialog(ADialog: PWindowsObject): INTEGER;
   VIRTUAL;
FUNCTION ValidWindow(AWindowsObject: PWindowsObject):
   PWindowsObject; VIRTUAL;
PROCEDURE Error(ErrorCode: INTEGER);
   VIRTUAL;
FUNCTION CanClose: BOOLEAN;
   VIRTUAL;
END;

{ Abstract notification PROCEDURE }
PROCEDURE Abstract;

{ Memory management routines }
FUNCTION LowMemory: BOOLEAN;
PROCEDURE RestoreMemory;
FUNCTION MemAlloc(Size: WORD): Pointer;
FUNCTION GetObjectPtr(HWindow: HWnd): PWindowsObject;
FUNCTION NewStr(S: String): PString;
PROCEDURE DisposeStr(P: PString);

{ Multi-selection support routines }
FUNCTION AllocMultiSel(Size: INTEGER): PMultiSelRec;
PROCEDURE FreeMultiSel(P: PMultiSelRec);

{ Stream routines }
PROCEDURE RegisterType(VAR S: TStreamRec);
PROCEDURE RegisterWObjects;

{ Longint inline routines }
FUNCTION LongMul(X, Y: INTEGER): Longint;
inline($5A/$58/$F7/$EA);
```

```
FUNCTION LongDiv(X: Longint; Y: INTEGER): INTEGER;
inline($59/$58/$5A/$F7/$F9);

{ Application OBJECT pointer }
CONST
Application: PApplication = NIL;

{ Safety pool size }
CONST
SafetyPoolSize: WORD = 8192;

{ Stream error PROCEDURE }
CONST
StreamError: Pointer = NIL;

{ EMS stream state variables }
CONST
EmsCurHandle: WORD = $FFFF;
EmsCurPage: WORD = $FFFF;

{ Stream registration records }
CONST
RCollection: TStreamRec = (
ObjType: 50;
VMTLink: Ofs(TypeOf(TCollection)^);
Load: @TCollection.Load;
Store: @TCollection.Store);

CONST
RStringCollection: TStreamRec = (
ObjType: 51;
VMTLink: Ofs(TypeOf(TStringCollection)^);
Load: @TStringCollection.Load;
Store: @TStringCollection.Store);

CONST
RWindowsObject: TStreamRec = (
ObjType: 52;
VMTLink: Ofs(TypeOf(TWindowsObject)^);
Load: @TWindowsObject.Load;
Store: @TWindowsObject.Store);

CONST
RWindow: TStreamRec = (
```

```
ObjType: 53;
VMTLink: Ofs(TypeOf(TWindow)^);
Load: @TWindow.Load;
Store: @TWindow.Store);

CONST
RDialog: TStreamRec = (
ObjType: 54;
VMTLink: Ofs(TypeOf(TDialog)^);
Load: @TDialog.Load;
Store: @TDialog.Store);

CONST
RDlgWindow: TStreamRec = (
ObjType: 55;
VMTLink: Ofs(TypeOf(TDlgWindow)^);
Load: @TDlgWindow.Load;
Store: @TDlgWindow.Store);

CONST
RControl: TStreamRec = (
ObjType: 56;
VMTLink: Ofs(TypeOf(TControl)^);
Load: @TControl.Load;
Store: @TControl.Store);

CONST
RMDIWindow: TStreamRec = (
ObjType: 57;
VMTLink: Ofs(TypeOf(TMDIWindow)^);
Load: @TMDIWindow.Load;
Store: @TMDIWindow.Store);

CONST
RMDIClient: TStreamRec = (
ObjType: 58;
VMTLink: Ofs(TypeOf(TMDIClient)^);
Load: @TMDIClient.Load;
Store: @TMDIClient.Store);

CONST
RButton: TStreamRec = (
ObjType: 59;
VMTLink: Ofs(TypeOf(TButton)^);
Load: @TButton.Load;
```

```
Store: @TButton.Store);

CONST
RCheckBox: TStreamRec = (
ObjType: 60;
VMTLink: Ofs(TypeOf(TCheckBox)^);
Load: @TCheckBox.Load;
Store: @TCheckBox.Store);

CONST
RRadioButton: TStreamRec = (
ObjType: 61;
VMTLink: Ofs(TypeOf(TRadioButton)^);
Load: @TRadioButton.Load;
Store: @TRadioButton.Store);

CONST
RGroupBox: TStreamRec = (
ObjType: 62;
VMTLink: Ofs(TypeOf(TGroupBox)^);
Load: @TGroupBox.Load;
Store: @TGroupBox.Store);

CONST
RListBox: TStreamRec = (
ObjType: 63;
VMTLink: Ofs(TypeOf(TListBox)^);
Load: @TListBox.Load;
Store: @TListBox.Store);

CONST
RComboBox: TStreamRec = (
ObjType: 64;
VMTLink: Ofs(TypeOf(TComboBox)^);
Load: @TComboBox.Load;
Store: @TComboBox.Store);

CONST
RScrollBar: TStreamRec = (
ObjType: 65;
VMTLink: Ofs(TypeOf(TScrollBar)^);
Load: @TScrollBar.Load;
Store: @TScrollBar.Store);

CONST
```

```
RStatic: TStreamRec = (
ObjType: 66;
VMTLink: Ofs(TypeOf(TStatic)^);
Load: @TStatic.Load;
Store: @TStatic.Store);

CONST
REdit: TStreamRec = (
ObjType: 67;
VMTLink: Ofs(TypeOf(TEdit)^);
Load: @TEdit.Load;
Store: @TEdit.Store);

CONST
RScroller: TStreamRec = (
ObjType: 68;
VMTLink: Ofs(TypeOf(TScroller)^);
Load: @TScroller.Load;
Store: @TScroller.Store);

CONST
RStrCollection: TStreamRec = (
ObjType: 69;
VMTLink: Ofs(TypeOf(TStrCollection)^);
Load: @TStrCollection.Load;
Store: @TStrCollection.Store);
```

INDEX

X

%x format specification, 131
Xerox Corporation, 49
Xerox Star microcomputer, 49

Z

zooming
 drawings, 324
 windows, 5

Selections from The SYBEX Library

LANGUAGES

The ABC's of GW-BASIC
William R. Orvis
320pp. Ref. 663-4
Featuring two parts: Part I is an easy-to-follow tutorial for beginners, while Part II is a complete, concise reference guide to GW-BASIC commands and functions. Covers everything from the basics of programming in the GW-BASIC environment, to debugging a major program. Includes special treatment of graphics and sound.

BASIC Programs for Scientists and Engineers
Alan R. Miller
318pp. Ref. 073-3
The algorithms presented in this book are programmed in standard BASIC code which should be usable with almost any implementation of BASIC. Includes statistical calculations, matrix algebra, curve fitting, integration, and more.

Encyclopedia C
Robert A. Radcliffe
1333pp. Ref. 655-3
This is the complete reference for standard ANSI/ISO programmers using any Microsoft C compiler with DOS. It blends comprehensive treatment of C syntax, functions, utilities, and services with practical examples and proven techniques for optimizing productivity and performance in C programming.

FORTRAN Programs for Scientists and Engineers (Second Edition)
Alan R. Miller
280pp. Ref. 571-9
In this collection of widely used scientific algorithms—for statistics, vector and matrix operations, curve fitting, and more—the author stresses effective use of little-known and powerful features of FORTRAN.

Introduction to Pascal: Including Turbo Pascal (Second Edition)
Rodnay Zaks
464pp. Ref. 533-6
This best-selling tutorial builds complete mastery of Pascal—from basic structured programming concepts, to advanced I/O, data structures, file operations, sets, pointers and lists, and more. Both ISO Standard and Turbo Pascal.

Mastering C
Craig Bolon
437pp. Ref. 326-0
This in-depth guide stresses planning, testing, efficiency and portability in C applications. Topics include data types, storage classes, arrays, pointers, data structures, control statements, I/O and the C function library.

Mastering QuickBASIC
Rita Belserene
450pp. Ref. 589-1
Readers build professional programs with this extensive language tutorial. Fundamental commands are mixed with the author's tips and tricks so that users can create their own applications. Program templates are included for video displays, computer games, and working with databases and printers. For Version 4.5.

Mastering Turbo C (Second Edition)
Stan Kelly-Bootle
609pp. Ref. 595-6
With a foreword by Borland International

President Philippe Kahn, this new edition has been expanded to include full details on Version 2.0. Learn theory and practical programming, with tutorials on data types, real numbers and characters, controlling program flow, file I/O, and producing color charts and graphs. Through Version 2.

Mastering Turbo Pascal 6
Scott D. Palmer
650pp, Ref. 675-8
This step-by-step guide to the newest Turbo Pascal release takes readers from programming basics to advanced techniques such as graphics, recursion, object-oriented programming, efficient debugging, and programming for other environments such as Vax/VMS. Includes dozens of useful exercises and examples, and tips for effective programming.

Systems Programming in Microsoft C
Michael J. Young
604pp. Ref. 570-0
This sourcebook of advanced C programming techniques is for anyone who wants to make the most of their C compiler or Microsoft QuickC. It includes a comprehensive, annotated library of systems functions, ready to compile and call.

Systems Programming in Microsoft C (Second Edition)
Michael J. Young
600pp; Ref. 1026-6
This book offers detailed information on advanced programming techniques for Microsoft C, as well as a comprehensive library of ready-to-use functions. It covers both the Microsoft C optimizing C compiler through version 6.0, and Microsoft QuickC (versions 1.0 and later). With complete code for converting a Microsoft Cprogram into a memory-resident utility.

Turbo Pascal Toolbox (Second Edition)
Frank Dutton
425pp. Ref. 602-2

This collection of tested, efficient Turbo Pascal building blocks gives a boost to intermediate-level programmers, while teaching effective programming by example. Topics include accessing DOS, menus, bit maps, screen handling, and much more.

APPLICATION DEVELOPMENT

The ABC's of ToolBook for Windows
Kenyon Brown
300pp. Ref. 795-9
Gain the skill and confidence you need to create sophisticated applications for Windows. This hands-on introduction teaches you how to build custom graphical applications, without the need for traditional computer language. Learn to use the Script Recorder to create scripts and add animation to presentation applications.

The Elements of Friendly Software Design
Paul Heckel
319pp. Ref. 768-1
Here's what you *didn't* learn in engineering school! This entertaining, practical text shows how the same communication techniques used by artists and filmmakers can make software more appealing to users. Topics include visual thinking; design principles to follow—and mistakes to avoid; and examples of excellence.

Up & Running with ToolBook for Windows
Michael Tischer
138pp. Ref. 816-5
In just 20 time-coded steps (each taking no more than 15 minutes to an hour), you can begin designing your own Windows applications. Learn to add visual interest with lines, colors, and patterns; create a customized database form; navigate the user interface; draw and paint with Tool-Book, and more.

FREE BROCHURE!

Complete this form today, and we'll send you a full-color brochure of Sybex bestsellers.

Please supply the name of the Sybex book purchased.

_____

How would you rate it?

_____ Excellent _____ Very Good _____ Average _____ Poor

Why did you select this particular book?

_____ Recommended to me by a friend
_____ Recommended to me by store personnel
_____ Saw an advertisement in _____
_____ Author's reputation
_____ Saw in Sybex catalog
_____ Required textbook
_____ Sybex reputation
_____ Read book review in _____
_____ In-store display
_____ Other _____

Where did you buy it?

_____ Bookstore
_____ Computer Store or Software Store
_____ Catalog (name: _____)
_____ Direct from Sybex
_____ Other: _____

Did you buy this book with your personal funds?

_____ Yes _____ No

About how many computer books do you buy each year?

_____ 1-3 _____ 3-5 _____ 5-7 _____ 7-9 _____ 10+

About how many Sybex books do you own?

_____ 1-3 _____ 3-5 _____ 5-7 _____ 7-9 _____ 10+

Please indicate your level of experience with the software covered in this book:

_____ Beginner _____ Intermediate _____ Advanced

Which types of software packages do you use regularly?

_____ Accounting	_____ Databases	_____ Networks
_____ Amiga	_____ Desktop Publishing	_____ Operating Systems
_____ Apple/Mac	_____ File Utilities	_____ Spreadsheets
_____ CAD	_____ Money Management	_____ Word Processing
_____ Communications	_____ Languages	_____ Other _____
		(please specify)

Which of the following best describes your job title?

_____ Administrative/Secretarial   _____ President/CEO

_____ Director   _____ Manager/Supervisor

_____ Engineer/Technician   _____ Other _____
                                                    (please specify)

Comments on the weaknesses/strengths of this book: _____

_____

_____

_____

_____

Name _____

Street _____

City/State/Zip _____

Phone _____

PLEASE FOLD, SEAL, AND MAIL TO SYBEX

-- --

SYBEX, INC.
Department M
2021 CHALLENGER DR.
ALAMEDA, CALIFORNIA USA
94501

SYBEX

SEAL

The ObjectWindows Object Type Hierarchy

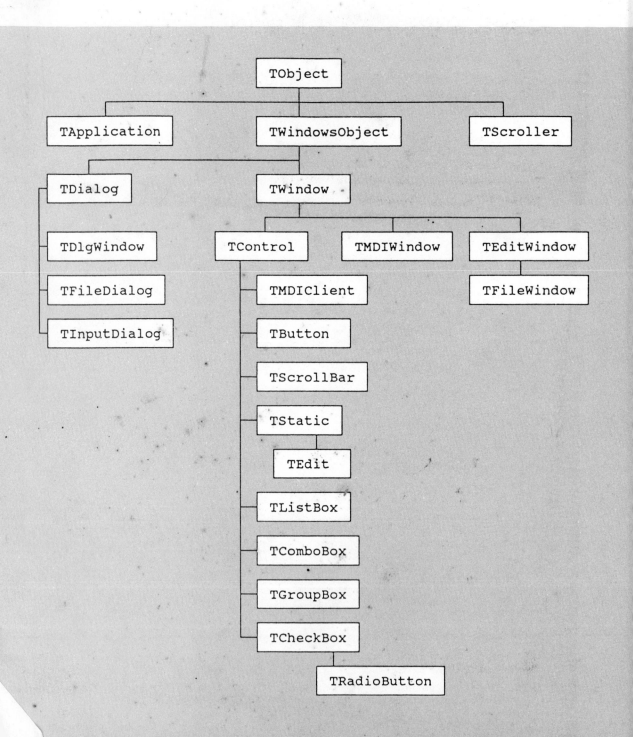